TRAVELLING TOWARDS CHEKHOV

'I carry the story of these Diaries with gratitude. No day goes by without a flutter of memory. My times spent in Russia over 20 years have enriched every part of my life with irresistible laughter beyond imagination . . . I miss them so much.

Миру – мир!

Peace to the World.'

— Caroline Blakiston, July 2024

This horse and carriage was a special purchase made by my parents during their trip to Russia when they found they were expecting me.

TRAVELLING TOWARDS CHEKHOV

DIARIES OF AN ENGLISH ACTRESS

with a Preface by Sir Trevor Nunn

CAROLINE BLAKISTON

CP

THE CHOIR PRESS

First published in the United Kingdom in 2024 by

The Choir Press

ISBN 978-1-78963-430-3

Reader's Comments

SIR IAN MCKELLEN

This illuminating memoir reflects the wit, generosity and enquiring mind of this remarkable "English Actress". Her unique journey is fascinating – a latter-day short story worthy of Anton Chekhov.

DAME SIÂN PHILLIPS

This is a magical travel book, mapping an expedition imagined in childhood and, remarkably, sustained throughout a long, successful life in the British theatre and, surprisingly, an age later, seized upon and made into reality. Caroline Blakiston goes, I would venture, where no actor has gone before, and she has a unique story to tell.

This is as unlike the usual theatrical memoir as can be imagined. Nevertheless, it is written with the sharp eye and open heart of a true actor.

SIR JONATHAN PRYCE

A unique memoir from one of the most exquisite, thoughtful and talented actors that I have ever had the joy to work with.

Russia and Chekhov, for me, are the beginnings of modern drama. For Caro to have experienced both and to share it with us in this way is a remarkable gift.

JULIET STEVENSON CBE

From its very first paragraph, I found myself entirely gripped by Caroline's account. Her style – understated, wry, witty, lucid and detailed – is an absolute delight and makes for a compelling read. Her two great passions – for the theatre and for all things Russian – combine to trace a fascinating journey by this wonderfully courageous artist.

MIKE POULTON

Caro Blakiston's memoir is a gift to any actor or director – or for that matter, for any translator or anyone wishing to get to grips with the brilliance and complexity of a Chekhov play. Caro is one of our most respected leading actors. She is the only actor who has studied and performed Chekhov's great works in its original language, in his own theatre and absorbed the processes, traditions and subtleties of the Russian rehearsal process. Rehearsing a Chekhov play with Caro – I say this from personal experience – is like having the great playwright with you in the room. Her insights and wisdom are now available in this fascinating book. And on top of all that, it's a real page-turner. Caro leads the reader by the hand into the world of Chekhov and stays with you as mentor and guide.

Read it!

FELICITY KENDAL CBE

A beautifully written diary of her Russian adventures by my closest friend and colleague Caroline Blakiston. Her passion for Russia, the culture and literature, the plays and the people, is infectious and compelling.

I first met Caroline in 1974 when we were both members of the Actors Company, committed to the idea of a touring company of actors and directors working on equal footing and involved in every step of the productions. Caroline and I bonded over work, wine, our passion for our jobs and our joy of being in a like-minded group of actors. At the same time, juggling with small children and divorce, Caroline was a leader and she led with grace and wisdom. Her wit and undiluted lust for life infected everyone and the work we did.

This book captures this glorious woman, her wit and enthusiasm, her infectiousness and endless energy. It is a marvellous Russian adventure and her personality leaps off the page. I applaud her. We need more.

JACK FARTHING

Caroline's diaries are an inspiring and deeply personal account of a love affair with Russia and all its rich theatrical history. Her writing bursts with warmth, wit and insight, and her passion transports you; you don't hear about it but see it for yourself, all told with natural humour and absolute honesty, humming with infectious enthusiasm.

MIRIAM MARGOLYES OBE

Loved it! As I expected, insightful – fascinating for an actress to read. Beautifully written – it is a lovely WISE story.

LEE SIMPSON, Artistic Director and co-founder of Improbable

Caroline Blakiston's inexhaustible hunger for adventure shines through this memoir of an English actress in Russia. Her writing is vivacious and full of wonder. Just like the author.

NELL DUNN

Caroline Blakiston was in the womb when she made her first trip to Russia. Ever since then she has been beguiled by all things Russian but most of all by the Russian Theatre. The book uncovers at a close level what it means to be an actress acting in a foreign country in a foreign language. The agony she goes through and how she survives is a moving story vividly told.

DR JEREMY HOWARD, Senior Lecturer, School of Russian Art History, University of St Andrews

Quick and curious, fleeting and penetrating, Caroline Blakiston's Russian diaries are a true gala of relationships, characters and humanity. With her unique blend of unstinting graciousness and bravura she reveals her pioneering immersion in the late Soviet theatrical world. In so doing, she offers her readers a rich and beautiful tapestry of life, individuals, professionalism and history: a marvellous boon that shows what can be gained through rising above politics and national intrigue. We are in her debt.

SHEILA REID

Immediately arresting. Full of fascinating anecdotes. What an adventure!

DEREK GRIFFITHS MBE

I did not want this synopsis of life in Russia to end.

The precise description of huge characters and dialogue are for me an exciting awakening of Russia's world and culture.

I doff my cap with much respect to the writer's courage, undertaking such a daunting adventure.

MAVIS CHEEK

Caroline's vivid and entertaining memoir of acting Chekhov in Russian, in Moscow, in the '90s captures the strangeness and delight of her time there and gives a window on a way of life that is sometimes funny, sometimes heart-breaking and always wonderfully engaging.

EDWARD PETHERBRIDGE

From Caro's encounter with the Moscow Art Theatre's night watchman to her becoming the first English actress to have played in Chekhov's legendary theatre, it intrigues and casts a special light on the beloved *Cherry Orchard*.

TIMOTHY WEST CBE

I knew about Caroline Blakiston's appearance with the Russian Taganrog Theatre Company, as Charlotta in *The Cherry Orchard*, and marvelled at her courage and audacity in taking on the challenge of involving herself in a major theatrical production in a foreign company whose language she didn't speak initially.

What I find fascinating about this account of her adventure, however, is Caroline's analysis, during rehearsal, of each of her colleagues in the company.

Beginning rehearsals for a production in the UK, one's first impressions of the actors with whom you are about to work (some of whom you will probably know already) tend to be quite simply: (i) are they going to be easy to get on with? and (ii) are they going to be good?

But having to form a close relationship with colleagues in a different land, with an unfamiliar way of working, Caroline has drawn fascinating vignettes, starting from the outside with clothes, hair, deportment, marital relations, and going on to reveal what their individual personal characteristics each of them have chosen to bring to their parts.

All in all, this volume is a witty, perceptive and fascinating diary of a courageous exploit into the unknown.

CAMILA BATMANGHELIDJH CBE

Caroline Blakiston has a profound gift. She can love and appreciate people because she can feel their soul. This makes her a brilliant actress, raconteur and philanthropist. In this book she makes history intimate, it's gripping. It is as if you've gone on a trip of a lifetime with your best friend and you don't want it to end.

Dedication

For Adam and Charlotte who have, as they always do, shown unconditional support and love.

And to Lily, Lola, Iris, Frank and Zac.

Acknowledgements

Help has been needed since I moved from London to the sea and decided to produce this book. The following friends have offered support: Alan Rankle, Tim Nathan, John Bostock, Ema Cavolli, David Holohan, Alice Platt, Michael Straughan, and Misha Bernatskiy. I am grateful to Miles Bailey, publisher of The Choir Press, Lyudmila Razumova, translator and lecturer in Russian at King's College London, and Rod Tweedy (former editor at Karnac Books). Finally, without Camila Batmanghelidjh, the book would never have left the ground.

Contents

Illustrations

Frontispiece
1. Anton Pavlovich Chekhov (1860–1904).
2. Kuindzhi, *Evening in the Ukraine* (1878).
3. My sketch of a lemonade machine.
4. Kagarlitsky family.
5. Konstantin Stanislavsky.
6. Cross found in Leningrad.
7. Misha Roshchin's sketch of Caro and himself as Aquarians.
8. Main stage and auditorium of MKhAT.
9. Muzei MKhAT – Henrietta in her office.
10. Gaga Kovenchuk's sketch of gallery opening, showing the crowd not paying attention.
11. Gaga's sketch of Caro at the opening.
12. Leningrad, Tovstonogov Theatre, chair made out of drinks can by garderobe attendant.
13. Cover picture of lgor Yasulovich and the bone sculpture, from monthly cinema magazine Ekran (Screen), June 1991.
14. National Hotel dining room: sketch of Kremlin.
15. Lily Glassby with her cat.
16. Ranevskaya/Lena.
17. Varya/Lilya.
18. Lopakhin #I/Yury.
19. Dunyasha/Zoya.
20. Borya/Yasha.
21. Volodya/Trofimov.
22. Octavy/Firs with Charlotta's dog Urzka.
23. Pasha/Yepikhodov.
24. Valya, Stage manager.
25. Sasha/Pishchik.
26. Kostya/Lopakhin #II.
27. Anya/Valya.

28. Matchstick house made by the son of Lopakhin #II/Kostya and his wife Valya.
29. Gaev/Lev.
30. Taganrog, Volodya Federovsky, Director of the Dramatic Theatre.
31. Juvenaly Kalantarov, Director.
32. Dramatichesky Theatre in Taganrog.
33. Taganrog, the cottage where Chekhov was born.
34. The weathervane atop Tchaikovsky's house.
35. Music School at Taganrog.
36. Clown costume.
37. Gown costume.
38. Chekhov bust.
39. Moscow MKhAT, Pilyavskaya – last living student of Stanislavsky.'
40. Moscow, flat of Sofia Pilyavskaya, drinking a toast. Caroline is holding a silver goblet that belonged to Olga Knipper who died in Sofia's arms.
41. Dom Kompozitorov: Sasha and Ksenia's flat. Left to right: humming fridge, Igor Yasulovich, Sasha, rubbish chute, and Ksenia.
42. Caro's MKhAT pass (interior).
43. Smoktunovsky with me in rehearsal.
44. Yefremov in rehearsal, 1994.
45. The plane to Taganrog, sans seat belts.
46. Caroline crossing the railway lines at Taganrog station.
47. Leaving Crimea on the train: guests of Mahomet and Mahomet with caviar.
48. Sasha Smirnov.
49. Poster on MKhAT billboard announcing the death of Oleg Yefremov.
50. Alexander Isaakovich Gelman.
51. Oleg Nikolayevich Yefremov.

1. Anton Pavlovich Chekhov (1860–1904).

Preface

How much can we ever understand of a culture different from our own?

'America and England, two countries divided by a common language'. Thus George Bernard Shaw, who would, I'm sure, be perplexed to read my declaration that the writer of this book is 'one of a kind'. Doesn't that mean she is just 'one, like so many others'? ... isn't that a way of saying she is just average? No, GBS, on the contrary, it means she is somebody very, very special. It's a street equivalent of 'unique'. And indeed, I have described Caroline Blakiston for many years past, as 'one of a kind'.

In terms of professional category, Caro would have to accept the definition of 'actress', but she is also writer, thinker, traveller, rebel and in her own way, poet and philosopher. To confuse matters a little more, I also think of her as a kindred spirit.

I have worked in the theatre with this multiplex woman, and found her vivacious, exuberant and possessed of deadly accurate comic timing. But I have also had many an extraordinary conversation with her, and most frequently about Russia.

Caroline knows that subject so much better than I do, but our conversations are partly fuelled by my experience of visiting Russia myself. In 1977, in company with two other chosen theatre practitioners (names on application), I accepted the invitation of the Anglo/USSR Society to be afforded a guided tour of contemporary Russian theatre. We travelled to Moscow, then to Leningrad (as it then was) – and then all the way to Riga in Latvia – seeing the work of Lyubimov, Efros, and indeed of the delightful Oleg Yefremov, meeting Tovstonogov, and the genius film director, Tarkovsky. This whirlwind experience considerably adjusted my idea of Russia. I was already fascinated by the seeming contradiction of their astonishing humanist literature and their absolutist politics. But I experienced an allure that I wasn't expecting.

In the plays of Chekhov and indeed Gorky, we reserved English can relate to intensely emotional Russians, who can laugh while bursting into tears, who can sob as they chuckle. Indeed, the

Russians of nineteenth- and twentieth-century drama tell us so much more about love and loss, than the characters of our own dramatic tradition. But visiting this vast and contradictory land engaged this Englishman in a highly emotional, all or nothing way, and so once smitten, I had to go back.

So back I have been, on several occasions, to both Moscow (where I was allowed to sit in Stanislavsky's rehearsal chair!) and to beautiful St Petersburg (where I was allowed to walk alone around the French Impressionist Rooms at the Hermitage) ... so many indelible and highly charged experiences.

But Caroline's attraction to all things Russian is clearly far, far greater than mine. But comparison of our magnetic strengths is not the whole story. Caro is an adventurer, a discoverer, and a researcher who believes in total immersion. She is not satisfied with observing. Her wanderlust can only be satisfied by experiencing, and ultimately living in a different culture. I suspect her acting instinct allows her, when immersing, to become somebody else. Her poetic instinct prompts her to find meaning and association. Her comic instinct prevents her from taking herself (and indeed us) too seriously.

This book, then, is in many senses a love story, while being a tale of two cities, and a human comedy; a multiple achievement, as we who know her would expect of this one of a kind.

Sir Trevor Nunn

Introduction

I can't remember a time when the words Russia, Russian, did not send an agitation of excitement through my body, releasing a nameless, familiar yearning. For what? Why?

In June 1932 my parents, Noel and Giana Blakiston, were among the first to take a three-week Intourist holiday in the Soviet Union. It cost £26 10s per person, all in. They sailed from Hays Wharf through the Kiel Canal to Leningrad in a Soviet ship, the *Felix Dzherzhinsky*. The party numbered around fifteen; among them a woman, travelling with her daughter, who in England had expressed a considerable interest in communism. The MP, Lady Astor, had paid for the trip so that the woman could see it for herself and be disabused of her enthusiasm. One of the English travellers, with problems of debt, jumped overboard. Seeing it happen, a Russian stewardess threw him a wooden board to hold onto; but although the ship circled and circled, the man was lost.

The food on board was exceptionally good. Caviar, with second helpings, was offered at every meal.

I had been conceived; so recently that it wasn't until a fellow passenger remarked how tired my mother was looking that she knew for sure I was on my first trip to Russia.

Two or three White Nights were spent in Leningrad. The traffic, including trams taking people to work, continued ceaselessly twenty-four hours a day. An overnight train took them to Moscow. They sat up, choosing Soft Class with padded benches rather than Hard Class without. The food, away from the ship, was generally unappetising and was given in return for a meal ticket.

Stalin was talked about (it was during the first Five Year Plan), though not with fear; OGPU, the secret police, with fear. Photographs taken by the tourists had to be left in the Soviet Union to be developed, after which they were forwarded.

My mother remembers the shop windows empty, save for handfuls of nails. Vodka was 1/6d. a bottle. In a foreign currency shop one traveller bought a Bishop's mitre.

The holiday included a visit to a car factory at Nizhny Novgorod, reached by boat down the Volga. There was great heat. My parents decided to sleep on deck to avoid bedbugs; they were devoured by mosquitoes. It was advised that a face could be cooled by covering it with slices of cucumber. The factory outing fell through. Later it was learned that a consignment of left-side car wings had arrived but not right-side. Echoes of left/right boots for soldiers missing during the Crimean War. No one was working.

My mother talks of seeing Lenin in his Tomb, of birch trees, of depression induced by the drab apparel of the citizens, and of the quantities of vodka drunk by the party in relief as they emerged from the Kiel Canal on the return journey.

I have only ever wanted one way of life – that of actress. In the meantime, in 1954, I spent a year as PA to Ismene, wife of Sir Pierson (Bob) Dixon, United Kingdom Delegate to the United Nations in New York. My qualification was that I spoke reasonable French, the diplomatic language, one-sixteenth of my blood being Gallic on my mother's side. I signed the Official Secrets Act. I felt proud to be left in charge of a locked briefcase while the Ambassador was away from the Riverdale Residence for a couple of nights. I took it to the tennis court and kept it in view throughout a game.

Each delegation had a register of their accredited diplomats to the UN. I devoured the entry for the USSR. One day, Bob Dixon asked me to look up the first names of the Minister at the Soviet Delegation, to whom he was writing a letter. 'Arkady A,' I told him, without moving. He was astonished but accepted my certainty. A heady evening in Manhattan was spent with some UN journalists, a Russian amongst them. I found him unbelievably glamorous, although we hardly exchanged words. I stared and stared, wondering which part of the country he came from; whether he had a wife and children; wanting to hear him talk his own language instead of English. We were told later that, being connected with the British Delegation, we should not fraternise with a Soviet reporter.

One hot summer evening at Wave Hill, on the banks of the Hudson River, Andrey Vishinsky came to a Security Council dinner.

We spoke French together. He appeared charming, teaching me my first Russian word, *zharko* – hot. I was wading into Russian novels, beginning with Dostoyevsky's *Crime and Punishment,* which was the most exciting book I had ever read. This year it was Tolstoy's turn. I wrote to my father[1] that I wished the diplomats in New York would talk about *War and Peace* instead of war and peace.

In the autumn of 1955, I went to RADA to train as an actress. While I was there, a Russian film of *Othello* was given a Gala showing at the Royal Festival Hall. I was among the students who sold programmes. We were invited to a reception at the Soviet Embassy to meet the stars, Sergey Bondarchuk – Othello, and Andrei Popov – Iago. The expanding confidence that follows a glass of vodka gave me the courage to approach Popov and invite him and Bondarchuk to lunch at my parents' house in Chelsea, before their return to Moscow. This was the equivalent of inviting John Gielgud and Laurence Olivier. They accepted. It was agreed that they would arrive at two p.m., bringing with them, after some persuading, a tense female interpreter.

My mother,[2] a generous and tolerant riser to that sort of occasion, bought beer and prepared lamb chops and other English typicalities. She then discreetly went out, leaving us waiting nervously. I had asked my American co-student, Elizabeth Hubbard, and her Swedish boyfriend, to help me with what suddenly seemed an egotistical folly. At a quarter to four – now thoroughly anxious – we looked out of the window and saw, coming round the far side of Markham Square, two enormous black limousines. They drew up outside the house. Out climbed, in addition to the two actors and interpreter, a pair of uninvited men in dark suits.

We gave them beer to drink; they asked about our studies. Then, into the dining room, laid up quickly for the gate-crashers, to eat

---

[1] Noel Blakiston was an archivist and Head of the Search Room, Public Record Office. He published *A Romantic Friendship: Letters from Cyril Connolly to Noel Blakiston* (Constable); short stories, *Canon James, The Lecturer, The Thoughtful Boy* (Chapman and Hall); three volumes of collected short stories (Constable).

[2] Georgiana Blakiston (née Russell) published *Letters of Conrad Russell* (John Murray); *Lord William Russell and His Wife* (John Murray); *Woburn and the Russells* (Constable).

the over-cooked food. The conversation moved comfortably enough. Bondarchuk seemed rather remote and austere, Popov very friendly. After eating, he went out into the little garden with a cine camera and took some shots. They gave us each signed photographs of themselves before they left.

Eight years later I was engaged to do a stint in a television programme, *Emergency Ward 10*. I discovered that BBC Radio intended to start a Russian language programme for beginners. The weekly lesson coincided with my recording day at ITV. I took my portable wireless to the dressing room during the supper break and sat in costume, listening, repeating, writing down, until the Studio Manager called 'Stand by, please, Miss Blakiston'. I used to transliterate the Evening Standard in Cyrillic letters, which looked glorious.

Work, marriage and a son and daughter: Adam and Charlotte. I made no progress with the language.

1974 took me to New York with the Actors Company, of which I was a founder member. We presented, among other plays, *The Wood Demon* by Chekhov, an early version of *Uncle Vanya*. I was not in that production. The two AC's, Anton Chekhov and Agatha Christie, both ignored me until Miss Marple swooped me up for television.

I visited an exhibition of pictures from the Hermitage and the State Russian Museum at the Knoedler Gallery in Manhattan, where I fell instantly in recognition with an oil painting by Kuindzhi, *Evening in the Ukraine,* painted in 1878. A group of cottages bathed in rosy light, nestling in a hillside. What is the chord that gets plucked? Did I once live there? I bought a postcard reproduction to keep by my bed, where it faded to wash colours.

Another opportunity to study the language came with BBC TV's *Russian Language and People,* devised and produced by arch-linguist Terry Doyle. Again, family commitments, travelling for work, made it impossible to do the minimum daily homework that is essential to build up the groundwork of a foreign language.

Years go by.

2. Kuindzhi, *Evening in the Ukraine* (1878).

The big step forward came in the spring of 1982. I was appearing with the Actors Company at the Lyric Theatre, Hammersmith, in *Bumps and Knots,* devised by Edward Petherbridge. The artistic director of the theatre, Peter James, for whom Yury Lyubimov was to come and direct his own version of *Crime and Punishment* the following year, invited to our first night Oleg Yefremov, Director of the Moscow Art Theatre, Tanya Lavrova, one of his leading actresses, and Alexey Bartoshevich, theatre critic, Shakespeare scholar and grandson of Kochalov, the first actor to play Konstantin in Chekhov's *Seagull* in the new MKhAT. They were on a visit to this country sponsored by the Great Britain-USSR Association. After the performance Yefremov graciously kissed my hand, murmuring compliments in his rich bass voice. Lavrova looked not at all well, pale, wearing shaded glasses. Bartoshevich, a quiet mysterious person, spoke exceptionally good English. The Lyric Theatre management had gone home, leaving the three somewhat bewildered with no prospect of supper or of a ride back to their hotel. I had to meet my agent and was unable to oblige. Eventually someone took pity on them and gathered them up.

John Roberts, Director of the GB-USSR Association, responded enthusiastically when I suggested giving a lunch party for them at my house, followed by a trip to Hampton Court Palace. Among my guests were Edward Petherbridge and his wife, Emily Richard, the director Julian Amyes with his wife, Ann, a cultured, witty woman, who has adapted Chekhov letters for performance; actors Vernon Dobtcheff, whose name sounds as though he should be Russian but isn't, and Jeffry Wickham with his wife, Claire. Jeffry learned Russian while doing his National Service. The Amyes brought with them the American writer, Jerome Kilty, who had had work performed in Moscow. Helping me were my son and daughter, Adam and Charlotte.

I picked up the Russians from their hotel. Yefremov in flared trousers, much commented on by my children, and a leather overcoat. Tanya wore a feminine black trouser suit. In the car they talked through Andrey, the only linguist, declaring that Alan Howard in *Good*, by C. P. Taylor, was the actor whose work they had most admired.

I had prepared smoked haddock, steak and kidney, apple pie.

Yefremov spoke no English. He offered *etwas* Deutsch. I thought he looked a little pinched and unhappy, but he enjoyed his wine. I took Tanya up to my bedroom for a breather. She explained that they were all three completely worn out, having seen thirteen performances in seven days. Her few words of English and mine of Russian helped us to exchange family facts about our children, work, the difficulties of divorce.

Before setting off to sightsee, I proudly showed them the signed photographs of Popov and Bondarchuk.

'We do not bring pictures of ourselves,' said Yefremov grandly, handing me a large photograph of Stanislavsky as an old man, which the three had signed.

At Hampton Court, Tanya and Charlotte went into the Maze together. They were lost for several minutes although we kept in shouting contact. When they escaped Tanya was weeping. We posed for each other's cameras outside the Palace. I knew that at last I had friends to visit in Moscow.

During the spring of 1983, I was working at Granada TV in a comedy series, *Brass*. I spotted a gap in my schedule. I rang John Roberts who was encouraging, telling me how to telegraph Yefremov, to make travel arrangements through an agency that looks after businessmen. He and his wife, Liz, were to be substantial friends to the Russian side of my life.

I asked Peter James to give me an introduction to Yury Lyubimov in Moscow. His Taganka Theatre was the most exciting in the city, and I knew that tickets would be impossible to come by without influence. As luck would have it, Lyubimov was in London doing some pre-planning with Peter, who suggested that I drop by casually to meet him. His designer, David Borovsky, was pointed out to me, a large shambling figure. Eeyore. Majestically down the stairs came Lyubimov. Two or three people accompanied him, but he created space around himself. After shaking his hand, I asked whether I might visit his theatre and perhaps watch a rehearsal. Of course. I felt that a curtsey would have been in order when I left.

What I had always wanted was about to happen.

Beginner's Luck

8–14 June 1983

8 June – Wednesday

Couldn't get to sleep last night; mind racing. Washed my hair in the kitchen sink, listened to John Timpson and Brian Redhead squeezing out their last BBC pre-election jokes. My visiting ex-husband Russell Hunter, with our daughter Charlotte, came down to see me off. Packed an umbrella. Forgot my sunglasses.

A duty-free bottle of Bell's whisky for Oleg Yefremov, Director of the Moscow Art Theatre, *Diorissimo* for me and boarded the plane. Seated next to a Polish-born lawyer from Chicago. He asked where I was getting off.

'Moscow. You?'

'Warsaw.'

'*Warsaw?*'

Miles of farmland, following the curvy sandy river, high-rise flats, children playing on dusty squares. At Warsaw most of the passengers trooped out, leaving two extrovert Englishmen, a silvery American, a smiling plump, gold-toothed man with a small daughter, a wrinkled man who might have been a woman, a wrinkled woman who might have been a man, and me.

I was determined to touch Polish soil. A teenager in khaki barred my way but David and Dennis said, '*Ne* problem', and came too. It was hot. A small empty airport, with about two hundred people watching from a balcony. We wondered if a VIP was about to land.

We took off again, so light that the plane rattled.

Two hours to Moscow. We turned right. They said, 'We've crossed the border now.' My heart pounding, I lay down across three empty seats, trying to rest, but too excited. The approach to Moscow, Sheremetevo, twenty minutes or so, is beautiful: forest, patches of green, gatherings of dachas amongst the trees; small

I

pines and birches with silver trunks. As we land, my heart feels as if it will burst. Into a modern, darkened-glass building with sliding doors.

'This is the bad bit,' warned David and Dennis.

Passports and visas – five minutes.

'Now we get to the really bad bit,' insisted Dennis and David.

From a bag, like Mary Poppins, they brought out six glasses and some wine.

'Waiting for the baggage can take two hours,' they announced.

'For eight cases?'

'Yes.'

We hardly had time to empty our glasses twice. Practical women put the bags through an X-ray machine. Less than half an hour. David and Dennis helped us all to find where to go for cars. I changed some money; my driver was there.

We drove fast and straight. About forty minutes. I saw war memorials; a baroque station – Belorussky Vokzal – where the international trains arrive. A statue of Gorky; Peter's Palace, red and pretty; a statue of Mayakovsky. The historic highlights stand out from the modern buildings. Up wide Gorky Street. A sudden opening out into Red Square with the Kremlin just there. All yellow paint, the Kremlin. Those shiny golden domes, just as I thought they would be. The National Hotel faces it across a huge площадь,[1] which you can't cross because of the rushing cars.

Reception offered that if I didn't like the room I could move in the morning when some people leave. It's a large, old-fashioned hotel. A wide staircase with relief marble statues sticking out from the walls, naked. On each landing there is an open space with a large desk and a chair for a woman who controls the keys for that floor. She also has supplies of mineral water, you can order tea from her.

A little cupboard of a room with a radio that worked when plugged in and a TV that didn't. The bathroom was tiny, the bath a Sitz. No hot water. I learned that breakfast was from eight to ten on the second floor. I approached Reception and arranged to swap in the morning.

---

[1] Square.

I had been warned that I must not telephone people in politically sensitive situations from the hotel. Taking my map, I stepped into the callbox on the corner of the street to ring Professor Julius Kagarlitsky. Later, it occurred to me that the callbox at the bottom of Gorky Street must be the most foreign-used and KGB-listened-to in the Soviet Union; both writer Julian Bond and actress Juliet Stevenson had seen him when they were there.

Juliet and I met on her first television job, *The Mallens*, by Catherine Cookson, at Granada TV. I was struck by her warmth, maturity and superb truthfulness, and have cherished and admired her since. While she was working with Peter Brook at the Royal Shakespeare Company, she encountered, sitting in on rehearsals, the distinguished Russian scholar. She was fired to visit his country, where she met his son, Boris, her age. He showed her all over Moscow, impressing her greatly by the level of intellect, curiosity and advanced education and positive thinking. For this reason, she recommended that I introduce myself, though she warned that Boris has been interned for dissidence. Julian Bond had recommended that I take soap to deliver to him in prison. I'd also rung his friends, Ronald and Laura Harwood, who help him in his aspirations towards being published in England. Laura told me on no account must I call on them because they were being eaten out of house and home by foreign visitors. Julian Bond told me to ignore that. My luggage was full of plastic packs of coffee, paperback plays by Stoppard, Pinter, Brian Friel, David Hare and two one-man plays by W. Gordon Smith, *Xanadu* which Russell does and one on Van Gogh. The professor answered the telephone. I told him who I was. He asked, 'Will you come and visit us now?'

'Now?'

'Yes, now. Get on the green line at Prospekt Svyerdlova and get out at Aeroport.'

'All right.'

It was ten p.m.

The Moscow underground is famous for being perfect. It's true. Easy to put the five-kopek coin in a slot, go down a moving staircase to a platform on the right or left, above which the name of every station the train stops at is written. If you can read the letters, you *can't* get on the wrong train. As the train stops at a station, a woman's voice announces the name of the stop, whether it's an intersection and what the next stop will be. As well as 'Осторожно, двери закрываются. Следующая станция...'.[2] I thought it was a friendly guard but it's the same voice on every train and I suppose an actress got a year's employment for doing the entire network. I wonder whether Ken Livingstone would allow me... Also, there's the marble, the chandeliers and the statues...

Julius said he would be wearing a blue-jeans suit, sitting opposite the last carriage. I was in black. He's around sixty. He took me a short walk to his apartment, showing me his parked car which he can't drive because it needs an unavailable spare part. Up some stairs into a narrow hall where he took my coat. I unloaded everything from my bag and tentatively brought out the soap for his son. He said, 'D'you know we have a miracle, he has just been released ten days ago.' I cried. He took me in to meet his wife, Raya, who was sitting at the kitchen table, wearing her dressing gown, with two crutches up against the wall. She, too, speaks excellent English. An obliging girl was cutting up cucumber with liver sausage, cheese and bread.

'Please, no,' I remembered to say. 'Just some tea.'

They brought out the vodka. I made a ghastly *faux pas*. I sipped mine and while talking, put the glass down on the table; Raya gasped, 'No!' and reached forward. Too late, I'd done it. It should be swallowed in one.

'Is it bad luck?'

'Yes. I'm very superstitious.'

I felt a chill. But it passed; time, too. He brought out the letter Trevor Nunn, Glenda Jackson and others had written to *The Times* about their son, Boris.

'Please thank them all and tell them our wonderful news.'

They are an impressive literary couple; she translates, he teaches students at the Theatre Institute, they both write reviews of TV series from England.

---

[2] 'Attention, the doors are closing. The next station is....'

They were feeling wounded because a notice they had written had been returned unpublished, thought too enthusiastic. They talked frankly about the difficulties, of the bad times their country has been going through. Not *them*, their *country*. Boris is at the seaside he visited as a child, trying to adjust to being free again. He will find it hard to get a job. Maybe a scene shifter at the theatre. He is brilliant and can't function unless his mind is engaged. He wants to write. I sensed the agony they must feel on his account.

Around one o'clock, tea was put on the table with some special cake. I felt overwhelmed to be sprung into such a powerful encounter on my first evening. Finally, well after two, I said goodbye to Raya. Julius took me by the arm, out onto the street to find a taxi. I left him like an old friend.

Outside the National Hotel, deserted at that time of night, the Kremlin behind me, I rang the front door bell. I showed my пропуск[3] to a sleepy porter through the glass door, he let me in. I fell into bed, feeling that even if I had to go home the next day, it would have been worth it.

9 June – Thursday, Election Day

Breakfast by eight. Put at a table with a French girl who'd been in Moscow for two weeks. Black bread, openwork greyish bread, butter and orange purée: two slices of cheese on my plate, two bendy pink sausages on another, a sweet shiny bun. Tea or coffee. I dropped the bangers in my bag in case I got into difficulties over lunch.

I moved into a more comfortable room with bath. Each room has its own telephone – you dial direct. I called the Cultural Attaché at the British Embassy, whose colleague could arrange a meeting with Yury Lyubimov at the Taganka Theatre, to whom I must deliver a letter from Peter James of the Lyric Theatre, Hammersmith. This was a ruse of *entrée*. From Intourist, I requested tickets for the circus and *Ivanov* at MKhAT.

Crossing into Red Square by the underpass, I came up near GUM, the State department store. The queue for Lenin's tomb

---

[3] Pass.

opposite was about four thick, stretching to the edge of the square. People were waiting for the Changing of the Guard – every hour, on the hour. An officer and two guards march like Rockettes doing diagonal kicks across their bodies with straight knees, crashing their feet straight down onto the ground. It must hurt dreadfully. The last people in the Lenin queue snaked through the doors of the tomb, which were pulled to, as the Kremlin clock chimed. Proud-making for a Russian. My eyes welled.

I decided to walk all around the Kremlin before going in. Красная площадь[4] looked more or less as I expected: cobbled stones, smaller than it appears during the May Day Parade on television. Getting my first impression of Russian people together in a crowd – they are as diverse as the Americans. Short, dark, tall, fair, bandy, slanted, fat, thin, deep-set eyes, Chinese, hanging jowls, sunburnt. Plenty of smoking soldiers in uniform amongst the spectators. A feeling of nonchalance.

People eat ice cream here. The ices are long thick sausages, wrapped in paper or cornets, which come from cold galvanized trays.

I made my way down a hundred-yard slope to the Moscow River, which is about two-thirds of the Thames at Westminster. It looks muddy, but people were fishing in the sunshine. As I walked, on the other bankside I could see the British Embassy with Union Jack flying, a pink gracious early nineteenth-century building inside gates, with a drive in.

Historic buildings are painted pink, peach, yellow, Wedgwood blue, duck egg, dark green, peppermint.

I strolled along the riverside of the Kremlin. Like Edinburgh, it's on a mound one side, though not so steep. Trees shedding white fluffy cottony stuff. Round the back from Red Square are charming gardens laid out with rose trees tended by women wearing headscarves; benches, scented lime trees. There are also self-service lemonade machines, in rows like lockers, maybe eight together. The glass, not plastic, is upside down on a nozzle that when you press it down squirts water and cleans it for the next person. You put in your money, place the glass under the taste you

---

[4] Red Square.

want – if it's working – drink, then turn the glass upside down again for the next person. Nobody seems to steal the glasses; there are two in each place.

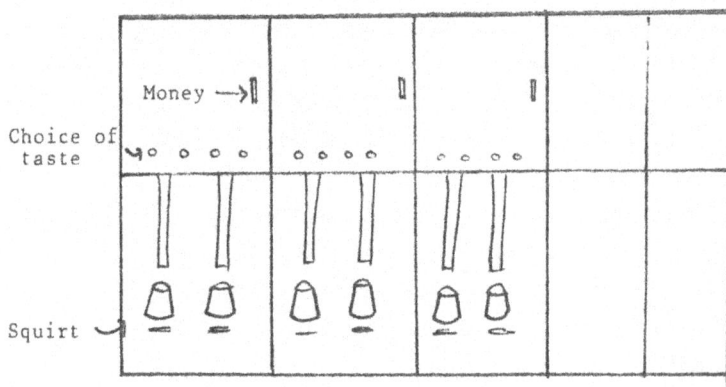

3. My sketch of a lemonade machine.

The three entrances to the Kremlin are guarded. Red traffic lights, signs saying *СТОП*[5]. The public way in is over a bridge. It was *ЗАКРЫТ*[6] until tomorrow, so I went into multi-domed St Basil's. Surprisingly small inside. Groups of people pushing to look make it impossible, but I got my first taste of icons.

It suddenly rained, I hurried into GUM. It is constructed on levels; floors with open balconies going up to the roof. Sections devoted to shoes, cameras; ice cream on all corners, with queues. Nothing I wanted to buy – clothes without style, cut glass. They are not fashionable in Western terms. Many dyed-blondes of all ages with roots growing out; some pretty girls, desirable men. When the older women give up, they go all the way; immensely stout with ankle socks or footlets inside their sandals. The very old wear headscarves, as in Eisenstein films.

Under the walls of the Kremlin is the Tomb of the Unknown Soldier, sporting a big flame, where brides come to lay their wreaths. They arrived in clutches of four and five, placing their bouquets – two or four roses or carnations. Stared at appreciatively

---

[5] Stop.
[6] Closed.

by bystanders, photographed, then bundled back into their cars. I feel so safe.

You can get almost anywhere on the Metro in twenty minutes. A woman in a fat red hat sits in a kiosk at the top of each escalator where you pay, with a green plastic disk. No ticket. After my adventure on the first evening I think nothing of a journey and want to see how few stops I can do it in by changing lines. Going to the Taganka, I went eight stops with one change. Coming back, I was told how to do it in three.

I tramped home, having passed the Bolshoi and Maly theatres; a big children's toy shop; people pushing through swing doors to buy meat. For dinner, I was put at a table with a Finn who is doing a deal in paper and plastic bags.

'Cutting down your trees?'

'Finland is all trees.'

Having eaten only my limp sausages walking around the walls of the Kremlin, I went all out for protein. The Finn helped me to order £5 worth of black caviar (£25 in England) and some vodka. The waiter looked shocked. It comes by the 100 grams, so I had 100 which is two strong glasses. Then I had sturgeon à la Moscow; the piece of firm fish is under mushrooms which are under potatoes, on top of which is a creamy sauce, accompanied by a cucumber salad with celery leaves and sour cream.

The Finn left after the band had played their first set; three balalaikas (one electric), drums, two female singers. Some Japanese businessmen got excited about one of the chanteuses. I joined some English-speaking people at the next table. A Canadian with his Russian comfort beside him and a German, speechless with fatigue after setting up an exhibition.

10 June – Friday

Led to a breakfast table.

'Oh, you're that television actress, aren't you?' asked an Australian, I think, living in Kent.

I wondered if she'd heard the election result. She hadn't.

I booked a trip to Zagorsk, which was sold to me as a museum. Pouring rain. In the bus, with our guide's enthusiasm, I began to get a picture of the Kremlin as the centre of Moscow; all roads leading into it, at the heart of Russia.

I've heard no aeroplanes overhead. The only birds seem to be sparrows, pigeons and a version of a magpie which is beige where ours are white; it caws like a Shakespearean clown. I've seen two cats but no dogs.

Zagorsk is the Vatican of the Russian Orthodox Church, a great walled complex with a gold-domed cathedral and baptistry; a refectory for when the tsars visited, the palace they stayed in, which is now the home of the students. This is where they train for the priesthood. There is a house for the patriarch who visits in the summer. In the cathedral such activity – lights, chanting, old women kissing crucifixes held by priests; kissing the Tomb of St Sergius at rest. We were shown garments and medallions belonging to Boris Godunov who is also buried here. The cathedral was founded, I believe, by St Sergius of Radonezh, the spiritual leader and founder of the monastic order in medieval Russia. Icons, candles; holy water and bread being bought; people writing names on pieces of paper that were placed on large pewter plates – perhaps asking for blessings. A feeling of pilgrimage. Artificial flowers decorating the icons; people crossing themselves and bowing. Not only women. A man with one arm was going at it like anything with what remained of his other, which wasn't much. War-wounded. The seat labelled for them in in the Metro is often correctly occupied. I lit a candle for peace and dropped some tears.

For lunch we ate cold pork and cucumber, followed by cabbage soup (not hot enough), followed by stew with rice on top in a deep pot. You couldn't get to the meat until you'd eaten the rice. Then a pancake with sweet purée on it, followed by ice cream. Two big bottles of lemonade on the table. In the lavatory we were handed individual linen towels to dry our hands. You might expect that in Germany – extraordinary service here.

Embassy message: 'Taganka, 6.30'. Lyubimov.

People clustering round the doors of the theatre, hoping for returns. I asked to see the *administratr:*[7] my name was known. I

---

[7] Administrator.

got a ticket for 1 rouble 80 kopecks and was led upstairs to meet the Master.

A comfortable office with armchairs and posters. Autographs on his wall. Pale-blue denim suit and red jersey. He clearly didn't remember meeting me with Peter James at the Lyric. I gave him the letter. We tried a little French, a little Italian. The leading actor, Smekhov, came in for a minute and tried a little German.

Lyubimov had sent for an older actress, tiny as Joan Greenwood, who spoke good English. Through her he questioned me about the cast he has for *Crime and Punishment*. I know them all, except two. I began telling him how Sheila Reid (whose name was on the list) and I had played Regan and Goneril to Robert Eddison's King Lear with the Actors Company. She is petite, I am tall. Whatever must Queen Lear have been like to produce two such disparate daughters? He was not the slightest bit interested in my imagery and cut me off, asking, 'Are they good, are they good?'

'Of course.'

His colleagues thought it splendid that I had gone to Zagorsk.

'The heart of Russia,' agreed Lyubimov.

They talked of the play that I was about to see by Trifonov, who had been a great friend of this theatre. He left me alone with the modest communicative actress from Leningrad. She had come to Moscow to ask if she could join him and was staggered that he took someone as old as her – not more than sixty, six years ago. She thinks he's the best director in Russia. She also has a way of talking about the difficult times their country has been through. Again, never the *people* – always our *country*. We welled up together. Lyubimov took me down to my seat. A public man. He was the centre of attention as he gesticulated his way down the stairs to the foyer. I remarked on flowers laid before a memorial in the foyer. They were for Vladimir Vysotsky, the poet-singer, beloved by Muscovites, who had performed Hamlet at the Taganka. His gravel-voiced records are still amongst those most often played. Unofficially. The Russians honour their dead heroes.

The play was hard to understand. My friend, Tatyana, had a tiny part. Intense, it has been in the repertoire for three years, still sells out. It's about the bad times.

I like watching actors in a foreign language; you can see who's being truthful. I found it an exemplary company. At the curtain call two of the leading actors were handed flowers from the front – half a dozen carnations or roses.

11 June – Saturday

Set off for Novodevichy Nunnery (recommended by Juliet Stevenson) soon after ten. Chekhov and Khrushchev are buried there. I asked a policeman the way as I came out of the Metro; proud that I understood him when he said, 'To the right.' I have carried a tired body today. Shimmering with fatigue and feeling that I must take it gently, I walked slowly to this lovely place. Once you've seen Zagorsk things can pale; but it's beautiful. Red and gold.

I strolled round and got the feel; sat on a bench with an old woman who was feeding bread to the birds. She wore corduroy gym shoes and held a stick; crossed herself vigorously when she'd finished. The public lavatory could have been no worse in the time of Ivan the Terrible. You hold your breath, stand over a hole and hope that no one else needs it at the same time.

I ambled to Tolstoy's charming, detached, red country house in the middle of Moscow. I'd like to live there. The rooms are the right size. It is a real family home. His study with black upholstered chairs and sofas; a low ceiling, small windows – you could imagine him chatting with Gorky *et al*. The housekeeper and dressmaker shared a matchbox bedroom that would be scorned as a bathroom in Britain. Four rooms on one floor made a sitting room, a drawing room, an inner room and a landing for receiving people. The writer slept in a room partitioned by screens from a sitting room near the large dining room. Two wooden single beds next to each other. Unpretentious. I stayed as long as I could to soak up the atmosphere of living there.

A trek down a wide, dull, circular avenue to Anton Chekhov's pink house, which doesn't have the same authentic feeling. The floors are modern; unlived in. I was interested, in both houses, by the tiled sections in the walls with brass flues where the heat must have come from. One comforting warm wall in a room to lean against and someone putting in logs somewhere, but not in sight. I was given uni-size felt slippers with strings to tie. They help to save and polish the floors. In the garden which was tiny and over-grown, there was one bright orange five-headed lily standing.

Back to Gorky Street, I walked the length of it (memories of Fifth Avenue). It's the shopping street, but the displays make you ache. Nothing to go in for. Women's petticoats; pale green and peach, arranged in the window. Queues waiting for the doors to open at a TV shop. A window devoted entirely to *petit beurre* biscuits or uniform tinned food stacked up. Two bookshops, government offices. *Izvestia*. Stanislavsky Theatre. Down side streets I caught a Chelsea sight of rows of lowish pale-yellow buildings opening into a piazza with benches, people sitting with their children under leafy trees. An old-fashioned domestic atmosphere. I was looking for the old Moscow Art Theatre, but didn't find it.

Seven stops on the Metro to Universitetskaya – one of which is in the open air right in the middle of one of the bridges over the river. What a brilliant joke.

The new Circus is a permanent, silvery domed building, glass at ground level. The usherettes pointed to the date on my ticket, 10 June – *yesterday*. I tried saying, 'Intourist' – they said – '*Administratr*'. I waited... they relented and shoved me round to a seat. I queued for a piece of smoked fish on bread and a slice of curled rubber cheese on bread. Everyone else was drinking lemonade as well and eating ice creams.

Some fine acrobats performed daring feats on a slanting wire. Others climbed up four tiers and did marvellous jumps in pairs off springboards, if they missed they tried again. No wires. They were best. Four muzzled bears in shorts and T-shirts on the high wire; then llamas, an ostrich, poodles, ponies, a chicken, white doves, two camels, a sheep and a zebra. They did their best. I couldn't clap and the Muscovites groaned in sympathy for the animals too; I felt I should applaud so they didn't feel a failure. They looked well kept and shiny, but it was hateful. Because performances start at seven p.m. you're out before ten, in broad daylight.

12 June – Sunday

OK, the Kremlin. It's free unless you want to get into the churches and museums. The space feels immense. Old buildings round a large piazza with a small *касса* for tickets and a kiosk for postcards. Ladies and Gents (always, everywhere) labelled'Ж'[8] and 'M'.[9] Here the Ж was a converted, domed place, lined with plenty of tiles. Hot air machines to dry your hands. Bright sunshine outside. I sadly missed my sunglasses. Took stock. The big cathedral where they crowned the tsars. Icons from floor to ceiling. Much gold. It's a small building compared with Western Gothic; square, a mosaic portrait of Jesus looking down on you as you peer up into the high dome. Ivan the Terrible's throne. Henry Irving would have appreciated that.

The place I most wanted to see, Lenin's study, was not open. There is a large, early nineteenth-century group of buildings, painted yellow, where the government offices are and where the leaders live. I think of Andropov 's head on his pillow not a quarter of a mile from mine on mine. (Wrong, as I discovered later.) A formal laid-out garden behind a statue of Lenin displays the oak that Yuri Gagarin planted after being the First Man in Space. It's the size of a large apple tree after only twenty-two years. Policemen with whistles make sure that people walk only on the pavements or zebra crossings. Sharp toots go on all the time against infringers.

Now Lenin's Mausoleum. I announced 'Intourist' and was allowed to join the part of the line that was already at the edge of Red Square. The patient locals had probably already been trudging for three hours. I felt guilty and grateful. I was about fifty yards from the entrance when we stopped so that the Rockettes could change the guard on the dot of one. They move at one step every two seconds. The swinging arm thumps against the chest as it comes up. They're standing on guard, with eyes flickering, as you file in through the door. Policemen insist you walk formally in

---

[8] The first letter of the Russian word *zhenshchina*/женщина meaning 'woman'; here, 'ladies'[toilet].

[9] The first letter of the Russian word for 'man' – *muzhshchina*/мужчина; here, 'gents'[toilet].

pairs. 'Take your hands out of your pockets!' 'Ts, ts – No talking': down steps, round to the right, into the chamber about twenty feet square, VERY COLD – up steps. There is Lenin under a canopy with eerie light. Set in crystal, they say; you can't see the edges from the way it's lit. He looks like a waxwork, with sandy hair and beard. Hands, one closed, one lying flat on the black cover. You can see him from three sides – the last as you go downstairs again to the exit. You can then walk beside the wall of the Kremlin which exhibits the statues and plaques of past leaders. Kosygin gets a plaque on the wall, but no statue. Brezhnev, a statue. I was standing exactly at the spot I had noticed when watching his funeral on TV in London. Stalin too, a statue. It was all over in thirty minutes, my trip would have felt incomplete without it. Lenin was an icon, you feel the homage to him all around. There are always flowers by his statues.

The new MKhAT is built on a *boulevard* – there are several of these gracious tree-lined promenades in the middle of wide avenues. MKhAT reminds me of shrapnel from the outside, strikingly unlike anything else I've seen. Inside, I asked once again for the '*Administratr*' and gave him a book and letter for Yefremov; he told me that the Director was in Prague with the touring company. I went to a good centre stall for a little less than £2 (two roubles). A large open stage, no curtain, sloping auditorium. The circle starts far back; upper circle and gallery; boxes sloping down like the Royal Festival Hall. A photographer in one of the boxes was taking shots throughout the performance. Not flashes – click, click. I'm surprised the actors didn't complain. Ivanov was played by Innokenty Smoktunovsky, which was a thrilling surprise for me, as I had admired him so much in the fascinating Russian film of *Hamlet*. The actors, all properly engaged; when the entire cast was on there was movement within groups. It was set in the courtyard of the house, playing scenes through ground floor windows and sitting out of doors on plain bentwood chairs or sprawled on cushions on the paving. It was fluid and believable, though I understood little of the dialogue. Smoktunovsky stood with one leg straight and the other slightly bent. He did fine acting. His agitation was marvellously discreet. There was measured pacing of the huge stage. His build-up to the shooting was masterly because of its ordinariness. Suddenly, bang, he was dead on the floor and the play over. The wife was excellent; the young girl truthful; plenty of convincing young actors standing about; a servant being comical with a tray of vodka; a funny character man who was cynical, then drunk, then crying. I enjoyed it. The woman next to me had seen a production at the Maly ('Small Theatre') ten years ago, which she thought was much better. The lighting was what I call stroking lighting, taking you from scene to scene tenderly. Flowers for the leading lady were handed up from the stalls.

In the foyer there was an exhibition of photographs of Stanislavsky in many of his roles. I shook hands with the *Administratr* and thanked him again, profusely. Amazing what you can communicate with a few words. Again, bright daylight at ten to ten.

I sauntered up to Pushkin Square where there's a celebrated statue of the poet, always with flowers at his feet. I greet the statue every time I pass it from now on. Dostoyevsky, when he was honoured with a large laurel wreath, staggered to lay it at the feet of his master. It seems to be a spot for drawing the young. Groups talking, smoking.

Strolling back down the other side of Gorky Street to search for the old MKhAT – there it was, all grey-beige and scaffolding. Peering through a workman's door in the wooden surround was a woman as anxious to investigate as I. We crept in. Out of a little hut came a character, the Gravedigger in *Hamlet*, the Porter in *Macbeth*, Luzhin from *Crime and Punishment*. A thick heavy voice. He explained that they've moved the stage to fit a revolve. Afterwards it will be pushed back again. It was bare and exposed. I explained that I was an English actress and wondered whether I could take a memento to London:

'*Можно?*'[10]

'*Да, да.*'[11]

---

[10] 'May I?'

[11] 'Yes, yes.'

The heavens opened. The other woman brought out her umbrella and went home. I sheltered in the hut with *мой русский друг*.[12] He gave me a boiled sweet, told me about the English authors he knew; Shakespeare, Oscar Wilde, Bernard Shaw, Priestley, Richard Aldington (very shocked I'd not read him), Dickens, Burns, *Gullsworty*. It took time to decipher John Galsworthy. I gained points when I divulged that I had played Marjorie Ferrar in *The Forsyte Saga* on BBC television, which was exceedingly popular in the Soviet Union. He told me he is sixty-four. How old am I? I teased him with it is not customary to ask a lady her age and told him twenty-one. He talked about his children Boris, thirty, married but no children, and Katerina, twenty-three. He is a pensioner now, works one night here, then has three at home. We discussed his war wounds. He clapped the left side of his head hard, then under his armpit, then his right leg (enough to re-open any of them). He did it three times.

'*Москва?*'[13] I asked.

'*Нет, Украина – Кавказ.*'[14]

'*Deutsch?*'

'*Да.*'[15]

He showed me his medal. We had a heated conversation about the chances of the next war. He quoted Reagan and Thatcher and did cut-throat gestures – saying the Russians don't want another war. I said I don't either; we both roared *Миру мир*[16] many times. This encounter must have lasted forty-five minutes. We shook hands warmly. He accompanied me to the gate where we shook hands again; he watched as I turned to wave before going into Gorky Street. The whole trip would have been worth it just for this.

13 June – Monday

I resolved to come to Kolomenskoe, recommended by my Australian breakfast neighbour, where I am now, sitting in hot sun

---

[12] My Russian friend.

[13] 'Moscow?'

[14] 'No, Ukraine – the Caucasus.'

[15] 'Yes.'

[16] 'Peace to the World.'

on a bench, on a slope above the Moscow River. This lovely derelict estate used to be a Moscow home of the tsars. A sixteenth-century cathedral of white stone going up into a spire. Relaxed people taking their children for walks, watching tugs on the water. It's the first time I've sat for a time out of doors in any place. There's a small ferry taking cars across, one or two at a time. In the Metro, on the way here, apart from getting lost and having to change four times, I noticed the only rural person I've seen. He had his trousers tucked into his long boots, a rich brown, lined face and small embroidered flat hat. Out of the Metro I asked the way and was taken onto a bus and paid for by a young man who simply wouldn't accept the fare.

I'm so happy. Behind me there's a church with five powder-blue domes studded with gold stars; angled golden crosses sticking out at the top, glittering in the sun. I gave a little boy along the bench my last piece of Swiss chocolate, then an old man who knew him came by and gave him a sweet. They love children; I haven't heard a cross, inter-generational word – even at the circus, which was crammed with tots of three and four.

I came home into the restaurant, ate caviar, cucumber salad, 'sturgeon on spits', which means one piece, with some olives and pickled cabbage. It came to just over ten roubles. For six breakfasts, two lunches and a dinner, I have sat and looked out of the window at the Kremlin – lucky me. It strikes me that the restaurant was jampacked from three till four thirty when I left. Maybe that is when they eat their big meal. I gathered a packet of coffee for Tatyana with two T-shirts to give to whom she wants, also a bottle of whisky for Lyubimov and his actors and various Western plastic bags, which are what people rate best at the moment. I came out of the wrong entrance at the Metro and had to walk all round a large square to reach Taganka. Hopefuls waiting for returns.

Loyal Tatyana Zhuraleva was waiting; I was given a free seat this time. She took me to Lyubimov's office as he wanted me to take a message for Peter James. He wasn't there but his wife made me a cup of coffee while Tatyana tried to tell me the story of Bulgakov's *Master and Margarita*, already in the repertoire for five years. Smekhov was in the play again, hanging round like a tall, sad Labrador. It is a highly inventive production with lots of effects. Excellent ensemble. Actors running through the audience, a live white mouse. I didn't understand enough to be moved but the audience clearly was; I was when the company held up pictures of Bulgakov at the curtain call and clapped him. Zhuraleva helped me to telephone *au revoir* to the Kagarlitskys. Also Tanya Lavrova, just home from the MKhAT tour of Berlin and Prague. We learned that she was in bed, completely wiped-out that Andrey Popov, with whom she was rehearsing Goneril to his Lear, had died suddenly.

The management had kindly allowed me to make the calls and waited to lock up the theatre. In the office, Tatyana and a young *administratr* had talked again about their political difficulties; they said that they only hear bad things about the West, as we only hear bad things about them from Mrs Thatcher.

'Why do people vote for her?' they asked.

I found it hard to say – used words like 'Nanny'. 'The English appreciate being smacked. It makes them feel safe.' I couldn't give a proper answer – only that I didn't agree with the way she goes on. Shaming.

Tatyana came with me to the train, also to the next when I changed lines; she told me about her brother being shot in the war... then about her father dying of starvation in Leningrad...

14 June – Tuesday

I had my last breakfast looking out at the Kremlin. Tatyana had shyly given me a letter from a sick friend of hers to pass to Metropolitan Anthony Bloom in London, asking him to pray for her. She was anxious that if it were found I might be in difficulty. I put it in an envelope with all my theatre programmes and ticket stubs.

Lavrova telephoned; we agreed to meet in my room.

'*Да.*'[17]

She rang back immediately to ask if we could meet outside. They are not allowed into the hotel.

'*Да, хорошо.*'[18]

---

[17] 'Yes.'

[18] 'Yes, that's OK.'

This being Moscow, I saw that I had time to hurry to the Tretyakov Gallery, which houses their best national paintings. I got there quickly on the Metro, shot in – glanced at the early paintings and began to pay real attention to marvellous portraits of Tolstoy, Dostoyevsky, Chekhov, Mussorgsky, Chaliapin, Diaghilev, Shostakovich. I was pleased that by racing through the early rooms I got literally a moving picture view of Russian history through the eyes of their painters. The pictures of Jesus don't show him at all as the late nineteenth- or early twentieth-century Chelsea Embankment girly sort of person that we are used to. They make him Eastern and male; much more convincing.

Back at the hotel to find Lavrova wearing a candy pink trouser suit with high-heeled white sandals and a pale blue jersey. The first sight of Western fashion since I got here. We hugged and laughed. She gave me presents for the children and vodka for me. She took me to her Film Actors' Club for a quick lunch; black and red caviar – very thin crisp little pastry cases filled with liver pâté or an egg mixture; cucumber and tomato with coriander leaves for salad and a small carafe of vodka. I managed to empty my first slug in one. At last I see what you have to do. We talked a bit about Goneril, as I'd played her in two different productions. She complained that the part is difficult because Goneril is so like a man. Popov, Iago – Bondarchuk, Othello. Tanya had told Popov that she too had been at my house in London, he remembered and wanted to meet me if I came to Russia.

I recounted how, when I was working at Granada Television recently, I had watched on a monitor in an office the storm scene of Laurence Olivier's Lear, directed by Michael Elliott, being recorded in short takes. He was having trouble remembering the lines, being prompted *sotto voce* by his colleagues. It was shocking and heroic. He refused to give up. I shall never forget it. She said he was an actor without heart, and anyway she was cross with him for saying all those bad things about Vivien Leigh in the television interview she had seen at the British Embassy.

We were brought two metal dishes – like Turkish coffee pots – holding mushrooms in a creamy sauce – very hot. Russians love mushrooms... and children. We had to leave before the fish. She had arranged for a taxi to take me back to the hotel for my luggage.

I asked for my telephone bill.

'Nothing,' they cried". 'Local calls free!'

I could feel Moscow draining away from me as we sped to the airport. I filled in my customs form. The airport was quite empty. The official looked in my bag, found the envelope with letters, pulled out the paper with the picture of Bulgakov, discovered that it was a programme, looked in my purse, each compartment slowly and separately. When he came to the bag of cloves that I chew after eating onions, he was uncertain. After asking me if I spoke Russian and I'd answered *нет,* I was through to passport control.

As soon as I landed, I called my son and daughter and asked them to meet me at Parsons Green with a bike to help with my heavy bag (mainly vodka and *Пепси-кола*[19]). A cheering cry of 'Mum!' as I stepped from the train. They'd managed to get onto the platform, shivering in T-shirts. It was nearly ten o'clock.

Postscript

It would be impertinent to draw too many conclusions at the end of this six-day trip.

Russia and the Russians. I felt safe. All the time. No threats. I sensed a profound innocence. In the UK – or the USA – I am accustomed to making assessments of people's way of life, aspirations, general well-being by the way they dress; how they present themselves, what they read on the underground, etc. In Moscow I was quite unable to differentiate between the better off and the poorer. I felt that there was a uniformity of everyday experience shared by all – I like that. The drabness, lack of variety and colour in the clothes might depress me if I lived there; at the same time I took pains not to dress garishly, if I caught the eye of someone staring (and they always looked away) I don't think I saw more than a passing curiosity. I felt that they are engaged in their lives – they love their children... and mushrooms and ice cream. I can see they must feel as bewildered by Mrs Thatcher's 'sworn enemies' speeches, as I am. I've just read in Willy Brandt's

---

[19] Pepsi-Cola.

Introduction to his Commission's first report, *North-South*: 'We judge ourselves by our good points and the other side by their failings. The result is frustration and deadlock.'

When Peter the Great sent an embassy to the West, in order to see how things really were, he travelled with the group incognito, part of the time working as an artisan. Hard to imagine a modern politician being so practical and open-minded, he misbehaved socially, too.

I feel that the Russians I met have little experience of how things are in the West and I can understand why Solzhenitsyn was shocked by the materialism. The lack of choice in the consumer sense, while frustrating and boring, must throw them into the real bottom-line, the truth about themselves; something we can divert ourselves from for a lifetime.

I am shocked that they are not free to come and go, to write or say what they like in public; to send and receive what letters they wish. I felt humiliated for them and for myself that to meet me at my hotel they were not permitted to enter but had to wait in the street.

I envy their directness, their spontaneous warmth, their concern for 'our country', not for themselves. The people in the street/Metro look neither happier nor sadder than we do.

I am quite inclined to the official view that the Iron Curtain is as much to prevent the infiltration of the Western forms of corruption/decadence as it is to stop people getting out. It is a vast country and must be hard to administer.

Once, in my room, I saw the door handle being turned – I always locked my door from the inside. Twice the telephone rang – once a woman, once a man – the voice rattled off something in Russian which I couldn't understand; I said so, they rang off.

When I was alone, I found myself thinking randomly and saying aloud, 'I love you'; it's definitely an easy place to express yourself emotionally, my last words must re-echo our shouts in the nightwatchman's hut in MKhAT – *МИРУ МИР!*[20]

---

[20] 'Peace to the World!'

Follow Up...

Following the London visit of Oleg Yefremov, I joined the GB-USSR Association, attending several interesting talks and sometimes meeting Soviet writers, film-makers, musicians there; or at the hospitable house of John and Liz Roberts.

One such talk was given by Mikhail Roshchin, the novelist and playwright, who was accompanied by Svetlana Prokhorova, an English-speaking woman with a post at the Writers' Union in Moscow.

I offered to repeat my previous Hampton Court lunch party, adding to my guest list Nell Dunn, Prunella Scales and Timothy West, (he was playing Stalin at the Old Vic), Robert Cushman (theatre critic of the *Observer)*, Guy Vaesen, theatre director and painter; another Russian-speaking actor, Michael Poole, and his wife, Sybil; David Gothard, who at that time ran the Riverside Studios in Hammersmith.

While I was collecting the Russians, I left a key under a brick so that English guests could get into my house and have a drink. At the Roberts' house I was introduced to and found I was instantly comfortable with Misha Roshchin. He spoke few words of English but there was something relaxed and accessible about him; I knew that communication would be no problem. He is not tall, has a moustache, beard and wears spectacles. He laughs easily. Completely unselfconscious, he was wearing a woollen jersey over his shirt, no jacket. Svetlana, with her splendid command of English, seemed content to be a channel for people to plug into.

On one wall of my kitchen I had, ages ago, pinned an advertisement for a festival of films, directed by Andrei Tarkovsky, that had been held at the Riverside Studios in Hammersmith. I had seen all of them, *Andrei Rublyov, Ivan's Childhood, Mirror, Stalker* and *Sacrifice*, and had been captivated by their profundity. I was not sure whether it would be embarrassing for Misha if I discussed it with him in front of Svetlana. 'Never speak to a Russian about another Russian in front of other Russians,' I had been warned before my first trip. It could put any or all of them into difficulty. There was something about Misha that made me feel it would be all right. I risked it. I pointed to the poster and told of my feelings.

'I want to marry him!'

'Me, too!' answered Misha.

He was, that evening, speaking at the GB-USSR Association; he gave us a dress rehearsal of his speech which was expertly translated by Svetlana, between indulging her passion for bananas. We didn't go sightseeing in the afternoon as he would have been too tired to do his performance, we paid a quick visit to the Soviet Embassy on our way back to their hotel.

For his talk, Misha wore a smart navy-blue pinstriped suit. He spoke without notes for about three-quarters of an hour, then invited questions. It was quite soon after Lyubimov's famous departure from the Soviet Union. The audience, being mostly English, tactfully failed to refer to what was at the front of everyone's mind. Finally, it was a brave thing to do, Misha said he had noticed that no one had mentioned what must be at the front of everyone's mind. Silence clattered round the room. He declared that Lyubimov was an important person in the Moscow theatre scene, that he was missed and that it was hoped he would return. The audience let out its collective breath. This is a writer, some of whose own work is under censorship, who holds a position at the Moscow Art Theatre similar to that of Chekhov in his day; who stood at risk by being so frank. He also made a joke about *Hamlet* that was so subtle it by-passed the audience and failed to get the laugh it deserved. He was speaking in Russian with a translator sitting beside him.

John and Liz Roberts gave a party for Misha's fiftieth birthday. My birthday would follow in three days so with Aquarian fellow feeling I gave him a whisky tumbler inscribed with his name and the date of his first London visit.

Andropov had died in the morning of that day. Their visit was to be shortened. Svetlana sat alone at one end of the room, suffering shock, unable to join the festivity.

At the end of the party, I was designated to drive Misha back to his hotel. We had both drunk enough champagne to think it would be funny if he drove my old automatic Volvo. He set off, gleefully, down the wrong side of the King's Road until, restored to sobriety, I took the wheel.

The night before Misha and Svetlana went home, John Roberts brought him to my house to say goodbye. I was giving dinner to eight people. We agreed in the hall that John and he should pretend to be each other for the benefit of the other guests. John took his jacket off, smiled broadly and spoke with a convincing heavy accent when I introduced him as the Russian writer.

'And this,' I led Misha forward, 'is John Roberts, Director of the GB-USSR Association.'

'*Goot efenink!*' struggled Misha.

John took him away to finalise the translation Michael Frayn was doing of an article that Roshchin had written for the *Observer* about his London visit.

Here, for sure, is a new friend whom I would really enjoy meeting next time I go.

A Moscow–Leningrad–Moscow
Long Weekend

11–13 September 1984

11 September – Tuesday

Julian Amyes, his wife Ann, guests at the Hampton Court excursion last year, with their daughter Isabel, an admirable, listening actress, are coming too.

Julian is a fast-thinking, accommodating television director; I've enjoyed working with him for the last six months. Their family atmosphere is sharp and entertaining. Ann loses things, appears calm on the outside, also indicates impending hysteria. She is funny, travels provided with every aid.

I had bought half a dozen newly published plays, including *Good*, by C. P. Taylor, requested by Julius Kagarlitsky; bangles and hair-clips for Misha's daughters, instant coffee and Earl Grey tea to share.

At Gatwick the guide carried envelopes containing our precious documents and, crucially, the itinerary. It was known that half the party were to stay the one night at the Rossiya Hotel on Red Square and the less privileged half – at the Sevastopol Hotel, away from the centre of Moscow. We had drawn the short straws. We got a £3 rebate. A regular haul of *Diorissimo* in the duty-free.

The brown glass building of Sheremetevo already familiar. I was preparing to recognise Irina, Misha's wife, who would meet me, as he is recently out of hospital and not very well. Misha himself walked through the door, looking all round. He saw me. Our hands went up. Another ten minutes before I got through and was speaking my first words to Misha in Russian since February, when I last saw him at Dancer Road. Wearing blue; jeans, shirt, sweater and windcheater. His hair shining. He had been talking to the Russian tour leader, who explained that I must travel in the bus to the hotel and may not go in his car. He was obviously disappointed that it was such a long way out. He told me that his new play has been censored. Another one too – they are still waiting to hear. Distressed, his eyes reddened.

We got on the bus. Tired and unwell, he followed in his car. The hotel stands in a newly built, characterless concrete area. Misha parked, he carried a bunch of pink chrysanthemums for me. He entered the hotel, saying that he was an Englishman, too. Being so tired, he was going straight home. I asked him to lend me some coins for the Metro, so that I could take the Amyes to look at the Kremlin, floodlit, when we'd eaten. Instead, he sat with the tour guide, Tanya, and waited while we ate steak for dinner. We ordered a bottle of wine which didn't come.

Packed into his car, this sick man drove us until we saw the Kremlin. He drove round it. We crossed the river and looked at it from the road near the British Embassy; stood by the riverside, drinking in the glamour of onion-domes by full moon. He described his love of Moscow, how he knows it and all its corners; it gave him pleasure to show it to us personally. He then took us past the hall, decorated and flag-draped, where Karpov and Kasparov are contesting the World Chess Championship and dropped us at the History Museum. Two minutes to midnight: 'Быстро, быстро!'[1] – we scuttled across Red Square.

I could see that the two young soldiers and their leader had already started their strange stamping, swaying, hypnotising march from the Spassky Tower to the door of Lenin's Tomb to arrive – as they did – as they always do – as I remembered – on the dot of midnight, which chimes, not martially, like Big Ben, but in a tinkling, Christmassy sort of way from the tall clock tower. The door of the tomb slightly ajar, a light inside, Isabel wondered whether the cleaning women were at work. Outside, people were taking flash photographs, following the two retiring guards as they set off on their metronomic return trek. I felt as if I'd watched it all my life.

We must get home on the Metro before it closes at one a.m. We only had one twenty-kopeck piece. I asked the red-hatted woman

---

[1] 'Quickly, quickly!'

at the barrier what to do for change. She beamed dazzlingly, took the twenty coin and let us through.

We knew the hotel was only fifty yards from the Metro exit, but all the buildings looked identical; it being a good night in every respect, the first entrance we tried was the right one. We waved our *propuska*[2] through the glass at the night porter. It was one o'clock. He let us in, said we could get tea or coffee from the attendant on our floor. She had gone to the ninth floor to chat to her friend. Julian went to find her. She made black coffee, also produced Fanta orange. We sat on the landing amongst potted plants and a fish tank. Ann, talking in a loud voice, brought out chocolate, biscottes. Isabel told her she was talking in a loud voice. Julian pretends to be vague as protection against her *persona* of being an Englishwoman-abroad-who-is-slightly-disappointed-by-things-that-happen-which-hadn't-quite-had-her-in-mind-in-the -planning.

At two o'clock I was looking up Russian phrases I might use tomorrow.

'Worth it already,' I said to myself.

12 September – Wednesday

We were among the first at breakfast, where we found generous plates of cheese and sausage.

'*Wursht*, it's *wursht*, not sausage, Julian,' Ann said, both mornings, as it turned out.

I got off the tour bus at the National Hotel. Misha was sitting in his car reading a newspaper. I got in beside him, saying I hadn't been able to sleep because of being over-excited. He answered, '*Я тоже.*'[3]

He drove to the Writers' Union where he suggested we might have lunch. It is easy to park in Moscow. Streets stop being main quite quickly once you're away from the centre, though you've not moved far; nothing like as far as, say, Fulham Broadway to Hyde Park – more Hyde Park Corner to Victoria Station. The pavement

---

[2] Passes.

[3] 'Me, too.'

becomes less. There are, soon, more trees than concrete; paths out of which buildings grow.

The Writers' Union is Art Nouveau inside. I am told it had been the childhood home until 1914 of Countess Olsufyev, who married a Frenchman. She now lives in Kensington High Street. She had memories of Nicholas II's sister-in-law. Her daughter, Darya, married a Sheremetev. A big double door at the front was locked, with notices pinned to it. Misha met and kissed a large woman outside. They disappeared through another door. I sat in the car. Out he came with Svetlana Prokhorova, the tour guide when he had visited England. If I'd known I would see her, I could have brought some of the fruit she most enjoyed in England.

I knew that Margaret Drabble was around – had been in Yalta with a visiting group of English writers – Michael Holroyd, Melvyn Bragg and others. Svetlana was looking after them – they were lunching there today. She still has the banana-shaped purse I gave her. She would surprise Margaret by leading me over to her. Also in the group was Jenny from the GB-USSR Association, who had given Misha the details of my arrival. A table would be booked for us at two thirty.

How much more I am seeing this time – to be in a car with a Muscovite is richly different from outsider tourism. The flowers, which had stood in a tumbler in the bath all night, were in the back of the car. Misha drove through a district which intrigued me because of the number of trees seeming to grow straight up from the road.

The Donskoy Monastery is the first decrepit onion-dome church I have seen. Red stone. The onion is lead – no gold. An overgrowth of undergrowth; Tennysonian, lush, gravestones. A small extra house and onion-dome church to the side. Like a toy almost, not more than thirty feet tall. Sections of marble carving from a building that had been destroyed. A morbid, romantic place. My eyes welled up.

'Let's go and see the statues.'

He led us to a separate building where a *babushka* let us in for nothing. It was like any family mausoleum with tombs, marble statues, plaques on the wall.

'I call it the little Westminster Abbey,' he divulged.

As we came out, the sky darkened, suddenly there was thunder and lightning, a drenching storm. Sheets of rain. We rushed past a party of teenage schoolchildren being led, culturally, by a large oldfashioned governess who was holding forth. They looked bored.

We raced to the car. Misha gave me a beautifully decorated wooden egg, painted by a friend of his – the sort people give for Easter. And an apple. I took my shoes off. He wants to write a novel about the Donskoy Monastery. We talked, haltingly but freely, as I would to any of my friends; mainly in Russian, though he certainly said some things in English. A little-known language demands gestures. We had difficulty over *половина*;[4] he said it again and again, making chopping actions with his hand. I was thinking 'axe', 'stop', 'enough'. No, 'half'. How would I have signed half? Written '1/2'. A study could be made of the signs – body language – people or nationalities used to express an unknown word.

I recounted how much I had been impressed listening to Andrei Tarkovsky speaking in St James's Church, Piccadilly, the first time he made a public statement following the news that he was not to return to the Soviet Union after making the film, *Nostalgia*, in Italy. I sensed an almost hysterical hero-worship of him in myself. I desperately wanted to meet him. I decided to write a letter which would reach him through a reliable channel. The first draft, full of praise for his work, included the wish that I might one day work with him. Re-reading it made me uncomfortable; it seemed inappropriate to be asking for something. I simplified the message, expressed my gratitude for the spiritual depth of his films, adding that I feel at one with them.

The church was packed with journalists and devotees of his work. The rector, the Reverend Donald Reeve, had invited Tarkovsky to talk on the Apocalypse. I had dressed in noticeable white and placed myself in the third row on the aisle. Irina Brown, an experienced director and translator, spotted me and told me that Tarkovsky had received my letter. Blimey. With ringing enthusiasm the rector introduced the great director, who was accompanied by his wife, Larissa. Of medium height, dressed in a

---

[4] Half.

smart Western grey-flannel suit, he was instantly recognisable from photographs I had seen; the thick black quiff of hair on his brow, deeply etched lines on either side of his mouth. There was tension in the lower half of his face. At the end of a sentence his jaw clenched. His young son still in the Soviet Union, living with his grandmother, unable to join his parents; it was hardly surprising that he looked strained. As well as the given subject, he talked about his films. He wanted people to stop reading symbolic meanings into them – a work of art must be at one with the viewer. Was he quoting *my letter*? Amongst many questions from the press and the congregation, he was asked if he knew what was the theme of his next film.

'Yes.'

Would he tell us about it?

'No.'

He was herded from the church. The event was recorded on video. I left, incandescent. Walking along Piccadilly towards my parked car, I was halted by a middle-aged Frenchman on a motorbike. He announced that I looked extraordinary; where had I been? I told him. He launched into a lecture in French about how I should bring up my children, how careful I should be of left-wing influences. He went as he came – delivering books, he said. It was as if he were a messenger in a Cocteau film, although I didn't plug into his message.

Misha revealed that when they were younger he, Tarkovsky and Vysotsky had been 'hooligans' together – women, vodka... He showed no great curiosity in how things are for Tarkovsky now. I learn from John Roberts that it is because he, Misha, feels that people should stay and struggle from inside the country. Never do I feel he yearns to leave – quite the contrary – I feel him intensely involved with loving his country – or Moscow, anyway.

We drove past his flat – he pointed down the street – *Chisty pereulok*[5]. We drove past a statue of Gogol standing, then out of his way, past one of Gogol sitting. He has a character in one of his plays complain, 'They have a statue of Gogol standing and a statue of Gogol sitting – why is there no statue of Gogol lying?'

---

[5] Clean Lane.

Like Chekhov – for him the novel is the first wife; the drama – the second wife or mistress. He's working on a new novel. We talked about his children, I learn that he has a son of ten. Then he must go to the Vakhtangov Theatre where they are rehearsing the reopening of his adaptation of *Anna Karenina*. I sat in the car quite a while. When he came back it was to say that the director has flown off somewhere to do filming; the leading actress is in a state, and everything is topsy-turvy.

'Now let's have lunch.'

Back to the Writers' Union. A very old man with twenty-five or thirty medals on his chest was stumbling up the stairs as we came into a tall, dark, oak-panelled room with high windows, a staircase leading up to a gallery. About eight tables with people sitting in groups.

Someone called, 'Misha!'

Hard to say what they looked like. Writers? Chelsea Arts Club? Neither dishevelled nor smart. Heads together – plenty of talk – plenty of drink – happy, I'd say. We sat down. A big friendly waitress approached. Misha asked what I would like.

'Fish, please.'

He ordered: champagne, vodka, black caviar, mushroom soup, black bread, carp, potato and red cabbage. Later he wrote in Russian:

Чёрная икра/Black caviar

Белая рыба/White fish

Чёрный гриб/Black mushroom

Белая водка/White vodka

Чёрный хлеб/Black bread

I added – Белая женщина/White woman.

Our order arrived; vodka first.

Svetlana came to take me to a dark private room, where there were perhaps a dozen people. A standing man was proposing a toast. She fetched Margaret Drabble and brought her to the door, flabbergasted.

'Why are you here?'

I tried to explain about my Soul – *Душа.*[6]

She had more reserve in her reaction to the country. We agreed to talk about it in England. Back to my table where the vodka lay in wait. Jenny joined us and agreed to a taste of champagne. Misha filled my vodka glass to the brim, saying, 'I never, never, never, drink', took a nip himself, but not before he had prepared for me from ice cold dishes – a mouthful of black bread liberally spread with butter and black caviar. I knew I must sink my vodka in one, so with three generous swallows, down it went. My eyes watered, I gasped, but croaked, '*Я не страдаю,*'[7] which made them laugh. The champagne was opened, to more mouthfuls of caviar on bread. A basket of radish, cucumber, celery was alongside, from which I must pick a crisp *crudité* to counteract the richness of caviar and intoxicating vodka.

Svetlana came to fetch Jenny away. We continued lunch. Suddenly overwhelmed (drunk) I burst into tears. '*Не плохо, не плохо, не плохо. Мне нравится всё, всё, всё!*',[8] I sobbed, wiping my eyes on the thick linen napkin. Misha waited patiently while I recovered. He sat, eyes down. I think of Russians being emotional, but in public they are under constraint to keep their feelings hidden, which accounts for some of the mystery and sense of inner life they convey. I suspect he was reasonably embarrassed by my loss of control. He felt in his pocket, took out a piece of paper and pen, and wrote – Мужчина редко понимает, чего достаточно или чего недостаточно женщине в данный момент.[9]

We discussed women – he said, 'A woman is like a flower and if you...' he gestured breaking the stem...

I enquired, '*Теперь женщина – как мужчина?*'[10]

He nodded and continued, 'A woman should be in a harem...'

I smiled, too weak to retort.

---

[6] Pronounced *dushà*, stressed on the last vowel; the Russians love talking about what they consider to be their unique, special soul.

[7] 'I'm not suffering/I'm not in pain.'

[8] 'I don't feel bad. I like everything, everything!'

[9] 'A man rarely understands what a woman needs or doesn't need at the present time.'

[10] 'So is a woman now like a man?'

The mushroom soup, in one dish, arrived. We shared it. They shut at four thirty; he went to fetch my coat, as two huge dishes arrived containing a large piece of carp, a vast helping of sliced potato baked in the oven and red cabbage. We groaned in submission and ate the fish, which was sublime. Finally, after Svetlana had guided me to the Ж,[11] we tottered out – me, red-eyed and exhausted. The Kagarlitskys had invited me to come straight to them. I remembered that I must buy champagne to put us to sleep on the train. Misha stopped the car, went through a door (shops don't always look like shops), coming out with two bottles of champagne, one of vodka, for which he would take no money; bars of chocolate for my children and postcards.

He dropped me at the hotel where guide/Tanya instructed me to be at the Stanislavsky Theatre at nine p.m. to join our group catching the train to Leningrad. Misha, with my luggage, promised to be there at ten, after a sleep.

At Metro Aeroport, a young man rose to meet me; I knew immediately it was Boris.

'You can always tell a foreigner,' he smiled.

We stopped at a kiosk to buy a square wedge of fresh warm cake with fruit at the bottom. He led me home, speaking marvellous English all the way. I explained I was a bit hungover. I certainly felt very tired.

Raya was wearing a green dress. She wept a little as we embraced. Boris talked non-stop in dense colloquial English. She joined in. They wanted to know what is happening in the West. Boris, I think, surprised and let down that I'd brought no papers or journals. Exhausted, I didn't contribute much. Julius was at the hospital. We reminisced about Juliet Stevenson, Adrian Noble, the RSC director, who took me on for two seasons, and Ronnie Harwood.

Raya recounted how Julius lost his job two years before he was due to start his State pension (after twenty years' work). He was informed as he came out of hospital. She needed to do translation work to make up the loss. I'd brought *Benefactors*, by Michael Frayn. She asked me to beg him to give her the rights to translate it. They feel cut off. The British Embassy doesn't make contact any more.

---

11 The Ladies'.

Nothing can be initiated from their side. When Julius returned, Boris immediately fetched sausage, bread, cabbage salad, tea tinctured with orange to make it delicious. He filled me a glass from a bottle.

'Please, no more alcohol.'

'It's water, we make it,' they reassured me.

They add flowers to give it fragrance. Raya pointed to the telephone and warned, 'Boris', whereupon he placed it in a saucepan, put the lid on and carried it into another room. On the way to the flat, I'd asked if it was all right to talk about everything. He'd answered, 'A way can be found.'

Julius, wearing a suit, was thinner, obviously depressed. I felt reproach when he said, 'You haven't given us enough time.' His description of their situation makes me feel guilty and dejected. Boris had to leave for work. They both implored that I try to get them back into contact with the Embassy. They'd talked at table of hope: Chernenko might die and things change for the better in a year or two. Such patience. He commented that the trouble with us in the West – it's too long since we were beaten – we are so accustomed to our freedom and democracy that we play at it and elect someone like Mrs Thatcher.

'You don't know how to use your freedom.'

I agreed. It was what I had felt after my first visit. He asked what we thought had happened to Andrei Bitov, the Soviet Editor who had come to England, written articles in the *Sunday Times* and recently disappeared. He knew there was conjecture that he had returned to Moscow to see his wife and son.

'He won't see them, of course, if he comes back,' pronounced Julius.

18 September 1984 – A Press Conference in Moscow with Andrey Bitov explaining that he had been abducted and tortured by our Secret Service.

I began to feel anxious about being in time for the bus. I hugged Raya, who asked warmly about my children and, again, brushed aside a tear. I had no cash: at the Metro Julius had to pay for me, which was absurd. As we walked, passing the statue of Pushkin – 'Hello!', the Rossiya Cinema, then down back streets towards the Stanislavsky Theatre, Julius proudly extolled Boris, his extraordinary gift for languages, already three and starting Spanish. 'He's twenty-six now and we'd like him to get married but in his present position (caretaker)...'

We found guide/Tanya pacing up and down outside the theatre. The performance would end at nine thirty – Misha wasn't coming until ten. At nine forty-five, our group in the bus left, leaving Julius and me together, still waiting and knowing that we must get to Leningrad Station, for train No. 4 at eleven p.m. I voiced my worry, not helped by Julius: 'Well, now you have been abandoned by everybody.'

I only had my passport, no ticket, no money. Panicky. Suddenly, Misha! We piled into his car, following the bus which had seen us and waited.

At the *вокзал*[12] there are three stations sending trains in different directions. Misha had to park elsewhere, he'd driven through the No Entry sign. He brought the flowers, the bag with plays, coffee and tea for Julius.

I stood while Misha and Julius chatted. Feeling desolate... I moved to put my bag and flowers on the bus; turning back, I wrapped my shawl round myself and winked at Misha, an involuntary, inappropriate reflex – I, actress, noticed myself doing it.

Julius hugged me, saying 'Give us longer next time.' Misha kissed me; they walked away...

I had spent twelve hours in the care and company of a man of exceptional courage, life-force, vividness. In the car, I told him he was *смелый*.[13] An easy word to remember – *smelly* – and I'd looked for an opportunity to use it. When I did, he repeated '*смелый?*'

'*Нет?*'[14] I questioned.

'*Да,*' he accepted.

'In England, both at my house and in public.' Two or three hours later, he brought it up again. 'You think I'm *смелый?*'

'*Конечно.*'[15]

---

[12] Station (main line).

[13] 'Brave', pronounced *smely*.

[14] 'No.'

[15] 'Of course.'

I sat on the front seat of the bus, feeling cold, evacuee-like. I put my trousers on under my skirt, and my socks, and sat talking with lively guide/Tanya. Julius had said of her when she was out of hearing, 'Of course, she's KGB – they make them nice nowadays.' Whether, indeed, she knew who he was; she asked me, aside, his name. Misha had called him *Yuly* all the time so I told her *Yury*, hoping she wouldn't ask his other name. She didn't. I gave her salted nuts for her son.

I joined the Amyes on the platform – lucky there were four of us because sleepers weren't allocated; I sensed a bit of jostling from people trying to avoid being with the Noisy Bore, who had surfaced early during the trip. I suggested, 'Let's open a bottle of champagne.'

'We've got one too!'

I woke in the night to hear yelling. The train had stopped. An Englishwoman's voice on the platform; a Russian man shouting 'Идём! Идём!'[16] Howls from the woman. Someone next door, urging 'John, John', he retorting, 'I'm not going to fucking-well get up.' After insulting the attendant, he'd tried to force his way into one of the compartments; they'd called the police who put him off without any identity papers.

13 September – Thursday

I drew back the blinds. We were travelling through wooded country, passing small stations with ornamental wooden palings.

Leningrad station. Commuters hurrying. The massive Moskva tourist hotel, at the Neva River's edge, we lurched into a vast ballroom for breakfast; found a table for six with an English couple from our group. Impatience for the hot tea and coffee.

Wursht, wursht on the plate, also an attractive curd mixture made with egg and sugar – golden, lightly fried, warm and squidgy, accompanied by blackcurrant jam.

An elderly man in a fine grey suit sat on his own at a table for six next to us and got instant service from two waiters, which made our table fidgety. Our profusely leaking coffee pot had to be substituted.

---

[16] 'It's leaving!' (*lit.* 'it is going').

Inevitably, a long queue in a very smelly (not *смелый!*) lavatory. Only three cubicles, the doors not reaching to the ceiling. The unwished-for shared experience of explosions discouraged me from anything more than a quick breath-held pee – no paper, anyway. A thorough hand wash, breathing through the mouth. Some people had brought their toothbrushes – but I escaped. Ugh!

Onto the bus. Along a wide street, shops displaying meat, cheese, milk, bread, clothes, books, shoes. Extraordinary, after Moscow's empty stores. It was the Nevsky Prospekt – people busying along.

Our young Leningrad guide took us to the spot that has the best view of Peter and Paul Fortress – with its glittering gold spire, as well as of the Winter Palace – blue-green and ravishing. We stood on the bridge and, having heard the statistics, thought about the thousands who died to construct it. He pointed out the main sights in a laid-back voice, 'as to the red building on the right of the bus...' Informative, educational, in my opinion a perfect first way to visit a city; an overall view to gauge what whets my appetite for next time. I feel that we have so much eighteenth- and early nineteenth-century architecture in London that I prefer to look at something less European, though it's interesting to see what they chose to copy in order to make Western contact and comparison – Peter the Great's aim and startling success. It is certainly glamorous. I shall go back one day to revisit the tsar's iconic Bronze Horseman and the Winter Palace, which was our last stop. We were allowed out for photographs. Knowing a smattering of history can be appealing or appalling. In front of the great iron gates of the Winter Palace, I saw on the ground and picked up a small metal crucifix, one inch long, with Cyrillic writing on the back. Made, perhaps, from a tin or zinc spoon. An illegal Christian talisman.

We set off down the same long, straight road the tsars had used to reach their country estates; elaborately decorated milestones, past the colossal wrought-iron and stone triumphal arch that is the symbol of wartime Leningrad. The guide had pointed out the Astoria Hotel, at which Hitler had planned to have his victorious dinner after the fall of Leningrad. Reputedly the invitations were printed – but due to the heroism of the people… the enormity is almost too hard for me to assimilate. There were many statistics concerning the city.

At the airport, similar size to that of Edinburgh, our conscientious guide left the bus to a smattering of applause. I bought for thirty roubles a man's black fur hat with ear flaps. At the final departure place, I put my bag down so that I could touch the ground to say goodbye. I like rituals.

Looking out, we were crossing vast lakelands – Finland, then Sweden, watery expanses. The safety belt sign went up while we were still miles over sea. A perfect landing at Gatwick after three hours exactly. Pleased to be quickly off, having only hand luggage.

Adam was at home. He gave me a fine welcome with his friend Lisa. They got some of Misha's chocolate. I unwrapped the flowers, scraped their stalks, put them in cold water and placed the vase outside in the cool of the garden. In an hour they were standing up like soldiers. It is Monday – I was given them last Tuesday, a thousand miles away. They look as though they will last another four days at least. They did.

When in Moscow, do as...

26–30 October 1984

24 October – Wednesday

I planned this short trip soon after the previous one to eradicate the scarcely contained hysteria of the last; less fantasy, more calm. This way I shall maybe understand better how they live their lives and what it feels like to be them – instead of my projections playing such a large part. The platform for this visit is theatre.

4. Kagarlitsky family.

Zoya Anderson, an interpreter with the GB-USSR Association, persuaded me to take a large green zippie, packed with everything her sister could possibly wear to get married; her bridesmaid sister's ditto, and the presents as well.

Taxi to Heathrow, with plenty of time to buy *Newsweek*, *The Times*. At passport control, I breezily handed over the Photostat copy that had been sent to obtain the visa. The piercing-eyed man asked, 'Why have you brought this? Where is your real one?'

Horror!

I raced to the BA desk which deals with Aeroflot. 'Is there someone at home who could bring it?'

Of course – Lena, my Sicilian cleaner would be there. I telephoned.

NO ANSWER. Her home – no answer.

'You must tell us if you're not joining the flight; your luggage must be recovered from the aeroplane because Moscow won't know what to do with it.'

Struggling to find a desk without a long queue, I saw Gennady Rozhdestvensky and his wife Alla (I'd met her at the Roberts' house); I had a message for her from John, who knew they would be on the plane. Both dressed in new, black Burberrys, accompanied by a young man.

'Alla!'

As she turned and recognised me, I burst into tears, sobbing that I'd left my passport, etc.

'Don't worry,' they consoled. 'Come on the next flight.'

Their compassionate agent gently guided and handed me to the right, kind woman.

She said, 'First we must get your luggage; it may already be on the plane.' She telephoned: 'It is. It must be off-loaded. Then we'll see if we can book another flight. Next one... is Friday. You can wait here. Would you like a cup of coffee?'

'Oh, yes please!'

Unable to stem the flood, I sat on the sofa. I, actress, noticed the intensity of the present. *In extremis*, there is the minimum of movement, as if time is holding its breath till the next onslaught of bad news; sitting in my smart coat, shoes, hair, make-up, swollen eyes, red nose.

The resourceful woman returned with a new flight – visit shrunk to four days. My bag would be disgorged soon onto one of those slowly revolving, scaly dragon's tail carousels.

'Dreadful weather isn't it, love?' a cheery taxi driver volunteered.

'Yes.'

'Have you come from somewhere nice and sunny, love?'

'No.'

The tears flowed silently all the way back to Dancer Road. In the house I let everything go and howled, square-mouthed, like a spoilt baby in a cartoon. I watched snooker on television. Just the thing. All that green, and no violence. Late in the afternoon, Adam came thundering upstairs. Telling him made me cry again. He patted me tenderly, saying it could happen to anyone. Then it was Charlotte's turn to care. She did. Off I went again. Exhausted, I went to sleep feeling nourished by the lack of criticism or scorn from my beloved, teenage, kind-as-their-father son and daughter.

26 October – Friday

I set out again – rather nervous. In duty-free at LHR I bought two half-bottles of whisky and more *Diorissimo*.

On the aeroplane I sat between a Japanese and an Indian. The intricate unwrapping of the eating tools gives us time to work out our own national strategy. The Indian was planning only to eat his roll. I offered him my roll, too. All was well when he discovered the meat was chicken. I'm Hindu, you see, I can't eat any big animals, only small ones.' He offered his caviar – good swap for a roll. The Japanese ate his pudding first, toyed with the chicken, enjoyed the salad and red caviar. Acceptance by all three; the joy of being human.

Arriving at Sheremetevo in the dark, I recognised Julius Kagarlitsky and Boris with him. I was touched. The taxi driver thought he knew my *Forsyte Saga* face – an open door to fame in the Soviet Union.

In their familiar kitchen, Raya was wearing her cheerful green dress. An air of greater optimism. Julius, pleased, his book is to be published. I brought him the recently acclaimed *H. G. Wells in Love*.

I had suggested to Raya that it might be good if Michael Frayn could see some of her translation work. After long discussion, she gave me the published copy of *The Country Wife*; this had been the hardest text to deal with.

Boris has a girlfriend. Much parental pride in this. She is so pretty – speaks excellent French; Irina, a.k.a. Ira. They are an overtly tactile couple. He's intensely intense. His mind has overed his matter (apart from Ira) with the result that he is brilliant and not at all lazy.

I gave Raya Earl Grey tea and a silk scarf; Ira – tights; Julius – one of the half-bottles of whisky; Boris got *Newsweek* and *The Times*.

Misha rang – on his way by Metro. Because of the forthcoming parade on 7 November, the centre of Moscow is shut to cars in the evening.[1] There are tanks all around.

'Let's eat,' they said.

One of the things that had altered the morale of the household was that, Julius told us, the Ambassador was anxious to help him and Michael Sullivan, the Cultural Attaché, and his wife had been to dinner.

Doorbell. Misha with white chrysanthemums for me, which Boris immediately put into water.

Doorbell. Oleg. I stood to greet him as he kissed my hand. He looked taller than I remember, showing much more personality. I had found him rather bleak in London. Everyone is clearly devoted to him. He smokes non-stop; has an expensive haircut; blue-grey windcheater and rather dispirited jeans.

We ate. Sardines, sausage, cheese, black bread, Danish pastry, tea. Oleg, star actor, held court at the top of the table, taking food without asking. It's common practice – you help yourself. He was pouring vodka and refilling my glass. My schedule was planned – the usual thing, looking through the list of plays.

'Well, there isn't anything really good just now; if only you'd been here when...'

It was decided – *Seagull* at MKhAT on Saturday night...

We had talked about me trying to find Tatyana Nikolayevna (Taganka), whom I ignorantly called Nikolayevich, making her male. There were then jokes about Oleg, who is Nikolayevich, being Nikolayevna, making him female – the gag kept running

---

[1] The actual date of the October Revolution of 1917 fell on 7 November (New Style) before Russia adopted the Gregorian calendar, hence the anniversary of the Revolution is now celebrated on that day.

gently during the evening. He has a rich bass voice and talks fast, so I didn't understand much of what he said. He told jokes. They laughed. There was ribaldry about the tanks. Boris told short jokes on the knock, knock lines, usually about a rat or something. They laughed but the translations didn't amuse me. I'm too sentimental, and always have been, to find *Tom and Jerry* humour funny. I relate to the violence in a hopelessly inappropriate way. It struck me many were Jewish jokes which in English always make me laugh. Quite a lot of Jewish talk. Boris declared he doesn't exactly feel Russian or Jewish; he feels both separately.

Into Oleg's car – a smart black one. Misha teased, 'Only a very important person has a car like this.' Driving through Moscow in districts obviously unknown to Oleg, Misha remarked, 'He only knows the centre.'

We passed tanks moving in rows to their parade rehearsals – a strange, not a threatening sight. Quite mild – warmer than London.

I was sitting in the back with my not-so-heavy-now bag. I had given Misha his art books, toy cars for his son; also letters from John and Liz (containing a 1985 diary to give him a feeling of hope and future, an incentive to travel when he's well enough). The same to Oleg (which he left on the Kagarlitsky dinner table).

We drove up to the Cosmos Hotel well after midnight, the hall still thronging with tourists. Oleg with his jaunty walk and smart grey tweed hat is a huge celebrity. At Reception, the girls couldn't find my reservation for swooning. After he had described me as an artiste from England, with plenty of jollity and '*Добрый вечер!*'[2] to all who passed, my entry was found. To my surprise, Oleg and Misha swept up my bags and marched with me into the lift. At the key desk on the sixth floor, my standing was immediately established. Into my room. Coats off, hats off. Two beds, own bathroom. Like any western-chain hotel. Built for the Olympics (1986). I presented the other half-bottle of whisky to Oleg. Also, scented geranium leaves from my garden – I gave them two or three each. Misha sat sniffing his, Oleg dropped his on the table and forgot them. He went into the bathroom and brought out two

---

[2] 'Good evening!'

glasses. We drank from one, Misha's flowers drank from the other. Jokes that they could stay the night in these beds.

Stretched out, Misha leaned against me. He had been all day at the Ministry, seeking a visa to receive treatment for his heart in Huston, Texas.

Oleg talked about a new two-hander play with Tabakov – '*Хорошая роль для тебя*',[3] (he used the intimate form of *you*). 'Ah, he's using *ty* to me, so I can, too.' Wearing his grey cap, I wanted it to go on forever. Finally Misha (whose way of showing exhaustion and strain is not to show it) said they must go. They left.

Looking out of my window at the inspiring, gleaming, space monument, I felt, as on both previous occasions, that the whole trip had been worth it by bedtime on the first evening.

27 October – Saturday

Zoya Anderson had arranged that her sister Lena would come to the outside of the Cosmos to collect all the wedding paraphernalia I'd brought. She would be wearing a red hat. It was quickly done, in good English. She hoped I could meet her actor husband, Yura, who would be free that evening; I knew that I would be at *Seagull*.

Outside the hotel, I walked round the rocket-taking-off, admiring its shine and enormity that makes me want to fall over when I look straight up at it, as do the World Trade Centre buildings in Manhattan which my children went up some years later, leaving me on the ground, fearing that I would have an uncontrollable panic attack during the three-minute ascent.

I was approached by a little boy doing writing motions on his hand. I didn't understand but realised afterwards that he'd wanted ballpoint pens.

Misha was pacing up and down outside the stage door at MKhAT.

'Where's the taxi?' he asked, preparing to pay.

'I walked from the Metro.'

He gave me my ticket to *Seagull* (two roubles); I would go to his house after the performance.

---

[3] 'A good part for you.'

'Пока!'[4]

'Да, пока!'

I walked past Pushkin, 'Hello!' into the street of old MKhAT, following Edward Petherbridge's directions, through a metal door, up to the top floor.

Moscow Art Theatre Museum

Three or four young women were smoking on the stone stairs outside; they were drama students from the MKhAT School. Announcing as I went in, that I had messages from Edward Petherbridge, I found I was amongst a trio of welcoming friends; Henrietta, Galina and Sasha. I stayed for three hours. We talked theatre, film and general goodwill. Galina loves Laurence Olivier, Sasha loves the Beatles and Henrietta loves Edward. I was given tea, black bread, cheese and spicy fat pork. Sasha cut up pieces of apple to put in the tea. 'We do this in the country or at home – not formally.' They were expecting an artist to arrive with his pictures for an exhibition. They introduced me to Palekh art, showed me illustrations, explaining that the tradition continues in its local district. They told me to remind Oleg Yefremov that today is the birthday of MKhAT; thus the performance of *Seagull*, with which the Theatre opened in 1898. Henrietta, a smiling, round-faced woman, toured me through the museum, showing me the original letter of Konstantin Stanislavsky, 'K.S.' as he was known, to Nemirovich-Danchenko, suggesting the meeting which led to the founding of MKhAT. Some Edward Gordon Craig designs for a 1911 production of *Hamlet*, which was never realised. I left saying that I would return with the presents from Edward.

I reached the theatre as the last stragglers shot in; parted with my coat and was directed to a seat on the aisle about three minutes into the play.

Quite an annoying set with trucks moving about for reasons I didn't understand. A marvellous Nina – Vertinskaya; and my friend Tanya Lavrova, a most credible Arkadina. All woman, all actress, and bravely, not all the most attractive aspects. In the interval, Irina Grigoraevna, Oleg's stalwart secretary, took me to an ante-

---

[4] 'See you later!'

room, where a table was laid with smoked fish or caviar on bread, cake and tea. She stayed with me, till Oleg, wearing the same jeans and windcheater as on day one, turned up. He said, *of course* he knew it was the anniversary of the opening of the theatre. I was then shown to my proper seat in the middle of the fourth row. Someone sitting in it was summarily turned out. Misha told me later that he had placed a message on the chair for me. It was not there. I never saw it.

I enjoyed the last act more. Oleg had directed the play with three acts before the interval, only one after. Vertinskaya, a great actress, played her last scene better than I've ever seen it. 'I am a Seagull' repetitions worked as never before.

I was taken by Oleg across the stage and up to Lavrova's dressing room.

Oleg asked, '*Можно?*'[5]

Tanya looked really surprised to see me. Out came tea, tights and greeting cards in the shape of apples, which Charlotte had asked me to give her. Lavrova said we must meet and gave me her number. I have learned since that she had been much offended that I had sent her three pairs of knickers via John Roberts, with a note wishing her luck. To a Russian actress this was in the worst possible taste.

5. Konstantin Stanislavsky.

---

[5] 'May I?'

Oleg locked his office, we left by the stage door, where a man asked for his autograph. Into his car. I don't quite feel comfortable with him yet. Perhaps I'm in awe – he seems a little larger than life. He's not easy to understand and, I sense, not as patient as Misha in taking the trouble to communicate. I had asked him at the theatre if he'd ever played Trigorin. He said 'No.'

'Why ever not?'

'*Время*,'[6] he replied.

There is a universality about the entrances to the apartment blocks. Stone stairs and lifts. To Misha's door. He opened it, I realised it was a party. Irina, an attractive, tall woman with a lean face and blonde curled hair – his relationship to her is unexplained. Though, in my house in London, I enquired whether, if I came to Moscow, I would have to fight my way through lots of wives and women, he conceded he was 'Sort of Vershinin'. A moment of not knowing how to be.

'*Нормально, нормально*,'[7] whispered Misha. People. The door opened into a room with a large table, eight or ten people sitting round it and a repast in progress or finishing.

'*Люди!*'[8] I gasped.

I was put at Oleg's left. Misha's eleven-year-old son, open faced, reddish hair, tall for his age. A vast dish of shrimps, prawns, back bread, white bread, smoked fish, which Oleg was already tearing at. Green leaves of a sort – coriander-ish. Some cold meat. Vodka poured out of a carafe with stalks in it, probably fennel, which gave an aniseed taste; when the carafe was empty, another bottle was poured into it to absorb the flavour.

Again, Oleg at the head of the table, was the centre of attention. All eyes on him. I was next to the plump wife, Vera, of a portly artist, Peter Ossovsky. She asked whether I could sit for him while I was in Russia.

'How long for?'

'Two hours.'

'Perhaps Monday afternoon.'

---

[6] 'Time.'

[7] 'It's OK, it's OK.'

[8] 'People!'

She gave me a card with his number to call. Next to her, an Englishspeaking woman who translated for me when necessary. Opposite, Irina's brother – an actor; next to him Misha's brother – a teacher – not like him at all. And another couple that I didn't identify.

Suddenly it became clear that Oleg was talking about seeing me performing at the Lyric, Hammersmith. An Actor's Company production, *Bumps and Knots*, assembled and directed by Edward Petherbridge; works adapted from R. D. Laing and a commissioned play by Gabriel Josipovici. I – English – self-deprecating – starting to say how bored he must have been by it, was mercifully not allowed to dishonour myself nor my colleagues. There were toasts: to Чайка[9] and lrina's brother did one to me as 'woman' – then I started. I explained how I feel this extraordinary bond: that what happens to them happens to me; when they laugh, I laugh; when they cry, I cry. I feel I belong to them and they to me – and that I find myself amongst them with a heart full of love. They listened in silence and received it with grace... Imagine saying that in England. I could be embarrassed reading this now, thirty years later, but I meant it then and still do. What a lot I have to learn from them. I told them how I found the cross on the ground in Leningrad but couldn't quite remember what the words were – *spa... sokhr...* Eventually, after they'd offered various suggestions, the words were found in a dictionary:

Спаси и сохрани.[10]

6. Cross found in Leningrad.

<hr>

[9] 'Seagull'.

[10] 'Save and preserve us.'

Misha asked if I wanted to see his *кабинет*.[11]

'Yes.'

'Come too,' he said to his son, maybe as chaperon. A spacious room with a large writing desk. A made-up single bed, I noticed. I'd seen a double bed through an open door on the other side of the hall. Bookshelves – lots. Pictures, Guy Vaesen's print, still in its polythene wrapper. Photographs in frames. A happy smiling one of John and Liz Roberts. I sat on his bed; his son wandered about, I asked him to get out the cars I had brought, to show me how they worked.

'What should I bring next time?' I asked.

'Just cars,' he answered.

Suddenly, Misha fell onto me. We sat closely for a minute. *Да*. He looked round for something to give me. A small brass bell from a troika. He opened his zip shoulder bag and showed me – almost secretly – a Bible. People came to the door, talking, trying to leave. Irina was being extrovertly friendly and intimate with him.

Misha's flat, according to John Roberts, is civilised compared with most Soviet flats. Even so, to me there is a stark, post-war utility-furniture feeling, which I believe is because there are no table lamps, only overhead lighting.

Oleg by now had moved to a sofa. I went into the tiny kitchen, following Irina to give her tights and tea. To quench the thirst there was bottled beer; I drank a lot but didn't feel drunk. I tried to explain how brave and splendid Misha had been in England... Oleg left the room for a pee, I suppose, just as I started so missed it... but I was glad to have the chance to tell Misha's friends about the marvellous way he'd talked of Oleg, that he'd called him such a good friend and colleague. Oleg, vodka'd, taking Misha's son in his arms, returned to the sofa.

People were beginning to leave. A lift was arranged for me. I sat by Oleg, trying to explain how it meant so much to me – being alone in Moscow – the way I was being included...

'You're not alone,' he interrupted.

I kissed him and Irina, and Misha, I expect, though I don't remember.

---

[11] Office.

28 October – Sunday

I was late to meet Boris and Ira at the stage door of MKhAT. They weren't there. Irina Grigoraevna took me up in the tiny lift again. When I asked to use the Ж, Grigoraevna brought out a special key and led me to the Director's *туалет*.[12]

Oleg arrived – same jeans and jacket.

'Let's go.'

He took me to the studio theatre – opened the door so that I could look. It was small and black; actors rehearsing. He vaguely presented me; some of them shouted '*Guten Tag*'. He apologised for disturbing them. Next, to a big rehearsal room filled with actors standing in groups; sitting round the walls. A piano – large windows. They smiled a huge welcome. He introduced me to an immense actor (Vyacheslav Nevinny), whom I had seen in *Seagull* the night before, and a slight man with a photogenic Hamlet face, surrounded by a striking curtain of silver hair. Dark-brown cords, shirt and jersey, short boots: could have been an English actor at the Acton Hilton (BBC Rehearsal Rooms). I didn't recognise him. I learned, another day, from Kagarlitsky that this was Slava Lyubshin, who had knocked me out months before at NFT, in *Don't Kill the White Swans*. Oleg had admitted, coming along, that he (Oleg) had a terrible head. (Vodka.)

This was a working rehearsal of the new Japanese play, *Avay Kovay* ('The Ghosts Are Among Us'), following a run-through the day before. Oleg held a small piece of paper with notes on it. He started with a short dissertation, it was clear that his actors adore him. He made them laugh – he performed for them, there was noisy accord – plenty of interruptions. Then he addressed himself a little to Lyubshin who nodded and got it. He explained that I am an English colleague. The actors invited me to sit in the one comfortable upholstered chair with arms, not too close to the draught which comes down from the ceiling.

The act started with two boys and two girls doing an introductory song and dance. He told the performers to look straight at the audience.

'Do it to Carolina,' he suggested.

[12] Toilet.

The young wore jeans and jerseys, the older ones – suits.

The play started. Two men selling ghosts, photographs and general skulduggery. Not easy for me to understand. Oleg stopped them frequently, acted bits with them. They were still struggling with lines; I understood there was a quiet desperation abroad. Nevinny brave and extrovert, risking things, getting laughs; also maddened when the watching actors talked. He exploded. Sometimes I couldn't tell if he was furious with Oleg too, but it didn't stop him continuing with the utmost humour. Lyubshin, rather tense and contained physically, nevertheless, played with complete openness and they both *listened* marvellously. Lyubshin also had to ask the talking onlookers to shut up.

'What I'm doing is very difficult! *Трудно.*'[13]

When anyone forgot a line, they yelled '*Что?*',[14] just like English actors; if the prompter gave a line that was not needed, they stared at her, wounded, as we would.

'That – was a pause.'

Boris and Ira arrived and sat beside me. Boris saying, 'We missed you.' He explained the story loudly. I tried to stop him, whispering that there is nothing worse for actors than having people talk while they are rehearsing. For three and a half hours they worked without stopping, even for tea... About one o'clock Misha walked in. Finally the session ended. They gathered round to hear Yefremov's words. In complimenting them, I declared that no English actors would have worked so long without a break. They insisted there was a crisis.

Misha said that he had to see his American translator, Maya; would I like to come too?

'*Конечно!*'[15]

In his car he handed me a single orange flower – bigger than a marigold. It was raining. We drove through plenty of streets, ending at a customary block of flats. He warned that Maya has broken her ankle, is using crutches. In the lift he complained how sore his shoulder was. I rubbed it gently. He said it hurt. I

---

[13] 'Difficult.'

[14] 'What?!'

[15] Of course!'

continued. Suddenly his arms were round me... Maya opened the door, showed us into her cosy, cheery flat, speaking perfect American.

'Coffee, tea?'

'Tea,' he answered.

In the kitchen we sat at a table with banquette, while she shook some of her best, newly opened packet of loose tea into a strainer; she poured boiling water through it, into each cup separately, half-full, then filled the cup with plain boiling water. The used tea leaves in the strainer will be kept in the fridge after this visit until the next brewing. There were little dark-red cranberries in a glass jar to stir into the tea.

Misha held my hands. There was something in the air. I felt I was being shown to her. She is warm and funny. They discussed Michael Frayn's *Noises Off* which, since she has decided not to, Misha is going to translate. She has daughters living in the USA. Her Russian ex-mother-in-law insists on coming to help her with housework.

'OK, make some pea soup,' Maya says.

The old woman turns on the gas in the oven and holds a match to a ring on the top, which is not turned on. As Maya, from another room, comes to help and lights a match, there is a huge explosion. The windows break. All the hair on her arms is singed away. Luckily neither her eyebrows nor her head hair are.

We discussed the difficulties of communicating without enough common language. I explained about a letter to Misha I had devised in pictures after my last visit. We should invent a picture code based on being Aquarians. Misha did a sketch of himself coming out of a flask, with me as the Water Carrier pouring from a pitcher.

'Supposing you, Misha, were in love with an Englishwoman and had to have every single thing translated?'

'It would make a good film,' I smiled, 'with a third party present all the time.'

Driving along he told me that his son is with his mother in church. I asked if he, Misha, is a Christian.

'No.'

7. Misha Roshchin's sketch of Caro and himself as Aquarians.

He dropped me at the Metro station, apologising for being 'Нервозен,'[16] not knowing whether tomorrow, Monday, they would say yes or no to the USA and he would have to be ready to leave on Tuesday.

'I am very happy – *Я очень рада,*' I said.

I found my way easily to the Sovremennik Theatre (Contemporary Theatre) which Oleg Yefremov founded twenty years ago in a converted cinema. Boris and Ira were waiting with one of the directors from the theatre. There were only two good seats, for Ira and me, Boris stood at the back, I guess. The auditorium enjoys much the same atmosphere as Taganka. Misha's play *Спешите делать добро,*[17] ran two hours without an interval. The story of a kindly husband bringing home a little waif girl; he and his wife making her human again, with care. Someone implies that she is the mistress of the husband and though the wife knows it's not true, it makes it impossible for her to have a continuing relationship with the girl, who eventually disappears. Episodic – it could just as well have been a film or a novel. The acclaimed film star, Lyudmila Kreilova – excellent, played the waif; the husband – a much-admired theatre star, Igor Kvasha, gifted with the same sort of sonorous, deep voice as Yefremov.

---

[16] 'Anxious.'

[17] *Hurry to Do Good.*

Julius Kagarlitsky was waiting at the stage door to introduce us to Kvasha, one of Russia's greatest actors. Now I've seen him, I can understand why he is so called. Julius had persuaded him to drive me home. Boris declared he and Ira must say goodbye, as he would be working for twenty-four hours and I wouldn't see him again. I thanked him for all he has done – kissed them both, hoping privately that I hadn't been ungrateful. In his car, Kvasha and I talked through Julius about the play.

'How long has it been on? Is it always the same cast?'

'A few years. Some changes of cast.'

'Do they rehearse every time it comes back?'

'Either it's on or off for a seasonal run.'

I admired that it has so much vitality. He concluded that they have reached the bottom of the play now. It's hard to keep the freshness. I asked if he has been in England.

'A person doesn't always have the choice – I have the money, but not the choice.'

'I have the choice,' I said, 'but not the money.'

'And which would you rather have?' Julius asked.

'The choice, of course.'

I felt disgusting. It was a cheap thing I'd said. Kvasha asked what I was doing the next evening as a play he is directing has a première. I apologised, being committed to Oleg's dress rehearsal. Julius said apropos choice and freedom – of course he, Kvasha, belongs to 'a most questionable Jewishness'. Meaning – I think, that his Jewishness must work against him. I thanked them profusely and went into the hotel feeling ugly.

Only ten p.m. I rang Lena who said she and Yura had waited in all day to hear from me.

29 October – Monday

Lena and Yura – tall, dark with a beard and specs – asked would I like to see Ostankino, as it is near? A trolley-bus, two or three stops. Their landmark soaring television tower has a lake close by, on which people skate in winter. Today, the first cold day. This beautiful Western-style, early eighteenth-century palace stands behind gates. A *babushka* attendant, with a headscarf as blue as much of the décor, scolded us, insisting we stand mute while the guide described every piece of glass, fragment of gold leaf. We were hushed when either of them tried to explain to me about the history of the palace. It was the summer retreat of the ubiquitous Sheremetevs. The elderly man had married a young serf singer and built a serf theatre for her, which in its day was the most spectacular and noted in Europe (as had Sir John Christie built Glyndebourne for his young, singer wife). Inlaid floors, crafted by serfs, original hangings. There had been a large collection of pictures by Rembrandt and others, now housed elsewhere. One or two interesting portraits of the kind-faced old man and of the young singer who lived only a year after he died. I guessed that in the summer with all the marvellous windows opening onto an enormous park, it must have been a blissful place to live. The theatre, with the stage entrance high up in the wall, needing steps down for the singers to make their entrances; some musical instruments; a chariot used in a Roman spectacle, all evocative of intimate chamber performances; I wish that, being so small, there were more such in England now.

We thanked the crone who had failed to thwart us, and set off for the hill-top Andronikov monastery where Andrei Rublyov, the most revered icon painter, lived and worked. In the middle is the small white-domed church, the oldest in Moscow. On a clear day I am sure you can see a marvellous view of the capital; however, the rain was drenching down, our umbrellas were up.

The icons are reputed to have miraculous healing qualities. Lena said she finds these works of art difficult to understand. I, too, feel no carry-over of my past Christian faith from them – I just don't get them. I am told by a living artist, with a particular interest in the genre, that each is a portrait of a real person, as are all the Chinese warriors of the Xian army.

Yura warmed to the task of explaining cultural historical aspects of what we saw, managing good English. He had to give a children's performance at three. Thinking of myself on a matinee day, having to trek round, say, Hampton Court in the cold and wet, with a foreigner whose knowledge of my language is minimal – I could imagine myself being very wintry. They had not allowed me to pay for anything.

I was astounded by one thing; Yura lit up a cigarette at the bus stop. Lena waved her hand at him, asking for one too, but he said 'no', explaining to me that he doesn't allow his wife to smoke or drink. She accepted this with a tolerance that made me wonder for a moment whether it was a joke.

I felt tired. I wanted to watch the Changing of the Guard, that's what I wanted.

Lena came too, wondering why I should find it so interesting. She acknowledged she loves Red Square. I explained that I am moved that those two young men are somehow guarding, standing in charge of the heart of Russia. For me the centuries of history seem to be what colour my feelings, the emotional climate that I am dealing with when communicating with a Russian. I was pleased to see the light of recognition in her eyes.

It was planned that I should meet Kagarlitsky at Filial MKhAT, the first Moscow home of the Art Theatre, for Yefremov's dress rehearsal. I would see Alexey Bartoshevich there. I knew I had to walk in front of Pushkin. 'Hello!' Past the gigantic Rossiya Cinema, left into Moskvin Street, named after an actor who appeared regularly in a private theatre founded by a rich barrister, Fyodor Adamovich Korsh, in 1882, after the state monopoly of the imperial theatres in Moscow had ended. I was to learn next day that it was he, the lawyer, who largely financed the original MKhAT. As I got near, I saw Kagarlitsky negotiating with an official. He was with an elegant, tall, blonde Englishwoman, Amanda Calvert; she was surprised that I was surprised to meet an Englishwoman married to a Muscovite.

Kagarlitsky gave me written messages for John Roberts, including the one about Raya receiving permission from Michael Frayn to translate *Benefactors*.

'I will remember,' I asserted.

'No, since you forgot the message I asked you to recover from the waste paper basket in your hotel about the offer of professorship at Cambridge.'

'But I didn't,' I defended myself. 'I picked up all the shreds and put them in an envelope and gave them to Boris last night.'

The other memos were for some matching jeans (with all the measurements) for Boris and Ira to be brought by a friend in November, and some medicine for Raya.

'I'm wearing my English jacket for you,' said Julius, revealing his coarse, checked tweed jacket, saffron coloured, the material as thick as the walls of a crofter's cottage – the sort of thing no Englishman would be seen dead in, unless played by an American actor in a Hollywood film. Brutally, I said how un-English it was and could have cut my tongue out at once.

'I bought it in Edinburgh,' he countered.

'Of course!' I leapt. 'A Scotsman would wear it, but an Englishman – never.'

Oh, Caroline!

Up came discreet Alexey Bartoshevich. I kissed him roundly on both cheeks, which he had not anticipated. Kagarlitsky explained that he was there as critic. Alexey reached into his briefcase and brought out a book for me – *The Golden Ring Tours of Exceptional Beauty and Historical Interest around Moscow*. Generous, as usual. We saw Misha's Irina in a stunning red felt hat and some of the people I'd met at their apartment. Smiling greetings all round, as we went into the auditorium.

There must have been twenty-five people scattered about; the customary roaming dress rehearsal photographer. Oleg's place was set with a table and lamp. He was already sitting with a youngish, round-faced Japanese. His customary pack of smokes – he always has to beg a flame from someone. A glass of tea was brought for him – I would have given anything for it.

The lights went down, the curtain drawn – yes, drawn; revealing – the young ones from yesterday in token Japanese costumes. I'd asked at the rehearsal the day before whether they would be using wigs and make-up, they said 'no', for Russians it was not necessary to make any changes in order to be thought Japanese. I realised how close their border is.

Oleg turned round before the lights went out: 'This is a black comedy. If you want to laugh, laugh.'

A plain setting with a moon in the sky. The piano in full view.

Nevinny and Lyubshin appeared. No sign of nerves. The rehearsed bits had been assimilated. No laughs. After about ten minutes, Alexey, next to me, sighed deeply. Often. Nevinny got a few titters.

At the interval Oleg said, 'Five minutes.' Some left their seats – I stayed.

I tried to discover from Alexey what he would like to see during his forthcoming visit to England. I guessed he would want to see Roger Rees's *Hamlet*. He guessed so too.

The second half went better. Lyubshin got plenty of laughs, talking to unseen ghosts, and the silliness of the machinations began to pay off.

No applause at the end. The actors, in traditional fashion, trooped into the auditorium to listen to Oleg. He introduced them to Utaka Wada who, Alexey or Kagarlitsky explained to me, had been the original director of the play. The actors clapped, he spoke a few sentences in Russian. Then the usual splitting up into groups.

Oleg came and sat in the row in front of us. He asked the critic what he thought. Alexey, uncompromising, said '*Интересно.*' [18] Nothing else. Oleg waited for him to say more – he didn't. I realised that was the most deadly thing he could say. Oleg looked at me – his arm hanging over the seat. I took his hand, '*Спасибо*' [19] – not ready with formulated thoughts and sensing such gloom on my right from Alexey. I could have spoken of the growth from the day before – the truthfulness of the two leading actors.

Kagarlitsky was talking with Lyubshin; I joined them, sitting in a seat on the front row. Kagarlitsky told him what I'd said about the film *Don't Kill the White Swans* and to me, 'You know that it was he you admired so much.' I wished my Russian was good enough to help me overcome my shyness by talking about his work.

Suddenly Misha was there standing in front of us. Lyubshin kissed my hand in a glamorous, intimate way and disappeared

[18] 'Interesting.'
[19] 'Thank you.'

backstage. Flustered, I begged a glass of water from Oleg's carafe, did an absurd actress's curtsey and toasted his production.

Driven to the hotel, I clasped Irina's hand in thanks. Misha kissed my hand: 'Завтра.'[20]

30 October – Tuesday

I made contact with my Intourist group. Two Americans, Bob Mackenzie, a sports writer for the *Scottish Daily Express*, a woman teacher, fan of Edward Petherbridge, on her fifteenth theatre-going visit. A man, visiting a girlfriend, returning to the hotel for breakfast in order to rumple the sheets of his bed. A young male employee in an unemployment office in Somerset. All enthusiasts, full of wonder.

Tanya, guide, directed us to pick up our own tickets at lunchtime. I explained I would certainly not be there. Bob Mackenzie would take mine for me.

With my last plastic bag, full of Edward's presents, I climbed the stone stairs to farewell my Muzei MKhAT friends. Gifts given, kissed and swooned over. Henrietta handed me two very old postcards of Moscow (1912) to give to Edward.

On the way, I had noticed a terracotta bas-relief of an eighteenth-century man in the wall of the building opposite the History Museum. I asked who it was. They'd never seen it.

'Come with me, I'll show you.'

It was Radishchev, a notable Decembrist.

'I have an hour. What should I go to see?'

'Stanislavsky Museum? But it's shut today...' Telephone call: 'It will be opened...'

Sasha will take me.

We talked to a watching dog on a high balcony, passed yet another church, arrived at Stanislavsky Street and the large yellow-painted house. A solid modern block of flats grew out of the ground beside it. Vladimir, a most conscientious guide, advanced. It is the next best house-museum to Tolstoy's; I was fortunate to have the place to myself I could imagine him with his actors; making notes with paper on his knees, instead of on a table.

---

[20] 'Tomorrow.'

The famous pince-nez, two pairs; the single bed he was ill and died in. The stage he had built for private performances. The actors' green room. The chair he used for *Othello*. Konstantin Alekseev chose the name Stanislavsky after an old Polish actor he admired in his youth, when working with Ermolova. Books, travelling trunks, costumes from the Edward Gordon Craig unrealised *Hamlet*, it smacked of enthusiasm more than anything else. They've reconstructed his dressing room exactly as it was at the theatre. Wigs, his make-up, costumes hanging in a wardrobe, lovingly preserved. Great emphasis made about K.S's astonishing attention to detail and correctness.

I find it disappointing that the photographs I've seen of Stanislavsky usually show him as an elderly autocratic guru rather than a stunningly handsome energetic young actor-manager, who met Nemirovich-Danchenko on a June night in Slavyansky Bazaar, to create the Moscow Art Theatre, for whom Anton Chekhov wrote his plays.

In the visitor's book I found the signature of my colleague and friend from the Actors Company, Ian McKellen. Characteristically modest, no flourish nor underline. I felt proud of him. Thirty years later I presume to feel even more proud. An actor of blest gifts, he has flung them joyously onto the world's stages and screens; sharing them tirelessly, as he has, also, his most private life. Coming out, smoothing the path for others in a generous surge of continuing global humanitarian aid. I hope his birthday wishes from now, till his 'second childishness' be granted, *sans* debate.[21]

Vladimir volunteered to get me back the quick way to Muzei MKhAT. I tore in, picked up my things, Sasha cried, 'Wait!'; he swept into the room with a bunch of flowers which he presented like a prince in a ballet. *Миру мир!*[22]

At the hotel, Bob handed me my ticket. We boarded a bus for Sheremetevo. Tanya asked, 'Has everyone got their ticket and passport?'

'My passport?' I gulped.

---

[21] *As You Like It*, ACT II, Scene VII.

[22] 'Peace to the World!'

The bus turned round and back we went. The document recovered, we drove through a most beautiful red sunset to the airport. The young man from Somerset had been much moved by his trip; done a lot on his own, watched the Changing of the Guard many times; listened, watched and picked up the essence of the place. He'd succumbed to the yearning. As guide Tanya said goodbye, she admitted that she had hoped Oleg Yefremov would be seeing me off. Suddenly welling, I choked, 'I love your country very much.' I touched her hand and turned away.

Things I noticed in the Metro:

I sit in my thick, black coat and Western shoes, often with a bright, silk collar sticking-up. Not ostentatious but clearly not Russian. Once, on the street, some people stopped and asked me the way in Russian. I apologised in Russian, I'm not a Muscovite; they moved on, bewildered.

A young man gave up his seat to an old man. A young woman gave up her seat to an old woman.

Two small children, four or five, with their parents – kissing each other tenderly on the mouth like cherubs in a Victorian illustration. I explained that I was English as I gave them a barley sugar each from my bag. They said, '*Спасибо*'[23] loudly and clearly. When they got out, their mother encouraged them, 'Say goodbye' – '*До свидания!*' – in piping voices, with waves.

On one train, I watched a woman with her dark hair haloed all the way round with a two-inch circle of bleached hair. Good idea.

I watched a blind person with a white stick on two occasions; noticed a couple talking sign language on the very long journey down the Metro escalator.

I picked up plenty of kopecks in the street. Well up to my London average. I gave one to Misha explaining how it's lucky to pick up and pass on. He said that for them, it depends on which way the coin is facing, as to whether it's lucky or not.

---

[23] 'Thank you.'

You ask what is Life?

20–30 March 1986

'You Ask What Is Life?
That Is Like Asking,
"What Is A Carrot?"'
A. P. Chekhov to his wife, Olga Knipper.

14 March – London

I have just returned from a week in New York. I had planned these trips adjacent so that I would get the full impact of culture shock, one to the other.

20 March – Thursday

This time, the anticipation of getting to know Leningrad better and of meeting Layla Alexander's artist friends, Gaga and Zhanna Kovenchuk, also Kostya Ivanenko, a friend of whom she spoke with exceptional concern; she describes him as a New Age visionary and poet who has endured many humiliations; but whose spirit soars above and around the world in communication with many beings, human and beyond. Layla was interpreter and archangel (his phrase) to Andrei Tarkovsky on his last film, *The Sacrifice.* A tall intelligent blonde from Uzbekistan, with blue eyes and long hair like a fairy on a Christmas tree; lives in Sweden but often comes to England; is in contact with most visiting Soviet film directors; works with Lyubimov; speaks tremendously good English; is a magnet to men until they discover that, being nearer to heaven than earth, she may not easily be seduced.

The Baltic we flew over was icy, as were huge lakes – one apple-shaped. Coming in to land, there were long, fine pencil-line shadows from the trees.

At the passport booth, the young man stared – up at me, down at the photograph, shaking his head. He was joined by a colleague.

'Yes, it's me,' I cooed. 'When I'm in the Soviet Union, I become younger.' He smiled me through.

The Metropol Hotel. In the same large open square, at right angles to the Bolshoi Theatre, a dark, old-fashioned entrance hall, without the style and grandeur of the National. An officious woman at the top of the three steps that lead to the lift and stairs. Difficult to get past without showing your hotel *пропуск*.[1] Dead mimosa and daffodils in the hall.

Kagarlitsky, out. Zoya Boguslavskaya, a noted women's movement writer, married to the poet Andrei Voznesensky, introduction from John Roberts – out of town.

I watched the Changing of the Guard at eleven p.m. I had difficulty understanding Irina telling me first, that Misha was at the theatre and would be back, second that he was at the theatre and wouldn't be back.

21 March – Friday

Disarming heat indoors, shocking cold outside. Dazzling sunshine. My feet, in shoes instead of boots, causing stares, as Lena walked me to Arbat, the historic street which has been restored as a pedestrian precinct. Old-fashioned standard lamps with large globes – like old gas lamps. A place for promenading. Antique shops – their version of the King's Road. We strolled to meet Amanda Calvert at the Pushkin Statue – 'Hello!' – to hand her requests from Vitya Borovsky for source material for his Chaliapin book.

Following my visit in October 1986, I had decided that I must take some serious Russian lessons. It is frustrating to understand so little in the theatre, and although I can make myself generally understood, it annoys me that I am unable to talk flowingly – my vocabulary is feeble; also irritating for Russians to have to reach for a dictionary when I am present. Not that they do.

I was introduced to Victor Borovsky by John Roberts. Vitya is an extraordinary man. I believe he has the fastest, most glittering mind I've met since *Hamlet*. He had lived in England nearly long enough to gain citizenship when I started going to him for lessons.

---

[1] Pass.

He would make time for me on Sunday afternoons and we sat for two enthralling hours while he teased and tamed me into a greater understanding of the grammar. He made tapes for me to listen to, write down, translate; gave me lots of homework. During pauses for coffee and hard black chocolate, his conversation and culture, his astounding grasp of English and of our literary and musical scene – we share a passion for opera – were entrancing. I can't remember when I laughed so much in someone's company. It was like being in the presence of a glorious crystal fountain. He himself was struggling with some tooth ill-health and the gestation of a massive biography of Fyodor Chaliapin, the Russian bass. I was lucky to be with him when he received the long-awaited call from his MP, David Mellor, saying that his citizenship had come through.

At the winter solstice my father died in his sleep. My mother, alone with him in the country, telephoned to break it to me. In shock, I telephoned Vitya to say that I didn't know what to do about the lesson as my father had died; should I come earlier or what?

'You go straight away to your mother in the country.'

In the spring, I was engaged in a series at Thames Television, *Mr Palfrey of Westminster*. Alec McCowen played Mr Palfrey. He is irreplaceable and can be dangerously funny just before the take of a serious scene. I managed to insinuate a few sentences of Russian into a scene that I played with Clive Francis, the Russian diplomat in the story. Vitya made sure that the text was correct and coached us both. He had plenty of experience of this, having prepared numerous actors and singers in Russian roles for film and opera. In Leningrad, where he lived before he came to England, he had been a distinguished musicologist.

Misha was waiting in his car outside the Metropol to pick me up. He noticed the improvement in my Russian at once. He drove us to the Actors' Club for lunch. It was crowded, noisy and jolly. He had arranged with the chef to plan a banquet for the cast of a play of his that was reaching an anniversary. The two men discussed the numbers, menu, drink, price. The whole deal seemed easy and comradely. I wonder whether one difference between

East and West is that in the East top people have money, power, position but know they are the same as everyone else, whereas in the West top people who have ditto think they're better than others.

Misha has new crowned teeth which please him more than the irregular ones he grew.

He took me to see Gastronom I, the huge food store on Gorky Street, with tiles and chandeliers out-Harroding Harrods. Jam-packed – we made no attempt to buy anything.

Later to MKhAT, where Irina Grigoraevna was waiting for me with Seat 1, Row 1, Director's Box. Also in the box was a voluble German, Birke Bruck, and a much younger man, Kurt von Hofman. He was qualifying in medicine, interested in alternatives. A previous night they'd seen *Nero and Seneca* and thought it terrific theatre, I must see that.

We watched *Uncle Vanya*. I found it uninspired. Borisov, one of the most famous and admired of their actors, seemed a bit old for Astrov. Neat, he gave a disciplined performance, not a passionate one. I could tell he is a great favourite with the audience. Vertinskaya again was superb as Yelena, exceedingly beautiful. I couldn't understand why Vanya seemed too small and lightweight to be Smokhtunovsky, who, I had noted with delight was in the production. I challenged Oleg at a later date, querying, 'It wasn't him, was it?'

'Yes, it was,' answered Oleg.

But he was playing Serebriakov, the professor, so I had missed him altogether by looking in the wrong direction. At the interval, my producer neighbour wanted me to agree that it was really wonderful: 'They're the only ones who can do Chekhov.'

The second half was better.

22 March – Saturday

Lena had agreed to take me to Gorky's house – *пешком*.[2] An uphill trek to a smaller house than Tolstoy's but something of the same atmosphere inside. Architecturally extraordinary, being the work of Schechtel, the designer of MKhAT. The unusual Art Nouveau

---

[2] On foot.

marble staircase climbing up out of the hall made me envious, as
did the wooden wall decoration in an upstairs room. The anteroom
for the male secretary is on the ground floor. (I recommend this
museum.) I am attracted to places where I can imagine people
living.

We walked on to the Yermolova Museum, her home. She had
been the great actress at the end of the nineteenth century –
perhaps the equivalent of Ellen Terry. She gave Stanislavsky work
as a young amateur actor, when he still went under his family
name, Alekseev. A friendly place. Photographs of her in roles;
costumes, citations, ribbons, garlands. I asked if I might buy a
guide book, postcards but the woman pointed apologetically to the
locked case and said *Закрыт*.[3] Lena begged for me, a visiting
actress from England. Hearts melted (they usually do). I was given
a plastic cameo brooch with her likeness on it, as a present. Lena
told me that her children are asking when I will come to see them.
We parted without a definite plan.

Two women followed me into the hotel Ж. I was carrying plastic
bags. While I repaired my hair and make-up, they watched my
every movement. Did they think I was a spy? Perhaps they were
waiting to see if I would offer to sell them something. It was rather
menacing.

I walked along the familiar boulevard to the theatre. In the
anteroom to Oleg's office, I talked with Irina Grigoraevna and two
or three others. I gave her some soap and chocolate; she opened a
drawer in her desk to find me a tiny scent sample. There was an
operatic feeling of people waiting for the door to open to reveal
the Commendatore.

In the inner sanctum, Oleg and Misha were working on the
script again. Eventually I was invited in to sit on Oleg's sofa, he
with his little book of *What's On*. I said I wanted to see what was
really interesting for me as a tourist. Neither he nor Misha were
keen on *Nero and Seneca* (I don't believe either of them had seen
it). 'Moderne,' said Misha scornfully, later. I was offered *Skameiki*,[4]
a two-hander by Alexander Gelman, with Oleg Tabakov – 'Or,'

---

[3] Closed/shut.

[4] *Benches.*

suggested Misha, 'you can go with Zaya Boguslavskaya to the Writers' Union to hear Nikita Mikhalkov who will be speaking there.'

This seemed more exciting, as I had seen a season of films that he'd acted in and directed at the NFT. His is a charismatic personality. Misha told me that we would now go to see the actress, Lyudmila Maksakova who is playing Anna Karenina in his adaptation.

'She needs to discuss some problems of the production. We will only stay a short while – I want you to see the flat.'

It is old and had been lived in by her mother, a renowned singer. Outside, the building is studded with plaques of differing shapes and sizes, dedicated to distinguished creative people who'd lived in the block.

It must have been two thirty or three o'clock when we knocked on the door, opened by a maid-servant – I didn't know such people existed here. The hostess was dressed up to the nines. An exquisite, pale-grey fitted suit made of dyed pony skin, with another sort of fur, possibly sable, on the collar and cuffs. Immaculate grey tights and new high-heeled court shoes. Lavishly made-up, honey blonde hair. She pulled us in effusively; 'Have you had lunch?'

Into the furniture-crowded sitting/dining room, where a meal had been finished but not cleared: two places, ours, still waiting. Formality – places laid with little linen napkins, decorations on the table – wouldn't have been out of place at a major wedding anniversary. Different sized glasses, etc. Food was ordered. An unusual dish of hot pasta with cherries. Also, the customary array of закуски,[5] champagne and, much more welcome, coffee.

She and Misha thrashed through whatever was causing difficulties at work. She was decisive. Her face grew rosier. We discovered that French was the easiest shared language for us. A tall, dark-haired man in a smart suit arrived and shook hands – her husband. He said he was German but I didn't ask whether from East or West. We disliked each other at once. When I told him that I was English and here as a tourist, he asked if I had a gun. I

---

[5] Starters.

answered smugly, 'I come in peace.' He retorted, 'They all say that.' That brought our conversation to a close, so I drank more coffee and tried hard to imprint the decoration of the room on my mind. Every bit of wall was covered with pictures, including portraits. Little cabinets and shelves stuffed with objects.

A girl of about eight came in carrying her school satchel. She was required to play a piece on the piano, at the end of which no one commented, except me. She faded into another room; the husband left. I walked round the room, noticing that on the door leading to the bedroom there was a huge poster of Andrei Voznesensky.

'Oh,' I said. 'I just read a whole book of his poetry in New York last week.'

She told me that she was the girl crying in the telephone booth in that poem. I confided that I would be meeting his wife in an hour or two.

'Give him my love, if you meet him.'

Then into the stylish, Western bedroom – mirrors galore. Also a piece of Perspex sculpture given her by Voznesensky, a photograph of Mastroianni with whom she had recently filmed in Italy. I believe Misha was feeling quite left out with our girls' talk. Although we weren't entirely on the same wavelength, I was drawn to empathise because of her chilly husband. She said she wanted to give me something and chose from the table top a charming blue and white china figure. I, in turn, said I wanted to give her something from my bag in the car, tights perhaps... Ignorant fool!

'You know, I really have everything.'

We parted warmly, having been there at least an hour and a half.

Misha drove me to the Writers' Union, alerted someone at the desk that I was expecting to meet Zoya Boguslavskaya. I knew her easily – she looked purposeful, believing that I was Liz Roberts's secretary. She felt comforting and real. Just time for a small strong coffee then into the packed lecture theatre. Zoya was greeted on all sides. Good seats.

Mikhalkov came onto the stage to great applause. Five minutes later his art director arrived to introduce him. Laughter. Mikhalkov talked for around forty minutes – of which I understood phrases and words; not enough. Questions were written on scraps of paper anonymously and put into a box on the stage. All were answered. Applause for several of them. Zoya said afterwards that many were quite testing in the political area – this sort of session draws people who want to feel the present climate; what's in, what's out, what can be said, what can't. I understood things he said about working with Mastroianni, wondered if this was the film my earlier hostess had been in. There was an attentive silence during his talk, two-way affection, humour shared. He made reference to his father who was sitting in the hall, talked of his brother, Konchalovsky, also a film director, working in the USA – having had a privileged childhood – meeting all the great artists and creative people of the time – Prokofiev, etc., came to their home. He stopped after two hours because *Пять вечеров*[6] was about to be shown. My favourite of his films.

Zoya led me to the dining room, introducing me to a film director who prevented me shaking hands with him in a doorway, saying it was unlucky. Zoya talked her way into a table against a wall, where we had black caviar, two glasses each of white wine; small filled pastry cases, cucumber, olives, hot peppers, spring onions, black bread, white bread. We talked in Russian as well as English about life, openness, inner life, Mikhalkov. She asked why I come to Moscow.

'Do you love someone?'

'I love lots of people here.'

She took me in her car to the Metropole, another new warm friend. Taxi to Leningrad Station. I found a vase with flowers in the compartment.

23 March – Sunday

Snow: clear sky; sun coming up; birch trees; a bird carrying long twigs in its beak; an old graveyard. Nearer Leningrad there are commuters waiting on platforms, reading books. No water to drink or wash with. Handed tea in my berth. Lost my spectacle case. Gave the attendant nail varnish and a Mary Quant comb.

---

[6] *Five Evenings* (1978) is a film written and directed by Nikita Mikhalkov.

An Intourist courier waited at the carriage door. Loudspeaker music in the station, as huge and heroic as the last reel of a war film.

The Astoria Hotel (Hitler's proposed scene of victory banquet) is glamorous, old-fashioned. An Edwardian plush bedroom, the bed in an alcove behind curtains, a glass display cupboard with china in it, a picture of Venice on the wall, a health and fitness class on television. I ordered tea in my room, put in a request for a visit to the Kirov Theatre in the evening.

The hotel is in a terrific position – St Isaac's Cathedral opposite, the Winter Palace in sight, passing Peter the Great's famous bronze statue on the way. I'd bought a map in the hotel. It was still early, nine thirty. I found a callbox on the river frontage on the way to the Hermitage and called Zhanna and Gaga, no answer; then Kostya, who answered after a long time; I must have woken him.

'Let's meet tomorrow.'

We arranged to meet outside a bookshop on Nevsky Prospekt and Herzen Street.

I needed a friend today.

I pulled myself together and made for the Winter Palace/ Hermitage. A student group was at a side door; I was in for nothing. It is overwhelming. Far too much to see. The portraits of those who fought Napoleon in a huge hall. A collection of Rodin sculptures. Just walking through the rooms – oh! The Malachite Room; the great audience rooms – like Versailles in its hugeness and grandeur. Up to a higher floor for the matchless Impressionist collection. The curators, men and women, though not in uniform, are involved and concerned about the pictures; they answer questions. You are free to move around at will, unlike a Дом-музей[7] ('house-museum') where you have to follow a route from start to finish. After three hours, I was exhausted.

Back at the hotel, yes, a ticket for Donizetti's *Don Pasquale* tonight. Enough walking. Is there a bus trip? Yes, to Pushkin. The great Ekaterinberg Palace, Tsarskoe Selo.

---

[7] Lit., 'house-museum', pronounced *dom muzei*; a place where a writer, composer or actor, etc., lived, subsequently changed into a museum and left as the inhabitant would have known and recognised it.

Pushkin is difficult to describe. The tour of the palace took an hour. It is enormous. In each room there are photographs on stands of how it was desecrated by the Germans during the war. Things smashed, used for target practice, stolen. It has been, and still is, being restored at undisclosed cost and to perfection. At one point I carelessly remarked to a young Austrian in my group: 'It must be so painful for German tourists to be reminded of what was done in the war.'

He answered, gimlet-eyed, 'What about Dresden…?'

I allowed plenty of time to get to the Kirov Theatre. I found it standing all alone in the middle of a vast space. On the way, passing statues of nineteenth-century composers on plinths – Rimsky-Korsakov, Glinka. Could ancient Rome have been set out a bit like this? People scurrying amongst grand architecture, their own appearance so humble in comparison; are their spirits raised by it? Huge distances to cross carrying shopping. I saw children being pulled along on sledges instead of in prams.

The Kirov is glorious, a wedding cake; the circles don't stick out or overhang the stalls. The stall seats are individual chairs. The best seemed to be occupied by tourists. My memory of the interior is of pale blue, white and gold. *Don Pasquale* was very poor. I walked home in a roundabout way along canals – I really am too lucky for words.

24 March – Monday

Today I decided to brave the crossing of the Neva River to see the Peter and Paul Fortress. The c-o-l-d, the w-i-n-d – make me gasp. They slow me down. The fortress contains a church where the coffins of the tsars are lined up. It's unexpectedly moving. All the wives and some children. Peter the Great's I expected to be much longer because of him being six foot seven, but it was the same as the others. There were flowers laid on his.

Being alone instead of part of a group is a blessing; you can move fast or linger, as eccentric as you like. Many people were imprisoned here, and dreadful things done to them.

As it is a lot of tramping to get round the exposed site, I tried to return by another bridge, but the distance was too daunting, so

I headed through the searing wind to the low, dark-red Menshikov Palace, which looked inviting but was shut.

A walk along the Griboyedov Canal before meeting Kostya at the art shop. Holding presents, standing for nearly an hour. It began to rain. Cold and wretched, I called Kostya's number. His mother said he was out. Could he telephone me at the hotel? Hot bath. I'd been standing at the wrong place... Abject, I took a nip of brandy, ate a couple of English Easter eggs and went to sleep.

25 March –Tuesday

Huge choice for breakfast. I stocked my handbag for lunch and dinner, just in case; trudged over to the Menshikov Palace again. Sold out. Frustrated, I trudged back.

Vitya Borovsky had given me a number of opera records for Marina. He'd offered a pile of ten but I brought only three, because of the weight. We agreed to meet in the small, bush-surrounded garden outside the hotel. There are benches, it is discreetly secluded from the eyes of vigilant doormen. She's round and cheerful, wore a headscarf, thick coat and boots, works at the Chaliapin House-Museum, which is high on my list.

I came across St Nicholas Cathedral. A gleaming gold cross at the top, people going in and out. My understanding is that it is still unusual, perhaps brave for people to be seen as churchgoers – but inside, like Zagorsk, there was no inhibition. Two services going on; a coffin. Coming out into the sunlight again, people busy living, getting about their business. I walked the length of the great curved backbone of the city; from the industrial, rather dingy end to the smart; the Fontanka Canal and Nevsky Prospekt. Melting, flowing slowly, majestically under the bridges, iceberg Poohsticks.

Down some steps into a white-washed cellar studio. Kostya is short and round with magnifying spectacles. We walked at a cracking pace along the Nevsky Prospekt, he having taken my bags from me. After a couple of trial conversational openings to do with reincarnation and the I Ching, and getting a listening response from me, he launched into esoteric New Age profundities in stunning, expert and expressive English – loud-voiced, ignoring other jostling pedestrians – occasionally seeing someone he knew

– sensing is a better word, as I understand he's nearly blind. He's a seer in the other meaning – walking and talking as if it might be his last chance to do either. We went in the Metro, then on a bus to the apartment block of the Kovenchuks. Large, bearded Gaga is a painter of repute, looks more life-worn than his wife; grandson of Kulbine, himself a well-known artist and associate of Mayakovsky. Zhanna, also a painter, half-Chinese, her mother having married the Chinese Ambassador. She's tall, exquisite – wears a hat or skull cap or bandeau or scarf on her head, which is a perfect shape. Their ravishing, darkly mysterious son, Alyosha is a student of architecture.

The flat is cramped and inhabited; alive with bright coloured rugs, paintings, cut-outs, typical of any artist's living place in any country. A terrific welcome. I brought out the gifts – some brandy from the hotel Beryozka shop, which Kostya commandeered, tights, nail varnish. He sat splayed in an armchair supping it down. Esoteric talk led by Kostya, the only one to speak English, though Zhanna has a word or two. There was food, beer. Alyosha gave me an etching he had made of 'disappearing Leningrad'. He's a conservationist and tries to record buildings that are being demolished.

They talked of Layla with devotion. Any friend of hers, a friend of theirs. It was good to be surrounded by a family busy with emotion and activity after being on my own. They pressed things on me. Pictures painted on glass by Gaga. How am I to carry them? Beautiful, delicate montages of New Age design – Mandalas, really, made by Kostya. Again, framed with glass.

They decided to give me the Dostoyevsky tour. Noisily, just inside the front door, they warned that if we met someone on the stairs we must on no account speak English, Gaga's position is sensitive. We met someone on the stairs. They all said, 'Добрый вечер!'[8] I, silent, must have stuck out like a sore thumb. We climbed into Gaga's car.

We visited the main venues from *Crime and Punishment*: Raskolnikov's house with the seventy-seven steps, which we walked up; Dostoyevsky's house with a balcony on the corner of

---

[8] 'Good evening.'

two streets – the building is being turned into family apartments. The Kovenchuks think it should be a museum and asked me to write to *The Times* about it. The bridge where Raskolnikov first saw the old woman; the step where the axe was hidden; the old woman's house. Entertaining, intriguing, happening in tiny environs.

We passed Tchaikovsky's house in Gogol Street. He died there.

We called on an elderly painter who, with his wife, had remained all through the war in a remarkable old flat that his father, who ran the Pushkin Museum, had lived in. An impeccably gracious couple. The wife had taught English long ago and spoke it well. The burnt orangey darkness of poor lighting gives these dwellings the look of a Rembrandt painting. Round the highest part of the wall in the oblong room where we sat were at least twenty watercolours which had hung in those positions for a hundred years. They survived the war. These two, our hosts, had had to burn their furniture to keep warm. A sizeable inglenook fireplace is where, they declared, Pushkin had sat to rest on the way to his fatal duel. They owned the first cat I had met in the USSR. We were given refreshing tea; biscuits and cakes were pressed on me before my 'rigorous journey' back to Moscow.

My new friends, dropping me off, explained that they must park round the corner, out of sight of the front of the hotel, to conceal their car number from prying eyes. We hugged.

I had the carriage to myself until an Englishwoman from Wolverhampton asked whether she could share with me rather than with an unknown Russian man. The news on the train's radio was followed by Prokofiev. Thank you.

26 March – Wednesday

A porter waiting for me with the Intourist courier. I mistook and mistimed. He went away without the kopeiki he had asked for. At the Metropol there was no room ready, so they allowed me a free breakfast, following which I secured my hotel card and a room key. I telephoned Graham Coe at the British Embassy; we agreed an appointment at eleven a.m. tomorrow, another ruse of John Roberts, who had given me a small job to do which would enable entrée. I rang Irina to leave my number for Misha. She said that he would be back at two.

I strolled to the Muzei MKhAT. Sasha no longer, Henrietta ill. I asked Galina if she could find some Chaliapin material for me to take back to Vitya Borovsky. I complained that on this visit I was not being offered *salo*, the spicy pork fat that Sasha had fed me last time.

I was at the hotel for two p.m. – no call. Slept. No call. I finished the stale food from yesterday's Leningrad breakfast, went to bed. Overnight trains save a lot in the cost of hotel rooms but they don't half wear you out.

27 March – Thursday

Misha rang. 'Come to my play this evening at the Sovremennik Theatre. Meet at six p.m.'

'OK.'

I walked to the British Embassy – over a bridge, down some sludgy, wet steps, across planks. I showed my passport at the gates to the couple of soldiers. Up the front steps to ring the buzzer. A Scotsman let me in. It was a strange Gothic hallway we were standing in – the odd comfortingness of being completely surrounded by my own language. Saying he was sorry that he couldn't let me in to look, he re-directed me to an annex where a friendly English secretary took me into a small low room, offering Nescafé.

Cultural Attaché Graham Coe was very polite. I remarked on the increase in the shops compared with earlier visits; some oranges, particularly, I had noticed. He answered dismissively that they were from Cuba, so no good. I decided then that we must be being overheard on KGB mikes; wondered whether he felt he had to be negative on principle or whether he meant it. I longed to start on my enthusiasms, but didn't. The cat called Pectopah came in, named after the Russian word Ресторан (meaning *restaurant*); read as English it makes a nice joke. He kindly offered to make an appointment for me to see Maria Grenkova tomorrow, the small job I'd said I would take on to save John waiting weeks for letters to arrive by post. It was agreed that she and I should speak French together. Graham Coe's Russian is enviably good.

'With the Ambassador away in Odessa, there is not a great deal going on, but I have to be in the Embassy, as I am on duty.'

'Why don't they have radio calls like doctors?'

'In Berlin they do.'

While he was talking, and for fear of being overheard, I wrote a question asking whether he thought I might have difficulty getting my glass pictures through customs. Should I declare them? I handed him the piece of paper. He read it in silence, then answered out loud, 'No, I don't think so, there should be no problem.' With gratitude for his help, I went to meet Lena for a trip to the рынок.[9]

A bus took us into unfamiliar territory, passing a crowd of people hustling to get into a liquor shop, also an unmistakable statue of Rachmaninov. The market has flowers in the outer part; up some steps and through doors to reach the fruit and other sections. People from different regions of the Soviet Union, in their own national dress with their own physiognomy and complexion, charging huge amounts for apples, which perhaps only the diplomats can afford. It was fascinating. The smell of fresh produce is delicious. We moved into the dairy area where they sell the most succulent curd cheese. They call out from their counter, inviting you to try it. Lena, seeing me enjoy a tasting, bought me a kilo – refusing any money, as indeed she did for every single bus or Metro ride that we took.

'You are our guest.'

Misha, wearing an expensive navy-blue cashmere overcoat, was accompanied by a theatre director from Minsk and another Moscow writer – who had a terrific giggle, talking so fast that I understood almost nothing. As we were driving along – I had been put in the front seat – a large cavalcade went by. Outriders with flags. The President of Algeria and Mr Gorbachev.

'Ah, they're on their way to see my play,' announced Misha.

Minsk got out at one theatre; Misha taking him in to arrange the ticket, being a noticeable and recognised celebrity. The writer and I were driven to the Sovremennik Theatre, where we made for

---

[9] 'Market'.

the basement cafe to grab smoked fish on bread, with a glass of fruit juice. My new friend screamed his enthusiasm at me with deafening intimacy at the speed of light. I smiled and nodded like a puppet. The theatre was packed. Good acting showing tough relationships. I found it hard to understand the words. At the end there were many flowers for the leading lady, also for Smekhov (from Taganka). He is conscientious, perhaps over-serious.

Boris arrived at the theatre, guided me back to the hotel, talking on the way about the new things that are happening under Gorbachev, so freely that I had to ask him if he would be carrying on like that in the hotel bedroom. He came in with me to collect the presents. Past the annoying doorman. No problem. He, still conversing with great vigour, was positive and cheerful. He said the Russians know no nuclear war and have no dread of it. He couldn't have tea for fear of missing the last train. Misha, who had not stayed to watch the play, had said that he would be busy tomorrow. I am losing my rarity value.

28 March – Friday

John Roberts had given me excellent instructions for finding Maria Grenkova. I had never been to Kalinin Prospekt before. A new atmosphere, not attractive. I passed the wedding cake building described by John and found my destination easily. To start with, the woman at the desk couldn't find Grenkova's name; I was invited to sit on a leather sofa until she came down. She was another formal Soviet. We had our conversation in French. I made notes; she did too; once or twice I tried using Russian words, she asked sharply whether I would prefer to have the conversation entirely in Russian.

'Non, non,' I answered humbly.

We concluded amicably. 'These things take time,' she conceded.

To *dom-muzei* Nemirovich-Danchenko for my meeting with Henrietta. I walked past an apartment block with plaques in memory of Kosygin and Timoshenko, a name I remember clearly from the war. All the soldiers that I see walking about have the same haircut, low and square at the back. They smoke on duty. I got lost and kept patient Henrietta waiting in the street with flu.

She insisted that it doesn't matter. We went up in a rickety lift – everything in Moscow is being repaired – ремонт. Into a modest apartment. I was shown round by a dignified elderly actor who smelt of Old Spice. He kissed my hand. He is allegedly the son of Bulgakov. Nemirovich Danchenko was at least as famous, if not more so, than Stanislavsky, in his time. His descendants still live next door; his grandson is head of music at MKhAT. Only three rooms in this apartment; musty atmosphere; piano; small room with a casting couch, evidently he was shameless in this way. Each room crowded with furniture. The museum being part of the MKhAT conglomerate, Henrietta is partly responsible for its displays and asked for help with some labelling in English under one or two framed photographs. A picture of Mary Pickford with Douglas Fairbanks. Nemirovich-Danchenko had visited Hollywood for a few weeks, according to Henrietta, and had written afterwards of being there for fifteen months. He and Stanislavsky had quarrelled. Our curator brought us tea. We sat at the velour-covered table for two hours. When he'd left us, Henrietta suddenly said that she wanted to ask a question – 'rather-strange'. She'd had a sort of vision of an aeroplane crash. Had I heard of such a thing in the West? A two-seater. I couldn't think specifically of one. Then we went off the beaten track. I'll listen to anything. Afterlife, Great Teachers, Dreams, I Ching, Atlantis. I gave her Kostya's number in Leningrad. Our relationship reached a new level of exploration. Knowing that her husband is an assistant director making television films, I asked whether I might go to a studio to watch a programme being made. She called Lena, whom I was to visit and arranged that I should get out of the Metro at Ploshchad Nogina and wait there.

We walked to her flat which is quite Spartan; in the process of being made ready, they moved recently. So far, they have no belongings except books. A son and daughter; Oleg was very serious, talking English in a low voice. Lena told me they had all watched in horror when the American space shuttle had blown up with the astronauts on board, and that the boy had burst into tears. Lisa, his sister, wore red gingham. We sat at the table and had a dish called vinaigrette. I would have called it Russian Salad. Also black bread and cucumber. I thought it was the whole meal and took two helpings. Then she said, 'Чай,'[10] and brought a hefty meat pie (пирог), cut into slices. Also jam and sweet bars reminiscent of nougat. I felt tired. Lena exudes simple humility. Oleg took lots of photographs with a birthday-present camera. He also washed up. Lena had to visit her sick mother.

I wanted to see the Changing of the Guard. There were plenty of people all around which helped to keep me warm. Eight p.m. Ding, dong, tinkle, tinkle. Stamp, stamp. Back to the hotel for a hot bath. I felt lonely so I went to watch some terrific TV serial on the landing outside. It is so popular that it draws the staff, the chefs from the restaurant, the old *babushki* from the landings. They forsake their duty and fill all the seats so that none of the guests can sit down. They commented loudly and emotionally on what was happening in the story, had a post-mortem at the end and went away. It was funny and completely charming. Also on television, the President of Algeria, Senator Edward Kennedy, and football on motorbikes.

29 March – Saturday

Misha rang early to ask where I had been yesterday and last night. He'd been trying to invite me to see a film of Lyudmila (grey fur-suit film star) with him and Yefremov and then to a party at her house. I wasn't going to tell him that I'd been feeling lonely sitting in front of a television set in a foreign country wondering what the hell I was doing wasting money when I could be tucked up in bed at home, near my children. I said I'd been with friends, which was true. '*Дура!*'[11] he said, vehemently. Did I want to go to the theatre banquet at the Actors' Club that I'd been in on the planning of?

'*Да*.'

Meantime, there would be a seat arranged for the matinee, a première, at MKhAT.

'Can Lena come too?'

'Yes.'

I made for the Theatre Museum.

---

[10] 'Tea'.

[11] 'Fool!'

Emerging from the Metro at a big main line *вокзал,*[12] I had to wend my way past outdoor platforms for local trains – people were using the station as a short cut. They carry parcels wrapped in string. I was struggling. At the entrance they asked whether I was a student. I answered, '*Нет, артистка,*'[13] and was allowed in free. Interesting, faded curators, maybe retired performers. It is a comprehensive museum. It could take a whole day to glean it. A room in the basement is devoted to Chaliapin. Glorious tapes of him singing; busts, self-portraits, wreaths, ribbons, accolades. In other rooms grown-ups were sitting obediently on benches, being lectured on Turgenev or MKhAT or Pavlova or Nijinsky. Too much to take in – I left, determined to come again.

Metro to Pushkinskaya – past statue – 'Hello!' and the trot to MKhAT. Lena waiting. We were put in Yefremov's box. It was the original 1908 production of Maeterlinck's *The Blue Bird,* a classic children's story. Stanislavsky got the director's credit in the programme. A small round woman played the little boy and did splendid, energy acting. The young audience laughed and clapped. Maybe it's their version of Peter Pan, roughly the same date. The actors appeal from the stage, in character, for the children to be happy, to find the Blue Bird themselves, now. Much joy in the full auditorium. Lena, when she discovered it was the Blue Bird, was disappointed, as she had seen it many times as a child. Première can mean the re-opening of an old production. She left at the interval.

At the Actors' Club before the banquet, I met Galina/*muzei MKhAT* and her artist husband; he wore a beret like any French painter. He's devoted to Turner. She delivered Chaliapin material. They'd also brought a sizeable piece of *salo* carefully wrapped and very cold. Horrors! Look pleased, look pleased! Misha arrived with his daughter and invited them in, but they thanked him and said they must go. We went into a private room, where a table for two dozen was set out in three sides of a square. I was placed at the centre of the three sides, next to Misha, with his daughter on my left. Brandy and vodka were presented in water bottles – a

---

[12] Station (main line).

[13] 'No, an actress.'

necessary disguise, Mr Gorbachev being against alcohol. There was also champagne, Georgian wine and mineral water. I stuck to champagne. A vodka'd, compact, middle-aged actress opposite poured and invited me to share a toast in brandy. (Oh, please, no.) She swallowed hers in one. I, warily, sipped mine, having raised my glass to her. Having emptied hers she put it upside down on the table.

'Why are you not doing the same?'

It meant I didn't wish her well.

'Of course I wish you well.'

'No, you don't.'

'Yes, I do.'

'No, you don't.'

'*Несерьёзна?*'[14]

'*Серьёзно.*'

Her raised voice attracted some attention. I knew I must concede, so I gulped it down and upturned my glass. Honour, but not friendship, restored.

Misha's daughter is extremely pretty, twenty-ish, with dangling earrings. Smoking non-stop. She wants to be a critic. The food came onto the table consecutively – the ideal way, in my estimation. Something new appears to set the imagination going again. On Misha's right the young director of the play, very thin, much loved by all, especially actresses, who will do anything for him, they say. He made a speech. Others did too. More food and drink. Misha spoke. More food and drink. I had my dictionary by me and planned a few sentences. When I stood up there had to be a lot of 'Shushing' by the director to gain silence from the far side of the table. I announced this was my debut in Russian in public. I praised their national hospitality, acting, etc., and sat down feeling relieved. Misha said '*Молодец!*',[15] which is what teachers say to children who get good grades. A young actress came and talked with me in excellent English, has appeared in some films, rather discontented with her roles; she doesn't want to play a boring Communist girl on a farm; wants to leave and work elsewhere; is

---

[14] 'You can't be serious!' 'Yes, I'm serious.'

[15] 'Well done!'

feeling watched and frustrated. Then another florid extrovert; as her husband arrived, she shouted like anything. I gave them pop socks from my bag. When I thought the meal was over, the main course arrived – it always does. Chicken Kiev with peas, desperate chips; finally ice cream and more speeches. We were invited to the home of the extrovert wife, where our hostess had taken off her shoes, turned on bright overhead lights and was playing loud music. A typical, relaxed actors' party. I noticed the silent young actor I'd sat opposite at dinner. He had stared and looked away alternately. People were telling me what an exceptional actor he is. The husband of our ebullient hostess came and sat with me. He is from Ukraine. We spoke French together, talking modes of work, payment and organisation in the theatre. His wife told me that he is in politics.

The party suddenly ended. Misha had been deep in conversation with his daughter. He, she and three friends were piling into a taxi. He came over – 'Maybe we'll go tomorrow to visit Zaya Boguslavskaya in Peredelkino.' He hugged and kissed me. 'I love you.'

30 March – Sunday

Already nine thirty – the clocks have changed. Peredelkino, the writers' colony I've longed to visit, where Pasternak lived and is buried. I rang Misha. Irina said he would be back at two. I asked her to say goodbye to him for me. I rang Zaya; she ordered, 'Get into a taxi; I'll pay, but don't tell him you're going to Peredelkino until you've started.'

'It must wait for another trip.'

I made a dash to Dom Kagarlitsky, asking them to make sure that I got away in plenty of time. They didn't. Rush for a taxi. Amanda – selfless and out of breath, arrived at the hotel with heavy tomes for Vitya.

Most of the strings of this visit tied up. I was exhausted.

The glass pictures gave no trouble at the customs.

A Carrot is a Carrot; nothing more is known about it'

November 1987

'A carrot is a carrot; nothing more is known about it'
A. P. Chekhov to his wife, Olga Knipper.

20 November – Friday

Seventy years' celebration of the Revolution.

I know, I should be getting used to it, but still...

The pilot had warned us it would be cold, but my! I have broken my smug rule about not offering death as presents. I give cigarettes to everyone. They like them. The drive so familiar; landmarks pointed out. I don't say, 'I know.' The National Hotel, more down at heel than during my first visit. The room. First Class, Fourth Grade. Shocking. Plaster peeling, electric cable joins showing, TV not working, telephone held with Sellotape. I learn early on to give my number to whomever I'm speaking within five seconds, to establish a lifeline. I rang Misha to find out if there were theatre plans. Irina said he would call me in the morning.

When I rang Henrietta, her husband answered; I gave my name, he sounded as if he'd been expecting my call. Gennady would meet me at nine p.m., as I was feebly unable to understand the name of her Metro station on the telephone. I couldn't see anything on the map that looked what it sounded like.

There had been a nasty half-hour when I could only find two of my Moscow numbers. The others turned up deep in my spectacle case.

We had no difficulty with recognition at Pushkin. 'Hello,' to Pushkin; 'Hello, Gennady.' I felt guilty but he is so charming, I forgave myself. They live in what I think of as a typical Moscow flat – a faceless, concrete block: small lift, entrance hall stinking of piss. Henrietta opened the door to one of the happiest evenings ever. Three warm rooms, kitchen and bathroom. Well-filled bookcases, comfort without luxury. A few treasured objects. He made me hot pork with potato salad, peas, smoked fish and tinned salmon that tasted of the sea – *море*. Their relations send fresh produce in boxes; cranberries, mandarins and parsley, which Gennady collects off the train from Sevastopol, Crimea, where he and Henrietta were born. They gave me vodka steeped in a root he gathered in Kamchatka, the land opposite Alaska – where he'd made a film of a fairy tale about whales. It has an ancient Friar Laurence taste.[1] I was lent his thick, felt slippers, *valenki,* to wear, which usually have longer legs and can be worn outside in dry snow. They have a long-haired tabby cat, called *Кошка*.[2] He lives high, like the Cheshire Cat, on top of a bookshelf in their living room. He didn't get me at all; wouldn't come close, stared accusingly, and later just stared, daring me to be without integrity, truth, love.

'He seems to be my conscience,' I volunteered.

'For us all the time, too.'

Henrietta gave me a shell which her brother had taken from the ocean; Gennady, a rack like an oversized abacus to massage my feet. They mix their alcohol without a thought, we hardly drew breath and got a bit drunk. Then tea. The Russians I like most manage to be intuitive, spiritual, open-minded and foul-mouthed. The best of friends, there's nothing we cannot discuss – nothing, without laughing. At two thirty a.m. Gennady went to find a taxi. He brought me all the way home.

I look out onto the inner well of the hotel where the dustmen start early and the large crow birds squawk.

21 November – Saturday

The Seventy-Years Exhibition is on at the Manège, the old riding school. Only forty kopeks to go in, not crowded, mothers with children. Conscientious for the first hour, I wanted one of the life-size wooden statues made from a whole tree trunk. A set piece with a familiar bronze half-Lenin leaning forward on an enormous

---

[1] A reference to the character in Shakespeare's *Romeo and Juliet.*

[2] *Kowka / koshka* is the Russian word for *cat.*

ornate framed mirror, some of the glass of which was broken; before it, a young man and woman, larger than life, cast in white plaster; at the front, modern; behind – constructivist, painted to look like bronze. A dozen or so were gathered *за*, voices raised *против*.[3] A small, bearded man in argument with any who would join, many did – old, young, a shawled woman, moving into the centre and out again – someone at the edge watching, smiling, detached, would find they couldn't resist being drawn in; a shuffle, confrontations, which at one point brought a soldier to look. Highly entertaining and un-English. People believe their point of view should be heard, no one fears scorn – this is what they enjoy – talking. I joined some elderly gents sitting on chairs facing a piano on a platform and watched.

I saw there was a cafe upstairs. I joined a queue for sardines, olives, sweetened coffee from a hot urn. If you haven't the exact change they give you a wrapped sweet in lieu of half a kopeck. I sat at a Formica-topped table, eating with a zinc fork and a white plastic knife taken wet from a tray. I walked through the Kremlin gardens to stroll opposite the British Embassy. It looks bigger on the far side of the Moscow River, which at this point is narrower than the Thames at Putney. Back up the steep hill – past St Basil's. How thrilling it must have been when the young German landed his plane in Red Square. He must have been so excited. They now jokingly call Red Square 'Sheremetevo III'.

Moscow Art Theatre – MKhAT

I felt anticipatory excitement, having waited four years to watch a performance in this world-renowned theatre. The restored Shekhtel building has a whole new block. The exterior is painted the signature grey-green. Misha led me through a corridor of marble, up in a minute lift to the Director's office. Irina Grigoraevna was there, warm, welcoming, speaking fast, as usual. When I don't understand, she uses German. As she made me tea, she recounted how she's worked forty years in MKhAT. Oleg's room is sparse as yet. A big desk: a long boardroom table with chairs, bookcase, portable turntable standing on a cardboard box – that's

---

3 *За* means for, *против* – against.

about it. A formal line of large, square glass lamps hang from the ceiling. It is civic, not yet lived in. Misha sat at the boardroom table working on the script of his recently opened play with a stage manager I had met before. I continued my diary which I carry everywhere. In walked Oleg with a slight limp, looking unwell. He glanced at me and walked on without comment. Misha announced, 'It's Carolina!' He realised. We hugged with real enthusiasm. He was to perform in the two-handed play by Alexander Gelman, *Наедине со всеми*,[4] with my friend Tanya Lavrova. He went to prepare, followed by Misha who looked seriously worried about him.

I was led to the smaller of the two auditoria. Like any studio theatre – black, with perhaps 200 seats. Lights out. The set comprised three rooms in a flat, with only the centre one lit. The upstage door stuck, so nothing could start. I heard Lavrova struggling to make her entrance. Eventually, with some shoving, she succeeded. It's a painful, funny play about a couple trying to leave each other and a son (not seen) who has lost two hands in an accident. I understood the acting but not enough of the words. Wonderful parts; they were both splendid. She hides in the cupboard. He opens the door, she tumbles out. The force of her fall knocked Oleg over and he cried out in real-life pain as he hit the bed. I thought he might have to stop, but he kept going. She smokes throughout, snorts and clears her nose. It was terrific honest acting by two artists, safe with each other. The ups and downs clearly marked. Throughout there was quite a lot of talking backstage which must have been distracting for them. The play runs without a break. At the end there were two rather desultory curtain calls. No curtain. Some people stayed in their seats, perhaps thinking there was more to come or discussing what they had seen. I picked up a discarded programme.

Misha was waiting to introduce me to the original restored auditorium. Exactly as it had been; inside plain, unfussy.

'Very democratic,' approved Misha.

Pale wood balconies. A lovely rounded carved prompter's box. I sat in Stanislavsky's chair No.12 and, of course, walked onto the

---

[4] *Alone with Everyone.*

large stage and said, 'Я чайка' – 'I am a Seagull.' The set for Misha's play, which I shan't see, was stacked at the side, as was the little arched platform they use for *Seagull*. A revolve and plenty of lights, but I'm told there were technical difficulties at the opening, as there had been at The National Theatre in London. Front of house – there is a long foyer, narrow and formal, where they have hung photographs of all the important people connected with the theatre from the early days. In an extension of the hall – foreign writers, Shakespeare, Sheridan, Dickens... Also, there were Dostoyevsky, Tolstoy, Ostrovsky... It is highbrow; not at all vulgar or red, or even very comforting.

8. Main stage and auditorium of MKhAT.

Instead of taking me to Lavrova's dressing room to celebrate, Misha whisked me back to Oleg's office. I asked Irina if I might see Tanya Lavrova (*narodnaia*/dame); but she would have gone home already. The leading actors are transported by car to and from the theatre. Her performance was even better in this than in *Seagull*. One of the dames, she has a massive, truthful talent. All-round first class, like Judi Dench. I asked tentatively if I might have a poster. Two or three people, including Leonid Ermann, Oleg's devoted assistant, kindly went on a hunt to find some. They came back with top-quality plain ones of the theatre façade, not yet overprinted with the name of the play. Also one of Misha's play, on which he, and later Oleg, both wrote for me.

Oleg came in jauntily and sat down at his desk, looking as actors do after they've acted well; cocky and vulnerable all at once. I told him that when I cannot understand all the words, I watch and sense even more.

'*Я верила*,'[5] I said, which is what Stanislavsky aimed for always.

He looked pleased enough, brushed off concern for his bruised back where he fell.

There was a bit of bustling to and fro, shutting up shop for the night. It became clear that we were going to Oleg's for something to eat and drink. Misha had warned me not to give him brandy as it is so bad for him but now he relented and told Oleg that I'd brought him a bottle; Misha had received his blue boots for the boy and I'd got my posters. We were all happy.

I was putting my boots on again but they said it wasn't necessary because we would drive – so my coat and hat only, but before I was ready, they'd trooped out of the room and switched off the light. I growled, the light went back on. Into Misha's car, we drove two yards when Oleg said, 'We must get some champagne. There's a place just here.' He got out and went through a door. A young man put his head in at the car window and asked if Misha would drive him and his girlfriend home, as in a taxi. Misha said, 'No.' The girl was completely drunk. Oleg returned with a bottle of champagne which had cost 100 roubles. We drove off, only to stop round the block, on Gorky Street. I thought, 'He's taking us to a restaurant.' But it was an apartment block with a *babushka*, wrapped in a shawl, sitting at a little table in the hall. A lift or stone stairs. I lingered for Misha but Oleg, already in the lift, said, 'Come on, come on, he's always so slow.' So, up we went. Quite a dishevelled landing with two flats. He was pushing the key into his door but it wouldn't go – wrong floor, I thought. Wrong building. Down we went, out into the street and tried the next. Better luck. Misha was already there, with the door open. Igor taking coats and hats. A young woman was preparing food. The kitchen, high, old-fashioned, all the door and window

---

[5] 'I believed.'

fittings seem pre-war – an electric stove, tall fridge freezer, kitchen table covered with a red paper cloth, vase of purple chrysanthemums, newspapers, box of chocolates. Against one wall, a china cabinet. All the kitchen units have a matching dark-brown, man-made surface. Misha showed me the bathroom, if I wanted. Oleg took me round. The flat faces onto Gorky Street and looks across to MKhAT. A hundred yards from work. His large bedroom with a low double bed covered by a red tartan blanket.

'This is where I sleep.'

Pause.

Stare.

A dressing table, maybe a chair, one or two photographs of himself, one large pastel, done by a student of his. The curtains are of open-work white net... boarding-school bleak.

'Is it noisy?'

'Yes.' He shrugged.

Through a door, a preformed, red armless sofa, two or three matching seats, a table.

'This is where one drinks vodka and cognac and coffee and watches television and plays tapes and talks.'

A room with no character, life or charm. Who cares? Russians naturally provide those qualities for themselves with their talk. Perhaps that's what I love them for most. The other side of the passage is his old father's room. Staying in the dacha.

'Is the dacha at Peredelkino?'

'No fear!'

'Why not?'

'Because that's where Misha goes!'

They are best friends.

Misha was trying to persuade Oleg not to drink but having no success. We sat at the table. Igor and his wife either were already or became guests. Champagne for me and I stuck to it, despite urging from Oleg. To eat – tinned crab, tasting of crab; smoked salmon or sturgeon, the whole fish taken from the fridge and slices cut from it; колбаса;[6] a plate of tomatoes and peppers. I remembered Oleg eating loads of tomatoes at John Roberts's

---

[6] Salami sausage.

house in the summer; a dish with loose pomegranate seeds and a slice of lemon. A jar with whole cranberries, sour; some extremely hot mustard; саΛo; an Armenian dish of cold spiced red beans; cabbage salad; a tin of pressed ham taken out of the fridge halfway through the meal, opened unnecessarily; black bread, white bread; an EEC butter mountain.

The conversation was going hammer and tongs. Oleg, thrice married, describing Misha being interviewed on television and talking like a 'greybeard' about how one should stay with a wife and be loyal. He (Misha) looked rather shamefaced and remonstrated about that story being told, but it brought much knowing irony from Oleg, who before now has said to me, 'Of course you love Misha.'

Misha took the floor with a story I didn't understand which made him nearly die of laughing as he told it, the others too. I hardly spoke, just bathed in the atmosphere. Oleg waved around and said, 'This is what it is like with my very close friends.' I felt included. I told them how I had been invited to read the letter from *Nostalgia* at the Memorial Service for Tarkovsky which was held at St James's Church, Piccadilly, on 30 January 1987. Time concertina-ed. His wife and son were present. Susan Fleetwood, leading lady of *Sacrifice*, his last film, read a poem by Arseny Tarkovsky, Andrey's father. Gennady Rozhdestvensky read a Pushkin poem in Russian, John Roberts the same in English; Lindsay Anderson, Ian Christie of the British Film Institute and Anna-Lena Wibom, producer of *Sacrifice*, all spoke; there was singing by Rachael Hallawell and members of the choir of the Russian Orthodox Church in Ennismore Gardens.

Misha reminisced about being хулиган[7] with Tarkovsky and Vysotsky when they were young men. They taught me a new word – мудила, which is affectionately derogatory, meaning *fool, prat,* centring on the uselessness of someone's balls. Things moved to politics and socialism. I volunteered that socialism will never take on in England, and how bad it is. I sensed later that this came out as 'socialism is bad' – not my intention at all. Oleg used several times the phrase, 'Please excuse me saying', very polite, but a small

---

[7] 'Hooligan'.

coolness had come down which I didn't altogether understand. He declared that he'd like to go to sleep now. It wasn't heavy or serious, I just felt it. We hugged goodbye warmly; Oleg didn't get up. Too tired, eyes drooping, blowing kisses from his seat. I was given the large pot of honey that was on the table at supper.

22 November – Sunday (President Kennedy)

I rang Kagarlitsky. To my surprise Julius answered, as Amanda had said he was at his dacha. He asked whether I could come this evening. I answered,

'Could I come now?'

'Come tomorrow, we'll see the matinee of an interesting new play and you can have food before the train.'

I was anxious about collecting my luggage.

'You will be seen to the train.'

I arranged to meet Lena at two.

'Get out at Kirovskaya, wait by the statue of Griboyedov.'

I started to catch up with the diary, feeling the socialism misunderstanding with Oleg taking hold.

I get out at Kirovskaya. My appearance provokes stares. Aunt Diana's brown fur-lined (hamster) 1920–1930 coat, long and Chekhovian; my black fur hat bought in Leningrad airport, pulled right down over the eyes and tied under the chin with two red velvet ribbons I'd sewn on, two pairs of gloves... I really need it all. The cold is intense. Eyes screwed. I walk past Griboyedov (literally translated, it means *mushroom eater*) – he died at twenty-five. There are children with sledges. An attraction is that the daily papers, *Pravda, Izvestia*, are put inside glass cases at eye level for anyone to read *gratis*. Towards me come Oleg, thirteen, and Liza, six. Sweet and friendly. He talks seriously in English, the little one being shy. They lead me onto a bus for one stop, insisting they pay, then a short walk.

I brought out the presents. The Beryozka in the hotel being shut, I was unable to offer a bottle. Yura declared since the Gorbachev decree on drink, he'd packed it in. Nevertheless, he brought three tiny liqueur glasses and we drank a toast, a sip of Chivas Regal. He is a dark serious man with a resonant voice. Lena

produced four or five courses. Oleg sat opposite his father, Liza –
next to her mother. I had my dictionary on the table which was
referred to frequently. Oleg – something so moving about him, I
don't want him to be in a war, ever. Lena jumped up and down,
fetching *smetana* to go in the soup, cranberry juice, fruitcake she
had baked.

Then everything was cleared away. Yura went to rehearsal and
I said I should go back to the hotel. Oleg asked if he could take a
picture of me as he'd done last time. I sat on his bed and he
flashed, then his sister sat on my knee for another. He and I shook
hands, before Lena and her daughter took me to Kirovskaya. Only
two stops. Out at Prospekt Marksa. I now know which exit to come
out at the National Hotel. I started serious work writing this but I
shall stop now, because the sneezing I was doing earlier has turned
into a cold and I must start on Olbas Oil. Henrietta says we can
store my heavy things in her office until I come back from
Leningrad.

23 November – Monday Morning

I am sitting in the dining room of the National. There has been a
fall of snow in the night. St Basil's domes are whiter than
yesterday. This room is rococo in style. A painted ceiling, sky and
cloud in the middle, surrounded by decorations and a frieze – the
walls gold damask, a large mirror hangs at one end. Twelve tables
seating six stand along the outer walls and six round ones for four
down the middle. There are wall tables on which are heavy brass
lamps with parchment shades and good white linen table cloths.
White and gold china, solid metal utensils; high-backed, tapestry-
upholstered chairs. The floor, wood parquet in a pattern of
decreasing squares – different woods, polished, suitable for
dancing. A large vase of gold metal flowers stands on a plinth
against the mirror which reflects them advantageously. This time
I'm sitting in the main room, away from the window. Many
businessmen today, seizing bread, butter, jam, so that I must stand
up, lean over and reach them. Rather slack service too, but I got
two boiled eggs again and cheese. This time I put nothing in my

bag. I was hungry from having done without supper the night before so I ate what was there and drank three cups of tea.

9. Muzei MKhAT – Henrietta in her office.

Packing.

A call from Misha: 'What are you doing today?'

'Going to Leningrad tonight. Matinee and supper with the Kagarlitskys.'

'I'll come to Kagarlitsky – see you there. Oleg slept all day yesterday.'

I half-packed then went down to meet Amanda in the hall. She's absolutely English, completely open. We talked on the sofa for a good half-hour. She left, replaced by Henrietta. She and I struggled across Gorky Street, carrying weighty things; honey, foot massager, etc. Henrietta persuaded a driver to take us the short journey to her temporary office, where she sits at a little table by the window. She thinks the *ремонт*[8] of the old museum will be finished in about two years. She made tea, offering Indian, green or mint. We had a ramble about socialism and communism. She asks what the West has to fear from communism, as it is so wonderful an idea. Too ignorant to answer the enormity of the question, I spoke the simplest, 'I guess we fear the loss of freedom.' She continued that there are, of course, many things wrong in the manipulation,

---

[8] Repair or refurbishment.

people can fight to get more, cheat and lie and push and pull, at least the ideal is pure and can be worked towards. She prefers to live clean and have less. She thinks it right that a female factory worker earns more than her, because she works harder.

I told her about the socialism debacle at Oleg's flat and asked whether she would help me write a letter to him to clarify my position. Re-telling it makes me cry. Again I discover the material surroundings amongst some people here are unimportant compared to the quality of the life they lead in relation to each other. It is inspiring.

'No doubt, we become confused with so much choice.'

'Tell them we see so much that is good in your life in the West, why should we want to take it from you?'

'They would not believe you.'

Henrietta decided to try the film director Elim Klimov – he answered. She explained I am a friend of Layla, and asks if the book about his wife Larissa is available for me to take to her? I am going to Leningrad tonight.

'Me too,' he said.

We agreed to meet on the train.

Ten minutes late, I felt genuine warmth towards patiently waiting Julius. We hurried along towards the decorative Puppet Theatre. A group of unemployed actors had got together to do a piece about Kampuchea, Vietnam – written by a well-known writer, Alexey Kazantsev, who with Misha Roshchin started *Dramaturg* magazine. Both these working for no money; the actors taking the profit from the doors. It was a three-hour piece of great savagery. Every sort of beating and violation. A man pretending to be dead on the ground watching two soldiers finding his wife who has just died of grief following her son's death. They decide to fuck her.

'Still warm, won't scream, what do you think?'

'Let's try then.'

Power turns people into machines; everyone can be corrupted from their own vulnerability. Systems destroy people. At the interval, Julius said that he found the text a bit agitprop. It had a profound influence on the audience. Julius said that it would take time for people to get used to this sort of freedom of expression. It will become more distilled. It was strong meat, and thoroughly disquieting. I asked what he felt about one of the actresses being topless for one of the scenes.

'We are beginning to get used to that sort of thing.'

A long Metro journey back to Aeroport with one change. Julius told me that I was the most 'laughable' person on the train. There is often an undercurrent of aggression in what he says; expressions of how insensitive we Westerners are.

'Over-civilised and silly,' he remarked at one time.

'If you say so, Julius.'

He continued, 'No one could understand this play unless they were Russian and Jewish.'

I guessed that in our country the equivalent might be for our black population, but apart from the splendid Black Theatre Co-Operative at present, I know of no constant company of black actors. Maybe one time I will ask him why he wants to have contact with us if he despises us so.

Two tall friendly young men who had been in the theatre, were on the escalator in front of us carrying Western plastic bags, smiling at my appearance.

'Is she warm enough?' they asked Julius.

I said, 'Я англичанка.⁹ We don't have such cold weather in England.'

At ten degrees below freezing it is not severe for them. Last winter it got to forty below. They were jolly.

Dom Kagarlitsky. Boris was at the door warning us not to wake the baby, Georgy. Eighteen months old and, although he can hardly talk, he is beginning to read. Raya, sitting in her green dress, looking not well at all, with a burning stricken face. Already nine fifteen and I had to catch my train at eleven ten.

'How could you come for so little time?'

I gave her three copies of The Dresser playscripts, specially signed by Ronnie Harwood.

'No, no, we wanted the Russian edition.'

⁹ 'I'm an Englishwoman.'

They gave me four copies in Russian to take back for him to write in. Raya's translation. It is obviously important to them. I wish I was not affected by their accusatory way. I'm sure it's only because they so long to see us and it is hard to have to share us with others. We talked quickly and ate some special food they'd prepared – smoked salmon, meat, potato salad, beetroot. A toast in vodka, then in brandy.

Raya urged, 'Can't you come again? It is such a short visit. You must come for longer next time and see more plays. It is your profession.'

'I like people too,' I explained.

'People are her profession too,' confirmed Julius, kindly.

'Maybe we should not have gone to the Kampuchea play,' I offered.

'I thought you would be interested,' he replied.

There was a lot of emotion and not enough time for it to come out. Clearly Misha was not going to turn up. Tired, well-mannered Boris was put in charge of getting me to the train. Ira, looking beautiful, arrived halfway through the meal bringing a cream cake – called *Птичье молоко*[10] – fluffy sponge, iced with chocolate and filled with layers of mock cream. *Bird's Milk* because bird's milk doesn't exist, therefore it is a luxuriously witty rarity. It was a generous offering.

Boris and I went out into the street and immediately found a taxi which he told me was extremely lucky. We went to the National to pick up my green bag, then straight to the station, me keeping an eye out for Elim Klimov, whom I had heard speaking at the GB-USSR Association in London. We chatted comfortably in the cab – I liked him more than ever before. He says something will be published in *The Times Literary Supplement* about a left-wing movement he belongs to, the *Red Arrow*. A compartment to myself, a busy Lizzie in a pot on the table. Boris asked for tea for me, refusing money for a taxi home, he left.

The train pulled out – I applied lipstick, sprayed *Diorissimo*, arranged myself attractively on my bunk with my guide book and waited for the famous film director. Nothing.

---

[10] Bird's Milk.

24 November – Tuesday

A good twenty minutes in a cab to the grand hotel Pribaltiskaya, the sea lapping at one side. I'm on the tenth floor, not looking onto the Baltic. Comfortable, warm; decent bathroom, hot water, television, plenty of hanging space. I had a shower and washed my hair for the first time this trip, before telephoning Gaga and Zhanna. Jeremy Howard, an English friend, would pick me up around noon. This gave me a chance to settle in and go to the Beryozka.

Jeremy turned out to be late twenties, tall and thin with spectacles. He's an art historian. He has lived here for fifteen months; now with a Russian wife, Ossetian, going home in a month – instantly sympathetic. He put me firmly into a taxi saying that he has plenty of roubles from his grant to spend before he leaves the country. Driving along I was struck by the registration number of the car in front – 1149, my telephone number in London. 'Phone home.'

We arrived at Dom Kovenchuk to a noisy welcome, like puppies, continuing and continuous and interrupting conversation. I wanted tea more than anything. We talked, laughed, and drank tea for two or three hours. I brought out the presents. The men put their new English shirts on over what they were wearing. Alyosha, beautiful, and brooding, brought some work to show me. A fine draughtsman. Etchings – for him, it's all to do with architecture; how to conserve beautiful buildings. We were invited to the State Russian Museum for the opening of an important collection of work left to the nation by B. N. Okunebo.

Leningrad *beau monde*. Gaga had forgotten the tickets so he had to go through a back door to rustle up some more. He came back waving two, to let in four people. He shouted, 'anyone want to come?'

A man joined us. The bored audience, hardly listening to a succession of speakers introducing the exhibition, began to talk louder and louder. Gaga brought out a biro and sketched – including me; finally a red ribbon was cut, there was a surge into three rooms of lively paintings from 1902–1968, including work by Roerich, Bakst, Golovin, Goncharova. Easy-to-live-with pictures of a period. Some decorative Art Nouveau stage designs, strong portraits in bright colours of revealingly clothed women. Here, at an opening, people look at the pictures; in London, they look at each other.

10. Gaga Kovenchuk's sketch of gallery opening,
showing the crowd not paying attention.

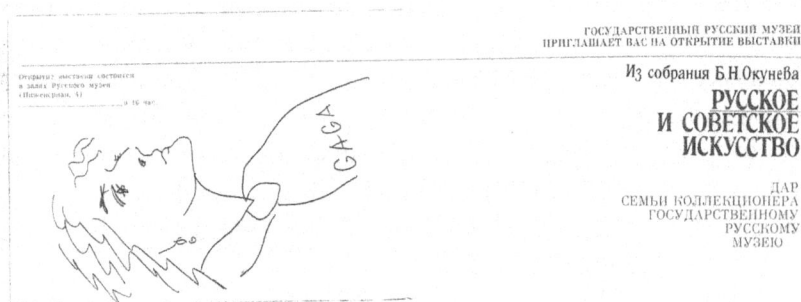

11. Gaga's sketch of Caro at the opening.

Gaga always removes the window wipers and locks them inside the car when he leaves it so they have to be re-attached, while Zhanna clears away the new snow from the windows with a tiny brush.

We went to the Artists' Club for coffee. It is a cellar, the cafeteria, quite cold and sparse, but as usual the character is established by the people. A man announced that Elim Klimov was going to speak later at the main cinema before the showing of *Interview* – Fellini's latest film. All ears pricked up. Into the car again to pay another visit. A drive through beautiful four-inch snow shining glamorously under the globe street lighting, which is ungarish and shadowy. The roads along the canals with their trees have a local character. You go in under an arch to a tiny courtyard, through a wooden door, up stone stairs. Two flats to a landing, front doors either old or painted brown or, in homage to modernity – perhaps for insulation, quilted, buttoned mock leather.

We went to a door and rang. A woman answered. We were on the wrong floor. Back down and this time the door was opened by a neat man of sixty-five wearing a maroon cardigan and slippers. He had many British mementoes. A hanging dishcloth, a calendar with pictures of Loch Lomond, which song he started to sing, so I joined in and we finished together. A long-haired cat sat in the hall. Lots of small Matchbox cars in a glass cabinet. We sat down and were offered miniature tumblers of brownish vodka and fruit cake made by his wife, who wasn't there. It became plain that he is a friend of Tovstonogov, the great theatre director. He was telephoned and told that an English actress friend of Vitya Borovsky was here. I was made to say hello. He had a fine voice and was kindly offering two seats for *Lower Depths*, by Gorky, for the following night. Thank you, thank you. The courteous host then helped us out, kissing my hand on the way. When we were in the street he opened his first-floor window overlooking the canal, and waved goodbye.

Zhanna asked me to confirm that his flat is English in style. I had to say not at all. The two main reasons are the wallpaper and the fact that the Russians light their apartments only from above with varieties of metal or wooden chandeliers – they rarely have table lamps.

Fix wipers. A careering, skidding journey to the vast cinema where there was a milling crowd. Gaga inventively talked to an *administratr*. Someone came and waved us into an inner sanctum where Elim Klimov stood. He reminds me of the actor Michael Jayston, though taller and rather stiff, like a schoolboy. Black leather jacket. He is one of the most important film directors of the country. He made *Agonia* (*Agony*) about Rasputin, quite an operatic film, affording wonderful glimpses of Leningrad and maybe an unusual point of view, for a Soviet, of the difficulties of being tsar. Also he finished a film started by his director wife, Larissa Shepitko, following her death in a car crash, about the population of a whole village being forced to leave because it was to be flooded and used as a reservoir. A strong, beautiful work. *Come and See*, his latest film about a young boy's experiences in the war; so dreadful that his hair turns white. I could not possibly stomach it. But Russians, many of whom have endured the same as the boy, do go to it and sit in tears. War is very close to them. As Lena explained – all mothers fear, when their sons have to do National Service, that they will be sent to Afghanistan. I saw on TV a ghastly piece of newsreel, in which a young Russian soldier, begging for mercy, was having individual fingers blown off.

We shook hands with Klimov. Gaga and Zhanna explained about Layla. He nodded. The book should be collected at Lenfilm the next day. We could see the Fellini now if we wished. His new position is head of Mosfilm and the Film Union. I had seen a programme on TV in England where film people, including Nikita Mikhalkov, had been interviewed and it is clear that things are changing. Scripts, long-buried are being brought out of drawers; films finally being shown, etc.

We were given good seats in a filled auditorium, 1,000–2,000 people – young and middle-aged; plenty of soldiers and sailors. They have to wear their uniform, even off duty, which is why I get the impression of much armed force about the place. Klimov was introduced. He talked generally for half an hour, followed by questions on paper, read from the floor. He answered them all, some at length. Several questions drew laughter from the audience, as did his answers. Asked if he believed in God, 'You mustn't ask me such a question, it is my problem to deal with whether I do or whether I don't.' There were also questions about Boris Yeltsin, the newly dumped mayor of Moscow – an innovator and freer of rules, much loved by Muscovites. Sacked, according to our English press, for making too much of a cult of himself; here, I'm told by Kostya, for telling Gorbachev he's making too much of a cult of himself. Another Ken Livingstone? The questions went on until at least ten. There was applause, the lights went down. Klimov left and Fellini began. I was so tired by now that I slept some. There wasn't enough room for my legs. Mastroianni looking old and fat (on purpose), Anita Ekberg likewise. As usual with Fellini films, in my view, the large and wonderful visions are offered in too expanded a way so that the image is distorted, though they demonstrate plenty of vitality and colour.

25 November – Wednesday

Breakfast at nine fifteen, self-service, huge choice. Meats, sausage, hard-boiled egg, baked egg custard, solid, cut in squares, the wonderful and disgraceful warm light cheesecake, potato cakes, beetroot salad, cabbage and onion salad, carrot grated fine, slices of cheese, grated cheese, cottage cheese, cream cheese, sour cream, yoghurt in mugs, porridge, smooth, rough, black bread, white bread, butter, soft rolls, rolls with currants and sugar. Tea, coffee, jams. Shocking, really. We tourists take advantage.

I had booked my ET call home to catch Adam and Charlotte before school. The operator rang at eleven a.m. (eight, London time) and relayed 'No reply'. It seemed odd. I tried not to feel anxious. On my way out of the hotel I booked another call for eleven p.m., Russian time, thinking I would surely be home from the theatre which starts at seven thirty. (Kostya telephoned to say that he was in the Metro station and would come to the hotel in ten minutes.) Jeremy was waiting downstairs. We stood together on the steps till we saw Kostya hurrying towards us carrying my great bag. The flaps on his fur hat dancing excitedly like Piglet's ears. A taxi took us to the recommended side door of the Hermitage; finding inside a grand door; through a room with fine furniture, two girls tapping notes onto typewriters. I explained my connection to Madame Dukelskaya through a personal introduction. She is a bright-eyed, highly esteemed, international art historian. I introduced Jeremy as an English art historian, Kostya – artist and philosopher. She honoured us by giving the tour of the Scythian Gold treasure herself. Kostya, unconcerned, was cutting across her, talking loudly about President Reagan's position in One World and his importance in the New Age. I saw Madame sizing him up unfavourably and felt obliged to suggest to him that we could discuss that later. He has grunting mannerisms which weren't appreciated as she took us from glass case to glass case. Her hostility was noticeable; if he spoke or questioned she answered sharply in monosyllables. I saw her several times standing back from him – he is not fragrant – and staring quite frankly. She was polite and gracious with Jeremy and me, but reacted strongly when I put my hand on one of the cases as I looked into it. We had a good hour of her time and saw great riches. Generously, she gave us permission to stay in the museum as long as we wanted. Parting with profuse thanks, I said that I should like to give her a small present which was in my bag in the *гардероб*.[11]

'Leave it for me in the office,' she acknowledged courteously, as she retreated.

---

[11] Cloakroom.

Kostya invited us to the Egyptian department, where he knows every sarcophagus and statue. His intimate passion; I feel no incarnations there.

We left the wrapped soap for Madame and made our way out into the street, where Jeremy left for home.

Kostya and I set off for the Pushkin House-Museum, in which the poet lived for the last months of his life – and died. We walked along beautiful Rossi Street, I recognised it from the single day trip I'd spent with the Amyes family, three years ago. Places needn't change. Coming and going this way and that we arrived at the museum which is on the Moika River.

The group leader takes her job seriously, acting the drama of Pushkin's last days as if it were her own family. Lowered eyelids, low voice, religious atmosphere. The group of men she was hypnotising stood motionless, cowed, as she enunciated the terrible story of the duel that led to his death. Kostya cleared his throat, snorted and talked to me until he was told to shut up as if he were in church. It is a spacious flat, the tragedy gathers momentum from room to room until we are where he died. The couch he lay on for three days, bookshelves to the ceiling, the clock stopped at a quarter to three. His is a powerful spirit with a great hold over the people. He stands for all that they would like to be. Passionate, unbowed, free-living, speaking their language and funny, though I wouldn't have known that today. There were flowers left by his desk.

It must have been nearly five when we were through. I needed a sit down and a cup of tea.

We had to be at the theatre at seven. Kostya took me to a *kotleta* cafe, which he was afraid would shock me. A basement floor awash from people's melting snow boots. He refused everything. I took two cups of milky sweet coffee, a piece of chicken on a plate. We stood at a table on a stalk. He advised me that it would be more hygienic to eat with my fingers than to use one of the available zinc forks.

We set off again, along Nevsky Prospekt. Suddenly, there was Gaga walking towards us. He came into the theatre, collected the tickets, gave Kostya some money to buy me chocolate and left. We dropped our coats at the *гардероб*, in care of a tall gaunt fellow with scarce teeth but a lavish soul. Into our smart third-row seats. The lights went out on a full house. President Gorbachev had seen this production on his recent visit to the city.

I was looking forward to watching *Lower Depths*, which I had neither seen nor read. Kostya's head gradually sank down onto his chest until he was snoring quite loudly, to the distraction of our neighbours. I nudged him for the sake of the actors. He said it was necessary to go deep into the subconscious. I understood minimum dialogue; though I didn't get the story, it looked to me a first-rate production. I believed the characters. A lot of tall actors in Leningrad. They spoke clearly without showing off. Good work. After two hours the curtain came down to a smattering of clapping and the house lights. I thought it odd the actors didn't come out for applause.

Collecting coats, we surprised our *гардероб* friend.

'That's only the interval!'

'What time does it end?'

'At the première, it was eleven forty!'

With the London call booked at the hotel, I had to pack it in. Our skilled coat attendant gave me an ornate doll-sized chair he had made by cutting and bending a food tin; the seat was the bottom of the tin; legs, arms and back curled into fancy shapes, the metal still joined in one piece. It was sad to miss the second half as I may not see such a production again, and embarrassing to leave a performance at which I had been a guest. There is nothing more obvious from the stage than empty seats that were previously filled. Kostya was kind and supportive. We came to a bus stop for No. 7 which would take me all the way home. Easy. I saw on the outside of the hotel that it was minus ten degrees C. The operator rang at eleven to say that the London number was engaged.

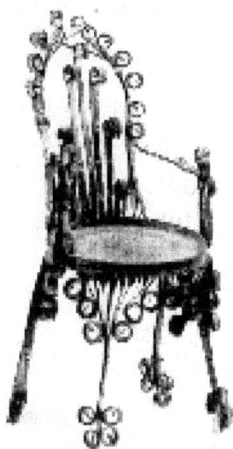

12. Leningrad, Tovstonogov Theatre, chair made out of
drinks can by *garderobe* attendant.

'Please try again.' I turned on the television.

Almost at once, Gaga phoned.

'Please, I'm waiting for a call from London.'

It rang, Adam's voice as clear as a bell. He told me he had eaten a chicken Kiev from the freezer without de-frosting it enough and made himself very sick indeed, so much so that Charlotte had left school in the afternoon to look after him. He is better now. She came on, they both sounded cheerful and all right. I carried the telephone over so they could hear a football match on television from Russia minus ten degrees. The telephone number on the car had been a strong message to me. I miss them.

26 November – Thursday

The morning rose heavy-misted. My limbs felt heavy, too. All tourist intentions seemed to drain away. I sat writing this diary.

Trying to pay for my call to London, a friendly woman could find no record of it at all. We laughed; I said I would accept it as a present from her country. A trip to the Kovenchuk atelier in Pushkin is planned for tomorrow. Back to the buffet for tea from a girl who was a bad advertisement for the Soviet Union; cold, humourless, charging thirty kopecks for a spoonful of honey; we spat at each other; as I was being a bad advertisement for the UK, I drank quickly and left. I wrote the diary until late.

27 November – Friday

I practised the T'ai Chi in my restricted space and liked it – not the restricted space – the T'ai Chi.

With Zhanna a sudden descent into a shop. You pay first, then get the goods for your receipt. An abacus does all the sums. She'd bought two bottles of fizzy water: I am suffering great thirst.

At three thirty, just before dusk, we set off for Pushkin as Tsarskoe Selo is now called. I asked that we might stop at the place where the poet fought his duel. We walked a little way into a copse, the remains of a summer estate, still known as Commandant's Field, surrounded by factories now. In a clearing there is a large memorial stone and two slabs, one of which carries a Lermontov quotation. I felt nothing.

It takes a long time to get out of Leningrad during Friday rush hour. Next stop Pavlosk, a palace built by Catherine the Great's son, Pavel. Small, classical, with a curved elongation on both sides of the house, making three-quarters of a circle altogether. A lovely central courtyard, with a statue of Pavel, one of the few monuments not stolen or destroyed by the Nazis because, they said, Pavel had been a Mason and the Nazi commander who could give the order to destroy it was also a Mason. *Pravda?* Enormous gardens, laid out in the informal English manner, with lakes, stone steps and informal elegance. We strolled for half an hour in the moonlight, then careered to the charming studio – could be in Paris.

There, irregular, oblong shape with a thick pillar in the middle, I notice straw packed between the inner and outer panes of glass. Jeremy, who had dinner guests coming at home, rang to tell his wife that he might be a little late – one guest had already arrived. It was warm from the house central heating, I suppose. They explained that their electric meter doesn't work so they haven't paid an electricity bill for three years. Zhanna knocked up fried eggs, bread, tomato, cheese, with various sauces out of jars – and *чай, чай, чай.*[12] Then we sat about, looked, lolled. Zhanna couldn't stop giving me things. A heavy glass paperweight, two trays painted by her, a fish painted on canvas, then a precious book to show in London; colour photographs of Gaga's paintings, taken by Jeremy here now. I spotted a small oil on the wall of two pigeons on a wet pavement with a railing and houses behind. Definitive Leningrad. Jeremy was putting paintings on an easel and flashing away, as I asked if he thought it would be in order to offer to buy it. He suggested I try. As I feared or guessed, Gaga presented it to me. After some remonstration, he relented: 'All right, give me a rouble...'

...I gave him a rouble and one fifty-pence coin and one penny; he stuck them to the wall of the studio and asked me to write my name. Zhanna was rolling off copies of a print she had made of old Lagoza. I did a little washing up. Jeremy gently said that he really ought to be going.

Nine thirty p.m.

We all managed to pull ourselves together, away back to Leningrad. They dropped Jeremy and me at our addresses, saying, 'See you tomorrow evening.'

28 November – Saturday

A note was slipped under my door to say, 'Please don't forget to pay for the telephone call – twenty-four roubles.'

Jeremy and I joined a rare taxi queue below the hotel with my tonnage of baggage. We aimed for the station. The driver slowed down several times for hopeful passengers but was not going where they wanted. Finally, in got a magnificent naval officer wearing a stunning uniform, blue-black overcoat and trousers, with hat, black leather gloves and smart briefcase. He talked all the time with the driver, gave him something at the end and got out in Nevsky Prospekt without a backward glance. In the back seat, I felt like an extra in a Cary Grant movie. We lockered the luggage in the Moskovsky Station and walked all the way to Alexander Nevsky Cathedral and Necropolis, where we lingered among the graves of Dostoyevsky, Balakirev, Rimsky-Korsakov,

---

[12] *Чай* is the Russian word for tea.

Mussorgsky, Tchaikovsky. Metro to the Russian State Museum where Jeremy expertly guided me through the Repins – one of the 'Travellers'. There, suddenly, was the full-sized portrait of barefooted Tolstoy that I have in postcard on my desk at home. Thrilling.

Our driver of the taxi to Chaliapin's house could have been a young rock star. He talked music very fast in a high accented way; admires Dire Straits, has a band. Jeremy engaged with him. There was a moment when Jeremy left the car to ask directions; the boy immediately probed to see if he is my husband, boyfriend; do I have any pounds to sell; make-up is very hard to come by, 'No, I can't sell money because of the Customs.' I gave him my last but one packet of BLANKS. Although he was full of vitality and energy, Jeremy said afterwards that he had painted a bleak view of the Soviet Union and did not hold out much hope for improvement despite *glasnost* and *perestroika*. He was an attractive wide-boy.

Dom Chaliapina[13]

We were taken on a solo tour. Atmospheric, lived in, undrab, undingy. Large gracious rooms. An allegorical portrait of Chaliapin on one wall of the sitting room. A grand piano with photographs on it, a desk with busts of Tolstoy and Gorky. People I had read about in Vitya Borovsky's brilliant book came back to me: Mamontov, with his passion for opera; Stasov, the critic. A big decorative pot, out of reach, on the ground, designed by Vrubel, which our guide kindly unveiled for us. In an ante-room there is the full-size nearly nude painting of him. She told us that on the day he died it cracked right across. Three hours later they rang from Paris to say he was dead. There is a bust of Pushkin in an alcove – always – plenty of photographs of the singer in a velvet dressing-gown. I sensed a lusty, exuberant personality. Immense energy seems to remain in the house. We share a birthday. I will remember the visit vividly. A hurry to the Metro to meet Jeremy's wife; also, a young English conductor, Martyn Brabbins,[14] on the same sort of British Council grant as Jeremy. He was waiting at the

---

[13] Chaliapin's House Museum.

[14] Brabbins became Music Director of English National Opera, at the London Coliseum.

station, wearing a hat that made him look like Shostakovitch. He is bright and witty. Finally, Jeremy's diminutive wife Albina, doe-eyed and beautiful, appeared carrying his guitar. We climbed onto a bus that took us close to the Kovenchuk flat, behind the fruit and vegetable market, still open at six thirty p.m. on Saturday. There were bruised apples, pears and onions. At one end, bunches of parsley and pickled garlic which I longed to try – but apart from the smell of freshness and a suddenly snatched cabbage, the goods weren't enticing. There were plenty of pomegranates which might have tempted me.

At the flat, the swinging party was for Gaga's student reunion, after twenty-seven years, with a Mongolian theatre designer. A small ripe apricot, the guest of honour was sitting in a chair, smiling. Gaga heaving about, Zhanna fussing confidently. The vodka was gratefully received and poured into many glasses. The designer talked to me from time to time; drinking vodka, he said, for the first time in five years, he was intimate in his approach; he invited me to come to Mongolia. I asked whether he was married – he shuddered 'No'...

Alyosha came in, still beautiful, still haunted.

Jeremy sang to his guitar on and off during the evening, showing a hitherto unseen, beguiling, performing side of his personality, the opposite of the retiring Englishman that he usually displays. On his advice, I had bought, in a Beryozka, two art books: *Pushkin and His Time – A Comprehensive Study* and a large volume of reproductions of Voznetsov's work in the matchless Aurora publications. I could have bought one of Vrubel, too – not sure why I didn't – weight-dread, I guess. Jeremy urges that these books should be bought whenever possible, as they go out of print. Around twenty roubles each.

Departing, I took Jeremy's mother's number in Amersham to call without letting on that he's married. We found the two-bunk railway carriage, on the lower of which were an attaché case and a pair of men's gloves. I froze. It was not what I wanted to tackle, sharing a room with an unknown man. Gaga went along to the attendant woman, who came back and said, 'It will be a woman.'

They helped me write, on an English postcard, my apologies and explanation to Tovstonogov for missing the second half of *Lower Depths*. With many hugs and kisses, the Kovenchuks were off to their Pushkin studio.

I sat looking out of the window, knowing how much I had to write to catch up with this journal. The train started. I heard a man's voice saying, 'Good evening – I am your companion.'

He was sixty-ish, neat in his buttoned, belted raincoat. I felt utterly hostile, and blurted that they had told me it would be a woman. He looked abashed and withdrew, coming back later to collect his bag and gloves. I managed to say, 'Thank you,' got into the bottom bunk and put out the light. Shortly afterwards the door slipped open; someone, a woman, came in, looked at the top bunk and left again. A while later, after I'd been asleep, the door opened once more. In she came, noisily, and climbed untidily into the top bunk with some grunting. I complained loudly in English. She reposted, 'I'm Georgian.'

We got through the night.

29 November – Sunday

The attendant had been told by Gaga and Zhanna that I couldn't possibly share a cabin with a man, as I was a famous English film star. She had brought me tea at night and now again. She asked whether I'd been in any films with Mikhalkov.

'No,' I admitted, regretfully.

This time a suite at the National Hotel. I went to breakfast taking this book, as I always do, and made my first sketch out of the window, staying there until around ten. Amanda rang to say I could go to the theatre with her – she has a ticket, well, Valery, her husband, was going to sacrifice his ticket so that I could go – which left him free to go to a friend's birthday party, what he really wanted to do. Pick me up at six thirty at the National with his car and he would drop us at the theatre.

The Museum of Oriental Arts is displaying some newly discovered archaeological finds, similar to but trumping, to my mind, the Scythean Gold in the Hermitage, including a glorious finely beaten gold wreath for the head; the leaves thin as paper and shining, shining; irregular shapes, not formal. In an extension, some modern Tunisian paintings; pieces of classical mosaic pavement, perhaps, formed of the tiniest coloured stones I have ever looked at, which gave the relic an extraordinary plastic quality.

Henrietta, with her gentle persuasive way, sought out the object of our visit.

Nikolay Roerich (1874–1947), described by Kostya as a visionary artist well ahead of his time. He was a voyager, a writer, a spiritual seeker, philosopher. Also a theatre designer; for the MKhAT 1912, Ibsen's *Peer Gynt*; in opera, Wagner's *Tristan and Isolde*. He shot to fame with the controversial *Rite of Spring* for Diaghilev, Stravinsky and Nijinsky, which turned Paris upside down at its première.

The first room houses traditional Russian scenes, then moves on to vivid, garish, delicate, spiritual Himalayan pictures; mountains, rose pink and tangerine, people in obeisance, completely surprising; this collection, coming at the time it did, must have caused a stir. A man's intense inner vision. Blake, I was reminded of, though the form and execution are different. There is a self-portrait in a cap and gown of the East, which are on show in a glass cabinet. Buddha statuettes from his collection. He lived a long time in India, settled in the foothills of the Himalayas. He said, 'Where there is Peace, there is Culture. Where there is Culture, there is Peace.' He was nominated for the Nobel Peace Prize in 1929.

The exhibition being officially closed, there was no crowd, although, as we left, a party of fifteen- to sixteen-year-old girls was being herded in. Enlivened, we made our way back to Henrietta's office to collect my clothes, all the presents and the pot of honey. On the way, she had talked about *mat*, which is a form of obscene slang much in use amongst the intelligentsia for a while, not quite so fashionable now. *Мудила*,[15] the word I learned at Yefremov's apartment, is a mild example. A classic *mudila* story

---

[15] *Мудила* (pronounced *mudila*) is a swear word based on the Russian slang word for testicle. Used in anger, it is insulting, rather like calling someone an *arsehole*.

goes: a woman tells her husband that he is a *mudila*; such a *mudila* that he would win second prize in a *mudila* competition.

'Second prize! Why not first prize?' asks the husband.

'Because you are such a *mudila!*' answers the wife.

We gained access to her work through a grocery shop this time. I met her colleague, Natalia Lyubanskaya, who has watchful eyes, a woolly hat to cover her hair, a liberal coat of creamy make-up and carefully painted pale pink thinnish lips that spread upwards like Mr Punch, rather than sideways, when she smiles. As well as fulfilling her museum job, she is an artist, healer, a bit of a psychic. She was carefully painting yellow and red triangles onto a large card which had astrological connotations. Her serious look at me was deep and slow – very clear that Russia will lead the spiritual rebirth that is necessary for the survival of mankind. We drank diverse teas. With horror, I learned that Oleg's fall during the performance that I'd watched had left him with two broken ribs and pneumonia, for which he is now in hospital. How can he have continued as he did, and entertained us in his flat? My admiration for him knows no bounds.

Any great leader of a theatre will be sniped at from one side or another. As Laurence Olivier at the National Theatre in London, so Oleg Yefremov plans and administrates, he also acts and directs. This takes energy, courage and health. Thinking of his broken-ribbed bravery is an inspiration – quintessential professionalism. Makes me proud to be an actress. It reminds me of the Virginia Woolf remark that the test of a vocation is the love of the drudgery it entails.

Henrietta's mystical colleague offered to help us carry all my stuff back to the National, so that I might be ready to go to the theatre at six. We marched straight in past the green-uniformed guard at the door. They wear mid-dark leaf-green coats and trousers with peaked caps to match. Sometimes they're polite, sometimes very rude and bossy, particularly with Soviet people trying to get in. They swing the door open by a diagonal, round brass rail. On the sofa in the hall sits, from time to time, and has sat since my first visit to Moscow, the same man in a grey suit. The hair on his flat head is considerably greyer than at first and he has shrunken down into himself, looking even more simian than before. Sometimes he talks animatedly to a large woman of similar style. I feel they must be KGB watchers. I've been looked at by them often, but have no sense that they recognise me. Sometimes he just sits, throwing occasional laconic words to the green hall porters who jealously guard the door to the cloakroom where people may leave coats and where I park my bags between quitting the room and catching a train or plane.

Amanda collected me from the National with her large handsome husband, Valery. He drove us to the Maly Mayakovsky Theatre, where we met Vladimir Zeldin and his wife: he, a distinguished actor from the Army Theatre, is seventy-ish and looks like Laurence Olivier – easy not to recognise in just the same skilful way. When I remarked on it he told me, wryly, that it is a commonly held opinion. We sat in marvellous third row seats. Both Amanda and the Zeldins had five carnations to give at the curtain call – a splendid tradition. The play was *Смех лангусты*,[16] by the Canadian writer John Murrell. It shows Sarah Bernhardt writing her memoirs with Pitou, her secretary. Living and reliving all the events of her life, making him play the catalystic characters; her mother, the Mother Superior, Oscar Wilde. The performers are husband and wife, Nemolyaeva and Lazaryev. He had previously come to the National Theatre in London with the Mayakovsky Company in a rather difficult play for English audiences to respond to, about wartime children in school; it concerns betrayals. For them still painfully relevant, it was offered with commitment and peerlessly simultaneously translated by Vanessa Redgrave.

This was quite a different evening. One of the most dazzling things I've seen for ten years. Lazaryev, we were told confidentially, was ill with flu and had only agreed to do the performance because Zeldin and party were coming. He's tall, attractive, dark and very expressive. She is tiny and comedic – Felicity Kendal or Giulietta Massina, a film star. I understood the acting but not much of the text. They both seem to me to be consummate performers. Light, mercurial moods changing with extraordinary speed. Tears ran down her face at least three times

---

16 *Laughter of the Lobster* (1991).

during the evening. I saw Zeldin watching and smiling generously, which is not always easy for actors to do about each other's work. Lazaryev wore a smart Mediterranean white suit and shoes. Nemolyaeva a variety of gowns; mauve-ish, green-ish, some Eastern trousers, a hair-covering lace cap, a turban which she suddenly pulled off to reveal a cascade of feminine fair hair – as had Vanessa Redgrave during her stunning debut, playing Rosalind in *As You Like It* at RSC. They were splendid.

At the interval Amanda and Zeldin[17] went to fetch their bouquets and sat through the second half holding them on their knees. At the end, several people came forward, handing flowers up to the stage. Zeldin stood, leaned over the people in front, and handed them direct to Lazaryev who, like Yefremov, had covered his illness majestically throughout the performance; finally, he dropped the mask and we saw clearly how much strain he had been under. We went out from the hall which reminded me of a wartime army camp cinema, to two undecorated dressing rooms, one beside the other, containing only a small table and chair with minimal mirror and lighting, opening onto a green room. Plainer than plain. Amanda handed over her posy, being too shy to do the public giving; much kissing, *khorosho*-ing[18] and warmth. Nemolyaeva, alight with achievement, humble and glowing. Lazaryev came in wearing a sweater and trousers; apologetic, shaking his head; hands splayed in sorrow that they couldn't invite us back to their home due to his illness. We left.

The Zeldins kindly drove us to the apartment of Igor and Natasha Yasulovich; friends of Amanda and the closest intimates in Moscow of Vitya Borovsky. Igor works with the Film Actors' Theatre Company. They live, third generation, in a block that Natasha's mother and grandmother had occupied. Developers are trying to rebuild it but the couple are doing everything they can to withstand a move.

Igor, a trained clown, opened the door and let us into the living room where his smiling wife already sat at a table beside a

---

[17] Zeldin died in 2018, aged 102, still a working actor.

[18] The Russian word хopoмo (*khorosho*, stressed on the final vowel) is very frequently used to mean *good*.

Georgian artist (*художник*) who wore a navy blue suit and had long sideburns under a shiny bald head, reminding me of my English butcher after a week by the sea. His wife was dark, attentive and silent. A divan in the corner, velvet upholstered, is where Vitya used to sleep when he was a guest. A large carpet hangs on the wall, as does a shoulder bone of mutton – bleached after being eaten in a stew and successfully painted to resemble a Modigliani head. The bath being in the kitchen, behind a curtain, adds a feeling of family continuity to the flat. Dark fruity Georgian wine and vodka. Natasha had prepared a hot meat stew and a heap of boiled potatoes with another Butter Mountain on top – not to mention the beetroot salad, *колбаса*,[19] cabbage salad, sour cream, tinned fish, cheese, black bread and a dish of dried fruits brought by the Georgians.

13. Cover picture of Igor Yasulovich and the bone sculpture, from monthly cinema magazine *Ekran* ('Screen'), June 1991.

The food is sequenced onto the table; people help themselves casually – as they feel – onto smallish plates. The eating can last for two hours thus; it is informal, unshymaking, sociable. Tea was

---

[19] (Salami) sausage.

made. I drank cup after cup, couldn't stop, raging thirst. I refused cognac.

After midnight, Valery Levental and his beautiful wife, Marina Sokolova, arrived. Both distinguished scenographers; she, Bolshoi designer of an admired *Golden Cockerel,* he, ex-MKhAT, now with the Bolshoi; he is compact, Jewish, with steely hair, shining eyes and excellent American-accented English.

Igor is the supreme mime artist to whom Marcel Marceau declared he would hand his crown. His comedy is irresistible. He acted a story about a man going to the doctor. It involved all the skill of taking ages to undress in mime; the denouement was something silly about one of his balls hanging lower than the other. It was received with uncontrollable laughter. He sat down again. I asked if he would mind putting his clothes on again, as I can't be at the table with a naked man. He told another about a man who felt a tickling up his bum. He went to the doctor:

'Doctor, I've got a tickling up my bum.'

'Let me have a look. You've got a newspaper up there!'

'*Pravda?*'[20]

'*Niet, Izvestia.*'

Good highbrow playmates.

I tried to explain how alarmed I am by Mrs Thatcher's ways. Not easy. I seem to end up with such banalities as, 'The rich get richer and the poor get poorer', which is easy to say in Russian. Levental suggested, 'Perhaps it's what the English need at the moment.'

We stayed until one thirty – Igor was describing a film *Mayo Mai Mayo,* in which he had been directed by Volodya Grammatikov, whose name rang a bell... I had a message for him from Layla Alexander. They yelped, they know her too. Igor rang Grammatikov who was in the bath – 'Sorry, must be at the studio early in the morning; too late to come out now.' Igor is planning a co-operative ensemble, similar to the Actors Company – to present seventeenth- and eighteenth-century classics; Corneille, etc., because only this strong material stretches performers, who

---

[20] 'Is that true?' However, *pravda*, meaning *truth*, is also the name of a major Russian daily newspaper, and *izvestia*, meaning *news*, is another famous Russian daily.

otherwise easily fall into personality acting; also, there are not many plays of this date performed in Moscow.

His company would be given a hall and a grant; if successful, a permanent home. Exciting.

Igor has worked extensively with Declan Donellan in Moscow, Paris; also at the Barbican in London. He is a *заслуженный артист* – 'meritorious artist' – similar to CBE. (Note – even more – *народный артист*/People's Artist – 'Sir', graceful in mind and body, Igor is not a *mudila.)*

Natasha, eternally hospitable, teaches History of Theatre Design at the MKhAT School. She leans affectionately against her husband while making tea.

30 November – Monday

I took this book down to breakfast and had a better shot at drawing the view from the same table in the dining room. I invited myself to Dom Kagarlitsky at five p.m. Henrietta recommended a specialist shop on Kuznetsky Most, as I wanted to buy a map of the Soviet Union. Many charts and globes on walls, counters, reminding me of the unexpected map of Africa in *Uncle Vanya*. Communist-oriented Central America. I feel there is a strong link with India; in the Seventy Years Exhibition there is more than one statue each of Mahatma and Indira Gandhi. After dithering, I chose a varnished map for two or three roubles.

Returning through an unfamiliar square, I was brought to the back of the Bolshoi Theatre. A man asked me the way to GUM. I pointed:

'*Напротив Кремля.*'[21]

I decided to join a queue for ice cream... At minus three centigrade, I must share the local idea of a good time. I got the last one sold from a zinc tray by a woman who is presumably refurbished every ten minutes. Obviously there is no danger of melting; always a queue to buy at eighteen kopecks. The taste was delicious, butterscotch in a castellated cornet. A man asked me where I bought it. I pointed:

---

[21] 'Opposite the Kremlin.'

14. National Hotel dining room: sketch of Kremlin.

'*Там.*'[22]

I found myself in Hertzen Street, named after a man later to become a socialist hero of mine.

I stared at the imposing Conservatoire; Tchaikovsky on his plinth outside, the words *Большой Зал* (Great Hall) over the pillared porch.

On my way back to Gorky Street I was stopped and asked for the Telegraph Office. He was tall with spectacles and a rucksack. After explaining I was English, I pointed:

'*Прямо и направо!*'[23]

He was amazed. We rocked with laughter. On my last day, I must look like a Muscovite, a *москвичка*.

From my room I collected a bottle of vodka for Henrietta and Gennady, put the pot of honey into my bag for Georgy Kagarlitsky and set off to Metro Aeroport. It was nearly five thirty when I got to the door of the flat. Julius started:

'You are late and we have so much to talk about.'

I sat down at the table beside Raya, Georgy there with his mother. He has a cold; puffy-eyed, white face, a formed character, vital, running around, talking on the telephone to imaginary people. They say *Hallo* in such a way as to make it sound very

[22] 'Over there.'

[23] 'Straight on, then right!'

aggressive; *Alluwo!* It is universal. He and I played hiding games over and under the table. Ira was so pleased and proud of him. Kiss, Kiss. A light in their lives.

Tea was brought and some plain biscuits, onto which at last the мёд[24] was spread. Julius and Raya asked me what I'd seen in Leningrad.

'*Lower Depths* at Tovstonogov's Theatre.'

'We hear that theatre is very run down,' they commented. 'Why are they doing *Lower Depths,* what relevance has that today?'

I described the Sarah Bernhardt play with enthusiasm and admiration.

'You see, we don't admire the work of that theatre, it is completely irrelevant. It has nothing to do with the real problems of life.'

I said I thought that Sarah Bernhardt was entitled to her problems, but they weren't having any – Julius, at one point, made a mildly slighting remark about the English, so I launched:

'You despise us so much, don't you?'

'What do you mean, "despise"?'

'You never stop criticising us.'

He looked quite taken aback – good. Bitch!

They have suffered dreadfully over Boris; Julius losing his job, however, I believe at last I can overcome the guilt I have felt, which unaccountably made me angry with them. Much healthier now. In their devotedness and enthusiasm for the Brits, they want to have absolute knowledge of all our movements. It's love, really. They gave me Raya's translation of *The Dresser* to take for Ronnie Harwood to sign.

Boris arrived; he, Ira and Georgy retired, perhaps to put the little boy to bed. Julius tells me they have a dacha now, where he goes at weekends with Ira and his grandson.

It was nearly seven before I knew it would be all right to leave. I felt a giant surge of love for dear, provocative battered human Julius as I said goodbye. He pressed on me two large Father Christmases, looking as if they were made of spun sugar.

'Can you eat them?'

---

[24] Honey.

'No, it's some synthetic material.'

One red and one white.

In the Metro I found a seat, changed at Pushkinskaya and again sat until it was time to get out. Gennady was on the platform, we hopped onto the bus. There had been a thaw; not nearly so cold as Leningrad, or Moscow previously. The snow had simply been pressed down to hard glassy, irregular shapes. Tough on the feet, and very dangerous. Henrietta was waiting, familiar. Her eyes and mouth smile in tandem. I presented the vodka. They wouldn't hear of it. Gennady went to his desk and showed me four bottles – for New Year.

'We really don't need any more.'

It was packed back into my bag.

There was smoked fish and bread waiting. They had already eaten. A full bowl of apples from Sevastopol sat under the table. When I left, three were put into my bag. Charlotte, eating one at home, was delighted by the delicious taste and thin skin. Кошка stared at me again. They told me that Gennady's film had been well received on television. I'd missed it.

All a little tired, we relaxed...

I asked Henrietta...

if she would ring Grammatikov, in case he wants me to take something for Layla.

...

She did, he does.

...

... They brought out their *pièce de résistance*. Positively their last present to me – a large electric samovar with a book of instructions.

1 December – Tuesday

Zoya Boguslavskaya called. She will pick me up at twelve – no, eleven thirty, no, eleven forty-five, and go to the Writers' Union for two hours, no, an hour and a half. She is free till one thirty, no, one. Misha will come to the Writers' Union too. All this was conducted half in Russian, half in English. I'm excited and impatient to get home to see Charlotte and Adam.

In the hall, I took the KGB simian's space on the sofa until Grammatikov hurried in and sat beside me, cheerfully handing over a heavy book for Layla. He doesn't have any English at all, so with minimum vocabulary, we beamed hopeful goodwill until next time.

I sat quietly on the sofa, wearing my coat and hat like *Cherry Orchard,* saying goodbye to the National Hotel. Zoya, punctual, wearing a long black, fur-trimmed mac was surprised and pleased that I was waiting.

'I'm an actress, I'm used to being on time.'

We zipped along to the Writers' Club and she negotiated with the driver Valery to take me back to the hotel after lunch, then to pick me up again at three for the airport, before collecting Andrey Voznesensky from Peredelkino.

'And no money,' she insisted.

Her profuse abundant generosity removed all anxiety about my departure. I had given her my last precious packet of jasmine tea. She thanked me and requested that next time, if it is possible, decaffeinated coffee would be wonderful, as they can't get it.

Under the grand coat she was dressed in a simple pale-blue jersey and black skirt. Her broad, benign face is encircled by light hair that she put into shape with a baby brush after taking off her scarf. We parked our bags at a small round table and went to choose a variety of luxurious foods. Russian hospitality is in a league I had no inkling of. During the meal, I was telling her how much I'd enjoyed *Smekh Langousty* and was intrigued to hear that Vanessa (Redgrave) might have bought rights to it.

'Tell me about Vanessa,' she asked.

I started, 'Well, she's an incomparable artist.'

'Yes, I know all about her work. As a person?'

'I've known her since we were students at different drama schools.

Sometimes her politics draw attention.'

'What are her politics? Is it true she is anti-Semite? All this Palestinian business...'

'No, of course not. She's a woman, an actress who plays Jewish parts too. She believes in human rights.'

Suddenly Misha was standing at the table. They shared great excitement, discussing the sensation that President Gorbachev had been at the Vakhtangov Theatre the night before to see Shatrov's new play about Lenin and Trotsky. Mikhail Sergeevich and Raisa had turned up unexpectedly and sat in the actors' loge. (I came home and told John Roberts who told the Cultural Attaché at the Russian Embassy who hadn't heard. Pigeon Post.) Misha gave me a small volume of his newly published stories – a wartime-looking little book, not more than four inches square, with his picture on the front. He inscribed it for me.

Zoya left us so that we could be 'alone together'. He was going to see Oleg in hospital. I sensed he is overloaded. He gave me a note for John Roberts which Zoya later snatched and wrote on too. I handed him the last snowball candle from Harrods, which pleased him. There was a sudden explosion of kisses all over my face and he left. My hostess and I gathered ourselves for departure. I dropped a flurry of coins onto the *гардероб* counter. Zoya saw me into the car, insisting that I am secure and the taxi will turn up at three.

I kissed her gratefully. A lot of her conversation had been about making contact with women writers. Round Table stuff. She is full of energy, open-hearted and strong. I can't guess the difficulties of being a woman writer in the USSR. She is clearly proud of having been elected chairperson of a particular women's group at the Writers' Union. They're lucky to have her.

Leaving. I looked at the familiar sights. We drove in silence. I gave Valery the last packet of BLANKS and put myself amongst a group of French travellers. When we got to the sonic machines, the single man in front of me was being given a bad time by a young official in a grey suit. Everything to do with money was taken from him. His bags were opened, the red light put up. In the end, he had filled his form in wrongly; he was released. An Orthodox Jewish man with a long grey beard and black hat pulled down low shrugged at me, as if to say, 'That's life!' Then it was my turn.

'How many bags do you have?'

'Five.'

He looked at all my papers.

'Have you got a lot of caviar?'

'No, it's *рыба,*[25] tins of salmon and...'

He nodded and stamped my papers. I loaded up my trolley and was going to move when he said, 'How many bags have you got?'

'Five,' then realised that I had left my handbag on the counter. I stuck my tongue out and made a face. He smiled. I was through. The Orthodox man had not known what was coming to him. He was done over from top to bottom. The red light went up. Everything in his case was brought out – all the careful plastic wrappings. His wads of notes were gone through again and again. An Englishman looking back at him said, 'Serves him right, he bribed his way through to the front. Obviously the man saw him do it and decided to make an example of him. If I was Jewish, I wouldn't flaunt it in a country like this – I'd cover it up. He'll think he's being given a bad time because he's Jewish.'

This Brit and his wife, carrying long Chinese boxes which could have held snooker cues, were on their way back from a second visit to a part of China which they think is matchless. Moscow was only a stopover.

We were now in a British Airways queue. Our plane had not yet landed. The air was foggy. We should take off in half an hour. A Kensingtonly-English British Airways woman came round, sticking on labels to save time once we got through the formalities. It became national and familiar. A French girl was being tormented by the customs man who had allowed me through. He had taken a large tin of caviar (we guessed) from her bag and however much she complained and remonstrated, he was adamant. She had to abandon it because her plane was leaving. The English queue agreed that he would probably take it home to his wife or mother. I sat on a chair in the waiting hall, drained and peaceful. Only one thing on my mind for a change. Going home. Safely seated in the plane, there was more delay, waiting for a flight coming in from Japan.

---

[25] Fish.

'We feel that they would not have wanted to be dumped at Moscow Airport without a connection any more than you would; they're human beings, after all, so please bear with us just a few more minutes.'

We got off the plane only half an hour late, having made up a lot of time. The captain congratulated himself and us:

'I'm afraid we've caught them with their trousers down. There is no tunnel for us to leave the plane by.'

One was found. I spotted Adam leaning against the barrier: what a sweet relief. We trolleyed over the road to the car park. A gentle drive into London. Charlotte opened the door. XXXX.

Prologue to Taganrog: Say Goodbye to Fear

8 February – 28 April 1991

I have been visiting Moscow and Leningrad greedily for nearly ten years, struggling feebly with the language for twice that time. I suppose I'm in thrall to Mother Russia. She has the power to cherish or hurt.

Layla Alexander had made a connection with an enterprising collective of Moscow directors, *kollektiv dramaticheskikh rezhissyorov* who, wanting to breathe life into the despised provincial theatre, as well as creating much-needed work for themselves, have chosen Chekhov's last play, *Cherry Orchard* as their first venture, staged by the Dramatichesky Teatr in Taganrog, the town on the Sea of Azov in southern Russia, where Anton Pavlovich as born.

Layla suggested that an English actress, with a few words of Russian and a lifetime's yearning, could add a singular slant, even invite useful publicity, in the role of Charlotta Ivanovna, the foreign governess.

The astounding offer came in October, 1990. The right friend was in the right place at the right time. I knew at once I would accept, despite the warning of Henrietta, with whom I rushed to celebrate on the telephone.

'You can't go to Taganrog, it's the provinces. You'll starve, it will be very dangerous. You must play the part at the Moscow Art Theatre.'

'I haven't been asked to play it at the Moscow Art Theatre.'

I flew to meet *режиссёр*[1] Juvenaly Kalantarov. He sat in silence the first evening, while the impresario Azat Rafikov, a densely built Tatar and I, tried to thrash out dates, finance and quality of life. Would I, for example, be able to speak to my children from Taganrog?

---

[1] Director (of stage or screen).

The following morning a working session with Juvenaly. I carried the text and an exercise book. He suggested that I write down what he was about to say. He talked about Chekhov as teacher, about his view of the play and about the developing importance of Charlotta's six entrances. He asked me to keep his ideas to myself. Disappointingly he didn't want me to read the part out loud, something I had been prepared for. I needed to test my early attempts against an authoritative ear. I wished to share with him my crude fear about the difficulty of learning and playing a role in a foreign language. That did not interest him. I said a little tremulously,

'I don't want to let you down.'

'You won't.'

I went to see *Cherry Orchard* directed by Oleg Yefremov at the Moscow Art Theatre, but had difficulty concentrating. During the interval Oleg, the Russian theatre person I've known longer than any other, asked:

'Carolina, why are you in Moscow?'

He knew perfectly well. He told me how Chekhov, spending a summer month at Stanislavsky's country house, Lyubimovka, had made friends with a diminutive English governess from a nearby estate, Lily Glassby. He gave her piggy-backs.

15. Lily Glassby with her cat.

'So, it is all right to play Charlotta as an Englishwoman; come and do it with us!'

'Oh, Oleg, thank you... Must I choose?'

'Of course not. Go to Taganrog. Chekhov is there. Then do it with us, if you like.'

What a man! I have been asked to do it at the Moscow Art Theatre.

I came back to England with two months to become word-perfect; to gather vitamins, prunes, lentils, Marmite – no, the glass jar is too heavy – soap, tea, coffee, Elastoplast, tights, etc, etc.

'Caro, you *are brave!!*'

'I didn't know you spoke Russian!!'

'What will you eat?'

'Will it matter having an English accent?'

'How are you going to learn it?'

I kept the Russian and English texts side by side, so that I should understand the exact meaning of each word. An actor friend in Moscow had made a tape with some colleagues of all my scenes, including the speeches leading to my entrances and cues, so that I would be familiar enough with the music of the scene to be able to time things properly. Because of my lamentably small vocabulary an agonising number of new words had to be assimilated. In the first act there are only four lines. I am familiar enough with the language that words I know can be learned with not much more difficulty than their English counterparts. It is the new words – 'nuts' and another form of 'eat' which take time and produce brain-locking panic. So, four days to achieve, 'AND my dog eats nuts.' A further eight days for the remaining three lines of the act. My RADA diction exercises are of no avail since the sounds are made in different parts of the mouth. A new tongue is needed. Walking in Fulham open spaces with my earphones. Looking round, then shouting the lines to be heard at the back of the Coliseum. I tested my outraged memory. After two hours' work, I would feel replete with fresh material. Next morning only one short phrase would remain. I started again from scratch. The shouting was so that I will not be frightened by the sound of my own voice when I first speak the lines in front of strangers.

Russian is a beautiful, musical language. I had asked Alyona and Volodya to write down some exercises which they practise, simply to bring my voice into the right place.

Русские скороговорки – *Russian Tongue Twisters*

Из-под пригорка, из-под подвыподверта, зайчик приподвыподвернулся.

(*Iz-podprigorka, iz-podpodvypoderta, zaichikpripodvipodvernulsa*)

Повар Пётр, повар Павел. Павел пёк, а Пётр парил.

(*Povar Pyotr, Povar Pavel, Pavel pyok a Pyotr paril*)

Вакул бабу обул да и Вакула баба обула.

(*Vakul Babu Abul da i Vakula Baba Abula*)

Only West London parks and the beach at Hastings know what a battle it was to get Charlotta's forty-six lines into my body.

I was to join the company, already two weeks into rehearsal, on 10 February. I decided to spend a week in Moscow first, getting acclimatised to the language and to the cold – fifteen degrees below freezing.

The official visa took a long time coming, but it allowed me to stay with a friend instead of in a hotel. I slept in earshot of the Kremlin chimes, not more than two hundred yards from the Moscow Art Theatre. From the kitchen window I could see the flat where Shostakovich had lived.

Azat Rafikov became the ruling personality. He whisked me round to meet possible sources of funding; the head of the Theatre Workers' Union, Ulyanov, and the Minister of Culture, Sulomen, both distinguished actors. The latter also runs the Maly Theatre.

I must give respect to Azat – he deserves it. Thanks to his atomic-powered determination, his ungainsayable will to artistic success, I found myself making theatrical history; the first English actress to play Chekhov in Russia, in Russian. However, the clash of our personalities – call it culture shock on either side – led to the most ghastly rows I've ever experienced.

I felt a stubborn streak resisting him from the start. I sensed he was not used to asking, he was accustomed to telling and being obeyed. The difficulty became clear when I gave him and his male colleagues cigarettes from my obligatory duty-free pack. When I moved to offer to two girl assistants he said loudly,

'No!'

'Why?' I asked

'I'm boss!'

'And I'm a person!' I retorted, making sure the girls got two each.

They blushed with pleasure. I could hardly have flouted convention more overtly. As his employee and even more (or less, according to how you look at it), as a woman, I had challenged him in front of his staff. Once he called me capricious. It sounded Mozartian. Evidently the word is often used of actresses who cry when they are in a tricky situation. I did. I was more highly strung than I had anticipated.

At exactly the right moment I was invited to a supremely hospitable lunch at the British Embassy, where the incumbents, Rodric and Jill Braithwaite, were friendly and encouraging. I realised, ashamed and grateful, that top rank could be pulled if things became unmanageable in the south.

I gave a House of Commons keyring to a staggeringly fast and accurate driver.

8 February

Warmer. Ten degrees below freezing.

Azat collected me to catch the night train bound, in three days, for Yerevan. We would disembark after eighteen hours. At the station I met Volodya Federovsky, the administrative director of the Taganrog Theatre. He's huge and humorous. I liked him at once. He carried a gigantic Chinese thermos flask which kept us in tea till Taganrog.

The midnight train left at three a.m. I had a double compartment to myself, the luxury a sign of managerial esteem that I appreciated. Azat explained to the attendant, this being an Armenian train, that he was Tatar, I was English and Federovsky Ukrainian, none of us Russian. Several windows had fly-sized holes where stones or bullets had been directed at a train traversing hostile territory.

'Why does the train travel so slowly?' I asked naively.

'In order not to have an accident.'

In the morning, I looked out at sparkling thick snow cradling small brightly painted wooden houses. Laden trees were like sprouting cauliflowers. A stolid couple emerged from whiteness, trudging across whiteness towards whiteness. I could see the silence that snow imposes. We were travelling due south, passing through Tula and Oryol, stations for the country estates of Tolstoy and Turgenev, the route Chekhov would have taken to Crimea.

9 February

Taganrog. As in German, the final *g* sounds *k. Taganrok*. We slowed towards the station. I was struck by the brilliance of the constellation Orion whose belt mercifully hung out of reach of the brown-belch industrial chimneys. A thousand miles south of Moscow it felt much colder.

Ten thirty at night; it hadn't occurred to me there would be a reception party from the theatre on the platform. I stepped from the carriage to a burst of applause, smiling faces, red carnations and a formal welcome in excellent English by a diminutive interpreter. I shook many hands before being swept into a car, the twenty or so others into a bus. We all ended up at the hostel where I've been booked to stay. My bottle of vodka provided a sip each for a toast before we *dosvidanya'd*[2] until tomorrow. A friendly young woman announced:

'I'll be back at eight thirty in the morning.'

I was accompanied to my door by a Sergey Bubka lookalike[3] – with eyes bluer than his jeans. Valery. He was my night guard. After he'd said goodnight he indicated his room across the passage. He reached into his pocket and brought out a small black gun. I gasped and giggled like a schoolgirl. Then he gave me a dazzling smile. I managed to smother my second gasp, his teeth were made of gold. There were to be other night guards; Volodya, Vassily, Sasha, Alyosha. Valery was my favourite.

---

[2] *до свидания,* – goodbye.

[3] Sergey Bubka (b. December 1963) is a Ukrainian former pole vaulter who represented the USSR; he won six World Championships and was awarded an Olympic gold medal.

Taganrog Actors And Actresses

'You are an artist and that is like being a good sailor: no matter on what ship he sails, be it a government vessel or a merchant ship, he remains under all circumstances a good sailor.'
Chekhov to the actress, Kommissarzhevskaya.

16. Ranevskaya/Lena.

Lena/Ranevskaya

Our leading lady is married to Volodya Fedorovsky, the Administrative Director of the Taganrog Theatre. She arrives for work wearing a generous fur coat, fox hat over fashionable jeans decorated with stitching down the seams; she changes into daily uniform of a turquoise jersey, with a long skirt borrowed from the wardrobe department. Lena is of average height. She has film star prettiness, a neat figure. Their grown son is doing Army Service.

Lena has dark hair which hangs in loose curls to the nape. Her generous lipstick-advertisement mouth opens in a completely spontaneous and frequent smile that lights her eyes which are also of screen beauty. Her vulnerability is her openness. She seems not to shrink from it. The pain is in her eyes, but she transforms it with laughter into credible optimism. I can't imagine her sulking. Her head is always peeping over the parapet in hope. Ranevskaya is the leading woman's part in *Cherry Orchard*. She came in for the biggest barrage from the director Juvenaly Kalantarov. He stopped her, showed her, showed her again – gave her no time to assimilate; demanded obedience, rather than compliance accompanied by initiative. If she cried – I believe she did – she recovered quickly and tried again. She carries a handkerchief for the last act.

Lena's rehearsal make-up was as complete as I would wear for a glamour role. For the play she added false eyelashes and plum-mauve shadows to delineate her eyes. Every day a fresh coat of ruby varnish was applied to her nails as the last bell rang. I was so intrigued that I forgot to ask whether Olga Knipper and her friends would have used those enhancements. Photographs of the original production lead me to believe that the actresses dressed their own hair. Lena uses a full-blown reddish wig which, she had to be persuaded, was a friend not an enemy. Her costumes were well-fitted and attractive and she wore them with ease. Except her shoes. She caged her toes in modern high-heeled patent pumps. The groans as she took them off were piteous. Her husband proudly showed me a picture of his ravishing young wife playing Nina in *Seagull* in this theatre some years ago. She's lovely now.

17. Varya/Lilya.

Lilya/Varya

Lilya is the most upfront of the women temperamentally. She is a dancer as well as an actress and is responsible for the choreography in the third act party scene. There is a Latin atmosphere about her flashing eyes and her long rich chestnut hair which is in prime shine condition and either pinned back in a dancer's knot or corkscrew curled and allowed to hang. Her trained, tuned body is at full pitch of activity while she teaches the actors the four different dances we must master. She's sexy and explosive and packhorse strong. Working to her own limits she demands as much from us. The cast are all competent at picking up dance steps; not least the rounder comics, whose sprightliness I have noticed as a gift of heavy actors worldwide. They are lifted by their wit. I am paired with Pasha/Epikhodov, who confirms this. He also remembers the steps. 'ONE two three four.' Lilya spits like a wildcat when Juvenaly complains that the dancing is not good enough or that too much time is spent on it. It is a no-win situation. She usually gets her way. The sessions warm us up for Kalantarov's work, so he benefits in the long run. Lilya/Varya and Yury/Lopakhin #I have a teenage daughter. Most of the couples put all their eggs into one basket. Our second son died less than twenty-four hours after he was born. Russell and I were lucky enough to get our daughter Charlotte within two years. Because of the earlier loss, my anxiety when either our elder son Adam or she became ill during their growing years rose to near panic if it was more than a usual malady. The vulnerability of a young life can be a source of excessive terror. I noticed that these actors and actresses have offspring who are highly susceptible to infection. The long-suffering, hard-working parents complain of the difficulty of obtaining drugs and remedies, but I don't remember any of them missing a rehearsal because of the ill health of a child. They are trained to mental as well as physical toughness.

18. Lopakhin #I/Yury.

Yury/Lopakhin #I and Lilya/Varya make a good pairing offstage too.

'He is a very man.'

I didn't know the word for masculine. But Lilya understood and appreciated my appreciation of her husband. He is a well-proportioned actor, with a chin length curtain of dark brown hair, eyes and beard to match. He could appear menacing or priestly, but his persona is unaggressive and shy. Yury leans backwards from conflict and allows the director to act his part for him, finally rising, exhausted by watching the surrogate performance, to throw himself into the travail. I find it easy to believe the journey this Lopakhin has made from the humble little boy visiting the great estate to the well-meaning, rough, financially successful, emotionally insecure suitor of Varya, and terminator of the shredded illusions hung onto by the improvident brother/Gaev and sister/Ranevskaya. Once or twice Yury raised his voice in frustration but he was usually shouted down and treated to a further demonstration of his role. He retired, shaking his head like a bewildered bear, then made a further attempt at what was being asked of him. He never gave up. He turned in a warm-blooded unpretentious performance which drew my unquestioning belief. His wife had no pity when it came to putting him through his paces for the solo dance he did with the Jewish orchestra. It was remarked what a hardworking artist he is.

'He's not an artist, he's my husband.' It leaped out of her mouth. As she got to the end of the sentence she burst into fits of laughter.

Yury was obliged, in his capacity as union representative, to call a protest meeting. The actors, who are under contract all year round, were complaining that there had been no day off since I arrived, and that with twelve consecutive performances to come – not to mention travelling to Moscow for the Gala and back – they were overworked and unable to spend time with their families. He led the discussion, which was attended by Fedorovsky and Kalantarov. The cast were promised a whole week off following the Moscow outing. Yury exemplifies a particular Russian male that scholars write and talk of. One who will fight for his country or for others, but whose innate humility makes it hard for him to be belligerent in his own cause. I can conjure the open, hoarse tone of his voice inside my head.

19. Dunyasha/Zoya.

Zoya/Dunyasha

A bright-eyed, tall, rounded woman – thirtyish – with a daughter under ten years old. Zoya has an attractive elusive personality. She has coiffeuse as well as acting skills and can be seen with Tanya sorting, cleaning and dressing heads of hair in the upstairs wig/makeup room. In a room that she shares with Valya/Anya she gets into her Dunyasha costume early each evening. She busies round at one end (the smelly end) of our dressing room where many of her props are awaiting inspection. She also brings to the three of us, Lena/ Ranevskaya, Lilya/Varya and me/Charlotta three or four sheets of tissue and a little dish of white powder for the performance. I had brought my own make-up. Tanya, however, presented me with a palette such as the other women use. It has three base colours in big sections and a line of stamp-sized bright tones for eyes and mouth. There is black and white and blue and red which deal with my clown decoration.

This actress's ear-to-ear smile fits well with Dunyasha's over-the-top ruched frock and exaggerated giggles. The serving girl's infatuation with Yasha and her attempt to rise above her lowly position throw the poor creature into turmoil – she is pushed and pulled this way and that – her excitable laughter turning to hysterical tears as she perceives that her mistress's servant/lover has toyed with her most cruelly. Zoya challenged Kalantarov beseechingly.

'There is no room to put the tray down by the mirror.'

Her pout quickly resolves into gaiety. More than any other, Zoya's description of Taganrog in the summer made me want to revisit this intensely romantic town. Acacia, roses, sun, grapes, apricots and warm sea were some of the blandishments to which I could feel myself responding.

20. Borya/Yasha.

Boris – Borya/Yasha

This actor struck me from the first as a loner. It takes one to know one. Being unpaired in life means that the business of relationship is absent. Other ways are found of filling the time that might be spent sharing food or picking fleas off the partner. Borya is big and strong. His head is topped with curly, goldy, brown hair which he wears clean and dishevelled. I feel that he longs to be asked to play. That he is waiting for it to be his turn. He homes in on *Cherry Orchard*. He brings an abstracted, callous quality to his characterisation which exactly suits and feeds the production. Yasha's flashy, apricot-coloured gent's suit displays him as a pseudo-Parisian smarty-pants. It makes him walk in a different way from the poor locals he despises. I find Borya's portrayal rather painful to watch. I can see that this jumped-up servant has no basis for his arrogance. I feel that he knows it and is marking time without joy until Something Else Happens. The uneasiness for me lies in my notion that for many Russians, then and now, a sort of helplessness in the face of too many odds is the actuality of too many lives.

21. Volodya/Trofimov.

Volodya/Trofimov

Volodya – Vova Babaev was not at the station for my night arrival. He entered the tiny rehearsal room on the first day bearing flowers. I am disarmed by the rituals of gallantry and am charmed when my hand is kissed. Volodya has a style which feels more Western than that of the other men. His physique is slight; that of a pantomimist, which is what he also is. His movements are light and fluid. The other men grow like trees from the ground. Volodya springs from water and air. I learn quickly that he is musical. He is rarely without his guitar. We duet at the piano. He sings the songs he composes whenever two or three are gathered. His brown hair is worn in cascading luxuriant locks around his shoulders or tied back in a rope or stuffed into the universal woolly cap. His jeans are the latest in elegance, with a complicated belt mechanism; he wears his jacket modishly with sleeve turned back. His face, however, is unlike any I have seen. There is scarcely a film of flesh on it. The bones of his skull are delineated in their entirety. Circling around him I might feel that I am viewing the history of mankind. His eyes are blue and aware. Although his reserve makes him shy like a startled deer, I feel that I have known him quite well for a long time. Charlotta addresses only one line to Trofimov during the entire play.

22. Octavy/Firs with Charlotta's dog Urska.

Octavy/Firs

Octavy has a bristly military moustache. He is dignified in an unprotected way. He stands his ground, gathering the strands of his life around him. He indicates, humorously, that he is out of control, out of sorts and out of breath. Certainly out of pocket. He is a devil at the chess board. His/Charlotta's little white dog, Urska – obedience itself, responds to the flicker of his eyelid.

Actors can communicate private matters on stage in carefully chosen moments which neither distract from the action nor from one's own portrayal. My time on the swing drew personal observations from the actors sometimes, and from Octavy quite often – mostly as he was making an exit. You wouldn't risk anything like that when you are coming on to play a scene. Dear me, no. These observations are always made in the character that the actor is playing. I have been aware of football scores zig-zagging in doublet and hose across the court of Brecht's *King Edward II*.

23. Pasha/Yepikhodov.

24. Valya, Stage manager.

Pavel – Pasha/Yepikhodov

Comedy is there for Pasha to dip into. Humour through relaxation is his theme. He has a spreading, buttery easiness. His blond hair is stranding. His laugh comes from the groin. His giggle makes his eyes run and his skin turn pink. His singing voice – oh, his voice! As Yepikhodov, Pasha makes a long slow entrance, singing, accompanying himself on his guitar. 'Mandolin,' Yepikhodov insists, when it is described as guitar by Yasha-distracted Dunyasha, whom he is trying to woo. The song starts off in the men's dressing room. Then the three of them saunter past me/Charlotta as I sit on my swing. They ignore me. I am not gentry. I am not one of them. Feeling horribly left out I follow them to a log and try to integrate. Nothing doing. Pasha/Yepikhodov must sing six verses of the song every night. He distorts the music with a ludicrous vibrato, even so it is like bathing in warm oil.[1]

Pasha is authoritative about what works and what doesn't. It was he who insisted that early plans for the difficult picnic scene must be abandoned for something faster and more concise. We know that Stanislavsky was worried by the scene when he was grappling with it in 1904. I would give the scene as an exercise to student directors. Nothing HAPPENS. How will he/she generate a reason for the actors to be on stage instead of at home or in the dressing room, playing chess. If they succeed, it becomes one of the most revealing scenes in the play.

Pasha/Yepikhodov is married to Valya/Stage manager. Their teenage son collects old coins which he swaps generously for some of my modern ones. Their younger daughter skips at the side of the stage or sits, patiently waiting. Valya wears a warm bonnet on her head during the performance. The stage is draughty, even though the radiators are on at full tilt. At the end of the play we are shown a display of golden princess curls that have been waiting for a chance to dance in the light. Valya has esoteric gifts – not the only one in the Dramatichesky Teatr. I told her that I love her husband warmly. I have his voice on tape. She can have it every day.

---

[1] The song is *На заре ты ее не буди/* 'Do not wake her up at dawn'; the words are from a lyric verse by the Russian poet Afanasy Fet (1820–1892), set to the music of Alexander Varlamov (1801–1848), one of the founding fathers of the Russian Art Song.

25. Sasha/Pishchik.

Sasha /Pishchik

Charlotta has only one person in the play who responds generously and personally to her. Simeonov-Pishchik. He is a flustered, worried adoring neighbour of Ranevskaya, from whom he borrows money that she cannot afford to lend. He is kindness itself. He is inclined to fall asleep without warning. I am fortunate to find myself acting opposite Sasha. He plays Pishchik with real depth of feeling. He, like Pasha, is a natural comic but, unlike him, arrives at his results through wound-upness, through a journey of stress and commitment rather than throwaway. He revealed to Kalantarov in front of us all one day that he has found that the most important thing for Pishchik is to make everything all right and everybody happy. With this as his motivation he can seize and swallow Ranevskaya's addictive pills, and he can and does co-operate fully with Charlotta's tricks and games at the party. Sasha/Pishchik laughs and laughs and laughs. This generous actor has thick straight black hair and cornflower blue eyes. He is young.

He is stout. He fears nothing. Under his instruction we did some proper circus knockabout, with prat falls. It is energetic, professional work. We come off breathless and satisfied. At the end of the play I am sitting on the trunks waiting for the final departure. I face upstage while Sasha/Pishchik plays his scene with Lena/ Ranevskaya. He is on his way out when she calls to him that they are leaving the house for ever. He stops in his tracks beside me. As the news sinks in, he flashes a look at me/Charlotta for confirmation of the shocking truth. Sasha's eyes invariably fill with tears before he mumbles his goodbye and rushes away. I am moved by his talent and artistry.

26. Kostya/Lopakhin #II.

Kostya/Lopakhin #II

There are tall elegant actors in England who resemble Kostya. He carries his height comfortably. His fair hair grows in an unruly intellectual style and his features are set in such a way that I expect to hear English when he starts to talk. How can this be explained? He is beautifully mannered, built for noble parts rather than for the drunk passer-by who makes a short disruptive entrance in the second act. The third of the blue-eyed boys, his are deep-set. I understand that phrase now. It means that his eyes are set deep into his head. They are not on the edge of his head. He understudies Lopakhin. I have not been asked to rehearse with him. I feel Kostya is quietly watching over my well-being.

27. Anya/Valya.

Valya/Anya

Valya, married to Kostya, is another out of whose mouth English could easily glide. She has a Bloomsbury look. A long face, pale skin, dark hair which is held back by a ribbon in the play. She is affectionate and enjoys twining her arms around my neck. She is not inhibited about looking deep into my face, to see whether she can read the secrets of my foreignness. Since she looks to me as if she comes from London WC1, I'm surprised that she needs to ask any questions at all. She shares a serious poetic outlook with her husband; even her clothes are in the shape and style that I associate with those literati. Anya is a prolific knitter; she wears original home-made sweaters, one of which has incorporated yarn made from the hair of her dog. I would have been interested to see inside their home. Their son, while trapped in a bout of flu, constructed a little log cabin for me. It is made from matches. How I long to spend time with these people individually and to delve into what brought them to this place in their lives. I also would like to answer any question they wish to ask me. I can't imagine holding any secrets from them.

28. Matchstick house made by the son of Lopakhin #II/Kostya and his wife Valya.

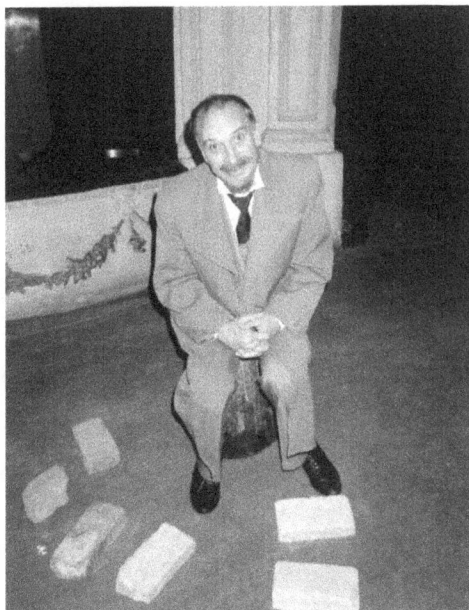

29. Gaev/Lev.

Lev/Gaev

This unobtrusive Armenian actor seems to hold a particular place in the affection of his fellows. He has trouble with his heart which explains his diffidence. He sits quietly with his hands in his lap when he is not needed in a scene. The others, men and women, lean in to stroke him or to enquire how he feels. He always answers, 'Fine,' but it is unlikely. His own delicacy of manners towards me inhibits me from intruding into his fragility, so what I know of him is revealed by what I see on stage, rather than through discourse. His Gaev is a broken-hearted man, floating almost without struggle on the tide that is sweeping his past, his present – his whole identity – into oblivion. I learn from watching his grieving acceptance.

30. Taganrog, Volodya Federovsky, Director of the Dramatic Theatre.

Vladimir – Volodya Fedorovsky/Administrative Director, Taganrog Theatre

Volodya, first and foremost, makes me laugh. I feel I can say anything to him. And I do. He has an easy personality. His mind moves fast, building on a joke or a bone of contention – sometimes the same thing.

His large form is usually clothed in a smart city suit – a chalk stripe or a brown or a charcoal grey. A few times I have seen him wearing jeans. He is an excellent history teacher – his sightseeing tour of Taganrog was instructive as well as amusing. I believe he enjoys talking as much as I do. Since he speaks no English I get a real shot at my Russian when we are together. We have hundreds of misunderstandings which make me laugh even more. Volodya is Ukrainian and proud of it. I asked whether he would nevertheless come to the aid of Uzbekhistan or Siberia.
'Without question.'

At my birthday party Volodya raised his glass to our absent children. He was visibly moved, had to distract himself.

He and Lena have a garden at their dacha down the coast. He tells me he grows vegetables. He never looks surprised – I've dealt him a few – worldliness prevents that. He is sophisticated. He seems to understand me perfectly and wants me to have a good time. I am shameless about asking him to heat his electric samovar for tea. He utterly despises the Earl Grey that I offer as my luxury gift.

'Tea must be so strong that it hurts.'

I came upon Volodya one morning emerging from a shed outside the theatre. He had been up all night trying to make the boiler work for the central heating.

31. Juvenaly Kalantarov, Director.

Juvenaly Kalantarov/Director

Juvenaly is a mid-height muscular man from Astrakhan. He stands, legs apart, hands on hips, claiming his territory. He has a beautiful Roman emperor's head which grows firmly out of his sturdy body. His personality is not overt. He is someone who has learned to keep himself to himself, not to be socially assertive. At first sight you could estimate that he has passed through a course of therapy which has left him calm and unaggressive. Even soft. I was inspired by the high-minded and sensitive talk he gave me the day after our first meeting. He outlined his feelings about the play, Chekhov and Charlotta. I was ready to give my life for his production. Nevertheless, I came away with the nagging sense that it had been a lecture, not an exchange between colleagues. When it came to rehearsal I discovered that he can be a bully.

Letter from Stanislavsky to Leonidov, an actor and director with the company; Director's answer.

7 Nov, 1906

'You will know, if you have not been through it yourself, how much blood, nervous tension, health and torment of soul and disappointment it costs to sit at your table as a director in rehearsal.

'... Say, in all conscience, how many actors can you find in the company who can or are able to work independently? Are there many who can bring a character and a creation independently to the stage without the help of the director's imagination?

'...Aren't most of them concerned to latch onto a few superficial features, or just follow their whims, especially those who do not work at home? ...Anything that can destroy the director's mood in moments of creative tension (the director cannot take one step without that mood and creative tension), everything that offends him in the sense of disrespect for his efforts, all this a director gets continuously, every minute as payment for his efforts. And all this is done, unconsciously, from Russian habit, to despise other people's efforts.

'...Everything that is said in rehearsal is related to the whole. All the details of the production create the kind of atmosphere in which the actor merges with the author and the other actors and every department of a complex theatrical mechanism. Is it possible for us to keep an actor in that atmosphere of his own free will? Won't we be told; "It's inhuman to keep an actor in a rehearsal when he is in the play, but not in this Act?" ...The director is stuck in his seat all the time and that is considered human, but for an actor it's considered impossible.

'...And so the director is obliged to say the same thing a dozen times to different people and that is not considered inhuman and the director doesn't have the right to lose his temper nor to reproach the actor for his coolness of attitude towards the business in hand.'

Chekhov to his wife, Olga Knipper:
'My work is nervous, disturbing and involves strain. It is public
and responsible, making it doubly hard.'

Chekhov to the critic, Suvorin:
'To divide men into the successful and the unsuccessful is to
look at human nature from a narrow pre-conceived point of view.
Are you a success or not? Am I? Was Napoleon? Is your servant,
Vassiliy? What is the criterion? One must be a god to tell successes
from failures without making a mistake.'

Taganrog = Chekhov

32. Dramatichesky Theatre in Taganrog.

My first sight of the theatre. The Mayor of Taganrog looks at it out of his office window. The interiors of the theatre were designed to look like a smaller version of La Scala, Milan; it was built in 1866, when Chekhov was six. He saw his first performance there, *La Belle Hélène* by Offenbach, when he was thirteen. He used to bunk off school and be first to the top gallery to grab his favourite seat. It is marked by a plaque, clearly visible from the stage. In his day members of the audience wore claque ties to show which performer they supported, so there would be competitive applause from different factions. I was told that Anton Pavlovich sometimes added his own spice by shouting the names of known citizens sitting in the expensive seats below him. All heads would turn to watch Mr and Mrs Ivan Respectable blushing. It became so predictably embarrassing that some couples hurried out of the theatre before the clapping began rather than risk humiliation. My cousin Alexander used to do the same thing to my parents in the Chelsea Palace, before it was pulled down.

Russian men, I've noticed, blush readily. It seems that, in general, they grow up rather shy and modest.

With scarcely time to do more than fall in love with the red, gold and white auditorium, I was led across the stage, up an iron staircase to a small dressing room where the rehearsal was to take place. Juvenaly sat behind a table. A lot of actors in a tiny space. I learned that some parts are double and triple cast to provide more roles for the company members, they had all turned up for my first day.

I was, and would continue to be, three people. Yesterday's cheerful girl was Zhenia, my every day guard. The gun was handed back and forth in a sock. Sometimes I found it in my handbag if I was looking for a pen or peppermint while Zhenia went to collect her son from school. I felt better about it after I learned that it was loaded with gas, not bullets. The third me was my interpreter, Nina. No matter what hints I dropped about how much English people enjoy their privacy, it was not until after the last performance, a full month ahead, that I actually got to be where no one knew I was. For fifteen minutes. I had to hide in a theatre box, with my head below the parapet. They sent out a search party. These hospitable people wanted me to be happy all the time, and wanted to witness the fact. They didn't want me to feel lonely, even on the way to the Ж.

Last night's faces, still smiling in daylight, were joined by new ones. Volodya/Trofimov brought me flowers. Kalantarov, rightly, threw me in at the deep end with my big speech at the beginning of ACT II and then ACT III/Charlotta the clown. I had practised illusions with a silk scarf and a pack of trick cards that my magician cousin had prepared for me; I have been juggling badly with three balls since The Flying Karamazov Brothers came to London. Another Charlotta joined in a discussion about the card tricks. It became heated. Everyone joined in. I did my whole part except the first entrance with the dog. I felt my character supported by bold original production.

At three o'clock there was a tea party to introduce me to the other actors and the theatre staff. A cake set in front of me said "HELLO! MAY ALL YOUR DREAMS COME TRUE!!" Azat, Kalantarov and Fedorovsky made speeches, so did I.

Azat had also stayed at the hostel where, this morning, there was no hot water. I didn't complain but was moved to a grander self-contained apartment, half an hour's drive from the theatre. Kalantarov asked me on the way home what I thought about the actors. I answered truthfully some seemed more prepared than others. In my new home I unpacked more completely, and went to bed feeling cherished, safe and worn out.

11 February

On stage today. Agonising cold. Actors huddling round radiators. Kalantarov gave a serious talk about lateness and discipline. A long morning rehearsal, starting with dancing. They all eat a big breakfast so can wait until three p.m. for the meal break. I'm not yet used to that.

I was introduced to the Ж at the front of house. Four in a row behind doors that reached neither to the ground nor the ceiling. Paper was not available, you are expected to bring your own. If there was time I made this journey from behind the proscenium arch. The alternative is not enticing. Below the stage there is a facility for either sex. The actresses looked at each other before directing me down the stairs to hell. My nose led me. I found a young woman, her hair tied in a scarf, sweeping around a battered door behind which I saw, embedded in the ground, what had been a white china or enamel fixture with a footplate on either side. I had seen something similar in a Parisian railway station in about 1950. The pretty girl, whose job it was to keep this Augean stable clean, stood aside charmingly.

'*Je vous en prie.*'

She spoke with an exquisite accent.

'*Merci.*'

I was trying to hold my breath as I spoke.

The stench on the men's side was even worse. Some days it penetrated the boards of the stage during rehearsal and performance so that even the residents remarked on it. Certainly one end of the girls' dressing room was a place I chose never to loiter.

The Russians I've met are clean. Their personal hygiene is felicitous. And they've dealt with the cold. They heat their homes.

I was emboldened to discuss the stinky bog with Fedorovsky. Not judgmentally, simply out of curiosity.

'How can you bear the smell?'

'We're used to it.'

There is a part of me, too, which welcomes the down to earth lack of pretence. In the bowels of the theatre it is the bowels which perform.

Fedorovsky, attentive to my needs, doesn't take much persuasion to switch on his electric samovar. He sits at the side of the stage, watching with the other actors. When I say that I am used to eating something around one p.m., a twenty-minute break is introduced at that time. All the actors race up to the foyer where, for a few kopeks, they buy salami on white bread and a mug of black tea. Sometimes there are sugary buns, and even a huge bag of sweets which they fall on, dropping ten or twenty into their pockets for moments of low energy. After two or three days gorging the tasty salami and buns with the others, I realise that my *avoirdupois* will not stand it, so I just drink tea. At least the others benefit from Anglichanka's national ways.

My first three-p.m. lunch choice was so delicious that it became habitual. The restaurant next door sent over sliced cucumber with sour cream and plenty of the black bread that I am a junkie for. Occasionally I indulged in a dish of potatoes fried to a crisp with onions and lots of salt and pepper. Large glass jars of pickles – cabbage and carrot, cucumber, tomato, tins of processed peas (I got to relish them) found their way into the room at the side of the stage where I camped during the day. Also, thick, creamy, pure plum juice, pear juice, apple juice. No payment could be made for these delicacies. I offered tights, bouillon cubes, make-up pencils, tea, coffee, Pea and Smoky Bacon Soup Mix, eye shadow, curry powder, chocolate. Cigarettes, best of all. One woman stage-door keeper gave me two golden apples, another a pot of honey.

Lopakhin #II brought walnuts which he cracked in his palms so that I would have some protein. Varya brought jam made of rose petals in case I develop a sore throat; she must have got the recipe from Mount Olympus. These nutritious home-made foods carried such love and warmth with them that, like a well-stroked pet, I enjoyed perfect health the whole time I was in Taganrog, which is a seaside town.

Rehearsal continues from six to ten p.m. Kalantarov has only had five days rehearsing on stage. He acts everyone's part. He makes huge energy input. They are not highly roused yet, apart from the comics – Pishchik and Yepikhodov. I ask why there is no stage manager with a script.

'She's ill. We prompt ourselves in performance.'

She turns up in a few days. Married to Yepikhodov.

Octavy, who plays Firs, introduces himself formally, kissing my hand. He presents me with a wrapped sweet saying,

'You have everything, so all I can give you is my heart.'

I frankly enjoy it. It is his dog, Urska, who is my excited companion in the play.

The actors go off into the dressing rooms to smoke – how they smoke. I make my way to the top gallery to sit in Chekhov's seat. I try the nearby seats as well in case history has made a mistake. I watch them rehearsing. The acoustic is terrific. A tortoiseshell cat darts across the stage.

12 February

Worse cold. They are greatly concerned that I be warm enough.

I'm not, despite thermals, salopettes and moon boots.

Today, minus fifteen degrees, is the beginning of the holiday to celebrate saying goodbye to winter – Pancake Day. I eat too many.

13 February – My Birthday

An elaborate poster pinned to the stage door proclaims the occasion and welcomes me. They must have looked at my passport. Shit. As I climb onto the stage, a burst of applause from the actors. Presents, tears, hugging, dancing, 'Happy Birthday' played on the piano by Volodya/Trofimov. I've been with them three days – it feels like three years of friendship. I expect we rehearsed a bit too.

In the afternoon, I'm taken to the little green and white cottage where Chekhov was born, then to the high school, called *гимназиум*.[1] This is a fine museum with sections devoted to different periods of his life. Tea and sweet fluffy cake decorated with filigree biscuits like mantillas is offered by the cosy blonde curator. Home-made cherry jam spooned onto a small saucer. You eat mouthfuls as you drink your tea.

Back at the theatre, more surprises. I find that we are to rehearse the difficult ACT II scene in front of cameras. Rostov TV. I'm definitely not ready for this sort of exposure. We stumble through the scene quite badly. Kalantarov sits with his back to the camera and doesn't open his mouth.

I'm put on a throne in the middle of the stage, well lit. Baskets of flowers are banked round me and a pair of teenagers do a skilled *Come Dancing* routine. The Deputy Mayor of Taganrog makes a speech welcoming me to the town. He hands me an oil painting of a typical local view. I make my second speech in three days. I am being treated like royalty; it's unexpected, it's moving.

33. Taganrog, the cottage where Chekhov was born.

---

[1] Grammar School; the word was borrowed from the German and was originally a borrowing from the classical Greek word *gymnasion*.

Earlier I had told Federovsky that I would like to buy the whole company a drink. That turns out to be a banquet for forty people in the restaurant that does my daily lunch. I don't remember being asked for money. I hope I paid at least for the vodka and ruby Rostov champagne. Where did the food come from? They have ration cards in Taganrog. Live band. Dancing. Speeches. I made at least two. Time to go home. These celebrations start early, so what feels like the middle of the night is only nine thirty. It's a clever trick.

14 February

Some people don't make it to rehearsal at all today. Kalantarov tells me not to play out front.

15 February – Religious Festival

The day winter and spring meet. If it's warm today it will be a warm spring. There is a huge thaw. Dripping water everywhere.

I see my costume designs. Splendid ACT I, III, IV. Not sure about the tea gown for ACT II.

Six p.m. Run ACT II. Felt unreal, without inner motor. I rushed the bit with Yepikhodov – made the exit too quickly, getting the lines in the wrong order. Everyone a bit muddled. Kalantarov said some useful things about characterisation and inner motivation to particular actors. I waited for him to tell me I was unreal. He didn't. He is very fierce and rude to Ranevskaya, Yasha, Dunyasha. He shouts at them in a hectoring way. He doesn't try to subdue the two comics. They're strong. People answer back like anything, then laugh. He demonstrates physically, talks every point into the ground, gives line readings. How will they arrive at their own performance if he goes on like this?

16 February

Orchestral rehearsal for dancing. Tempers. Kalantarov asks why people don't get dances right. Choreographer/Varya says there is no time to practise. Orchestral players, rightly, feel the rehearsal is for them. The actors get hot, confused and snappy. Useful for me to get to know them all in a physical sweaty way. I feel loyal to their individual work and performances. I shall enjoy ACT III. It will take a lot of energy, but I like the 'plastic aspect'. The tricks are going to work.

17 February – Sunday

Day off. I am taken sightseeing with a simple history lesson from Federovsky. In 1698 Peter the Great laid out plans to build Taganrog as the capital of the south. Situated on the then deep Sea of Azov, it could be a useful trading outlet. The Turks, however, repulsed him. He went north and started on St Petersburg in 1703. Taganrog was the first town built on straight lines, instead of in circles.

When Chekhov was young it was a thriving port, with merchants of differing nationalities plying successfully alongside each other. Greek Street, the most impressive of many elegant roads in the town, is a glorious extended tree-lined avenue with fine large houses painted in the same stylish colours chosen by London house-owners now.

On one corner stands the great house where Tsar Alexander I died, and where Pushkin stayed on his way to exile in the Caucasus. He wrote a poem about a wise cat who lived in the old oak tree that still grows outside. Perhaps T. S. Eliot was familiar with it.

Tchaikovsky's brother, who worked in the port, lived in an eccentric red-brick building. It has a square tower which displays a large weathervane shaped as a galleon in full sail, and N S E W in Cyrillic letters. The position of the house is breathtaking.

34. The weathervane atop Tchaikovsky's brother's house.

It is on a balustraded clifftop beside one of the prize sights, the steps descending to the sea. A statue of Pushkin stands at the bottom. A short stroll through willows planted to hold the earth stable, where a tourist hotel complex is planned but not yet executed, leads to the seashore. At present the sea is frozen so solid that people walk out more than a hundred yards, bore holes and fish in rows. From a distance, they look like penguins. People have been known to trek for seven hours across the ice to Rostov.

The Tchaikovsky house, now a music library, is the one I would most like to live in. Chekhov felt the same. He left Taganrog when he was nineteen, but continued to love the town, second only to Moscow. Had the local water supply been more reliable he would have bought that house and lived there during the long summers, instead of at Yalta...

One of the theatre musicians lives in a spacious converted flat on Greek Street. He took me yet further along to the oldest Music Academy in Russia for a concert in Anglichanka's honour. I had a solemn face ready for Rimsky-Korsakov, Borodin and Mussorgsky. I got Gershwin on elderly traditional instruments, followed by seriously good jazz and tea.

Generalization: Whenever possible, Russians are funny.

35. Music School at Taganrog.

In the town, Garibaldi signed a declaration that he would strive to set his country free, with a statue to prove it.

18 February

Men's dressing room. Actors playing Racing Chess. Trofimov beats Lopakhin #II three times. Firs, growling to terrorise, beats Trofimov three times.

19 February

A call from London. I am rushed to Federovsky's office, but the line has gone.

I find I don't want to be separated from the other actors. I go into the girls' dressing room, needing intimacy. All four are mothers, between thirty and forty; pretty without exception, highly made-up. They talk, like most actresses I know, of fatigue, of having no time to shop, of their children's health and school problems. But for them there is no car nor Sainsbury's nor even certainty of anything worth having at the end of a three-hour queue. *Кошмар*[2] is a popular word.

'What can we do? We are slaves,' laments Varya, in French.

They are apparently unresentful of the cards being so heavily stacked against them; contrary to weary myth they are extremely feminine and as strong as packhorses. They laugh and laugh. Oh how they smoke!

Varya tells me not to stress the T at the end of words, make it softer. First advice I've had from anyone. Very helpful. My Rs and Ts make them squeal with sympathetic laughter. 'TTTURRRGENEV!' I declare to everyone I meet.

They're building the set on stage today. A wonderful noisy activity.

A call from London had been alerted but didn't materialise.

20 February

Rostov TV again. No warning. I feel tired and don't want to be looked at. While I am being looked at, a call from BBC Kaleidoscope. I had been interviewed before I left England and this is their first successful contact since. Quite a flurry, emptying

---

[2] Nightmare.

Federovsky's office so that I can be private. I relish the opportunity to let off a little steam in English about the glories of the town, the theatre and the people. I feel a flicker of disloyalty when I tell how maddened we are by aspects of Kalantarov. Perhaps they won't put it out.

Federovsky took me across the road to meet the Mayor. He was sleek and attentive, presenting me with a bronze medallion of Anton Pavlovich, some flowers and a large biography of the writer illustrated with many familiar photographs; Tolstoy with Chekhov, Gorky with Chekhov, as well as plenty of others I hadn't seen before.

We sat down to open sandwiches, cake and tea. I was asked almost at once from the far end of the table about my political views. Twelve people sat in silence as I tried to nutshell my feeling that the time will come when socialism, maybe even communism, will be accepted universally. We are simply not good enough yet. I don't find that view goes down well anywhere, really.

Generalization: For them, socialism/communism is what they're supposed to have had, for seventy years, not what they might have one day. I never understand why people bunch the two together. Even more do I not understand the lazy thinking that allows my right-wing friends to say, as Eastern Europe changed its mind about totalitarianism: 'There, I told you socialism doesn't work!'

My hosts changed the subject and gave me the opportunity to express my infatuation with their town. With more allied historic sights than Stratford-upon-Avon, six months of summer every year, a seaside to relax by, it had already implanted a wish to bring about a twin connection with Shakespeare's birthplace.

A huge injection of money would be needed. Some giant philanthropist might just fall in love with the idea of awakening this Sleeping Beauty with a golden kiss. The Mayor took me seriously and responded with enthusiasm. I promised I would do my very best to put in motion at least an *en principe* twinning of the two theatres. I failed completely even when, years later, I was working with the RSC.

22 February

ACT III. Meant to be a run. The dancing is hard. Kalantarov
interferes. Tempers start to rise. It seems to me that he insults
people at the core of their professionalism. He decides to change
what I do at the end of the act. An exciting new bit of business. I
do it. It feels good. He says I haven't understood and starts to
demonstrate. He does exactly what I did, but at a different
moment. I call out that he is insulting me. I know *what* to do, just
tell me *when* to do it. I can feel the pent-up frustration of the entire
company being channelled through my mouth. Why does he play
everyone's part for them? Why doesn't he let the actors do their
job? I use his hectoring style. I repeat myself loudly several times.
(He hasn't really insulted *me*, just actors.) I believe he is so intent
on his way that he doesn't listen, and ends up not even hearing
the actors' creative offerings. He looks bewildered and says he
hadn't meant to insult me. Later one of the actors takes my hand:
'We're with you.'

The actresses say, 'Thank you, thank you.'

I went down to the frozen sea and walked upon the water. Six
p.m.

ACT IV. Straight run. Kalantarov stopped immediately and
throughout. The actors somewhat revivified by my outburst. I feel
very tired indeed.

Eight fifteen. Short breather. Another run immediately without
rest or refreshment. They are strong people. As I leave to go home,
Federovsky comes with three arum lilies saying,

'These are from the admirers of your talent in Taganrog.' He
smiles obliquely.

23 February

Before rehearsal, Kalantarov does a preamble about yesterday.
Perhaps our reproach of him playing all the parts was right. His
dictatorship will recede now. He will watch and help. He is
convinced his method is right – to push and press actors.

While I was eating my lunch, he came to my dressing room. His
eyes welled. He hadn't meant to upset me. (This is awful.) I told
him he spends more time acting than the actors.

'I am a teacher,' he stressed.

'If the piano teacher plays scales all through the lesson, he will be good at scales, the pupil won't be,' I countered.

'The director has the right to be hard. The actor wants his barriers broken down.'

He said he believes the director understands the actors better than they understand themselves. I forgot to say that the director can attack the actor's vanity, but there is no one to attack the director's vanity.

I was glad of the opportunity, since I have been avoiding him, to say that I feel it's an original and dangerous production and that I am happy to be here. I had said earlier that, in England, if a director demonstrates all the time the actors call him a wanker – at least I do. This had to be translated as *onanist,* as I didn't have the Russian slang to hand. I am confused by the violence of my feelings. Am I getting my own back at a safe distance and not face to face on bullies who have given me a bad time in England? He is not being critical of *my* work, I wish he would be more demanding. Anyway, the extremes are in play and it's fascinating.

Today is National Man's Day. The men shake hands, the women wish them 'Happy Holiday!'

Home to watch the armed forces singing music of all sorts on TV. Very little about the Gulf War.

24 February

Run ACTS I and II in the set. People trying out costumes, I have my wonderful clown outfit and the large white picture hat to go with the tea gown in ACT II. I am already planning how I can dump the hat as soon as possible after the entrance. It feels as big as a satellite dish, I hate it.

Sveta, the chic assistant director comes for coffee in my dressing room. She says the actors are slaves, that is why they must be beaten. It is clear to me, and bewildering, that this is tacitly condoned by everyone. Collusive victimisation. I insist that it can change – but from the top. Whoever has power should not abuse it. She agrees wryly.

I'm invited to the three thirty meal at Volodya/Trofimov's flat. He lives there with his attractive artist girlfriend and her little boy, also her artist mother. He tells me that I am stressing my first line in the wrong place, also that I'm overdoing the last entrance. I wish he had told me earlier. I ask him why Kalantarov doesn't direct me the way he does the others.

'He's probably afraid you'll pack up and go back to England.'

I'm home by seven thirty. My feet ache from the dancing. I get hot water for a bath by boiling large cauldrons that I find in the kitchen. Two make the water hot enough to get into, two more top it up for another ten minutes. There is hot water out of the tap not more than half a dozen times while I'm in Taganrog. I don't mind a bit. Federovsky laughs when I complain about the shock on the days it's there. What consistently winds me up is the abuse of personality. Henrietta puts it brilliantly: 'We have not yet found an agreed way of behaving to each other.'

I watch the nine o'clock news, *Время*.[3] Allied forces are fighting on the ground in Kuwait. I see President Bush, John Major; Tariq Aziz in Moscow. It seems Mr Gorbachev is working hard for a result. It is said that Americans won't eat chicken legs, only breast. The fat juicy legs are imported from the United States and are known as *Bush's Legs* – *ножки Буша*. The scraggy, meatless homegrown legs are named after the country's thinnest and greatest ballerina: Plisetskaya's Legs.

25 February

The costume designer has arrived from Moscow. An ally, she doesn't like the hat. She has ideas about the clown make-up.

It is worked out that I will give the music cues to the orchestra with a handclap.

The three days that we have started wearing our costumes coincide with a coat of paint being given to all doors and passages to and from the stage and the dressing rooms. The smell brings near walk-out from the actors. I am invited to do a mock faint on the stage so that Federovsky will think I've been overcome by

---

[3] *Время.* (pronounced *Vremia*) is a popular news programme; it means time.

fumes and call a halt. My tea gown gets stuck to a wet wall but it's not serious.

After the paint-faint, Federovsky talks to us about the possibility of doing the play at the Vladimir Festival (impresario Azat), and maybe Yalta. In April. We already know that we are to give two or three performances in Moscow mid-March.

The actors take the opportunity to complain that they have not had one day off since the beginning of rehearsals and that they will have to re-rehearse with Charlotta #2 after the première next week. I record some of their raised voices, led by Union representative Yury/ Lopakhin #I, on my BBC tape recorder. Everyone is called all of every day whether they are needed or not.

36. Clown costume.

37. Gown costume.

Six p.m. Run the whole play.

First time with Urska. She barks noisily as we make our collective entrance. I try hard to stress the first line properly.

After the second entrance in ACT I (in the tea gown) I move to a swing upstage and stay on it for the rest of the act, about twenty minutes. I swing as discreetly as I can. Kalantarov says,

'Don't swing so discreetly. Do it more.'

'Juvenaly, if my friends in London could see me swinging while other people are trying to speak I would never live it down.'

'No. If you swing sensitively to what is being said it will be like a musical accompaniment'

I get to enjoy it and use the time to let this unique experience engulf me. I beg my psyche to remember and not to let me go back to England and generalize about the Russians.

I make a bridge by playing a bit of Chopin on the grand piano and we start ACT II. The costume change between ACTS III and IV is very quick. I miss my entrance.

We did the whole play without interval or pause. It lasted two and a half hours. No serious complaints from musicians or stagehands. The usual free movement of actors and actresses into each other's dressing rooms. The concentrated drifting that goes on when people are thinking of their next entrance.

A stage entrance here is called an exit. You go out onto the stage. The actors endure without tea or anything till ten p.m. Federovsky joins us in the stalls and is funny about the working conditions.

The Moscow dates have changed. We will perform only once – the 18th, Federovsky's birthday.

26 February

Though tired I am feeling more relaxed. I am making the role mine. After two and a half weeks that's about right.

Another talk with Kalantarov.

I must try to be amused and not get sucked in. Kalantarov tells me the same thing. I must not take on the problems of others.

'I am interested only in making Chekhov happy,' he rejoindered. 'So I forgive myself and the actors and you.'

During Notes, he said he does not praise he only criticises: 'That is my nature.'

I was chastened by being told not to interfere in things I know nothing about, yet I find I don't trust his processes. He complains greatly about the System. He goes to church.

He appears to be an intelligent person. The conversation trots along nicely. Then you come to a halt. You know that you are in a cul-de-sac. Like being with a drunk. Reality is no longer the basis. The essence of the person moves out of sight from the front of the face onto a back burner, in a darkened room far from danger, and will stay there until it is safe to come out. Was there so much brutality dished out from the beginning of his life that he has no idea that he is passing on the brutality to the next lot?

27 February

A disagreeable day. The interpreter is sacked and another much younger girl takes her place. I shall feel more comfortable.

28 February

Ten a.m. Azat has arrived from Moscow. We ran the play. I was quite nervous. The other actresses are overtired and not very well. I have a much smaller part than they.

Six p.m. The Dress Rehearsal turned out to be a stopping affair, with Kalantarov making a lot of changes. On Azat's instigation, I imagine. Then suddenly Azat was giving direction too. Shouting his head off. I went down into the stalls to shake his hand as we hadn't yet greeted each other. Later, tea in Federovsky's office. Azat came in and said baldly,

'It will be a success not because you are in it but because it is an ensemble.'

'Sounds good to me!'

He came to my dressing room later to explain that tomorrow people would be here from Moscow to watch the performance. He looked uncomfortable.

'I don't believe you are happy here.'

'I am happy. I am being very well treated.'

'You can't be happy, you didn't look pleased to see me. You sat in rehearsal looking angry.'

It didn't occur to me that maybe he needed approval from me. I am kept awake by these perplexing relationships. I must concentrate on the work.

1 March

Eleven a.m. Full Dress Rehearsal.

Throughout the rehearsal period we had done imitations of Kalantarov's most frustrating directorial mannerism.

'Нет, нет, нет. *Смотри, смотри, смотри!*'[4]

Now, as the girls prepared, it was being used as a mantra.

The emotional temperature rose while people lacked costumes, props, sleep, attention. Ranevskaya needed a lot of stroking by the other actresses when she put on her wig for the first time; and her white dress; and her black dress. She has been given a lousy time by Kalantarov. A sweeter gentler woman would be hard to find.

---

[4] *Hem/Niet means no; смотри / smotri – look.*

A dozen and a half outsiders in the auditorium. Cold empty feeling. I began to work with good concentration. Tanya, the wigmaker, and Vera Panteleyevna, the warm-hearted dresser, whispered kindly comforting words to keep me calm during the very quick change. It went better than I had done it before. The Literary Director's mother, also an actress, was first into the dressing room after the run with encouragement and a jar of pickled cabbage. My turn to well up.

We trooped into Federovsky's office for the Collective Meeting. I switched on my tape recorder. Azat and his Moscow assistant; cast, director, designer, literary director, publicity woman, box office manager, town representatives, other members of the company, etc., etc., around twenty-five. Each in turn spoke their mind about what they had just seen. A critics' forum *after* the last Dress Rehearsal and *before* the First Night.

Lit-director Sveta said that Kalantarov's method of working is right. It is necessary to push. She had never seen the company act so well. Federovsky also declared that he would not have recognised Ranevskaya as his wife.

The BBC rang in the middle of the meeting. Twenty-five people obediently filed out. The call was to plan the next call. Twenty-five people filed back.

The actors and actresses whose work was being discussed in positive and negative detail sat with their back burners operating. My contribution was acknowledged. The publicist and ticket saleswoman spoke frankly about a scene which had caused a rumpus in rehearsal. Dunyasha was required to do something explicitly sexual to Yasha. The actors involved had thought it too rude. The colleagues had thought it too rude. The publicity lady understood that this was a production with a contemporary slant, but the town would find it too rude. It should be cut. It was not.

Azat's turn. He declared that the work was not good enough for an International Festival. (Vladimir.) He added that the English school (me) was no different from the others, maybe a bit more professional. It was ensemble work. His assistant announced that the British Ambassador and all the English newspapers were invited to the performance in Moscow. Federovsky asked if I would like to speak. I declined.

The meeting was followed by Notes. I asked an actor whether it was not humiliating for Kalantarov to have had Azat take over his rehearsal last night.

'Not at all,' he answered, surprised by my question.

There was a peaceful feeling of contentment in the stalls. People had performed and been received. Confidence was much higher all round.

We rehearsed the curtain call. The musicians were to play reprises of all the dance music. This was changed without warning to a thundering orchestral version of *Feelings*. I succumbed to its glorious inappropriateness, its vulgarity.

We came on in pairs. I was with Yepikhodov. I worked with a director in England who declared at this point that he has 'an illness about rehearsing the curtain call'. He couldn't bear it if the actors did funny walks or made silly faces or blew raspberries while the routine was being practised. I would say in general that actors have an illness which allows us to be completely asinine, especially after a serious play. No constraints in Taganrog. We came on to whoops and giggles.

The stage crew, dressed as peasants, had played useful roles as extras during the evening. When they had a pause they repaired to the men's dressing room, stage left where they played draughts or chess with anyone who was free. The women – never.

Kalantarov, also feeling light-hearted, directed the cast, once everybody was on and Firs helped to his feet, to go back and forth *Russky,* meaning very slowly. No bowing until about the third time.

'What about the musicians?' I suggested.

So we turned to clap them. This was followed by cries of *Режиссёр!*,[5] the actors ventriloquising for the absent audience. Kalantarov acted himself to chants of *No, no, no! Look, look, look!* from his affectionate, forgiving slaves.

Back in Federovsky's office Azat chooses a different approach. He said he is responsible for what is coming in Moscow, where everyone believes they know best, and that we will have to work

---

very hard to make sure we are best in Moscow. Taganrog is not the judge; He is clearly suffering from managerial nerves. And why not? We grapple bravely with the problem of communication. I tell him that I am very happy and excited by the work. I find I can smile at him with some warmth. He is trying to bring about a unique project with no official support. Deep down I am on his side. I sense we long to like each other, I even feel that we are aiming for the same thing, but the periods when peace breaks out and we look at each with trust are short-lived. We will get it together one day.

Generalization: Russians have yearnings. In the West, we have expectations as well.

Free until four thirty tomorrow, with the première at six.

2 March – Mr Gorbachev's Birthday. The First Night

The only person I wanted to see today was my open-hearted piano teacher, Volodya. We met on stage at three p.m. He made me do heavy finger exercises to help me concentrate. I wandered around the theatre, trying to forget that Salvini, Rossi, Ira Oldridge, Sarah Bernhardt had all appeared here and that I would be the first foreigner to step on this stage for over a hundred years. I began to feel nervous. Too much time. Federovsky handed me two telegrams from Moscow, one from England.

Slow preparations. Cheerful Tanya puts my hair up and attaches the blonde switch I brought from London. If she inadvertently sticks a pin into my head it becomes a Soviet pin. Vera Panteleyevna is in attendance. Her tenderness and love for her actors can hardly be exaggerated. I can hear that her accent is different to Moscow's. She coos and soothes, using diminutives. 'Our Carolinichka, our Charlottichka, clever-ichka to talk Russian to speak Russian to act in Russian, the actors all say how clever-ichka the actors the audience our/наша Carolinichka...' It's hypnotic and as comforting as a change of nappy.

The build-up backstage was without panic. Quiet concentration.

The lights went down on a packed auditorium. A man climbed onto the stage and made an introductory speech which lasted not less than five minutes. The actors waiting in the scene dock at the back patiently went through their final first-night rituals yet again, in pitch darkness. The speaker stepped down to a smattering of applause.

Tender dawn light and chirruping birds lyricised the beginning of the play. After the opening dialogue, a frolic of tiny bells, an excited rush of greetings, announced a family arrival. I twitched the lead of the little white mongrel beside me:

'Пойдем!'[6]

We stepped into the light... So the play began.

Definitely not a laughing audience early on. Chekhov paced Charlotta wonderfully. There was an entrance round when I came on in the tea gown and hat. It happened every night thereafter; I spotted that it was started by Pishchik on stage. Did the tricks all right. The clown stuff went well. All in all OK. After the last scene we ended up where we'd begun, in the scene dock. The actors fell on each other using their ritual phrase 'S primeroi', meaning 'We've done it!' For about ten seconds I felt I might die of loneliness. Then I was hugged, too.

'We've done it!'

I was looking forward to the curtain call, as the unknown part of the evening. We made our tableau. Then the slow serious walk forward without bowing. We stood and stared without smiling, then moved backwards. Then forward again. People started to climb onto the stage from the stalls, handing flowers to actors as well as actresses.

They were standing up in the circles as well as the stalls and the clapping was rhythmic. It was quite unlike anything I've experienced in England. I felt foreign.

I was last to the foyer where the party was in full swing. I took two or three gulps of champagne on an empty stomach. Quite soon Federovsky made the first speech, followed by one of the actors. I got up.

'Я пьяна!'[7]

---

[6] 'Let's go!'

[7] 'I'm drunk!'

As I spoke, my body was flooded with the realisation that I had done what I came here to do. I allowed myself a fiery thrust of achievement. Up went my arms in the Olympic gold medal gesture. 'I'VE DONE IT!' I yelled in English. Then to this cheering, beloved group of generous hearts I released their most familiar expletives. 'YOB! NA KHUY!' F U C K! (Fuck it!) Laughter and applause. I embarked on what I felt about the actors being treated with contempt during rehearsal. (Applause from the actors; Azat, next to me, was barracking.

'*Solidarność!*'

'Yes,' I threw at him. 'Certainly!'

He growled. I paused, then decided to pack it in.

'That's all.'

Azat got up from the table and marched out of the room.

Music started. People came towards me, soothing, calming. Kalantarov feels that I don't understand things here. That love is close to hate. He loves and hates the actors for having the possibility but for blocking the way. In turn, I apologised for causing embarrassment. It must be obvious to everyone that I find Azat difficult to get on with. Maybe it is because he is an Eastern man and I am a Western woman. Having been truthful, I found that the hostility could be dropped. I was suddenly free to express my gratitude and admiration to Azat for having brought me here, and for his wish to break down the barriers between our cultures; for our projected trip to Moscow. I then begged them to insist on better working conditions.

'Kalantarov has worked hard too, he has had no rest, but you have homes and children to look after. Shopping to do. I know. I brought up two children and did the shopping and learned my lines and got to rehearsal on time.' I banished mental pictures of a cleaner; overstocked supermarkets disgorging their multiplicities of choice into my comfortable ecologically-sound Swedish car.

'Ask him to call you only when you are needed. He's a clever man, he can do that.'

They don't seem to show it when they've had too much to drink.

Yepikhodov, with the voice of an angel, sang to a guitar, then we piled into the theatre bus to go home.

3 March – Sunday

Twelve noon matinee. Really nasty hangover. Everyone in the play suffering horribly. Full house. The actors under-energised, pouring with alcoholic sweat. Painful and humiliating.

It had been arranged that I should talk plans with Azat at three p.m.

It turned out he has a temperature of forty degrees. Relief at not having to talk overrode guilt.

After the second performance at six, straight home to telephone Moscow, thanking for telegrams. They told me the Gulf War has ended.

4 March

The car taking me to the theatre was half an hour late. I wondered whether I had been sacked. In Federovsky's office *Kaleidoscope's* Natalie Wheen came on the line. She graciously agreed to ring my agent and home before the crackling line put an end to it. No chance of recording.

Best performance so far.

'When the audience responds like that it means success beyond success,' said Varya in the dressing room afterwards.

During the evening one of the musicians had told me that though some people had thought I shouldn't have spoken, he felt that a lot of what I said needed saying.

I had sent a card to Azat wishing him a speedy recovery. He appeared at the dressing room door during the interval. I perceive a Tom and Jerry aspect to our relationship. We deal each other annihilating SPLATS. In the next reel we're bouncing back, apparently undamaged.

Back to my apartment.

'We can't talk in the theatre,' he insisted.

Azat came, his assistant, Kalantarov, Zhenia and Larissa, my delicately tough new interpreter.

'What about you?' I asked Federovsky as we left the theatre.
'They don't want me.'

Eeyore. Whatever was in store?

We had a most friendly meeting. Vodka, tea, English biscuits. I plan to go to England for Easter, following the Moscow showing, and will return for the Yalta Festival, a single performance on 10 April. I understand why Federovsky has been left out. Yalta is his scheme. Azat doesn't want me to go. Yalta is not an International Festival. It is not under his umbrella, he will not be there to guarantee my safety, living conditions, money. He wants me to be the queen of the Vladimir International Festival. He would like to invite my son and daughter to come. Taganrog can be dropped now, it is not important. He is polite and respectful. I, too, am grateful for the offer to my children, though of course I could not answer for them. Naturally, I want to go to Yalta to see where Chekhov lived and to do as many performances of the play as possible. I would happily do more here if they invite me. I love it here. Diplomacy carried the night. Kalantarov is silent in Azat's company.

5 March

Zhenia and Larissa take me sightseeing. First to Chekhov's father's corner shop, filled with barrels and tubs, as well as glass jars. The family lived above it for five years. The ground floor, where the theatre sometimes do reconstruction scenes, reminds me of a Beatrix Potter shop. Upstairs there is a nursery and several bedrooms as well as a light, airy sitting room containing some early paintings by his brother, a talented artist, alas an alcoholic, who died young. There is a portrait which I guess is Anton Pavlovich at around the age he first visited the theatre. The father's stern piety is shown by the number of hanging icons. It is easy to imagine hymn singing round the piano in the sitting room.

We visited a 'History of the Town' Museum, housed in a dazzling 1904 tiled building produced by Shekhtel who designed the Moscow Art Theatre. More and more I would like to share this town with Western friends. We dropped into a basement coffee bar for refreshment. Coffee can be had in a cafe but not bought in a shop. An electric samovar on each table means that you can go on pouring hot water onto the tea leaves in your cup until there is no strength left in them.

The rouble denomination is written on the paper money in fourteen languages.

6 March

Winter's back. Snow falling. I made myself sleep longer. Later I wrote forty-five postcards.

Agreed with Federovsky that I will not go back to Moscow with Kalantarov after the last performance but will stay a day or two longer to see some more of the town and have an evening with the actors so that we can ask each other questions. I have pushed aside any idea of a Victorian spinster. They accept that London is no longer blacked out by fog. We need to share more day-to-day experiences.

Six p.m. I gave a poor performance. Muddled some lines in the card scene. Ugh! In the autograph queue a boy of around nineteen told me the following story.

His grandfather, alone, had emigrated to England; Derby, where he bought a house. He never married. When he died the neighbours had said that they would send the young man an invitation so that he could visit his grandfather's grave. He had waited a year but the invitation had not yet come. Was there any way that I might be able to help him?

With several people still behind him I felt I could not take on such a huge problem. I suggested, knowing how much I would hate to be told the same thing, that he write to the British Embassy in Moscow. I felt sure they would be able to help.

7 March

At bedtime my guard, Valery, knocked at the door with flowers for Women's Day tomorrow. Tulips and mimosa. Tiny elastic bands keep the tulip heads shut.

8 March

More flowers, more postcards. At the theatre more travel talk.

9 March

Performances twelve noon and six p.m.

10 March – Sunday

Matinee twelve noon. Lopakhin #II played. Graceful, gentle, he had rehearsed with the others and with me for a short while between the two performances yesterday. Valya/Anya, his wife, watched from the wings whenever she was not on stage herself.

Six p.m. Last performance in Taganrog. I feared an overwhelm of nostalgia nerves, but knowing Moscow was to come helped me through.

There was a goodbye speech from Federovsky on stage. I made rather a conventional reply, thanking and asking that I might come back.

I'd bought drinks for the end of term party, the actors brought home-made food. We danced communally, not just in pairs. When it was my turn to speak I first of all congratulated Lopakhin #II on his debut. He answered from his seat that it was a pity that the director had been unable to say the same. Kalantarov had told him that he had done bad acting. I declared that I would not be provocative this time.

'Come, Carolina. Time to go home.'

I sat down on the stairs.

'No, I'm not ready yet. I've been guarded for six weeks. I've given my last performance and now I'm free. I don't have to do anything I don't want to. I'm English and I'm free!' Poor people! Oh, Caroline!

I decided to hide. I gave them the slip and dashed up to Anton's Balcony, concealing myself in the box nearest the stage. I heard them calling. I saw them. Fifteen minutes was all I needed. I went back to the foyer as if nothing had happened and allowed myself to be wrapped up, packed into the bus and taken home.

11 March

Kaleidoscope rang my apartment. Could I sum up my conclusions? No, but a key word is resilience.

In the afternoon to Nik, one of the violinists. His high-ceilinged flat in Greek Street is more like a Western apartment than any I've been in, and already buzzing with company members. We take our boots off as soon as we get indoors. Men sit in their smartest suits with socked feet sticking out at the bottom.

The plan had been that we should exchange ideas and ask questions.

I volunteered what I had told the BBC about their survival gifts.

'How do you explain it?' they enquired.

'I feel you believe in something.'

'What do we believe in?' they asked but did not wait for a reply.

It was a cosy family evening. My piano teacher and Nik played a concerto by Vivaldi which was the last piece for violin that I had learned before I gave up the instrument. The musicians gave me a glossy book on Russian ceramic art. No speeches. Feelings.

12 March

A calm efficient pack; intermittent with preparing fried potato and onion for Zhenia and I to eat on the train. I also filled a massive glass jar with spicy rice for the actors to enjoy on their journey two days later. The housekeeper put it out in the snow to keep cool. She gave me an old-fashioned travelling mirror in a small bag.

Zhenia and Larissa took me to the Post Office to send a birthday telegram to Charlotte. We walked in glorious sunlight to the sea, round about. On the way back, we passed the wigmaker's flat. She made us tea. Everything I was doing was for the last time.

Federovsky's office.

The money I had been paid lived with my passport in Federovsky's safe, the only key to which hung round my neck on a red ribbon.

Federovsky asked whether I would be willing to pay for my apartment and claim the money back in Moscow.

'I am asked to change my travelling day to suit Azat; if that is the way he does business, I won't go on the 13th.'

'What about the Press Conference?'

'That's his problem. I'll travel with all of you.'

I sat there. I couldn't tell whether he wanted to kill me.

I was given, as I left the theatre, perhaps the most personal of all my presents. The stage door keeper asked me to accept the Red Army jacket I had admired on her several times. I fought a ferocious internal battle, then put it on. It fits perfectly.

On the first night I had given tights to the women, socks to the men. Their ration cards allow them to buy two pairs of socks a year – if there are any.

13 March

I didn't feel wound up about leaving Taganrog. I kissed the stage and whispered, 'I'll be back, of course, but no tears. We nearly forgot my passport and money in the safe.

Seryozha, who drives the theatre touring bus, is another wheel-wizard. The roads in Taganrog need repair. People make for the bits without holes no matter which side they are meant to be driving on. Their skill allows a fast-lane attitude. You career towards inescapable collision. The collective intuition makes them veer correctly at the last moment. I found it quite invigorating and was never frightened. I trusted Seryozha absolutely as he took us the two-hour drive to Rostov in an hour and a half.

Larissa had wanted to see me to the train.

'Ask me questions, anything.' I pleaded with her.

'There are too many and I don't want to be a nuisance.'

Instead she copied out two poems that she thought I would enjoy. She made a little vocabulary of the difficult words at the side. I had recorded for her a tape of English vowels and consonants, and three Shakespeare sonnets.

Then Seryozha carried four heavy bags, any two of which would have defeated a Western porter, in one go to the train. I tried to picture his internal organs taking the strain. He's not big.

A flurry of hugs. Suddenly Zhenia and I were behind glass. The farewell quartet, having spotted two handsome men to take us to dinner in the restaurant car, stood on the platform waving. Then the tears came.

14 March

Charlotte's birthday. I wonder whether they will remember to deliver the basket of flowers I ordered before I came away.

I drew back the curtains for a better view. Zhenia and I drank tea together and talked girl's talk for a couple of hours. She longs to visit the West with her boyfriend.

I decided to give myself the luxury of an olive-oil bath with the uncalled for can I had brought from England. I laid out the towels and poured the stuff liberally all over myself I rubbed it in a bit, then lay there reading a book. I forgot that we would be stopping at stations.

We reached Moscow at three in the afternoon. Outside the window as we slowed down, I saw Azat, Kalantarov and the Moscow cigarette gang. Azat was holding up an astounding poster. A coloured Art Nouveau design, West End *de luxe*, advertising the performance at the Hermitage Theatre on the 18th. Chekhov's head above the title. My head, three times bigger, beneath. He really does want to please me.

(Thirty years later, I write, 'I failed to thank him.' Bitch!)

They crowded into the carriage, looking askance at the Red Army jacket I was wearing.

Hardly were we settled in the car than Azat began to reel off the names of the notables who would come to the performance. The British Ambassador, Smoktunovsky, Yefremov. I stopped him in full flood. I asked him please to take particular care not to tell me who would be there. Later I was describing my last interview with the BBC. That took the lid off the volcano of suppressed information.

'The BBC will be at the performance and all the London newspapers,' Azat boasted.

I exploded. McEnroe.

'You can't be serious. You don't listen.'

'He forgot,' interceded Kalantarov.

'I'm the one who has to give the performance.'

Even at the time I could see that from their point of view I must be completely mad. They were incapable of putting themselves in my shoes. You don't frighten the horses before a race.

The journey continued in silence. Fuming bewilderment on all sides. We arrived at the flat and unloaded.

'What time is the Press Conference tomorrow?' I asked.

'What Press Conference?'

'That's the reason I came two days earlier.' I roared at Kalantarov for confirmation.

'Look at me! You were there when it was discussed!'

His face was white. Back burner. He denied.

Azat marched out.

'I'll be back at six.'

Kalantarov followed.

Liars! Cowards! I hate them!

Henrietta, hard-pressed go-between from the October Day One of this adventure, came by on her way home. She stayed for Pavel, Azat's cash man, who arrived on the dot of six. He makes me laugh. We have a good rapport in French. His wife works in Africa. We drank tea. He opened an attaché case and brought out many roubles. The three of us, giggling like children playing Monopoly, counted and counter-checked until we made sense of the piles of currency. Later, Charlotte rang from London. The flowers had arrived.

For two days I kept myself to myself. I wanted no distractions before the 18th. I walked and walked. Like New York, pitted roads. Like New York, glittering surprises just around the corner. Like New York, people exercising their dogs in the evening.

17 March

I was called to the Hermitage Theatre at five o'clock.

The Hermitage Theatre was the first home of The Moscow Art Theatre. It was there that they had the famous success with *Seagull,* following the notorious failure of the play in St Petersburg. It stands in a small public garden, attached physically to another much more modern theatre. Easy walking distance from home, past the statue of Pushkin, 'Hello!'

The theatre is now in the hands of Willi, Azat's cosy romantic teddy-bear stepfather. He is one of the most warming people I met during my autumn visit.

The Taganrog party was sitting in the smaller studio. It felt a year since we were together.

Azat appeared, apologised for not staying long as he has bronchitis, gave a short summary of tomorrow's plans and left. I sat with most of the company to watch a modern three-hander, splendidly acted, in the main auditorium.

18 March

Run through called at eleven a.m. The walk seemed much longer, as I was carrying my make-up, boots, lunch, and a dress for the party after the performance.

The theatre seemed to be completely locked up. No stage door to be seen. I trailed round with my load wondering whether I was mistakenly an hour early. I sat on a bench in the little garden. They'll be here soon. They weren't. I tried to ring Henrietta. She was engaged. It was nearly twelve o'clock. I was feeling desperate and foolish. A man was watching a snow plough at work.

'Please, could you tell me how to get into the theatre?'

'Yes, the stage doors of both theatres are side by side round the corner past the billboard.'

Close to tears, I pushed my way through to the comforting sight of our prop lady unloading her wicker skip. The actresses told me not to worry, everything was '*нормально*',[8] they hadn't started yet. I calmed down a bit as we ran ACTS I and II.

I was asked to get into my clown costume as *Время*, the nine o'clock news programme would be covering the rehearsal. A small independent film crew were taking film of the TV company taking film of the rehearsal. Would I mind being interviewed on film now/later?

It became apparent that there was to be no rehearsal of the second half of the play.

All the actors were invited to the Theatre Workers' Union, not far away, for lunch, guests of Azat. I felt I had more to gain by remaining quietly alone in the dressing room, eating my picnic and signing the fifty copies of the poster that were to be handed to the Important People in the audience.

---

[8] OK.

I went in search of information. I found Kalantarov, wearing a smart, grey-flannel suit, sitting in a small office with Sveta and Vera, the Literary Director. They welcomed me.

'Come in, come in.'

I looked at Kalantarov.

'When will the dog be here?'

'I don't know.'

'Well, who has arranged the dog?'

'I don't know.'

'Will there *BE* a dog?'

'No.'

'No dog?'

He shrugged.

'How come the play needs a dog for twelve performances in Taganrog, but in Moscow it no longer matters?'

He laughed.

'Do I have to find a dog? Is it the actress's problem to find a dog? Fine. I will go onto the street and ask a dog if it would like to act in a play by Anton Chekhov.'

I steamed back to the dressing room and burst into tears of frustration.

'Do they really want *ME* to find a dog?'

'Unprofessional,' soothed Ranevskaya.

Her husband, Federovsky, came into the room. It was his birthday.

I'd given him a Mickey Mouse balloon.

'Why is she crying?'

'No dog,' explained Ranevskaya.

'They're not professional, I'll deal with it.' A dog was found.

Perfect after one rehearsal.

Dresser Vera Panteleyevna was in tears because she had forgotten to pack the bag in which I carry my juggling balls, silk scarf and cucumber. She made a new one, much nicer, in half an hour and the sun came out again.

The film crew stood me at the side of the stage and asked me questions that I must answer in Russian to their camera. They freed me half an hour before the performance was due to begin.

They came into the dressing room without request or warning, zooming in to watch me take a last look in the mirror, or flick my hands up and down to relax them.

Azat made a speech before the play began.

As I swung sensitively on the swing during the second half of the first act, I saw Vera Panteleyevna, carrying my quick-change clothes, walk unostentatiously from one side of the stage to the other in full view of the audience. No one had shown her an alternative route.

A metropolitan audience usually feels different to a provincial one. Does it lack innocence? Is it sitting in leaden parental judgment? Cameramen, press and TV, seemed to fill the first two rows. Flash, flash. Little red light.

I feel there is some protection to be had from acting in a foreign language. The foreigner speaking my language has an intriguing otherness. They know I know they're foreign. Chekhov's Englishwoman Abroad. I spoke the very best Russian I could manage.

The reception was more enthusiastic than I had expected. The British Ambassador made a speech emphasising the European-ness of the Russians. ('What is he talking about? We're not European, we're Eastern,' said an actor later.)

Azat had not spared himself to make the evening memorable to the Muscovites. The sort of stunt that we are used to – prefixing the actors' names with Lord and Lady, providing an army band to play appropriate music as the audience arrived, tricks which raise the level of expectation of enjoyment – these can be managed without too much difficulty in the West. To do it in Moscow must have stretched our impresario to the limit. The party that followed, too, offered a greater spread of more delicious food than was usual. One friend said it was the best-organised evening of its kind they had ever seen. He'd succeeded in getting us on the nine o'clock news, which is the only thing to be seen on television at the time it goes out across the huge soon-to-split Union. I write, I failed to congratulate him... Bravo Azat, shame on you Caroline!

None of the people from whom he most would have liked acknowledgment turned up; the Minister of Culture, the Head of the Theatre Workers' Union, the Director of the Moscow Art Theatre.

The parting from the cast was softened again by the knowledge that we would meet in three weeks. I was completely high on the fact that I had broken the tourist barrier which allows a person restricted movement and classified bed space, I was beginning to talk of Yalta and Vladimir as I would of Bognor and Walberswick.

The evening before I returned to England Azat invited me with Henrietta, Kalantarov and his assistant to have a meal. I was being taken to a gala at the Bolshoi Theatre afterwards and arrived at the Minsk Restaurant in unaccustomed high heels and finery.

I had two expectations. One was that two pictures I had bought would have been officially licensed for export and could leave with me, the other that all necessary arrangements had been made regarding the visa for my next trip. That I would have only to pick it up and buy an air ticket. I had emphasised all business must be complete before Good Friday.

The meeting started well. Azat handed me a set of photographs taken at the Hermitage party. We talked quite openly of the difficulties we'd experienced in relating to each other. I saluted his achievement but said I was his natural enemy because of his master/slave attitude. He felt in turn that they had treated me better than anyone had ever been treated.

Henrietta declared that he was treating me as a human being for the first time. She is usually so diplomatic this came as a shock. Then he dropped his bombshells. The invitation had been sent but the visa was not fixed. They had not got the export licences for the pictures. My goodwill disappeared.

He felt hurt that I had excluded him from my proposed efforts to twin Taganrog with Stratford. I explained that he had clearly expressed his loss of interest in Taganrog while we were still there. He thought I owed it to him to write to the Minister of Culture and the head of the Theatre Workers Union to say what a great collaboration this had been. I told him that he had left it a bit late to ask for such letters. Perhaps when I come back. I dumped my confusion and made for the Bolshoi. I'd never been there before. I found it, like Venice, as glorious as people say.

At the Sheremetevo departure desk I had a great deal of luggage and was asked for $800 overweight. I could fly round the world for that.

'Please, I am an actress. I've been working here for two months. Presents...'

A helpful passenger organised four others to take an extra bag each, while the young official watched impassively.

'Have you got any dollars?' asked the helpful passenger. 'You should give him ten or fifteen dollars. [BRIBE?!] No, not in your hand: put it in your passport and give him that, he'll understand.'

Clumsily, I did as he suggested.

'There's no need,' said the young official.

It was with a heavy feeling that I made my way to the plane. I dislike damaging Russia by leaving unresolved quarrels in her capacious lap. She has had enough harm done to her from outside to last a millennium, and from within – eternity. I feel the need to return quickly to take this painful unfinished business toward healthy completion; towards Chekhov's 'most absolute freedom imaginable, freedom from violence and from lies'.

At home, an hour-long telephone conversation with a close friend drew the headlines of my experience from me as easily as a wobbly tooth, draining the poison and releasing the joy and excitement which had been temporarily submerged.

'Heaven and hell!' I cackled.

Far too soon to go into detail, particularly where feelings were involved. I couldn't distance myself from something that was still going on.

Within twenty-four hours Charlotte said, 'Go, Mum, go!' I went. To the healing seaside which had been midwife to my line learning.

Back in London three faxes were sent to Moscow begging for the invitation necessary for a working visa, and for the contractual deal proposed for Yalta and Vladimir. Nothing.

I wrote letters to the Minister for the Arts and his Shadow Minister, to Peter Ustinov (fondly remembered by the Literary Manager of the theatre in Taganrog), to the Royal Shakespeare Company, asking for some response to the notion of a Stratford-

Taganrog twinning that I could take back as encouragement at the first stage of communication.

I was offered a tasty comedic job for a week at the end of April which would repay my entire financial investment in the Russian adventure. It didn't occur to me that the three remaining performances of *Cherry Orchard* might fall through. I turned down an opportunity to make my English livelihood.

The official invitation arrived.

Something was manipulating the strings in my favour, I was invited to an interview for an important new TV series about women taxi-drivers, *Rides,* to be made by Warner Sisters for the BBC.

I headed to the sea for Easter. I gardened, slept deeply and felt renewed.

Every day I spoke Charlotta's forty-six lines out loud.

Looking out of my window at the English Channel I feel tugging surges of affection for the actors in Taganrog. I can't wait to see them again. I miss them. I want to make their external lives easier. What can I give them, apart from a million pounds?

As I believe Channel 4 was originally invented to please me, so were the charity shops in Hastings. Skirts or jerseys for the girls, shirts for the men. Also, riskily, leather boots and shoes; and for me, tall red rubber boots for £1. Wedging the stuff into my car I had a momentary gloomy visualisation of myself at LHR.

I knew that the MKhAT Company, possibly led by Oleg Yefremov, would be playing at the Yalta Festival. Henrietta, Theatre staff, was paying a visit to her sick mother in Sevastopol, on the other side of the uvula peninsula of Crimea that hangs down into the guffawing mouth of the Black Sea.

I decided to telephone her from England to see whether she would be corning to Yalta too.

I found myself connected to an International Operator in the Midlands. We were subversives colluding to bend a potentially uncooperative system to our will. A silly intimacy is built up in seconds with a complete stranger. I love it, be it man or woman. In this case, a woman.

We discarded Latvia and Moscow as routes to Crimea, and settled for somewhere I'd never heard of beginning with L.

'*Allwo?*' *(Hello?)* Male Russian operator.

'Hello, this is England calling. Please can you connect me with SeBàstopol?' English operator, very loud.

'*Allwo?*' Louder.

'Oh dear, this is England calling.' Louder still.

'May I try, please?' Me, urgent, to English operator.

'Oh yes; please do. They don't seem to speak English at all.'

'*Allwo?*' Me, respectful and humble, in Russian. 'Excuse me, please, I am speaking from London. Is it possible, please, I need SeVastÒpol.'

'SevastÒpol? Moment.'

While he engaged his professional skills I gave my friend in the Midlands the reason for my call. The response encouraged me to divulge some of my TV-CV. Enough of my work had been seen for us both to feel safe and pleased.

'*Allwo?* Sevastopol?..' New male operator.

'*Allwo?* I need...' I gave the number.

'*Allwo?*' Henrietta...

'See you in Yalta.'

Anything is possible if you want it enough. Some people like to spend their money in restaurants and bars. I like to make international telephone calls without counting the minutes.

Local calls in Russia are exceptionally cheap. In Moscow, you can feed two kopecks into a callbox and talk all day. Even long-distance charges are minimal. Visitors from there sometimes have to be reminded that here British Telecom operates from a profit motive.

I carried this unusual topic to my TV interview. At stake was another unique possibility – to play a transsexual minicab driver. How do I dress to market myself for such a part? I went along as me and got the job; though I was not to discover that until I had been further tempered in a foreign place.

I had a ticket with an unchangeable date for return in a month.

Having rented my dollar trolley, searching either for a notice displaying my name or a familiar face, I spotted Igor, the young set designer who had been at the first night in Taganrog. His beautiful tall wife was exquisitely dressed in a tomato tailored suit which, I learned later, she had made herself. It was because she spoke some English, I guessed, that they'd been sent. Certainly Azat was not involved, as Yalta was nothing to do with him.

I had hoped, while experiencing the acute responsibility of mothering, to teach my son and daughter at least to clean their teeth well; and to show by my example that it pays to travel light. They had, before they were of school age, accompanied me on massive provincial tours, both with Prospect and the Actors Company. I had also taken them, with a small zip bag each, for holidays abroad from the earliest age, so that we might share the pleasure of foreign living; smell and taste, language and weather. Pancakes in America; *moules* and *boules* and Boulogne, choosing not to get sunstroke in Northern Cyprus, drinking water.

I have the utmost gratitude for this aspect of my own childhood. I remember perfectly the French doctor painting my back with something to cure me of pneumonia when I was four in Le Lavandou; and, during the same holiday, dropping a flatter longer lump of sugar into a large blue and white spotted cup of boiled fresh milk; and the curious satisfying taste of pine kernels which my sister and I collected and cracked with a stone on the warm wall, legs dangling. Foreign travel broadens everything.

My professional visits to Russia introduce a different set of priorities. I don't know the subtleties of seasonal change. Federovsky, during one of his entertaining potted history lessons, said unequivocally that in Russia everything is done to extreme whether it is happiness, unhappiness, revolution or weather. I should be prepared for winter and summer, for a possible lunch at the British Embassy, or a television interview not in Charlotta costume. I must be clothed for extended rail travel and the dirty, physical work of rehearsal. It remains a matter of clout to have appeared in the *Forsyte Saga* even when I succeed in challenging the received belief that I played Irene. I had also managed to capture Prime Time by being in *At Bertram's Hotel,* the Miss Marple episode that was shown on 1 January, the evening when most

Soviet citizens would be slumped in front of their sets following the greatest celebration night of the year.

Igor and Elya didn't blink. Their friendliness made me relieved to be sharing the long journey to Yalta in their company. Next day, I felt a shiver of excitement when I read the sign *Крым/Crimea*. Elya and I had a carriage to ourselves. Igor was elsewhere. Depressed by the resort to vodka of his sharing companion, he asked most politely whether he might sit with us. Igor's curved spine makes him shorter than his wife. He wears his coppery hair to the shoulders. His spectacles magnify pale sensitive eyes. There is a huge smile waiting to light up his delicate face. His hands, too, are almost girlishly fine; but his physique in no way limits the mule-strength that I have seen and increasingly admired in Russian men and women. He was able to shoulder his own tiny bag and two of mine without flinching.

Generalization: Russians do what has to be done. Except when they don't.

It has become known in England that the cost of living in Moscow has brutally doubled in the last day or two. The financial shock and the cost of their generosity to me, however, must be biting Igor and Elya. On the train Elya unpacked a cake, a carton of fruit juice and some sweets. I had brought with me from London a chicken leg, the end of a loaf of bread, a slice of cheese and a couple of brownish bananas. I had no idea whether any food, even bread, would be available to buy in Moscow, nor whether I would be travelling alone. Or, if accompanied, what contingency might have been made for meals, as with Azat, in the restaurant car. Maybe there wouldn't be a restaurant car. Or a samovar at the end of the corridor from which I could refill the new blue thermos that I had brought as a present for Ksenia and immediately requisitioned for the trip.

Elya laid the little table in our cabin with the concentration and reverence of someone preparing an altar for Holy Communion. She lovingly spread white paper napkins over its surface, leaving triangles hanging down, and placed a candle, a short fat white one, in a corner. Her plastic travelling mugs were of vivid red, introducing a celebratory Christmas look to the setting. Our meagre provisions were being sanctified through ritual. I also offered a glass jar filled with the crispy potato and onion delicacy, hastily cooked, that had been so pleasing on the Taganrog-Moscow journey. Establishing patterns of behaviour. This is how I travel on a long-distance train in Russia.

Kinaesthetic memory. When I was learning the violin I discovered that I could sing a concert A at perfect pitch from nothing. So, in physical recollection, I believe I could demonstrate the exact speed of the steps taken by the Changing Guards at the Lenin Mausoleum. Now, to this odd couple, I would like to add the timing of the clackety-clack of the southbound train in Russia. Not the train to Leningrad, which I have been on several times, the train to Chekhov town.

The countryside that we passed through was no longer plump-covered with snow, it was energetically green and busy. A map of the territory to be covered hangs behind glass on the wall of the corridor of the train. Also an unusual and useful timetable which gives not only the time of the train's arrival at the station, but the number of minutes it will be stationary. Maybe fifteen. It means you can take a leisurely stroll along the platform to a stall where rare fresh grapefruit or oranges may be bought.

A train journey can be used, like a song in a musical, to further the story; a time for learning. Elya told me that she had been married only four months. I saw no sign of intimacy between them except once, when Igor gave her bottom the sort of slap a person might throw at a horse's flank to encourage it to move over; they certainly talked with each other in a friendly way. Male travellers usually change into tracksuits as soon as they've settled in the carriage. Igor did not.

Elya has an ecstatic highly strung way of being. Her dark eyes burn with the sort of fervour I associate with consumptive heroines or people consumed by uncompassionate religion. She has a clear spiritual stance. She approaches life with a will to innocence; looking for the best, and greeting the worst (there was plenty of that in store) with a lovely choc-a-block laugh that rescues balance when it has vanished in conflict.

She told me that she is hungry most of the time and often has severe pain inside from lack of food. I was nudged into a shocked examination of how very desperate the food shortages are. She told me she believes she might die of starvation. She was serious. But I was still too closely in touch with Western plenty to be able to make the further leap to share her conviction.

Until this week the Metro fare was a five-kopeck flat rate. The poorest could still get about at that price. The beggars I have seen in the road subways don't look that much poorer than anyone else. Have I been sharing carriage space with many people who were suffering the same hunger cramps that Elya described? What will happen to them now that the fare has tripled to fifteen kopecks? Will they be reduced to sharing the experience of some of the poorest in England who have to stay at home because unreliable public transport is so expensive?

I had procured a few pieces of brightly coloured material for Elya. She immediately offered to make them up for me to wear. Igor gave me a copy of the brochure with his *Seagull* designs in it. When a man came along the corridor carrying a basket of cigarettes and milk chocolate, Igor bought a bar for each of us, and our present-giving was complete. We ate and went to bed early.

One way to escape from hunger pangs is to sleep. This Elya did until nearly midday. I, an early riser, had the excitement of watching us reach Crimea. For a short thrilling time we were on a length of track that had water lapping on both sides of it. Gradually the peninsula widened, showing itself flat and fertile and densely farmed.

History closes in. I can easily be overwhelmed by suggestibility when I am in places which are associated with huge events. I felt a thudding fearfulness as I drove, pregnant, through Glencoe with my baby son strapped into a seat beside me. The light was fading on a golden autumn afternoon; the challenging prospect of crossing majestic, deserted Rannoch Moor, covered with coppery bracken and heather, defying calendar reproduction. We didn't pass another car for thirty miles.

Before that there had been Galilee, my husband's secret holiday choice – our first as a couple – which was heart-stoppingly beautiful, domestic and pastoral. It was unexpectedly small and instantly cancelled misconceptions I had harboured from childhood. We were there a couple of weeks before the Six Day War. Our car got stuck in the mud below the Golan Heights. The strong, red-haired *kibbutznik* who rescued us with his tractor was Russian, of course.

Now I was entering British knitwear territory (Raglan/Cardigan/Balaclava)... Forgive me... We gently clackety-clacked our way past orchards of fruit trees. I had a clear feeling of being in a milder southerly landscape. More relaxed.

I would like to have got out of the train at Sevastopol, but Simferopol is the capital town. The railway line stops there. That is where we were being met. A smart white minibus attended our arrival. My orchestrally various luggage was somehow shifted to it from the train. I adopted an attitude of lofty non-involvement with the seven embarrassing pieces. I carried as many as I could manage and treated the others like recently introduced foreign relations for whom I was responsible but felt no natural affection. They were taken on by capable hosts.

Simferopol, situated in the middle of the Crimean peninsula, is about fifty kilometres from both Yalta and Sevastopol. The three towns are more or less triangularly equidistant; Sevastopol to the southwest, Yalta to the southeast, facing back up to the Sea of Azov and Taganrog.

Tall pillars hold up the pediment of the entrance to the station. Outside, there is a large sunny piazza where cars, vans and buses wait. My impression of the town is golden, with broad generous avenues displaying ochre and white mansions. I found grandeur in the buildings. It felt like a resort although we were still an hour and a half from the sea.

In ancient times Crimea was called Tauria. It is now one of the riches of Ukraine; although in the new order it has made itself autonomous within the Republic.

To reach the Eastern sea from the capital of the region, you must cross the Crimean Mountains, a range that so far has been too daunting for the railroad pioneers; Yalta cannot yet be arrived at by train. Each peak is individually named. I was told that in a prehistoric age, the back and ears of Cat Mountain had been densely forested, and that on these high places burial grounds had been discovered. The excavations had uncovered the graves of Tavr people, three metres tall. I forgot to ask where I might go to study the skeletons of these giants, about whom I felt such curiosity. I was disappointed when I visited the Fortress of SS Peter and Paul in Leningrad, to find that the box which contains the remains of Peter the Great is no longer than that of any of his ancestral neighbours. I've seen articles of his clothing in exhibition and feel had I met him, I would have been awestruck by his size. I have a particular curiosity about the way men and women contend with the peculiarities given them by nature.

An alternative way of travelling from Simferopol to Yalta is by trolleybus. We are used to seeing these in towns. It is most unusual to see one travelling between towns. It is not surprising to learn that this mountain-scaling journey of nearly a hundred kilometres is the longest trolleybus route in the world.

My pleasure in approaching and arriving at the seaside is one of the absolutes of my life. Maybe the sea is the oldest friend I have. The sun is the lover, and the sea is the one who knows. I lean forward for the first glimpse. I notice with relish details of the road; the vegetation and buildings on either side. I look for signs. TO THE SEA. MAJESTIC HOTEL. PROMENADE. TOWN CENTRE, even, can wind me a notch higher, it never fails.

Following the curve of the mountain my first view of Yalta was from above, at a distance of four·or five miles. The similarity with the Côte d'Azur is immediately apparent. After a fleeting vision of the sparkling Black Sea, my eyes were drawn back to a collection of large white sanatoria, strategically placed like a hand of blank dominoes in the shielding palm of the mountainside – well above the town, which nevertheless seems to stretch its fingertips to touch them. With vigorous building sites on both sides of the road into the town I guess Yalta will spread all ways like Cannes and Nice until the valuable holiday coast is outlined with a crust of habitation; subject to the intrusive lucrative scrutiny of outsiders. That is the price bathing beauties have to pay. Then, perhaps, the money will be found to extend the railway line.

Our bus took us to the theatre down narrow tree-lined back streets, intriguing, curving streets meant for walking not traffic. We came to rest at the stage door. The driver went inside. A cluster of smokers were standing about. We waited five or ten minutes, then I could bear it no longer. I subverted Elya, another committed oceaniste, to come with me in search of the seafront. It was less than fifty yards away. Expansive; to the left, the mountainous skyline and the port with steamers, time to notice little kiosks and shops facing onto the promenade. A woman, sitting at a crate-table, was selling greenish-yellow pock-marked apples. She offered me one to try. It was luscious with a sensational taste. I bought some, then we hurried back to find a thoroughly put-out Igor searching for us amongst the trees. I've always liked trees growing up out of pavement, especially when they are surrounded, as these at earth level, by wrought-iron grilles. Paris.

We felt like naughty girls with their fingers in the cake mix, but we'd had our taste and were satisfied. We were driven the few yards to my digs. The Palace Hotel, built in 1904, the year that Chekhov died. The front of the building, on Chekhov Street, faces away from the sea. There is a continuous wrought-iron balcony around each of the three upstairs floors. Heavy wooden double doors swing into a cool, dark marble-floored hall. Having still not experienced hot weather in this country, I don't yet feel the benefit of cool halls.

I signed in at the desk. The chic blonde receptionist asked me for which town in England I have a permit to live. I felt a momentary internal collapse. Of all the difficulties that I have watched my provincial friends enduring, the hardest for me to put myself in their shoes is over being confined to live in one place. Caged birds. I can't imagine not being free to move to Bristol should I want to. You live where you work. You work where you live. Of course, there are people who defy the rule, but they are at risk. Someone I know, who lives but is not registered in Moscow, pretends to be out when the police come to check his papers. I don't know how often they call.

During my earliest visits to the Soviet Union it was not done to telephone a friend from my hotel room, for fear of endangering them by association with a foreigner. I was excited and appalled to be close to such danger.

I used to bend over backwards to be tactful; not to be critical of the system, for fear of being patronising or voyeuristic. But each visit I took more and costlier presents, thereby compounding 'You know that I know.'

Now that my friends have the freedom to speak their minds openly, I find myself wanting to interfere with the natural process and to jolt them into taking greater steps faster.

My sense of urgency on their account, I realise with clanging self-jolt, may be prompted by my overdue effort to totter towards my own freedom.

Am I drawn to the Russians because we're actually in the same boat?

My luggage was heaved up an old-fashioned shallow-stepped marble staircase to a room on the second floor, which is numbered as if it were the third.

First a small entrance lobby with plenty of hanging space. On the right a more than reasonable tiled bathroom with a bidet, and a spacious bed-sitting room, a huge fridge, a vast television set and a sofa on which a rug had been spread. Its design was of a fearsome orange and black tiger. As well as an ordinary sized window there was a tall double French window leading out to the balcony. The space had distinction and was clearly from Before. Elya busied round me like a nursemaid before she and Igor went to find their abode.

I opened the French window and stepped out onto the wide balcony overlooking a road without pavement. It has an intricate railing. Half a dozen cypress trees, almost within reach across the street, vied in giving shade to the gardens and courtyards of whitewashed houses topped by sloping red-tiled roofs. Most days I was to see the same man bounding up an outside staircase to the first floor of the setback house opposite.

Cars, dogs and people share equal passage in the street. The town reaches away towards the mountains; these, reminding me of the striking Kyrenia range in Northern Cyprus, are not high enough to frighten me the way the Alps do. They start as tree-covered hills and gradually build, the stone flecked grey, to a knuckled, irregular unthreatening skyline.

A dignified sand-coloured edifice with a decorated cornice caught my eye. Maybe it is a row of shops, or a civic building, or flats. Behind it, a blink later, waiting to shock, is a revel of a church. Perched a little higher up, it shows itself to the sweetest effect in the bright light of the afternoon sun. Atop its pink wedding-cake body are jet black onion domes. Palm, pine and oleander can also be seen emerging from the panorama of modern apartments and pylons.

I hastened out into the old town and down to the front. Couples strolled arm in arm, sat on benches, peered into kiosks for souvenirs. I came across a hoarding which shows our coloured poster hanging beside the one for the Moscow Art Theatre; another advertised *Seagull* to be given by the Komsomol Theatre of Leningrad. The Chekhov Festival is in full swing. It was too breezy to sit and stare, so I kept moving past gazebos, 'Have Your Photograph Taken!', the Post Office, until I reached the busy harbour. I went past a large grey naval vessel, saw a hovercraft in dry dock, spotted an elegant pointed waterbus that looks as if it might do speedy trips around the coast.

Next I found the market. Covered stalls displayed an astonishing range of meat, fruit and vegetables. At a price.

I was captivated by a stall which offered grated raw vegetables; carrot, cabbage and beetroot. Separate and mixed; spiced, medium and hot. Samples were on saucers as tempters. The mixtures were packed into long plastic sausages and tied at each end with bright coloured thread. I tasted them all and finally chose a hot carrot mixture, leaving for another time enormous stuffed aubergines and peppers. Further on I spent time sniffing spices and herbs and was delighted to come across saffron which I buy whenever I see it abroad. It is always expensive and of variable quality, but I am attracted by the colour which turns alchemically to gold in cooking. It is non-baggage to carry and I enjoy the dry/armpit taste. I bought a kilo of oranges for twenty roubles.

At the gates of the market were more impromptu settlements. Traders who, perhaps, could not afford the rent of a regular stall, or who only come when their speciality is in season. I saw some frail lettuces, and postponable green coriander. I wanted to gauge what the hotel food would be like before I set myself up with a complete salad bar in my room.

Making my way back to the hotel using my mental Minotaur thread, I turned up a steep side street and saw a queue which I joined. A young woman was selling potatoes, short cucumbers and apples through the window. No door was apparent. I had spotted large glass jars of fruit juice and needed one to add to the oranges and apples that would make my breakfast. An elderly man waited patiently in front of me. When his turn came he bought a few potatoes and a couple of cucumbers. I pointed to a jar each of apple and plum juice and asked how much they would cost. She held out her hand. She wanted my ration card. I would have to breakfast without fruit juice.

Above the entrance to a building further up the hill I saw a yin-yang sign advertising (in English) The School of Alternative Health Methods. This did not surprise me. I have met a strong body of esoteric work in Russia.

A few steps later I was stopped by a couple, rather shy, who told me that they had seen the première of *Cherry Orchard* in Taganrog. They were here on holiday and might come again to the play on April 10th. They handed me a sweet-smelling bunch of freesias.

Buoyed up I went back to my room and made tea with my new essential electric element. Opening the doors to the balcony, I quickly turned on my BBC tape recorder, the church up the hill was chiming its bells ring-a-ting-tinkle. Enhanced by even clearer light, sharper detail was discernible. The black-capped beauty was now flaunting an apple-green waistband and a pale blue collar to the evening sun. I share out loud with myself a whoosh of gratitude for such good luck.

At six I was in the hall to meet Elya, Igor and Juvenaly for dinner. The latter had spent the day attending the Festival seminars in the Museum at Chekhov's house. We greeted each other politely. Elya had discovered that the restaurant was unable to feed them as they hadn't booked earlier in the day. She hustled me into the dining room so that I would not miss my meal. They would wait for me. It was ten past six.

At three of about twelve tables in the restaurant people were finishing their food. I sat down in front of two rissoles which had probably been laid at six when the meal was advertised to start. On another plate was an apple. The waitress poured sweet milky coffee into my cup and went out to the lobby for a smoke with her friend.

Thinking this was the first course I scratched a little at the greasy patties. I drank the coffee before it became cold, and waited. Nothing. I picked up the apple and walked to where the waitress was sitting on a red vinyl sofa.

'*Это всё?*'[9]

'*Всё.*'[10]

'*Конец?*'[11]

'*Конец.*'

Perfectly friendly. So, I must definitely buy provisions whenever possible.

Elya, a more virtuous vegetarian than I, flurried on my behalf and went in search of the chef returning with promises of extra effort from the kitchen. Why does she feel that I should be treated differently from anyone else?

The genial hotel manager had earlier dealt courteously with my enquiry about a telephone in my room:

'I'm sorry, we don't have them.'

The question was not as crass as might be judged; in the original hostel in Taganrog there was a bedside extension. Now he lifted a ration card from his pocket and handed it to me. Everything solved. I offered to pay for it. He shook his head, smiling:

'No need.'

There are good as well as bad surprises.

Scarcely had we sat down in the reception area than Juvenaly asked, 'Have you any money?'

---

[9] 'Is that all?'

[10] 'That's all.'

[11] 'Finish?'

'Yes, I have money.'

He told me they have no money. Only because he had insisted, will I be paid three thousand roubles when I return to Moscow. They can only pay me one hundred roubles (four to five pounds) for my performance in Yalta. The hotel costs a hundred and thirty roubles a night. Will I pay it here and get it back in Moscow? I'd heard this before. Remembering my stubborn sit-in at Taganrog, I dredged deep for an answer...

'No, I will not pay.'

'You don't understand, Carolina.'

'But Juvenaly, do you understand they failed to send me the invitation until it was too late for the flight I had booked? (I always pay my own airfare.) I've had to give an extra forty pounds to the Soviet Embassy for a last-minute visa, on top of my airfare. I don't know whether I will get it back. I have learned not to trust.'

I had never seen him angry before. This was quite different from the bullying stance. His face reddened. He was at a loss for words.

'I am a director. We invited you here.'

'Why did you invite me? Nobody gives me information.'

'These are the problems of our country. I could have been doing another job. I could have made some money.'

'Me too!!'

He seemed not to hear.

'Here we do Chekhov without a car. *We* don't have a house by the sea.'

'Juvenaly, why didn't you tell me you can't afford me?'

'I could have told you five years ago. Seven years ago. Our country can't change. We have problems that can't be dealt with. You can't deal with our problems.'

'I'm not trained to deal with your problems. I come here to act in a play.'

We went round in circles. He addressed me through Elya, making her translate everything, because he doesn't trust that I understand and he didn't listen to my replies.

'I hope you will do the same for me in England.' (What's he talking about? Is he coming to England?)

We were gaining an audience. Juvenaly indicated that we should go up to my room. There was something comic about the four of us stomping upstairs; the agreed action shared in the midst of throat-grappling conflict.

Juvenaly brushed me off irritably when I tried to relieve him of his long black mackintosh. I made tea in the toothmug and the two plastic lids of the thermos. I brought out a packet of fig rolls.

I'm relatively new to rows. It was my son and daughter who taught me that anger can be expressed without it being the end of the world. These intense confrontations have, on one level, been liberating.

A row has its own life span. Ours lasted for an hour and a half. In the end Juvenaly said he would pay the bill himself and get the money back in Moscow.

I could see that Elya was uncomfortable on my account.

'Please don't be unhappy. You must be happy when you're here. Your mission is to come here. Everybody's talking about it. Moscow is talking about it. It's very important what you are doing.'

'It's important for me too. I'm here because I want to be, not because I am doing anyone a favour.'

Anxiety overwhelmed her.

'You must eat the food in the hotel. It is paid for. You must have enough to eat.'

They took their leave, thoroughly warmed by the heat of passionate argument. Nevertheless I was sure we would be good friends tomorrow.

Thirty years later, I am aghast at my lack of cooperation; however, I clearly remember feeling, as in all the conflicts in which I fought during these extraordinary times, the battle was not personal to me, it was a struggle to gain respect for the work – the existence – of the actor.

My evening finished in front of the television set watching a programme about Nicolay Roerich. I know his work well from the permanent collection in Moscow and in reproduction. We sometimes talk about characters in a well-written play having vivid offstage life. I feel that Roerich's addictive paintings have intense off-canvas life. The source of light is usually dramatically strong and often comes from low over a horizon that is nearly out of sight. Three of his works were brought up from the cellar of the Taganrog Art Gallery in response to my enquiry. Roerich and Kuinji are the two I ask for first.

I've had two Good Fridays in two weeks, both enjoyed by a sea.

6 April – Saturday

Igor came alone to escort me to the conference. We stood at a dusty interchange waiting for a bus which didn't come. A taxi carried us about a mile along a rising road, past a small hospital, dropping us on a plateau. We climbed down some steps. To the right the house that Chekhov built, to the left the small modern museum where the seminar was being held.

Forty or fifty experts and critics heard each other delivering papers, one every twenty minutes or so. A woman got up from her seat during a colleague's speech and went to the chairman's table where she had quite a noisy conversation until she was hushed by the others who wanted to listen to the lecturer. I understood only a little of what was said, but I picked up that one person was talking about Komissarzhevskaya, the actress who created the role of Nina in *Seagull* in the original production in St Petersburg.

Igor and I sat a few seats away from Juvenaly who turned and acknowledged me formally.

There was a break. People stretched their legs in the spring sunshine on the terrace. I had been mistaken in my anticipation of the emotional climate. Juvenaly was not feeling friendly. Not at all. Elya arrived in a fluster. She had been raised from un-wellness in bed by a telephone call from her husband insisting that she come to look after me. They forget that I have been coming to Russia for eight years. She had hurried to save a crisis. There was none.

When the others returned to their seats I felt I couldn't wait another minute to get inside the house that has always been the focal point of Chekhov's life in my perception of him. The Chekhov House-Museum on the Garden Ring Road in Moscow carries no recognisable imprint of personality compared with Tolstoy's Moscow home, or Stanislavsky's, in both of which I could imagine gigantic personalities working, eating, talking, sleeping, ruling. Chekhov, the unjudgmental observer, is more elusive.

Mikhail Roshchin's plays are widely performed in the Soviet Union. He has a special relationship with the Moscow Art Theatre. His theatre *opus* is much larger than Chekhov's, he has lived longer; although he too has endured violent ill health. His appearance is not unlike photographs of Chekhov; the same beard, flop of hair, short-sightedness, gentleness of eye. He loves women and sometimes marries them. He enjoys talking, is a tranquil listener and although I once saw him near to tears of frustration over censorship of his work, I believe he is largely amused by the vagaries of modern Russian life. That may be because he is a good pupil of Chekhov, whom he describes as a hard teacher. Sometimes in his company I feel it might have been a little thus with Anton Pavlovich.

How will the master reveal himself to me as a day-to-day man in the house that took nine months to build, and in which he lived from 1899 to 1904? His mother and sister continued to live with him after his marriage.

In general, Russian House-Museums are faithfully decorated with reproductions of original wallpapers and, where possible, with actual furniture and belongings. The wish to satisfy the voracious tourist can lead to a 'unique' picture or object being on view in more than one place. I have found myself asking whether I have not seen a particular painting already in another museum.

'Oh yes,' answers the guide, unabashed. 'That is the original. This is a copy.'

The front door to the house carries the brass name-plate off which A. P. Chekhov has almost been polished. There is a small knob which tings like a bicycle bell when it is twisted.

The caretakers allowed us special access to the study and to the inner room where they are certain he wrote *Cherry Orchard*. The small corner room can only be reached through a fretwork door from the larger study. It contains a single bed, a washstand, basin and jug. The donkey brown wallpaper keeps the room dim. The wardrobe that stands between the two windows was spoken to as a friend by Chekhov's brother and, by tradition, is the model for the one addressed by Gaev in *Cherry Orchard*. Hanging on the wall a brownish canvas bag, nearly a yard square, which he had carried to the convict settlement in Sakhalin in 1890. There is a hatbox on a chair and standing in the corner a cluster of what appear to be cherry wood walking sticks, which open out as a tripod with a leather seat. The baize-covered table next to the bed has a glass case over it, covering a green glass lamp. I did not find Anton Chekhov in that room.

The main study is dominated by a large baize-topped desk, again encased in glass. Behind it, in an alcove, a sofa, over which hangs a painting by Levitan, his great friend and rival for women. There must be half a dozen other works by this artist. One, dedicated to Chekhov, hangs low over a brick fireplace which feels too modern to be right. I have to take historical stock. How am I to place him as a man, not as the object of biography?

There is very little daylight in this room, too. An extravagant cherry wood telephone hangs on a wall only a few steps from the desk in either room. It has a handle to turn, a ledge to write on. It was made in Stockholm. Family photographs crowd the wall space. Every surface is covered with objects and mementoes. A carved wooden traditional Russian village lives in a glass case. Fifteen or twenty little houses and onion-domed churches are laid out in an orderly way. The collection was given to the playwright to celebrate the première of *Cherry Orchard*. This, his last play, opened at the Moscow Art Theatre on Chekhov's last birthday, January 17th 1904; his death was on July 2nd of that year. The roofs of the buildings are painted white. I can think of no reference to snow in his plays which are set in spring and summer and have outdoor scenes which cause no discomfort to the characters. As an outsider I feel that cold and snow are the most famous things about Russia. Napoleon and Hitler might have agreed. Chekhov doesn't mention them in his plays, Tolstoy does in his novels.

The dining room next door is cosier. There is a large table, an upright piano, a dresser designed by Maria Chekhova, his sister, and comfortable sofas against the walls. The eating space in a Russian household is the most relaxing and welcoming now, too. Meals are episodic and can continue for hours. The last picture that Nikolay Chekhov painted hangs at one end. It is a sad portrait of a young woman, seated, an arm dangling despairingly. Nikolay's earliest flower paintings, still lifes and portraits of young Anton show delicacy and optimism. He died at thirty-one of alcoholism.

This room was where the Moscow Art actors crowded to eat and drink. They could overflow into a glass veranda which looks out over the garden. In every room there is at least one couch to lie on. The house is built on a slope. The ground floor at one side becomes upstairs, facing the sea. In a cupboard on a landing hangs the worn black leather coat which protected the writer during the harsh journey to Sakhalin. He was tall. A pair of long-footed leather ankle boots are so narrow it is hard to believe he could have worn them. I find that the women's costumes in Chekhov's plays usually take me further from a recognisable recent time than those of the men, which could be worn now.

Imagining visits from Rachmaninov, Chaliapin, the writer Kuprin, and Stanislavsky with his actors, brings the house to life. I did not take long to work out why the rooms looking seawards are gloomy.

We are told that Chekhov planted the garden himself. I found delicate bamboo, bay hedges, box hedges, large yellow celandine, daffodils, gooseberry bushes, holly, iris, ivy, japonica, yellow winter jasmine, laurel, marigold, pansies, periwinkle, primroses, rosemary, roses, as well. Two or three shallow gulleys carry racing water from a pipe at the top of the garden. Refreshing rivulets gush alongside the flower beds, inviting a dipped finger or toe. There are plenty of green benches in this peaceful haven. He lived up to his belief that if each person left a well and a garden when they die, the country would be enriched. He had only five years to enjoy his.

Chekhov built his house with a fine view from terrace and balcony. The sloping shoulders of the hills on both sides took the eye down to the sea. Not any more. He also planted trees. He forgot that trees grow. The tallest bay tree I've ever seen; cedar, cypress, a cumquat immediately outside his study; a huge magnolia, palm, pine, a cherry tree almost against the house. The hills, completely built over, are probably more obscured now. I wondered aloud whether the trees could be trimmed to make the house lighter and the garden more authentic in matching the way the house has been preserved: no one took it up. He delivered a real teaser to his respectful followers.

A sturdy walk took the conference participants to a set-lunch restaurant. I sat with Elya opposite the keeper of the Sakhalin Chekhov Museum. His Eastern eyes were agog with curiosity. He expressed with vigorous good humour his wish to have a copy of the black leather coat for his museum. His neighbour enquired whether I was a *professional* actress. The meal, at eight roubles, was deemed exorbitant by the experts and the restaurant will not be visited again. Elya and I stuffed the remaining bread from the table into our handbags as we left.

A presentation of *The Lady With A Little Dog*, the afternoon's film entertainment, seemed less engaging than another walk by the sea. First to the market for more raw vege-sausages and, today, bursting aubergines and leafy coriander. The woman hid behind a pillar while I photographed her stall. Elya insisted that we bought ten-inch candle sweets.

'They are nuts in solid fruit juice, very good for us,' she enthused. The solid fruit juice looked and tasted like pink wax. We bought recently baked buns at a kiosk, as well as some more apples.

Along the promenade are striped umbrellas, yellow and red, shading tables and chairs that face the Mediterranean-blue Black Sea. I wished for less wind, but the sun was brilliant. We drank first-class Turkish coffee, which we ordered at a kiosk window, followed by another and another.

A waiter approached me, having discovered that I was English. He wondered whether I could help him. His grandfather had emigrated alone to England where he had died. He had been buried under the ground at Derby. An invitation had been promised so that he could visit his grandfather's grave, but it hadn't arrived. It was a repeat of the story I was told in Taganrog. From what lexicon of English susceptibility do they draw this tale?

At the neighbouring table a well-groomed black poodle was sitting with three girls and a man.

'Would you like to act in a play with me; one rehearsal, one entrance, one performance, on 10 April? Anton Chekhov.' I asked the agreeable animal. The answer was yes. We learned that Verushka's owner's mother works at the theatre. Telephone numbers were exchanged. Good. That worry was out of the way.

I fared better this suppertime in the hotel restaurant. I was given vegetable purée, boiled cabbage and four slices of cheese.

In the lofty pillared foyer of the theatre Juvenaly formally handed me a ticket for *Seagull*. He and Igor sat in one row, Elya and I in another, beside a television crew who had been working during the day at Chekhov's house. I took in the light, unpretentious auditorium. Why did it remind me of St James's Church, Piccadilly?

As I assimilate new aspects of Russian life, I feel I'm gaining a greater understanding of Chekhov's plays. From living Russians I can learn about him, from him I can learn about them. Our English mask of everything being all-right-really doesn't apply here.

The Leningrad Komsomol Theatre had not cast the play to type. This was challenging and, in the case of a Nina plumper and older than I am used to, searingly successful. She joins the great Vertinskaya, the first Nina I saw in the still-running production at the Moscow Art Theatre, as the best I've known. She and Arkadina, also a committed and truthful performance, sat at dressing tables on either side of the stage whenever they were not playing a scene. A barred gate made an intriguing obstacle for the actors who spent some time also sitting with the audience. I've yet to see a bad Masha. Some of the men were a bit less successful at transcending the casting. I found it a gripping production. The interval came after three acts, one to follow. Elya decided to go to bed. Igor told me that he and Juvenaly were also leaving. I returned to my seat. Just before the lights went down the two men pushed through to the row in front without a sideways glance.

My television screen overflowed with the approach of Orthodox Easter. The Grand Patriarch, gloriously gowned, crowned with gold, led his priests, nuns and congregation in the rituals and processions that would climax at midnight. Through the open door to my balcony the bells of the church on the hill joined their anticipatory chimes with those of the great cathedral in Moscow on my recording tape. We were shown Boris Yeltsin. He held a lighted candle, as did the other intent worshippers. Only at the finale of a Bob Dylan concert have I seen such a quantity of individuals flaming a light in company with their fellows. I felt that a surging supportiveness was being enjoyed by the participants. I was unable to find an English equivalent. The Coronation, perhaps, but not everyone gets to join in that. Some of our public celebrations are about soldiers' work. In the end we're on our own.

As I waited for twelve to strike I mulled over the day. Much of the best comedy is found in humiliation and outrage. I know that I am engaged in some sort of farcical encounter with Juvenaly. It feels alternately funny and upsetting.

'Christ is risen!' was proclaimed. I watched for another hour then got into bed.

7 April – Easter Day

'Christ is risen!' they confirmed as I approached the counters with my ration card to buy fruit juice, oranges and cakes.

I sat in warm sunshine at the boat end of the promenade. Children raced round a wide space in hired go-carts. There was a special look of celebration on the faces of the strolling couples. They were dressed in their best clothes, eating ice creams, carrying bunches of flowers. Some violets were thrust into my hands by a pair who knew me from the poster. I felt energised and determined to enjoy the day. My plan, learning that boat excursions do not start until the summer, was to walk as far as possible along the seafront in both directions. I must drop my shopping first and have lunch. As I turned towards the hotel I saw a bunch of the *Seagull* actors. I spent the rest of the day with them. They enveloped me with fellow feeling. They'd noted the poster. Some had seen Vremya from Moscow and others a programme showing the juggling and tricks. They asked whether I actually did them myself.

We drank coffee and generalized about directors before they whisked me onto the very boat I had wanted to travel in. Our group leader was the actor who had played Konstantin Treplev. He was the entertainer, the decision maker. His manoeuvring gifts contrived that within minutes we had climbed up a stairway and were sitting over the heads of the other passengers on the captain's deck, lolling on comfortable upholstered seats in full sunshine, sharing a bottle of sherry that emerged from someone's bag. The captain had succumbed to one of my packets of BLANK cigarettes, deadly fag bribes.

After travelling in the direction of Sevastopol for about forty minutes, we rounded a rocky promontory, on the top of which is perched a minuscule turreted castle, the Swallow's Nest. My eyes were drawn still higher to everlasting grey crags leaning back against the most absolute pale blue sky. The Russian word for *pale blue – голубой* is slang for *gay man*. We passed the tsar's palace, Livadia, where Stalin, Churchill and Roosevelt rearranged the world. Treplev chose at which stop we got off. I left my tiring violets with the woman in the ticket kiosk where enquiries were made about our return journey.

A steep climb took us up shady lanes to a clearing where, fortunately, we found a cafe. The choice was limited. They ate ravioli, I, cucumber and the familiar vegetable purée. We all drank tomato juice and sour cream which they encouraged me to mix together. In ten minutes they had emptied their plates and were outside, smoking in the sunshine, while I toiled over some desperately sweet cake they had pressed on me.

We were on a grand estate, open to the public. More hard climbing brought us to the Vorontsov Palace, located in the town of Alupka and built for the field-marshal, Prince Mikhail Vorontsov, who had spent his childhood in London, where his father served as Russian ambassador. The palace was designed by the English architect of Buckingham Palace, Edward Blore.

Two guards melted to Treplev's blandishments and reached into their pockets for keys that would open gates, latches, padlocks. We had a huge terrace to ourselves. The guards stayed to enjoy our enjoyment, theirs heightened by another packet of BLANKS. Marble steps, flanked by statues of informal dozing lions, led down to other terraces, fountains, walks; countless varieties of trees and scented shrubs. We found a lake with white swans. There was appreciation that, as post-Revolution citizens, they have free access to this top quality national beauty spot, that it belongs to them now. Lewd bowing and scraping accompanied the gratitude.

The easiness of the negotiations, the relaxed pliability of the guards, the sun and the sea air. A day like this helps me to define a little more clearly a perception that I have about this country. Intertwined with extraordinarily ugly things that happen, there is a feeling of humanity at work. In the end the human response will come. Often it comes immediately.

As we waited for the bus to take us down to the boat the entertainer told us a current Russian version of a Nancy Reagan Story.

The Opening of an Art Exhibition.

Picasso arrives at the door.

Curator. 'Please can I see your invitation?'

Picasso. 'I'm sorry, I forgot it.'

Curator. 'You can't come in without an invitation.'

Picasso. 'I left it at home. I'm Pablo Picasso.'

Curator. 'How do I know you're Pablo Picasso?'

Picasso. 'I'll draw you a picture.' He does.

Curator. 'Thank you, Pablo Picasso, do please come in.'

Raisa Gorbacheva arrives at the door.

Curator. 'Please can I see your invitation?'

Raisa. 'I'm sorry, I forgot it.'

Curator. 'You can't come in without an invitation.'

Raisa. 'I left it at home. I'm Raisa Gorbacheva.'

Curator. 'How do I know you're Raisa Gorbacheva?'

Raisa. 'I am, I've just told you.'

Curator. 'Pablo Picasso forgot his invitation, and when I asked him to prove that he was Pablo Picasso he drew me a picture.'

Raisa. 'Pablo Picasso? Who's Pablo Picasso?'

Curator. 'Thank you, Raisa Maximova, do please come in.'

It was cold outside so we travelled steerage back to Yalta. While some of his colleagues dozed a tall, gentle, English-looking actor described his baby daughter. (He doesn't look old enough to be married.) He and his second wife (*What?*) had spent a holiday in

Brittany. He told me that in Russia a person of mixed race is called *Vinaigrette.*

After the exchange of addresses we parted lightly. They had embraced me with the generosity of our profession. Mother Russia had been in a cherishing mood. The sea air sent me into deep early sleep, from which I was woken before midnight by urgent banging on the door.

'Carolina! Carolina!'

'*Ha xyǔ!*'[12] I thought and went back to sleep.

8 April – Monday

Prompt at nine thirty Juvenaly, Igor and Elya were standing at my door.

'We came to find you last night but there was no answer. Did you know that Oleg Yefremov was playing at the theatre?'

'How would I know that?'

'There will be a trip to Gurzuf today, we must be at the Chekhov Museum quickly. They will leave at eleven.'

We set off up the hill in a straggling crocodile. After about half a mile Juvenaly, who was leading, turned round and said,

'The trip to Gurzuf may leave at two o'clock.'

When we reached the museum we discovered that indeed that was to be so. We had three and a half hours to wait. I felt violence rising in me.

'Thank you, Juvenaly.'

Elya led me to the trickling water and green benches. Her releasing laugh eased my passage back to humour. We found ourselves at the coffee shop on the front. Returning for the two o'clock departure we dallied in the girls' room. We walked cheerfully up the steps to see an overcrowded minibus driving away. This was too much for Juvenaly who retired to his hotel. Elya and Igor haggled a price with a free-market taxi driver. Exorbitance and mistrust led us to a state taxi driver. He charged exactly the same price for the fifteen-minute journey as the bandit, but we wouldn't be mugged. We decided not to visit the great Botanical Garden on the way.

---

[12] 'Fuck off!'

Olga Knipper, leading actress with the Moscow Art Theatre, married Anton Chekhov in 1901. She did not get on with her sister-in-law, so her husband bought a three-roomed cottage on the beach at Gurzuf, to which the actress could escape when his family became more than she could bear.

Gurzuf was and remains an artists' colony. Korovin, a contemporary of the writer, lived in a house which is now a co-operative holiday home for painters. It was Chaliapin's favourite seaside place.

The taxi dropped us in a small square. We walked past balconied higgledy-piggledy dwellings, down a lane ablush with cherry blossom, to a cluster of tiny cottages of which only Chekhov's had access to the hundred-foot stony mini-bay that he also acquired. The sea pounds noisily against four or five rocks which welcome being climbed up and sat on.

'This is the room where Chekhov wrote *Three Sisters*,' declared the curator confidently. The bare little building is awaiting formal association with the Moscow Art Theatre Museum whose representative is none other than my friend Henrietta, due to arrive in Yalta later in the day.

There was scarcely room for the busload of experts to turn around on the plot of ground in which grew cypress and palm. Elya and I were somehow accommodated in the minibus for the ride home. Igor was left to find his own way.

A knock at my door revealed Henrietta. We laughed and laughed and laughed and laughed and laughed. Then we had tea.

I met Henrietta on my third voyage to Russia. Her massive command of English coupled with a mixture of sunny reliability and imagination make her a treat to look forward to like a summer holiday. When she came to England people queued to have her as a guest. Playwright John Mortimer, QC, who followed my plea to visit her when he went to Moscow, said she was easily his favourite Russian. Her husband, Gennady, is a film director, whose warm dark eyes beam out of a shy, gracious smiling person. It is not usual to find a Russian husband who so willingly cooks Bush's Legs for a tired wife. One day I will know enough words to speak more freely with him.

Henrietta was feeling humiliated that her bus from Sevastopol, not a trolleybus, had arrived too late for the Gurzuf outing which was her only official justification for being here.

At the theatre we watched an evening of dramatised short stories given by some of the most distinguished members of the Moscow Art Theatre Company. Oleg Yefremov charismatically held the audience on seat edge not to miss a word of his delivery. At the end of the performance he accepted on behalf of the company an oil painting of a local sea view.

'We will have to find a place for that in the museum,' muttered Henrietta.

Oleg greeted me with familiar warmth at the stage door. Extraordinary to think I've known him for almost ten years. He flicked his middle finger under his jaw. This makes a hollow sound which means, 'Let's have a drink.' I climbed into his royal limo. We can't have travelled fifty yards. Henrietta had found colleagues; the actors, staff, managers and the Yalta reception committee eased into seats in the restaurant where cucumber, salami, tomato, hard-boiled egg in plenty were placed in front of us. I asked if I might drink champagne instead of vodka which annihilates me. There is always mineral water to protect a weak head.

Oleg made a speech celebrating Yalta. His gift is to be at once imposing and accessible. Whomever he is with feels that he chose them, specially, for that moment. His leading lady congratulated him that this was only the second performance he had given in his role. Later he drew attention to my time in Taganrog.

'Carolina does not despise our provinces, nor should we.'

With Henrietta's help I told of my first meeting with him in London. I hoped that they, whom I have watched so often in Moscow and whom I feel I know, would wish me courage for my performance on Wednesday. Oleg told me that he would be there to watch. His employees hover devotedly; to be at hand, to protect him if necessary.

I was dropped at my hotel. Tomorrow my actor buddies will arrive, after a day and a night in the train.

9 April – Tuesday

Henrietta's professional duty called on her to make curator-contact.

On the terrace of the museum, waiting to be raised onto a plinth, was a larger-than-life composition statue of Chekhov wearing a hat. It was painted gold. I'd noticed it stored in sections in an office passage while Elya and I were titivating instead of catching the bus to Gurzuf. It was being put in place by two workmen of such dazzling male gracefulness that I wanted to photograph them. They took a break for a smoke on a sunny bench. I stepped forward. Henrietta showed momentary frailty by begging me not to go in tight for a close-up.

Juvenaly appeared, suffering symptoms. He told me the television crew wants to interview us separately in Chekhov's house. I persuaded him to allow me time to change out of my shorts and prepare some photo-allure. I begin to weary of the two-mile dusty trek twice a day.

The interview took place in the dining room. I was relieved to be able to offer my good impressions of Juvenaly's introductory talk about the play and my role. Our troubles were irrelevant. What was important was to make as large an audience as possible want to be at our performance tomorrow night. Interviewers are generally happy to hear rapture about their country, town, people, theatre, author. No problem with that. As I was answering a question I saw Juvenaly's head peering over someone's shoulder.

The cameras and microphones were next set up facing the front door, around which a crowd of about a hundred had semi-circled. A priest was coming to give a blessing for the seventieth anniversary of the opening of Chekhov's house as a museum. Henrietta remembers coming in her youth to the house. The students were greeted by an old lady who walked down the stairs in a long dress. She was Chekhov's sister, Maria, the first curator of the museum.

A disabled boy, twelve or fourteen, an elf, was exploring the crowd; staring up into my face for minutes, then into someone else's. He didn't speak. He was given holy passage.

A young, black-bearded priest strode into the house and reappeared wearing resplendent red Easter vestments. He carried a crucifix and three tasselled candles of different colours. These were lit and patiently re-lit, in defiance of a gusty wind, by an old man with a fairy-tale beard, carrying the censer. He was busy with his matches and refilling the censer with incense. A man, wearing jeans under a mac, carried a large missal from which the priest read. On the steps waited what *couldn't* be a champagne bucket with a bottle leaning in it.

An informal mixed choir stood beside the steps, wearing hats and headscarves. When the cheerful priest finished his opening speech before the service, they burst into such happy unaccompanied harmonies that I knew we really were here to celebrate. For nearly an hour he and they supported each other with word and music. Lorries rattled past. The gathering crossed themselves and joined in the responses. When the service of thanksgiving ended, the joyful celebrant walked forward, calling, 'Christ is risen!', moving around the congregation, who echoed, 'Verily has arisen!'

The champagne bucket was full of holy water. He flicked it, with a long brush, generously and a little mischievously at our faces as he passed. I found him the very best example of a confident, faithful believer. The elf, carrying a lighted candle, had place of honour in the procession that followed him back into the house to disrobe.

Henrietta, leaving tomorrow, must make a lonely early morning hike to Gurzuf. She tactfully understood that I needed to be alone to concentrate on the performance in the evening.

'Till Moscow!'

I looked in at the theatre in case any of the newly arrived Taganrog actors were going to be watching the last Moscow Art performance. Fedorovsky and Lena/Ranevskaya were the first I saw. Then more, and more. Family. I presented them with copies of colour photographs I had taken in Taganrog.

Zhenia had talked her way into the trip. She was exactly the person to help me apportion the clothes. We agreed about the suitability of what for whom. She's a detective, I'm an actress, we should be good at reading people. I explained to Zhenia that I, and many people I know, buy things in second-hand shops. Some have grand cast-offs. The garments I had picked for my friends were mostly unworn, but I wondered whether there was an unpatronising formula.

'Of course the *комиссионный*[13] shops are all right, we all use them, too.'

10 April – Wednesday

We were called to rehearse at eleven. Zhenia came with her muscles to help me carry the bags to the theatre. The actresses, props, wardrobe and wigs were squeezed companionably into one sunny dressing room.

The hour during which they unpacked their presents and tried them for colour, size and approval from each other, was rewarding. Thirteen times I had watched Lena/Ranevskaya wrapping her toes in cotton before squeezing them into agonisingly pointed patent shoes. I was on tenterhooks. Rounded suede pumps.

'Do they fit?'
'Oh, they're perfect!'
'Really?'
'Wonderful!'
'Not too small?'
'No, no. Marvellous!'
'Are you sure?'
'Well, maybe just a little.'
The others crowded round to look.
'They will be all right.'
'Wear them for a while.'

The television cameras were in place. We played the second act for them. I had misunderstood, having dressed in my black opening costume for a run of the play. The TV crew left. No more rehearsal. What about ACTS III and IV?

The company was called into the stalls. Juvenaly gave his talk. It is a very important performance. All the critics will be there. We must relax. And be at ease. And try very hard. We must arrive an

---

[13] Second-hand.

hour before the performance. We mustn't eat anything after seven o'clock. The performance begins at eight. We mustn't have anything to drink. We can drink after the performance. We may drink coffee, but mustn't have anything at all after seven. These are professional actors he's talking to. *They accept it.* I can't look at him while it's going on. I keep my mouth shut.

'Carolina, Carolina, Oleg Nikolayevich Yefremov is waiting outside to talk to you.'

I put on a dressing gown and scuttled out with my hair in pins. J O K E!!

Verushka arrived and needed only one quick rehearsal of her entrance. She sat calmly beside my dressing table for the entire evening. The television crew were back, wanting to talk with me just before the start of the play. Absolutely not. How about the interval? OK. By then the most difficult bit is over.

Sasha/Pishchik came running in, ecstatic – that the shirt I had brought him fitted so well. The young crewman for whom I had brought a cassette of my favourites, Salif Keita and The Penguin Cafe Orchestra, was delighted that I had in fact chosen them instead of Prince, for whom he had asked.

The lack of substantial rehearsal had reached everyone. The actors were infectiously jumpy. The light bulbs over the dressing table were not working. We had been warned that the acoustics were rather poor.

'Loud and fast,' ordered Pasha/Yepikhodov. The actors' password.

The company members chose this time to give me serious mementoes of Easter. A crucifix, a statue, an icon; offered from the soul.

Despite being asked to wait until the interval, the cameraman pressed around us with his lens until we left the dressing room to go on stage.

The audience felt a little stiff to start with but the laughs came in the customary places. The performance was as when there has not been proper preparation. An unusual thing happened in the third act. I had performed Charlotta's card tricks and ventriloquism. We had reached 'Guter Mensch aber schlechter Musikant!'[14]

I was about to launch into the line when I thought to myself, I shouldn't be talking German I'm in a play by Chekhov. I managed instant translation into Russian. As I reached the end of the line I realised my mistake. From their eyes I could tell that my colleagues were as surprised and amused as I was. Incorrectness paled beside the fact that I had improvised in Russian.

At the curtain call Gennady, the humorous curator of the Chekhov Museum, and leader of the trip to Gurzuf, presented me with an oil painting, an autumn view of that village, in memory of our outing. It is imbued with southern light. It lives beside the English Channel.

What drives me to extreme feelings of outrage is lack of information, lack of consultation, lack of choice. For want of all of these, I guessed there would be a reception similar to the one I enjoyed with Oleg and his company. To this end I had put on my most extravagant party frock.

'Come quickly, they are all waiting!' Kostya/Lopakhin #II had been sent to fetch the actresses. He led us to a foyer at the front of house. The banquettes round the walls were filled with unsmiling men and women, including Juvenaly. No one moved as we appeared. No one spoke. Not a glass of water, not a slice of bread in sight. This is not a party. We were not introduced. We were stared at. This is not going to be jolly. We sat down. A young man began to speak. I switched on my tape recorder.

This was a critics' forum. We listened to them telling each other what they thought of our work until a nightwatchman began to flick the lights on and off. We were not addressed. We were talked about. There was no invitation to reply. Our director, also being treated as an object, was mute. I longed for him to jump to his feet and challenge things he didn't like. Maybe he liked it all. The actors were safely on back burner. I joined them, enthusiastically, for the first time. Am I in such a foreign country? Is it a society which is proud of, but behaves with contempt, towards its creative artists, who in turn sometimes behave contemptuously to each

---

[14] 'Good man, but bad musician!' (German.)

other? Is this what they are used to? Do they like it? Have they a choice? Who can I ask?

Fedorovsky approached me about the delicate matter of my fee for the performance I had just given. It was such a pleasure to see him again I laughed out loud. Ah, this is what makes me uncomfortable with Juvenaly. We do not communicate with humour. Is he going to offer me less than the hundred roubles Juvenaly promised? We set up a bazaar, it was delightful, Eastern. Funny. Would I accept five hundred roubles? Of course. Could I sign this paper as unfortunately he must charge me a small figure for tax purposes.

'You owe me seven roubles (five pence).'

I gave him eight and a big hug.

An affectionate cluster outside the theatre. Goodbye Taganrog actors for another ten days. Tender, capable hands helped me carry my bags to the hotel.

11 April – Thursday

Elya, Igor, Juvenaly and Zhenia were on the bus to Simferopol.

We got to the station two hours before the train was due to leave.

The waiting place is not a room, it is an echoing domed assembly hall, with stained glass windows and cinema rows of about two hundred seats facing from each end towards the middle. Having slid into a chair, you have a clear view of how the other half waits. It seems to be a place where people consolidate their relationships. Couples who are newly-wed or have been married for fifty years and still pleased about it. Lovey-dovey heads on shoulders, cooing. Absolute sweetness. The seats lean gently backwards. This is a real resting place. The babushkas sit with their hands crossed, as grannies do all over the world, in their headscarves, their woolly caps, booties and elastic bandages on their legs. Unusual faces of different races. They have the beauty of rarity for a foreigner. I feasted my eyes. Occasionally a single baby's cries multiplied to a chorus around the vaulted ceiling. Two hundred of us were eating ice creams. I dozed off.

Only when Zhenia said goodbye and remained on the platform did I realise that I was sharing a four-berth cabin with Juvenaly and Igor as well as Elya. Urgent adjustment of expectation. As usual it is lack of information not mixed-sex sardines that irritates me. When I discovered that the men plan to go on the top bunks and we women underneath, I said immediately and fiercely that I want to be on top. There is at least the possibility of being out of sight upstairs.

'Oh no, the men always go on the top and the women go underneath.'

Elya said she wanted to be on the top too, so we won that.

Privacy. Train radio. Chopin waltz on the piano. Verdi, *Trovatore*. I'm on the train, now, from Simferopol to Moscow, I'm leaving Crimea. What a thing! So much has happened. There've been good, bad and things that just shut me up.

'Carolina, *чай?*'

'*Без сахара!*'[15]

Elya laughs.

From My Tape Recorder...

We've had a picnic from a jar of tomatoes pickled in garlic-spiced brine; juicy, tasty fruit; some bread I brought from the hotel, then biscuits and tea. We went along the carriage to fill the thermos from the boiler. The woman was lighting newspaper, pushing it under a great urn. Federovsky asked me, while we were bazaaring in the theatre, 'What do you think you've come to when you're here?' My answer is, 'I think I've come to a country that's having a nervous breakdown.'

The trouble is, I'm a junkie for all this. When I get back to England I shall be relieved and exhausted and probably cry a lot; but I shall want a fix almost at once. A nervous breakdown in the sense that there is no norm; somebody says something, they then say the opposite, with as much candour and commitment as they said the first, and you can see that both are true, and neither is true, so everything is improvised. It's revolution and evolution, and nobody's in control of anything, it seems. I feel I'm part of an historical... I wish I'd been alive in Chekhov's time to see if it felt like this then.

---

[15] 'Without sugar!'

12 April – Friday

The train has stopped at Tsernye. I was just too late to photograph the last stop, Mtsinsk. I'm looking at a farmyard; white chickens, cockerels flapping their wings, an old woman shooing a cat.

Birds are making their nests in bare trees – the black and beige magpies; every two feet there's another up in the branches, you can watch big twigs being arranged.

The railway workers wearing their orange jackets so they can be seen in the dark, the women in headscarves, brilliant sunshine.

Everybody's still sleeping. We'd turned the light out at about nine thirty. This morning the attendant came by with tea at a quarter past nine, shouting and knocking on the doors.

Somebody told me Kalantarov declared that I treat him like a porter – he has often conscientiously carried my heavy bags. I would never treat a porter the way I treat him – no porter could offend me the way he does. But I want it to continue so that I can learn some more.

I'm walking up and down the corridor to loosen the limbs; there's a bar at the right height, I'm alone swinging my legs. When you go to – when I go to the Ж on the train – the first thing I do is roll up my trouser legs.

It seems to me that life consists of doing what you do from one moment to the next. That's what's happening the world over. People are just doing what they do. If you look out of a train window, people are walking along on their way to something, or walking back from something, or carrying a wheel, or watching us doing what we're doing, which is watching them.

We've just had a typical flare-up. Juvenaly, a short while ago, was asleep, breathing heavily, I was dozing. Suddenly the music is turned on loud, he's shouting (in English), 'Stand up! Stand up!' I can see that we're not near a station; he's trying to marshal us so that we are all standing on our feet at the door of the carriage. I lie back. He changes his clothes and shouts again.

'What's the problem? I'm ready.'

I dismiss him. He looks at Elya, saying, 'Tell Carolina that it's time. We're going to come into the station now.'

'I'm absolutely *ready!*' I bark. 'Hooligan! '(Their word; I'm such a bitch!)

'I'm *sorry!*' he subsides.

'It looks as if the train is going to be half an hour late,' Ely soothes, helpfully.

I suddenly have an insight; perhaps common sense is absent. It becomes a matter of something happening by the book. Perhaps that's the reason why we got to the station two hours early for the train. I overheard a discussion going on in the lower bunks about getting my luggage from the train to the flat. There was a bit of groaning. I leaned over.

'Will Ksenia come to meet you? Does she have a car?' they asked.

'No. I will pay for a porter and I will pay for a taxi.'

It was with a mixture of submission and heroism that the men took something in each hand and something more on their backs. Elya and I were not in the same league as the admirable men.

Sasha and Ksenia welcomed and fed me; then dressed in smart clothes, went to visit their relations. This is the custom for each day of the week following Easter. Ksenia had painted hard-boiled eggs with bold traditional designs. She carefully selected from a basket exactly the right egg for Sasha's grandfather.

I was alone with the floorboards and fridge. Alarming to discover how many of my belongings, heavy books and presents from Taganrog are stacked in the flat for carriage to England. Well, they must wait their turn, even if it takes years. Some telephone calls indicate there are promising theatre visits in store. I dropped peacefully into bed.

Another phase of my adventure, the Crimean eye-opener has been passed through. I saw ample evidence of Chekhov having lived in that still-favoured glamorous corner of land, but his presence? I don't know.

13 April – Saturday

No aeroplanes, no sound of traffic. What a delightful way to wake in a capital. With no immediate problems to distract me I can allow myself to integrate with my surroundings. Having sightseen avidly during early visits I am now free simply to live here. But there is one more attraction to look at; Chaliapin's House-Museum.

It is spring. Amanda and I set off. All of central Moscow seems to be within walking distance. On one long solitary trek before the Hermitage performance I took in two or three different regions. A similar two-hour outing in London would scarcely have allowed me to encircle the borough I live in. Looking at the map afterwards, I knew I had a permanent bird's-eye view of the districts I had passed through and need never get lost. I have an instinct which returns me to the Kremlin from no matter which direction. I really must visit a seer who specialises in past lives.

Stylish Moscow. Civilised Moscow. Made for walking. Reassuring architecture calling out from the pages of *War and Peace*. Calming, tree-enhanced scenery. Please walk some more, you will find Turgenev's house; this is where Pushkin was married. There is time for leisure and pleasure. Plenty of benches to sit on. Mothers with sledge-happy children, old men exercising their dogs, earflaps tied high on their fur hats, watching the ever-raised hindleg. A couple, their bottoms on the curved back of the bench, their feet on the seat, protecting themselves from the frozen ground. Dogs and smokers everywhere. This is a humane tolerant place, built for the delight of her citizens. I feel gratitude at being given the chance to assimilate pre-Revolutionary Moscow on foot instead of through a careering car window; to shed conditioning which tempts the unknowing Western mind to patronising feelings of block pity for a nation of victims. I have not yet visited Gorky Park.

The town is not crowded. Town is a clear clean word. Above board. City includes drains and crime. People go away. There is considerable dacha life, which, of course, can mean collective dacha. The writers' dacha at Peredelkino could house at least a *разговор*[16] of literati. These dacha people are, I suppose, privileged *intelligentsia*. I first saw the invention of this word ascribed to the nineteenth-century critic Vissarion Belinsky. I don't like it. It smacks of self-proclaimed superiority of understanding, judgment and, worse, separation of head from heart. It seems to be a boast.

---

16 'Conversation.'

It is commonly used in the circles within which I move in Moscow, and I have more than once believed myself in the company of intellectual snobs. They laugh when I tease them about it. It was they, however, who took the full force of Soviet disapproval, so it is not necessary for me to add my jaundiced view, except that it brings me back again to the painful tension between those who do, and those who expound. I have devised a shocking punishment for some sports commentators, by the way.

Fyodor Chaliapin. The great singer's name has been in my consciousness since childhood. On early visits to Moscow I kept asking whether there was a *house-museum* of his. Yes, but it was under *ремонт*.[17] He emigrated to the West during the nineteen twenties, from which his body was returned, honoured, some sixty years later. I absorbed details of his surging life when I was able to offer English theatrical colloquialisms to Victor Borovsky while he was writing his definitive biography of the genius.

The house used to stand on a wide leafy boulevard which has given way to the dusty Garden Ring Road, conduit of mud-spattered lorries and occasional convoys of armoured vehicles. Further along the Ring Road Chekhov's small pink house asserts its rights between sturdy modern blocks. It is a landmark, similar to Christopher Wren's diminutive house seen from a Thames steamer, opposite St Paul's Cathedral.

Apparently shut, the Chaliapin house responded to tenacious prowling, and a small side door admitted us to an entrance hall where we were welcomed by three enthusiastic attendants eager to show off their treasure. I usually try to avoid being accompanied around museums by possessive curators.

'This is a beautiful room, table, picture.'

But without a guide book it is foolish to deprive myself of intriguing detail and any opportunity to practise colloquial vocabulary should be seized, so in Russia I welcome the knowledge that is shared in an unfailing response to an *artiste* from London.

The house has been dazzlingly restored and decorated. Unlike the Chekhov home at Yalta this seems to be filled by a huge generous vivacious personality. I cannot imagine where the money

---

[17] 'Repair' or 'renovation'.

came from to pay for the luxurious reproduction wallpapers and silken hangings; sheet upon sheet of gold leaf. Though extremely rich, the impression is not pompous; it is a cheerful, very well-off family house.

The rooms lead one into another. First, a feminine sitting-room filled with a hotch-potch of memorabilia. Delicately displayed on the sofa are a minute dress and pair of pumps belonging to his first wife, a ballerina, and the favourite doll of one of his daughters. He had five children. In a vibrant green damask-walled room, the one most favoured by his intimates for coffee, tea and talk, there is an HMV gramophone and horn. Pictures by his friend Korovin hang on walls throughout the house; these include one of Gurzuf, immediately recognisable to me, also an astonishing portrait of Chaliapin painted on a single canvas by Korovin and Serov together. It glows with fun.

The white and gold ballroom holds the grand piano where Rachmaninov sat when they rehearsed together. We were invited to rest on small gilt seats to listen to some of the singer's recordings. Rich, golden, free. His popularity was partly due to the fact that he was also a great actor. He made detailed study of his roles in a way that was previously unknown in opera. He was an inspiration to Stanislavsky in his work with the Moscow Art actors, teaching them how to build a characterisation. His small study, painted dark Wedgwood blue, has walls crammed with photographs; of his first teacher, of the painter Repin (the image of Claude Rains), of Rimsky-Korsakov, of Stasov the respected critic. An unusual sketch of Tolstoy, ancient with sunken cheeks. A statue of Pushkin on the desk. A joke photograph of Moskvin seated opposite Chaliapin at a table, both huge, napkins tied round their necks, stuffing food into their mouths as if they had not eaten for a month. The names cross-refer to Chekhov's life, as well as to the Moscow Art Theatre and, with those of shared artist friends, it helps to build up a picture of a closely knit group of well-known creative people, similar to the Bloomsburys, perhaps. I would guess rather jollier and less acerbic.

A replica dressing room has been staged, containing wardrobes, trunks, hatboxes, make-up, a vivid red dressing gown thrown over the back of a chair. Next door, Chaliapin's weighty costumes for *Boris Godunov* and *Ivan the Terrible*, as well as one designed by Roerich, hang in glass cases. Sketches, some in charcoal, of his father, in life and in role, made by an exceedingly talented son. These demand attention, leaning on an easel or framed on the wall. I had admired the singer's gift for sculpting in the Theatre Museum. Genius is not only about having exceptional gifts, it is about having extra voltage with which to present them.

Our second guide shared her anecdotes with as much passion as if she had known him personally. She showed us the blue billiard table at which he must win or become enraged. If his daughter beat him he stormed out of the room. She had to telephone Rachmaninov or Korovin to beg them to hurry round and play a more tactful game.

Hugely famous, he lived in this house with his second wife for twelve years. Our tour ended on the balcony terrace at the back of the building. It looks onto a group of elm trees which Chaliapin planted. Our guide was unable to show us a well-known photograph of him bidding them farewell before he departed his home for the West. We learned that when the Museum was opened by his daughter recently she described how they used to pick mushrooms and berries on their land which, in those days, reached down to the river.

It was coincidentally during this visit to Moscow that I learned that the first live opera I ever heard, *Rigoletto* at Sadler's Wells, was almost certainly conducted by Warwick Braithwaite, the father of Sir Rodric Braithwaite, the present British Ambassador who, with his wife Jill, invite me to meals at the Embassy at the moments when I most need moral support. Besides saving me, they have earned a rare reputation amongst the British community during their term, known to be passionately interested in and knowledgeable about the country as well as unsentimentally caring about the future of the ex-Union.

14 April – Sunday

One advantage of knowing people at the Moscow Art Theatre is that I can get a seat for any performance and sometimes, as today, can watch a rehearsal of a forthcoming production. In Yalta Oleg Yefremov had talked about a production that he is engaged on. The play is by Alexander Solzhenitsyn. It was forbidden at source. Now, entrusted by the author to Oleg only. I could see from his face, as he described the situation, that it is a massive, troubling enterprise. A cast of nearly sixty, many of them young. The first time a play by Solzhenitsyn is seen on stage. Inevitably it raises, in times of 'glasnost', issues from which many people are hoping to have a rest. I know only that it is set in a prison camp and that Oleg has been preoccupied with the project for months. I believe I have at last hit upon the reason why we have the idea they rehearse a play for months and years. It's because it's true – with interruptions...

The Moscow Art Theatre has a repertoire of plays and a payroll of actors and actresses, some of whom might be in one or two productions only or, if very elderly, none. Plays are presented for a season, each with a fixed number of performances; rarely on consecutive nights and never, to my knowledge, the same play at matinee and evening on the same day. Evening performances are at seven o'clock, matinees at noon. Sunday is a matinee day. Except when it isn't.

All the plays of Chekhov are produced, but may not be in repertoire during a particular season. I have seen *Seagull* three times in eight years. The same actress, Tatyana Lavrova, has played Arkadina brilliantly each time, ageing not at all. Some of the older parts are also played by the same players as when I first saw the production. Treplev, Nina and Trigorin have changed. The designs by Valery Levantal and the *mise en scène* are as they were.

Many performers, of course, appear in a variety of productions and these are committed for months at a time. If plays are scheduled in which an actor is not appearing they may take other work, in film or television. My understanding is that they continue to be paid their monthly wage which is based on long-term service status rather than on flavour-of-the-month and, therefore, not huge, but comfortable compared with the provinces. A leading actor or actress may be able to afford to run a car, if they can find one that goes. If they know a mechanic who can mend it if it doesn't. Who knows how to get spare parts on the black market. Who will accept my bribe instead of yours to do the work within a fortnight. If there is time to queue for petrol.

Two or three rehearsals are all the players may expect when a play is re-introduced after a gap, or when they take over a role in a long-running production. The stage may not be available to work on because the evening performance is being set-up. Rehearsals of a new play, therefore, lack continuity in the early stages. The growth of a production is fractured and dependent on the availability of performers and director.

MKhAT, with its continuing reputation for great work, undertakes foreign tours every year to countries which can afford it, and brings home much needed hard currency. Lavrova, with *Seagull* in Australia, where there is a large Russian immigrant population, told me that the Russians stayed away, that it was the Australians who wept, cheered and stamped. It is possible to see why a production can take more than a year to come to fruition.

Alyona, with a small part, was called to a run of the Solzhenitsyn play in the morning. We went through the stage door together and down into the auditorium where some of the actors were standing about, others sitting in the stalls, as we all do, with their legs over the seat in front. On stage an actor was practising coming through a door quickly and neatly, another couple rattled through a row scene. Other necessary actors had not turned up. Oleg was away on business. After a bit of a wait the assistant decided to call off the rehearsal. Disgruntled actors who had dragged themselves out of bed to be there lit up their smokes.

'It's because Oleg is not here to keep discipline.'

The play is already being performed in front of audiences, under the heading Première. Critics have not yet been invited to attend. I decided to come in the evening. During the last day or two I had picked up that it is dreadful (someone who had seen it), ditto (someone who hadn't seen it), that I will be bored to death (both). Amanda agreed to take her chance with me.

We were confronted by a wall of cage as we took our seats. Did I imagine that the audience was more subdued than usual?

'There will be no one here without some connection to what we're going to see,' she alerted me.

The cage wall slowly sank out of sight. A useful revolving set showed us the prison reception yard, a boiler room, the commandant's office, a building site. The play is written in many short scenes. Oleg keeps his five dozen young actors racing about like ants, up and down ladders, in and out of fights, with huge stage energy. Early on Alyona and another young actress played two nippy comic scenes before being sent to their deaths at another camp (and getting home before the nine o'clock news).

Was it on purpose that Solzhenitsyn shows us two places of work where no work is being done? In a labour camp, I guess. I was not watching the experience of hard grind which was so telling in Martin Sherman's *Bent*. Ian McKellen and Michael Cashman lugged heavy stones from one side of the stage to the other, then lugged them all the way back again. On the building site I saw no building being done. In the boiler room, too, although some work was going on in the background, generally we were shown periods of rest. Or skive. Mustn't we see slog first in order to respond to the opposite? Any community, school, convent or prison is a microcosm of the world; naturally the corrupt characters smoked throughout, had access to vodka, girls, bread and *salo*. I didn't quite feel the desperation of these prisoners, that they would do absolutely anything to anyone in order to survive.

Oleg uses music to enhance the movement between scenes but the music seemed to let me off the hook. I felt safe in my seat. I missed the *terror* of Irina Ratushinskaya's harrowing autobiographical prison book. I believe that terror includes silence.

15 April – Monday

'Usually I try to protect you but now I must tell you the truth.'

Henrietta had been woken in the night by Azat Rafikov – first time his head has appeared over the battlements – bursting with rage at my refusal to write to the Minister of Culture and the head of the Theatre Workers Union, praising him and his managerial efforts. He told her that I must be at the Theatre Union building on Friday 19 April to go to Vladimir, and that I will travel on the bus. My status has gone down a notch...

Henrietta scarcely mentioned her lividness at being woken up.

It's no use pretending I wasn't upset by it. He's made no contact with me about appearing at Vladimir, hasn't spoken to me since I came back to Russia more than two weeks ago. For the first and only time, my spirit gave out. Anglichanka wept.

'I hate this fucking country! I want to go home!'

Ksenia was enchanted that the System had cracked me at last.

'Please cry some more, it's so beautiful.'

Trying to get it into proportion. What feels intolerable is the non-communication. I know that I can't carry my luggage. I know that I can't go in a taxi by myself – too dangerous. I will just have to sit in the flat and wait for them to come and get me. It will make a good story in ten years, but I don't want to behave unprofessionally. More than once since February I have been encouraged by friends here to tell them to stuff it, and go back to England.

I've turned down expensive work in England because I didn't want to let them down and because *I want to be here*. We'll see.

17 April

The Embassy had been trying to invite me to dinner on Monday but had been ringing the wrong number. Never mind, can I lunch today? You bet. The walk takes me past the Kremlin, downhill after St Basil's, turn right along the river looking at the Embassy on the other side, double back after I've crossed the bridge, now looking at the Kremlin. Brilliant sunshine. Half an hour on Moscow's various road surfaces makes my feet throb.

Watching television correspondents talking their items to the camera against a night background of lit-up Kremlin and glistening water and moving cars, I've often wondered why they race down to the Embassy gates to set up; for what we see is what is seen from the Embassy. The Ambassador put into my head that there could be a piece of back projection of that view in a studio against which the reporters stand. Well, why do they wear overcoats and scarves indoors?

Once again the informality made the party fun. Nora Beloff confirmed my feeling that enthusiasm as a trait is hard to beat. We were given the same warm sweet soufflé with cream as on my previous visit and was I glad. The Ambassadress made an introductory call to an English journalist whom she felt could open a door for me to write an article about my adventure when I get home. I was given a warm hug when I left, as Jill went, without pause to renew herself to greet the newly posted envoy of a small European country. He was making the round of formal calls that were *de rigueur* in my days at the UN thirty-five years ago. As I crept past I could see him standing stiffly with his back to the door, looking out at the unmatched view of the Kremlin. The correctness of the Dixon household is the only other diplomatic experience I have. The Ambassador was called HE (His Excellency), that is now considered a little old-fashioned. 'Ambassador' is favoured, or 'HMA'.

As I entered the flat...

'Carolina, a FAX from your agent in London, you must ring her immediately.'

Usually a call from Russia must be booked at least twenty-four hours ahead. Luck can strike. The quickest I've got through from Moscow to London was in an hour. Not today.

Oleg Tabakov is one of the Moscow Art Theatre's cast-iron comedic assets. I saw him play Oblomov in a film of the Goncharov play during a Russian season at the NFT. I can think of no one with a naughtier demeanour except Benny Hill. Chubby-cheeked and agile, he will look eight years old when he is eighty. He loves his audience and they leap into the palm of his hand as the curtain rises. When he's not performing he is a respected acting teacher. He turns out highly energised talents, whom he presents in the little studio theatre which bears his name.

It was there that I was going to watch my 'Russian son', Vladimir Mashkov, making his debut in *The Government Inspector* by Gogol. The play is called *Revisor* in Russian. This was a first production for the theatre by a new young director. An audience of colleagues and fellow ex-students chattered in a healthy agog way as we wheedled spaces for ourselves on the crowded benches, next to Oleg Antonov who'd given me his play to get read successfully at the Orange Tree Theatre in Richmond. It was an inventive, believable treat from the start. The set was the façade of a house with a tiny terrace and a balustrade for actors to lean against. He cleverly allowed us to see deep into the interior which was extensively furnished. There was a dining table with lighted candles. Some of the time complementary domestic scenes were being played out by characters not engaged in text at the front of the stage. I've never seen such convincing and varied drunk acting by young, or old, performers. Each person had found his/her own outrageous mode and followed it through and through. Bold, gross performances from mother and daughter made me laugh out loud. The Government Inspector made his entrance through the audience and set up camp in an alcove, not arriving on stage for half an hour. I felt enlivened and enchanted. To listen. To laugh. To laugh, perchance... You can't aim a gun if you're laughing, can you?

During the interval, having failed with the telephone at home, I was allowed to send a FAX to my agent suggesting a time to call me. *URGENT* takes on lateral value when it's impossible.

Sitting behind us was big, tall Igor (these men are huge) who had been to my house in London during the visit of the Moscow Art Studio Main Company to the Almeida Theatre with Lyudmila Petrushevskaya's play, *Cinzano*, brilliantly directed by Roman Kozak. It starts with two characters appearing through a door, laughing. They laugh for about five minutes. Without a word. Think about it. It is one of the bravest and most confident pieces of work I have ever seen. So, laughing Igor and, a few minutes later, Arkady, his company manager. The world contracted to a ping-pong ball. It begins to be a different, more responsible experience when you share history with people in their country as well as your own.

Arkady took me home to meet his flu-gripped wife. *Gripp* is the opportune word for that illness. With the acquiescence of a non-Western woman, beautiful Zhenia developed a feast before my eyes. Their daughter was staying out with friends. The flat, high in a modern block not far from the Taganka Theatre, is neat and attractive, not unlike a single person's apartment in New York. Wooden floors always score with me. Many bookshelves, more lamps than usual, an answering machine and a microwave. A second nip of whisky sent me to sleep on their spare bed.

18 April – Thursday

Sight-seeing goals. I yearn for Tolstoy's country estate, Yasnaya Polyana; for Tchaikovsky's Klin, for Abramtsevo, devoted to creative arts. None more than today's Melikhovo, where Chekhov made a home with his family for seven years before the necessary health move to Yalta, and his late marriage. He bought the estate unseen because it was cheap and the right distance from Moscow.

The outing had taken careful planning. Tanya Lavrova volunteered her car and a giant pizza. Igor Yasulovich (Mime-Igor) his driving; Amanda, Sovietsky chicken legs and hard-boiled eggs; I, salads, sweet biscuits and a camera. Tanya brought a friend. Knees were overlapping in the back seat.

Leaving the city takes time. We had the country road to ourselves. Igor stopped to ask directions more than once. A great mime, even his walk on such a mission is comedic. We parked and followed a path through shrubs until we reached the estate. 'Estate' I visualise as a mansion house surrounded by miles of parkland, Chatsworth or Blenheim. Chekhov's estate covers about two square acres. You can see the perimeter fence from any position as well as the brightly coloured neighbouring dwellings.

Two main buildings. The kitchen is a large room housing a tiled stove built into the wall, which must have comforted chilly visitors before they continued to the single-storey painted wooden dacha, where meals were prepared and carried through a covered passageway to the dining room. I would never have guessed that the buildings had been completely renovated from crumbled ruins.

We were the only visitors. Tanya Lavrova, a great star, was a bonus for these curators who painstakingly drew our attention to another of Chekhov's Sakhalin travelling bags; a pair of his spectacles; the last painting by his brother of the poor woman with her hand hanging down. Comfortable, bohemian and decorated sympathetically in warm rose pink, dark green, honey. I thought of Duncan Grant's farmhouse, Charleston, although of course there is no hand painting on walls or furniture. A grand piano crowds the stone-coloured sitting room. The writer's bedroom faces onto the pond which corresponds with the lake in *Seagull*. I wonder how recently double beds were introduced to Russia. I've yet to find one in a house-museum.

Several rooms lead into a long hall down one side of the house. It was called variously the Pushkin Room, the Stained Glass Room, the Library, the Sofa Room, according to the mood, indicating which feature was to be noted that day. Visitors might be taken into it from all directions, each time being told a different name. Although the rooms are not big there is an impression of greater space than I guessed from outside.

In the garden stands the little two-floored summer house where Chekhov wrote *Seagull*. An outer wooden staircase leads up to his writing room. Tanya Lavrova, distinguished present day interpreter of Arkadina, showed no sign of being overwhelmed by her proximity to the cradle of the great role. Tanya is wholly feminine. We had a conversation once about Goneril, King Lear's eldest daughter. I had twice played the part, she was about to. She was bewildered and worried by some aggressive aspects of the character.

'She is a man...'

Chekhov flew a red flag from a pole on the balcony of the hut to signal to the village that he was available to his patients. They arrived sometimes at five o'clock in the morning. The poor were not charged.

A cart is still sheltering in the tumbledown shed, known as the Coach House. People could ride horseback or be carted to the nearby station to catch the train to Moscow. Crocuses are popping through, yew branches have been laid against the pruned rose bushes. A section of the garden was named The South of France. In this were grown exotic vegetables, such as artichokes, never indigenous beetroot or cabbage. The property was lived in with humour and charm. I found it easier to feel him here than at Yalta; like Chaliapin, Anton Pavlovich planted elm trees too close to the house here, as well. They now tower over the building, blocking the light from the pleasant rooms.

We followed a track past the old village school. Chekhov donated money so that more windows could be added. A wooden church built in 1757 could nearly have doubled as a bird-box. The collection of small wrought-iron enclosures for individual family graves are decorated with vivid artificial daffodils and carnations, stuck into the ground. Tinsel caught the light, making the graveyard a glittering rather than a sombre place.

Walking down the centre of the village, we saw painted cottages on either side, each with a plot in which chickens and a brilliant-plumed cockerel free-ranged.

Dogs stood about like children out of school, watching as we sauntered by. One, with short legs like a dachshund, had an Alsatian body. An old bath collected water. A triangular shed had a door to match. A plump woman milk-maiding an overloaded carrier in each hand, approached from miles away. It must have taken her the whole morning to go where she'd gone to get what she got and come back with her shoulder-cracking burden. A supermarket trolley or a pram would have eased her travail.

We repaired to the car shivering from the wind chill. Inside, a royal repast was spread over ten knees. Distribution was a problem, as it always is in Russia. It was funny and made the meal last for ages. It was reinforced, for those who enjoy day-drink, with brandy and whisky consecutively.

The return journey was taken up with a conference about my situation. Tanya and Igor concentrated. Their advice was sensible and professional in a way that I understand and agree with. I should try making myself a representative of England rather than a person on a battlefield. My behaviour should be beyond reproach and on this basis it is safe to go to Vladimir tomorrow and negotiate when I get there. Integrity is the key. What a relief.

We put through a call to my agent successfully. She told me that I am offered the transsexual part in *Rides*, at the BBC. Good. I must return two days earlier to start rehearsing. Tomorrow they will call again to confirm.

The honourable – we've taken a moral stance now – thing to do is to give my employers my information; waiting for the BBC call, the early departure for London, to warn them now that this is why I will not come tomorrow. I hoped to arrange the meeting with Oleg Yefremov, if he has returned, to discuss the possibility of appearing in his *Cherry Orchard* in the foreseeable future.

Henrietta felt that if she made the call it would be safer. All the neurotic detail of the negotiations serve to reveal that we start from a different premise of acceptable behaviour; producing bullying from them, mulish stubbornness from me.

Henrietta returned the information that Azat's office were surprised that no contact had been made. Did I not know that I was to be Queen of the Festival, that I was to open the Festival on Saturday, and that my presence, including giving prizes on the last day, was essential.

There are universal rules of behaviour.

19 April

Kalantarov, formal and polite, rang to say we would leave at four.

20 April

Today I am a tourist holding my handbag tightly. Arkady took me to Ismailovo, a district in south Moscow. There is a large open-air market which has been running at weekends for four or five years. Similar to the Portobello market in London's Notting Hill, but arranged in a curve around a great stadium.

People bring what they want to sell and set up stall. There are rickety tables displaying dregs of kitchen cupboards and wardrobes, many of which items, nevertheless, are picked up and examined curiously. There are grander stalls offering amber and other jewellery; books, I saw a biography of the Beatles next to a sex manual. Wooden icons, the paint flaking nicely to look old. A large selection of Matrioshka dolls which fit inside each other. More entertaining than the traditional, headscarfed, diminishing women is the political sequence. Tiny Lenin inside Stalin inside Khrushchev inside Brezhnev inside Gorbachev. The one I bought for my son gave top billing to Boris Yeltsin, the topical hero. There were those that showed the tsar all the way through. One shocker had Saddam on the outside. Mine cost me about five pounds; in roubles not far off a month's wages for a regular Russian worker, so it was not a particularly comfortable transaction in front of Arkady.

Another friend, whom I had believed to be beyond nationalistic pride, bridled when I described my purchase.

'It is absolutely wrong for them to sell stuff like that. It's unpatriotic. It's all right to do it for us, to make us laugh, but not for foreigners and tourists.'

I tried to comfort this person with descriptions of the much more delicious scurrilous subversiveness of *Spitting Image* and *Private Eye*. To no avail.

In Arkady's company a relaxed day was assured. He and his company of actors with their author Petrushevskaya had dined at my house, so he's an old friend. He has excellent colloquial English, has travelled widely in Europe and America. He is a critic and director as well as administrator. Being fellow professionals gives good base for laughter. We noticed, separately, and remarked to each other that in certain company in Moscow there was delicate but unmistakable hostility towards him.

'It's because I'm a Jew.'

My stomach clunked.

In two hours we glanced at most of the wares. For Charlotte I bought two tiny malachite rings of original design at fifty pence each. As we left I stopped to enjoy an energetic Dixieland band who were filling the air with tune. These days, different parts of the world are assimilating each other's cultures, wanting to taste all the possibilities. When we've all tried everything, shall we go back to how we were, or what?

To enter the Central Market must be quite a torment for a Muscovite. It bursts with goods sold by southern suppliers at prices only diplomats or people with access to hard currency can manage. Mushrooms at forty roubles a kilo made Arkady blanch with rage; he's been going there all his life. I am learning that to throw in half a dozen dollars, which would be enough to feed twenty, is not appropriate. Strongly scented blue hyacinths, hot fresh bread unloaded from a hatchback car, hardly touching the counter before it is pressed down the sides of waiting carrier bags. Beautiful to look at but desperate in undertone, the Central Market.

We were contributing to a meal given by two of Arkady's closest friends; a comedian and an actress, with a daughter the best friend of Arkady and Zhenia's little girl. The apartment is unlike anything I've yet seen in Moscow. Open plan, white, luxurious, bare. Large plants in pots on the floor. All the kitchen gadgets are ultra-modern. A recently acquired toy is a meter to record the level of nuclear pollution in the surrounding environment. The machine squeaks the news that every breath we are taking is hopelessly unsafe. Buying in the Market, too. Who knows in which dangerous areas these succulent fruit and vegetables are grown.

Our hostess, who had previously been married to Oleg Antonov, and who had already given a matinee performance at the Children's Theatre, prepared a banquet – I've never been offered less than a banquet. I'd earlier promised not to let Arkady down by refusing vodka. Two tiny slugs meant that I must ring Misha Roshchin to say that I would not succeed in visiting him today.

'I am sorry, Misha, I'm *пьяна*.'[18]

'It doesn't matter, darling Carolina, come tomorrow.'

21 April – Tomorrow

Kropotkinskaya Metro station opens onto a region of Moscow, Old Arbat, which feels upper crust and elegant. Belgravia. Space between the buildings. Misha lives with Irina and his youngest son in a sturdy block of flats, in secluded *Chisty pereulok* – Clean Lane. Quiet. I have visited them by day and by night. Today is mainly varieties of fish, accompanied by two or three vegetable and crispy salads. These apartments were built before the Revolution. Wooden floors smell nice as well as feeling good. Misha's study is dominated by an imposing ministerial desk, similar to Chekhov's at Yalta; it, also, is piled high with books, magazines, objects, writer's paraphernalia. The desk is set at right angles to the large bay window; behind him, bookshelves to the ceiling; opposite, framed posters, photographs; of Pasternak, of himself with Oleg Yefremov as dashing young tearaways. I switched on my recording

---

[18] 'Drunk.'

machine to cover the guided tour we made of the walls. He is amused and amusing. He told a joke which I just understood. Many Russian stories are about people who are *unbelievably stupid.*

I explained the enthusiasm English actresses feel for the role of Charlotta; how much Chekhov has presented to us in the forty-six lines.

'Ah, I can't learn to do what Chekhov did which is to write sparingly. I have yet to learn to write few words to say what I want to say.'

He gave me a rare, worn postcard colour reproduction of Chekhov's favourite portrait of himself.

The inquisitive marmalade cat wanted to drink from the vase which held the blue irises I had been lucky to find at the Metro station. CRASH.

Later in the afternoon I failed to make an important delivery of heavy gifts, taking a wrong turning, I ended up at the TASS Agency building. I telephoned for instructions.

'It's Carolina. I made a mistake. I'm at TASS.'

'*Час?*[19] It is 5.30.'

'No, Tass. T – T – . Tur-r-r-rgenev.'

'TurGEnev? What about him?'

'Sorry, I'm not coming. I'll ring you tomorrow.'

At the Moscow Art Theatre, were waiting Tanya, Amanda and Oleg Antonov. We agreed to meet again tomorrow to see Oleg playing Lopakhin in a much-heralded production of *Cherry Orchard* which, being a co-operative project, only gets an occasional airing.

Into MKhAT went Amanda and I; we watched a smash-hit play by popular, prolific Petrushevskaya. She puts her finger on the sore spots of modern Russian experience.

The audience, facing each other across the adaptable studio, rocked and howled. I understood more than I expected and felt that I would enjoy to die laughing.

---

[19] 'The time?'

22 April

Talking English. Tall, grey-haired, friendly Peter Pringle of *The Independent* met me at Taganka Metro. He led me to a dining club used extensively by foreign journalists. Grand, cool interior decor. Poly-national management with strong Yugoslavian involvement. There was nothing to tell me that I was not in London or New York. We were joined first by Robert Haupt of the *Sydney Morning Herald*. We ordered trout in English.

Things went badly early on. I must have been feeling particularly sensitive. Peter told me that he had left our Hermitage performance at the interval because he found himself sitting behind a television camera. Robert had been in Moscow for five months, Peter for three. I felt my hackles rising at some of their generalizations. No different from any I've been making for ten years. I was commenting how odd it had been to have little information in Taganrog about the Gulf War; lucky to be spared the horror of battle details.

'It wasn't a proper war,' said both men cheerfully.

'You'd have thought it a proper war if your son, husband, father, mother, uncle, daughter had been killed in it!'

I could feel my hand shaking under the table.

'We have upset you, haven't we?' said Peter, kindly. His elegant wife, Eleanor, who represents *The Washington Post*, arrived for coffee. I decided to stop being critical and enjoy myself.

Robert offered me a ride uptown in his official car. The correspondents have chauffeur/minders. I saw that in many ways I get easier access to ordinary life than they do.

'Would you like to use my earphone?' offered Robert. There it sat on its executive plinth, inviting. I dialled home. No answer. Instant connection to my agent.

'I'm in a car stuck in a traffic jam in the rush hour outside the Kremlin it's Lenin's birthday it's pouring with rain have you got anything to tell me?'

Satisfying reverberations. Yes, there was a choice of flights on the 28th. I chose British Airways at teatime. Robert's indulgent laughter, as I dramatised over the radio waves, kept me at it longer than the business required. Revealing himself a true Russinfatuate, like me, Robert persuaded me to accompany him further, wanting me to share his enthusiasm for the *Sydney Morning Herald's* bureau/home. He showed me a secret door which had been used for silent exit by a former politically threatened tenant. We stood on his balcony and sighed tenderly at the sight of a playground below. He's got the illness, all right.

Mime-Igor and I had talked of the necessity of acting together. How could we bring it about? He met me at the Metro station. Sniffing the air, I declared that it will snow later.

As Natasha placed dish after dish in front of us we tickled some of the possibilities. Igor had ideas about one or two Chekhov short stories which he has already adapted and performed pantomimically. Language difficulties would be obviated.

Alyosha, their son, also a trained actor and mime, said he would drive me home.

The snow was already a foot deep. My Russian nose had not let me down. The family car wouldn't start so we used the excellent method of asking any motorist to be a taxi at the going rate.

23 April. Shakespeare's birthday.

Lunch in Moscow Art Theatre canteen with Henrietta. There we found Arkady, Roman Kozak and Laughing Igor. Also Isolde, the new, gracious personal assistant to Oleg Yefremov. She screens visitors and telephone calls and cares for him without fuss like a mother. The more robust administrative details of his life are dealt with by Irina, whose office is a meeting place, a negotiating chamber.

Amanda whisked me to a monthly meeting of Chekhov enthusiasts, hosted by interested diplomatic wives in turn. Today it was the Irish Ambassadress, who is Polish. We were given coffee and cake before settling on comfortable sofas for a couple of hours. Sleepy from my late night with Igor and Natasha, I had difficulty staying alert. I asked the visiting expert what made Chekhov decide to marry Olga Knipper when he was surely already aware of the severity of his illness and had previously philandered freely without feeling the need to leave his mother and sister who, in any case, stayed on in the marital home. Did Knipper want to be Mrs

Chekhov so much that he couldn't refuse her? The answer is on
tape. One day, someone will translate it. The widow of Trifonov
dropped Amanda and me at Pushkin's statue, 'Hello!,' in time to
be picked up by reliable Tanya Lavrova with her car.

The Satyricon Theatre is a large unatmospheric modern
auditorium some distance from the centre of Moscow. Tanya,
leaning forward to see through the snow, doggedly followed her
instinct and parked by the stage door. There was time for fish on
a slice of bread and a chocolate milkshake before we found our
seats. The more productions I see of a play I am familiar with, the
more intriguing they become. This one, severely handicapped by
the wide stage, was more uneven than the curate's egg, but
Vasilyeva, who played Ranevskaya, turned the evening on its head.
With the containment of a great performer she wasted energy on
nothing. She revealed to us her riveting view of the woman-
mother as a destroyed drunken junkie. I couldn't take my eyes off
her. Her smallest gesture carried in the huge hall. Her modern
blonde hair and poster paint make-up seemed to add to rather
than destroy the reality of her vision. Thrilling acting.

As I prepared for departure tomorrow, I was told that Azat has
been taken ill and is no longer in business. This could explain the
vacuum. I learned, also, that I must be packed and ready
punctually at eight a.m. I will be picked up in a car and taken to
Vladimir.

24 April

I was seen into the car by a Volodya I had not previously met. He
has become the calm link with whom Henrietta can negotiate on
my behalf. Crumpled and friendly, he kissed my hand and
introduced me to the other two travelling actors: Sasha, curly-
haired and comedic, plays the leading part at the Mossoviet
Theatre in Mikhail Roshchin's translation of *Noises Off*, by Michael
Frayn; Zharkov, tall and saturnine, I have seen in several
productions at MKhAT. They staunchly promoted each other's
starriness for me. Zharkov plays Lopakhin in Yefremov's *Cherry
Orchard*. He saw me faltering, not remembering his performance.
Fortunately, backdating, we discovered that when I saw it he was

away from the production with his leg in plaster following a filming accident. He still walks stiffly. I was given the front seat. The two men in the back of the car hardly drew breath during the journey. Sasha was going to give a performance in the afternoon, returning to Moscow at night; while Zharkov must stay a day or two to be a celebrity.

We were driven at audacious speed weaving in and out of the traffic – I do relish these wheel-spinners – to reach Vladimir in two hours instead of the predicted three. Again I felt exhilarated and safe.

I picked up quickly that for them tyrannical directors are normal. It is gradually seeping through that they expect to be treated without much respect and have developed the resilience that can sustain them through humiliations that would flay my protective skins. Solzhenitsyn, being ordered to go somewhere, followed by the command 'Run!', wrote that, until it has been experienced, the humiliation cannot be imagined. I've suffered shame, probably of my own making, at the hands of one or two directors in England, but I don't expect it and it's not usual.

I must remember this particular indigenous experience. I am in company with Russian actors, in a Russian car, on my way to a Russian Theatre Festival, travelling across their land, Russia.

Katya, assigned to be my carer, took me to the eleventh floor for my two-roomed apartment. The entirety of one wall in the sitting room is a charming blown-up photographic view of golden autumn woodlands.

Later, in the hall, I found Juvenaly. Zharkov and I were driven to a restaurant in the middle of the town. We sat at a long table, where we were joined gradually by Festival organisers. A five-course meal was laid before us. I didn't realise at the time – it was my only meal of the day.

The room was filled with jocularity, smoke and privilege. Not another actor to be seen; Juvenaly told me I would meet the Taganrog actors at the theatre in the evening. Juvenaly's interest was in a talk that the distinguished writer, Andrei Bitov, was going to give in the afternoon. Julius Kagalitsky had talked about him during my second visit.

A cluster of us followed a young enthusiast to a basement where he showed a short film he had devised about Andrei Sakharov. When it ended, the others left with scarcely an acknowledgement of his effort. I was reminded how dangerous it is for a creative person to offer their wares, especially to other creative people.

Juvenaly persuaded me that I must not miss Andrei Bitov. Having limited vocabulary does not make me try any less hard to understand what is being said. It is an exhausting process. I recorded the first hour of his relaxed discourse before I left to give a pre-arranged interview with a woman reporter from the local radio station. Later, I lay on my bed enjoying the wooded scene on the far wall opposite, but unable to relax; without information, not yet having a context. Seeing my friends was going to cure that.

I was taking off my coat in the foyer of the theatre when a young girl approached me with, 'Now you will come onto the stage to make your speech.'

'What speech?'

'You will be introduced and then you will make a speech.'

I was led through the pass door to the side of the stage, where Andrei Bitov, Juvenaly and Zharkov were waiting.

'Why did no one say anything to me about this?' I geysered.

'It's the same for us,' answered Zharkov, drily. 'It's normal.'

'How can I suddenly make a speech in Russian, without preparation?'

I expleted loudly in English for my own benefit, and perhaps to give me courage.

'I understood that,' remarked Andrei Bitov, in Russian.

My name was announced, I whisked out onto the stage, full of energy and confidence, greeted by applause and partisan cheers and whistles. Ah, my friends are here. I was handed a fine-art book about Vladimir. My speech of thanks in Russian, focused on my favourite film director, Andrei Tarkovsky.

After Zharkov and Bitov had done their bit Juvenaly, Master of Ceremonies, indicated that we should leave the stage. I went down into the stalls to find Taganrog sitting in a long line. I kissed and hugged my way to a seat which had been kept for me.

We will watch Andreyev's version of *Three Sisters*. Two of my neighbours left within a quarter of an hour.

As soon as the interval came, our enthusiasm for each other outweighed our loyalty to the spectacle. We did not make our way back to the auditorium.

Back on floor 11, Moscow and Marseilles playing football on TV. We will rehearse in the morning, perform in the evening. I hope to keep warm in bed. No hot water. Telephone: Lilya/Varya with details about breakfast. Later, another call, male, 'Do you want to be together?'

'*Кто вы?*'[20]

'*Я*' – *(pause)* – '*человек.*'[21]

Maybe I misunderstood the message. I put the receiver down.

25 April

A clear blue sky. Looking out of my top floor window I understand why Vladimir is so cold. It is on high ground, surrounded by a neverending plain. The wind whistles around the hotel's kidneys.

At ten o'clock a smart knock on my door revealed an extrovert young man in jeans. Boris. Borya. The Director of the Festival in place of Azat, I guess.

'Any problems?'

'Of course not.'

Boris offered to drive me to the theatre via some of the best sights. I'm not surprised that Andrei Tarkovsky chose this town as setting for his film, *Andrei Rublyov*. The layout of mediaeval wooden houses in attendance on a dazzling white church is almost too good to be true. While I stood entranced another car screeched up.

'This is the money,' confided Borya.

I photographed them in front of the church, then we dashed to the theatre. It would be foolish to be late for a rehearsal that I need desperately and feel lucky to get.

At one o'clock, we collected at the back of the stage, preparing to rehearse. A shivering little dog has been dragooned. The stage

---

[20] 'Who are you?'

[21] 'I'm...a person.'

was not ready for the Dress Rehearsal. Juvenaly gathered the company to give a pep talk. An actor's growl of discontent escaped. Relaxed despair prevailed. To raise our spirits, we talked about food. They look tanned and well. They told me that now it is very warm in Taganrog, all the flowers are out. Everyone of them had come to the theatre wearing clothes I had given them. Parting from them will be like leaving school. I shall have to grow up.

Of course we didn't rehearse. No, No; we did some of the dances, then it was lunchtime.

I pleaded with Peter, the gentle business manager of the Taganrog Theatre, 'Do I have to go to the critics' *razgovor* after the performance?'

'No, you don't have to.'

But I guess the other actors will go, sit and be humiliated. I feel quite angry with them. They say they have many directors like Kalantarov. When Lyubimov came to England, it was whispered the English actors stuck their tongues out at him.

Walking back from the restaurant, I see Azat Rafikov in his blue suit, coming out of the hotel. He's not in hospital.

'I thought you were ill.'

He takes my hand and shakes it.

'Ill? What do you mean, ill? I'm never ill.'

From My Tape Recorder...

Background hissing noise of open taps throughout...

I've come upstairs to have a rest. I turned on both taps in the bathroom. (Laughter.) Neither is giving water, they're just howling. Eleventh floor – maybe the water's having trouble going uphill. I know that feeling. (Loud laughter.) I've only got one more day. I feel so angry with Azat already, just for being there. How DARE they not discuss a contract? Assume I will come and play the part and make a speech without a word of warning? Oh, come on, Caroline, you must remember to laugh! (Despite the words, this section is delivered lightly, with relish.)

I'm having my rest when, suddenly, three hours later, this happens... (Sound of running water. Helpless laughter.) I believe it's symbolic. Pushing water uphill. This is the experience of working in the Russian theatre, 1991.

(Long laugh.)

I lie here, looking out at the beautiful sky, beginning to prepare myself for the performance tonight. Pasha/Yepikhodov is in Moscow, supervising exams. Poor young understudy, Sasha, didn't rehearse today. What must he be feeling? I can't understand, with the growling that goes on, why they don't say, 'You may not do this to us. Our bodies, minds, can't stand it.' But they can, and do. I'm not trained for it, so I'm still fighting.

Evening – ACT I

This showing feels dreadful, as it always does when there has not been rehearsal. But the audience clapped and laughed on practically every line. Whether it's because I'm English and they think I'm something out of the zoo, I find it nerve-racking; I *hate* the feeling that I'm working badly. There's general anxiety. A lot of smoking.

I had requested earlier that Peter arrange the contract discussion with Borya, which brought the latter hurrying to me just before the performance, waving a piece of paper.

'How much do you want?'

I reassured him it could wait till after the performance. Did he believe I would refuse to go on? The other Charlotta has been brought from Taganrog to stand-by.

The second half felt more satisfying. There was a flurry of cheerful visitors backstage, who thumped Kalantarov on the back and hugged him with spontaneous enthusiasm for the success of the production. It was the first time I have seen him being given praise or encouragement. Certainly Azat has shown the contempt for him that Juvenaly shows for his actors. Now he looked as happy as could be. He kissed my hand. I explained that I would not be coming to the *разговор*[22] as I have a meeting with Borya to discuss my contract. It was announced that a rehearsal is called for eleven o'clock in the morning on the last day.

'I'm going to Suzdal in the morning.'

---

[22] 'Discussion' or 'conversation'.

'You can't go to Suzdal in the morning,' declared Kalantarov. 'You'll have to go in the afternoon.'

'I have a television interview in the afternoon.' Bitch!

I sat with Peter in my dressing room feeling muddled and stubborn. I needed a showdown against arbitrariness, some form of reality and honesty and person-to-person responsibility.

They say, 'You must do this (speech), you must go to that (TV interview), you must see this (person)', *never* 'can you? will you? please?' Suddenly he wants to rehearse on the *last morning?* I've done everything they've wanted since February 10th – except when I flouted Azat's second-hand order to catch the bus to Vladimir – and all they do is shit on us!

I did all the rude Russian gestures I know, (theirs are different from ours) and listed all the filthy words I've been lovingly taught.

Peter's face reddened. He became convulsed with rage.

I thought, 'That's it. I've done it. I've gone too far. I've finally insulted the Russian self-esteem in a way that is beyond the pale.' The paroxysm produced a turn-around in my fortunes that I could hardly take in.

He declared that they are an incompetent management, hopeless and irresponsible. He was on *my side!!* Suddenly water could flow in the right direction. He found a Suzdal solution. We would go early in the morning and be back in time for the rehearsal and for the TV interview.

Vera, my literary manager, hospitable in Taganrog, supportive here, encouraged me to join the *разговор*. Light-hearted, with allies, of course, I agreed. Nothing could be easier.

Eight men faced the gathering. The actors' faces had already glazed. I sat for nearly an hour, watching body language when words left me in the dark. At a loss, I started my favourite defence against boredom. I imagine the people I am watching as seven-year-olds. Politicians make excellent subjects for this game. A couple of Kenneths have afforded me no end of pleasure.

I suddenly felt reckless.

I got up, saying, 'Excuse me,' politely, followed by Peter and Vera who neatly guided me to Borya's office.

'Who *is* Borya?' I asked on the way. 'What does he do?'

'He's a businessman.'

The businessman bounced, smiling, towards me holding out a bottle of cognac, indicating that I should put it into my carrier. Then he reached into his pocket and produced a tooled silver bracelet.

'No, no, no, please, I mean, thank you. It's not like that. We must talk business.'

Was I flouting Eastern bazaar routine? Borya, with his zappy American haircut, showed no sign of it.

I needed a drink. I reached into my bag for the welcome bottle.

No, no, I mustn't drink from my bottle. Another one emerged from Borya's desk and we were each handed a glassful. There was a toast.

'Now,' said Borya, waving the paper again. 'How much do you want?'

It felt more complicated. I was determined that this transaction should be scrupulously honest. I needed them to understand that I'm not interested in cheating or being cheated. Both sides had struggled with difficulties that needed airing. Much the greater part of this experiment has been a wild, glorious success. An adventure of unparalleled importance in my life. I wanted to clear the cons out of the way so that we could celebrate the pros. I started, 'I know you have very little money.'

'There is money. How much do you need?'

A young woman had been summoned to translate, in case we got into difficulties; I heard quickly that she was being consistently inaccurate. When I questioned it, she replied that she thought she should say what she thought I was feeling, not what I was saying; I continued unaided.

'Would six thousand roubles do?' offered Borya.

'Too much.'

'All right, five.'

'All right.'

'You'll have it at nine o'clock in the morning. Do you trust me?'

He looked at me steadily. His warm eyes holding mine in an open gaze of candour. A film director would have cut between us a couple of times before I managed: 'Yes.'

'Good.'

'If you're not there in the morning – what I have learned in Russia, which is not to trust, will be true.'

Eye laughter.

'I will be there.' Eye laughter.

Peter made a most earnest toast to the recovery of my trust. We raised our glasses.

26 April – Last Day Of This Job

At nine o'clock I was sitting in the car with Peter, Vera and Slava from the Ministry of Culture. A performer, a comic, he told me; an old friend of Vera.

Borya darted breathlessly into view. His arrival was a matter of faith in himself, in Russia, in human beings in general. I photographed him laughing, handing me five thousand roubles tied up with string. Then he photographed me receiving it similarly. Life can be a game. Oh, don't let this stop.

Another racer sped us to Suzdal in half an hour. I wonder if I've been duped about journeys that they say will take twice as long and don't. Is it a ploy to gain respect, or a sensible safeguard against breakdown? Who cares, it's one way of having a nice surprise.

Also built on ground rising from plain in every direction, Suzdal spreads aggressively over a distance that would take a day to walk round.

Founded in the eleventh century and, in the twelfth – a capital, the town exceeding London in size and population; it is preserved as a museum. At one time Suzdal had fifteen monasteries. In 1573 there were four hundred households, seven churches and a cathedral inside the Kremlin (fortified town), fourteen churches within the city ramparts, and twenty-seven monasteries – a rival, almost, for Venetian Famagusta in Cyprus, which had a church for every day of the year.

At one end of the town stands the outdoor Museum of Wooden Architecture and Peasant Life. A community of eighteenth-century churches and nineteenth-century wooden peasant houses, barns and granaries rises from the green sward. These buildings were collected from various villages, and are presented in an array to make a tourist's jaw drop. Open-air performances are given at the site during the summer.

A pair of young artists, their sketches and watercolours protected by cling film, had already leaned their work against a wall, hoping to make an early sale.

Slava, an expansive host, took me by the arm to show me details that I might miss. He discovered that we share an alternative language. The computer in my head nearly exploded as he translated into French something which was being explained in Russian and which I was trying to assimilate in English.

The view of meandering rivers and copses, stretching out of sight, tapped me into perceptions of the mediaeval. A day's ride on horseback; a glint of sun on metal, warning of unwelcome visitors. Extreme cold. Survival. The panorama of the town itself – churches, blue domes starred with gold; originally, each street had a wooden church. These, vulnerable to fire, were replaced by stone, built on the same site and given the same name.

We gazed from a vantage point, knocked out by the confidence of what we saw. My companions, moved and proud, said again and again, 'This is Russia, the heart of Russia. This is where our culture comes from.'

Time was racing and we forced ourselves from one resplendence to an exceptionally delicious building with an unappealing history. The Convent of the Intercession was a place to which lords banished their ladies from early in the sixteenth century. It could be punishment for barrenness, excessive liveliness leading to childbirth, or for simple boringness. Ivan the Terrible's fourth wife was dumped there – to weep and do needlework.

We found a quadrangle surrounded by a single storey whitewashed block. High cell windows with bars. This was used as a prison in Soviet times, too. Now the gate is gestured wide open for ever. The prisoners could have looked at a sky dented by a dazzling gold dome – on a sunny day. Heartbreaking beauty.

Every now and then I asked anxiously whether we should get moving to rehearsal. Finally, it dawned on me that they had no intention of getting me back on time, so I relaxed.

They took me to a shut cafe and persuaded the proprietress that we were there to help promote her day's business. She responded (they *always do*), producing hot strong coffee and *medovukha* – honeyed vodka – a cousin of mead.

Before we reached the outskirts of Suzdal, a small church caught the attention of my hijackers. Drawn by fate, Vera insisted afterwards, we went inside to find a wedding being celebrated. A youthful priest with long black locks was in charge. The bride wore a lavishly decorated full-length white dress, the groom a suit. A congregation of thirty stood in the body of the church, to one side – half a dozen unaccompanied choristers. Peter indicated that it would be acceptable for me to take photographs. It surprised me that my Anglican background made me shy of using a camera in church.

The pair, each carrying a lighted candle, made a circular promenade led by the priest who held a crucifix in front of him. The couple were followed by an attendant each, bearing a crown a few inches above their heads. I overcame my reticence, took two or three shots. The film came to an end and noisily rewound itself. I bent double, wrapped my coat, scarf, hat round it, nothing could stop the whirr until it was done. Vera, Slava and Peter had bought candles and were following the service devoutly. Each revealed a crucifix around their neck.

In Vladimir, no sign of rehearsal or actors or director. We continued to the local television station, housed in the eighteenth-century residence of the governor of the region. The nearest neighbour, rising impeccably from a floor of neatly cut lawn, is the Cathedral of St Demetrius. It's perfection silenced me.

Onto a roof terrace in numbing cold, overlooking the cathedral, I was interviewed by the most charming kind of Englishman – but he is Russian, a poet. I asked his parentage. He would get through an identity parade of Britons. A tenacious radio journalist cadged a place at the table for her microphone.

My restricted vocabulary has taught me the politician's trick of answering the question I want to answer rather than the one I am asked.

Back in the first-day restaurant, I found myself next to Borya. The sound *h* doesn't exist in the Cyrillic alphabet; *g* is substituted. GAMLET, GIMALAYAS, GOMOSEXUAL. During lunch I learned that Borya had been to GOLLYWOOD and BEVERLY GILLS. Kalantarov, at another table, gave no indication of his feelings about me missing the rehearsal. Behaving unprofessionally on my last day, felt satisfyingly inconsistent and Russian.

Still friendly towards me, members of Tovarichestvo Rezhissyorov asked whether I would come back again to do another play in Taganrog; and would I spend the evening with them after the performance. I explained that I needed very much to have time with my family, the actors. I couldn't help finding these cosy men old-fashioned for puffing cigarettes throughout the meal without enquiry.

I was given a badge; the latest joke, with Kommunist printed on it. An historic time-placer. Previously I had felt Badge Culture to be a serious matter. I have a huge collection from Moscow, Leningrad, of Lenin, Baby Lenin, Chekhov, Moscow Art Theatre, Soldier's Day, fiftieth, sixtieth, seventieth anniversaries of this and that. Here, indeed, a badge with my name, another carrying the name of the Festival, one to give me credibility on the bus. All indications that I exist and belong. In the West, do we patronise with a badge? I was here, not *here* was here and allowed me to join. Maybe the unsettling changes are making the straight-faced badge unnecessary.

To learn about a country I must stop thinking *they*. Think *we*, and see what that feels like. If I say *they*, I am observing *zoopark*, as they say.

At five to seven – two bells, one to go – I leaned against the radiator by the window and looked out at blocks of flats. Children playing football, others circling on bikes, people coming home from work, three policemen in their greatcoats strolling along. It had been a very cold day. I wanted these ordinary sights to direct me away from unwelcome emotion. I was quite glad to see the last of the second act, apart from the sensitive swinging. It never felt as if we found the proper rhythm. It needed breaking down and putting together again. I shall treasure the memory of Pasha/Yepikhodov singing to his guitar/mandolin. His melted-gold musicality comically distorted by excessive vibrato. One evening in England, watching an operatic gala from the Met in New York on TV, I saw a tenor walk onto the stage and sing Pasha's song, verse upon verse. I gave a long silent howl.

For the first time since the opening of the play our director didn't join us on stage for the curtain call. He didn't come to our dressing room. Clutching some pink roses and three daffodils, I was led to the lobby by the entrance to the stage. Volodya/Trofimov presented me with a golden amber necklace from the actors and actresses. Now the performance was over it was permitted to cry. My friends invited me to be their guest at a farewell party in the hotel, but first we must attend a ceremony in the foyer of the theatre.

A three-piece band was playing. Before I could put down my handbag I was seized by a stranger who fox-trotted me furiously from one side of the floor to the other until a pause in the music gave me the chance to disengage. We had been the only dancers. I hurried over to my friends who closed around me like an oil slick. I had failed miserably to learn not to expect refreshments after a performance. We sat watching the empty dance floor. The music played on. A group of Tovarichestvo Rezhissyorov stood to one side, smoking. To fill time in lieu of stomach I held my recording machine in front of each of our company in turn for a farewell message. Juvenaly came and sat with us. He presented each of us with a small plaster plaque, a memento of the production. I thanked him.

'I've learned a lot,' I said across the divide that separates us.

'Without irony?' he asked.

'Without irony,' I answered.

'I would like to say,' he said, 'that I've learned, too. It's been a very interesting experience to work with you as an actress.'

We were called to stand in line like at a school prize-giving. Thirty or forty people applauded as Zharkov fulfilled his celebrity role and handed prizes to Lev/Gaev, and to Sasha/Pishchik for being the best actor in the Festival. Juvenaly gave me some beautiful lacquer earrings. The Taganrog Drama Theatre Company was given a crystal vase as an ensemble prize.

When loss is imminent you attend to bodily needs; food, drink, physical closeness and music. The resourceful southerners, actors, *musikanty*, technicians and all converge in the room shared by Sasha/Pishchik and Volodya/Trofimov. We interleaved like sardines and ate hard-boiled eggs, fish and sausage on bread, slices of cucumber as fresheners, drank champagne and vodka. Each person in the room recorded a song or snatch to the accompaniment of Volodya/Trofimov or Pasha/Yepikhodov. I wish I had chosen anything but 'Auld Lang Syne', but I must live with that until I edit the tape. Pasha/Yepikhodov is the one who makes them laugh most. He told a story which very quickly had them in stitches. As he approached the climax their laughter went more and more out of control. The pay-off word *'Tractr!'* produced such gales that the more responsible members went out into the passage to see if anyone was on the way to complain to the manager. I was too shocked and exhausted to make a speech. I was just there like a running river. I ate their food, drank with them and listened to their love.

27 April

Vera/Lit. She told me the actors were having breakfast if I wanted to say a last goodbye.

'No, that's the last thing I need.'

One or two of them turned up and I began to cry, then I wanted to see them all. We stood in the rain.

'Carolina's crying,' remarked Juvenaly, usefully.

'Yes, Juvenaly, I'm crying.'

In the end, my heart cracked. I was able to hug Kalantarov. I believe we made peace. His eyes welled up. The sour taste left me. I was grateful. They piled onto the bus. I took two or three cheerful, smiling photographs of them, asked them to shout, *'Do svidanya, Carolina!'* into my tape recorder.

They drove off in the bus to catch a train to Taganrog, where I guessed I would never set foot again.

Vera and Slava helped me into the car for our drive back to the capital. I sat, the tears running down my cheeks, for nearly an hour.

Russians, tuned to feelings as a nation, are the best people to be with in such a situation. They let me be. Did nothing to jolly me out of it. They are used to grieving and honour the process.

I shared an historic moment with my fellow travellers. On the car radio the name 'Saint Petersburg' was used instead of 'Leningrad'. They howled at this *FIRST*, looking at their watches to see what the date was.

'It's an historic moment when you actually hear it on the news. You are our fate, Carolina,' said Vera, not for the first time.

28 April

Rested and calmer, I sat in the kitchen listening to the fridge.

'We have a hundred empty seats on British Airways this afternoon.

Whoever told you that we were fully booked?'

Henrietta called to say that Volodya/Rezhissyor would come for me in half an hour. No time to be sentimental.

His speedy driver got us to the airport in less time than it would take a circus bear to change his tee-shirt and shorts. Volodya talked non-stop all the way. We shared some of the areas where culture shock had made insurmountable barriers, based on misunderstanding.

'Here actors are just the same as ordinary workers, whereas in your country actors are paid more. They are not like ordinary workers. We do it – and directors – it's almost like a hobby.'

I forgot to ask him what he lives on, how does he earn his living?

I said I found it sad that the work they do is so little valued, that people are treated so rudely. I always believed that the artist is a revered species in Russia. I explained for me the most difficult thing has been the lack of information and consultation. But I regret nothing. It has changed my life for ever. I love his country. Nothing can change that. Nothing.

We hugged with new, added affection. He waited by the barrier for my last wave before going past the smoked screen.

On the plane, I pondered two aspects of life which I had not noticed before. One was some unconcealed anti-Semitism. I had not noticed it before.

The second has a faintly sexual context. I was visiting an apartment while the husband was out. The young wife had been washing clothes in the bath and had removed her skirt. She was sitting talking to me in tee-shirt and tights. Her husband walked into the room. She flushed and apologised to him for being without her skirt. She felt really shy at her state of undress. This same young woman told me once she had a foreign guest who left her bed looking like a bed all day; it was like an invitation. The normal practice every morning is to fold away bedclothes and sofa bed. I have found a slightly more modest attitude to physicality and sexuality in Russia than is usual in England amongst the people I know. My Anglophile hostess Ksenia relaxedly allows me to leave my bed as a bed.

Two expletives continue to catch me out. If someone calls your name across a room, you answer 'Ow!' as if you are hurt. If something is good, interesting or amazing, you say 'Oo-augh', as a Western man might when he is admiring a sexy girl.

The captain announced the descent twenty minutes earlier than expected.

***

This is the end of the trip. I love you, my darling Russia. I love you. I love you. A hundred feet from the ground I understand that I shall need to mourn.

Adam, meeting me for the second time that day, without a dime, had had to leave the car for several hours. The parking charge was nearly ten pounds. Worth it just to see his dear, dear face.

'Hi, Mum... Char's waiting for you at home.'

Moscow Art Theatre

December 1991

You know I can't stand Shakespeare, but your plays are even worse than his.'
Tolstoy to Chekhov on *Uncle Vanya.*

38. Chekhov bust.

Nothing prepared me for the difficulty of putting into print what I've lived through in Russia. My notebooks and cassettes opened caverns of dread. Especially the tapes.

I bought an electric typewriter. I begged forgiveness, in a mental bubble, for any criticism I have made of any writer. Ever.

With the small cast iron bust of Chekhov, presented to me in Taganrog, standing within inches of my fingers, I churned and dredged for three months, staring out at the English Channel. I saw nothing, was in a dark cinema of memory. Reel upon reel. Clear as a dream. My occasional calls to Moscow elicited enquiries.

The putsch has changed everything and nothing. I had no difficulty getting through to Henrietta on the telephone.

'Are you all right?'

'Yes, of course.'

'What's happening?'

'We go to work, as usual. When are you coming back?'

'Don't know.'

'Shall we see if Oleg Yefremov will invite you to play at MKhAT?'

'Yes.'

I had typed about 50,000 words. Some of the emotional congestion was eased. Lighter, I was also in need of a fix. I would be more likely to entice set dates from Oleg if we were face to face in a room. I'd better get over there. Henrietta, having set up the trip, had to rush in emergency to her sick mother in Sevastopol.

On the news, stories of how Boris Yeltsin has failed to energise the economy. What will happen when the severe cold clenches the country in its grasp? Will there be riots? Starvation? Muggings? Have they made a mistake in dumping Gorbachev? I knew I must take extra provisions for my deprived friends.

Igor Yasulovich met me at the airport. Also waiting were my Russian son and daughter, Volodya Mashkov and Alyona Khovanskaya. I had been lucky to be handed them when Brian Cox was finding London homes for his theatre student swap. Volodya/Vova, increasing diminutives of Vladimir, is beginning to be a film star and has bought a car. He is attached to Oleg Tabakov's Studio. Alyona is a rising star at MKhAT.

I chanced to be in Moscow at the time the Art Theatre was celebrating the hundredth anniversary of the birth of Mikhail Chekhov. This greatly admired actor and teacher was the son of Anton's elder brother, Alexander.

I was invited to come to Oleg Yefremov's third-floor room before the symposium began. Isolde rose to take my coat with affectionate endearment: she is the widow of one of the Art Theatre's greatest late stars, Gribov. I had heard, there is always gossip about people in power, Oleg has not been well.

He looked fine to me. He always has a superb haircut. Some days he looks tall, others less so. His actor's hands are clear and to the point – oblong fingernails cut straight across.

He embraced me, motioned me to sit at the long boardroom table, then chose a chair and pulled it round so we were facing each other. In public he sometimes uses the formal 'you', but in private, always the informal. A great person provides a silence into which you can put things.

'*Я дома,*'[1] I said.

'*Хорошо.*'

His cough racks up from the depths of his frame, but I bring him cigarettes because he likes them. And whisky. And, this time, a pair of black socks. He felt the bag and gave a satisfied grunt. Then he began to talk about the man we were about to celebrate. Irina, his executive secretary, put her head round the door and beamed.

'When are we going to talk?' Oleg asked her. 'Are we going to have a meeting?'

'Yes, of course, we'll arrange something.'

Stepping out of the minuscule lift, we walked towards the foyer where television lights had been set up and from which came an expectant crowd. A woman I had seen at the Chekhov conference in Yalta greeted Oleg warmly. She was Natalya Krimova, an eminent theatre critic, widow of the distinguished director Efros; he had stepped into Yuri Lyubimov's shoes at the Taganka, when that master was enduring a troubled time abroad. We exchanged grace notes, then she and Oleg led the way into the space where Stanislavsky and Nemirovich-Danchenko, the founders of this great institution, used to take it in turns to rehearse their productions.

The first person I saw was Azat Rafikov. He came towards me in the friendliest way; bursting with health and *bonhomie*, wearing a brand new tailored three-piece suit. He kissed my hand, we hugged each other. Splendid to feel so pleased to see him after all we've been through. Not a vestige of resentment on either side. He explained he is now a film producer working on a project. Where am I staying? Can he get in touch? The straightforward

---

[1] 'I'm (at) home.'

energy of his positive thought reminded me of why I came to work with him in the first place. He's courageous in a tough arena. He's real. I like that.

A seat was found for me in the front row. Krimova took the Chair. As the session was about to begin, an old lady was led, like royalty, to the seat beside me. Wearing a long black skirt, a fur collar round her neck, a diamond ring on her finger; India-paper skin, white hair pulled back, holding a little black velvet bag, she sat bolt upright with full attention. I squinted at her profile. Remarkably like Stanislavsky. Could she be his daughter? She was *народная артистка*[2] Sofia Pilyavskaya, the Polish actress, last living student of Stanislavsky.

Oleg Nikolayich got to his feet first and spoke extempore for about ten minutes. When he sat down, speaker after speaker came to the front, bowed deferentially to my regal neighbour and read a paper. This continued for three and a half hours. One of the contributors, Galina (whom I'd known since my first visit to Muzei-MKhAT) is an acknowledged expert on Bulgakov and married to the painter Igor Shneitr, spoke without text, her arms neatly crossed like a marble saint on a tomb. In mid-sentence she became aware of me looking up at her. Russian good manners compelled her to acknowledge me by name, which she did with formality and grace, making me feel shyer than I can remember. Oleg, before the first hour was up, responded to an out of sight summons, made his excuses and left, not to return.

---

[2] *народная артистка* means 'people's artist', an honorary title awarded to women in recognition of their contribution to the performing arts. There is a masculine equivalent for men, i.e., *НАРОДНЫЙ АРТИСТ.*

Дорогая Каролина!
Бесконечно рада, что я встретилась
с Вами, на Вашем прекрасном пут

39. Moscow MKhAT, Pilyavskaya – last living student of Stanislavsky.

40. Moscow, flat of Sofia Pilyavskaya, drinking a toast.
Caroline is holding a silver goblet that belonged to
Olga Knipper who died in Sofia's arms.

Eventually there was a short break to stretch our legs. This was followed by a demonstration by students from the Theatre School. Their teacher guided them through a set of physical attention/awareness exercises, drawing indulgent applause from their elders. Michael Chekhov moved to America in middle life, where he taught and wrote about acting; it was his method of work that was being shown.

Theatre performances start early in Moscow. Seven p.m. is the norm. Misha Roshchin was waiting for me inside the stage door. There is a heavy outer door at the marked Workers' Entrance. A stage door keeper sits at a desk in the small lobby – to whom you must identify yourself – and there is a beam to pass before you go outside again into a yard where the two official cars wait. They drive in and out under an archway through electronically operated gates. One is a creamy yellow Volvo estate. Pulling open another heavy door, meeting a blast of hot air, safe now from the weather, you find yourself in a large marble-floored hall with another keeper, this time a woman behind a windowed wooden partition enclosing a much-used telephone. There are two comfortable upholstered banquettes where people sit and wait for each other. On the left is a dark panelled section, with another kindly keeper, where the actors and staff leave their coats, boots, umbrellas and hats. There is plenty of room for everyone's outer coverings. One of the original rules of behaviour had been that, as the Art Theatre is like a home and the people who work there a family, it is good manners to take off your coat when you go indoors, no matter how long you are staying, and that every day you greet each person as you meet them for the first time, the way you would a relation. I don't know how successful it was ninety years ago. I've read of desperate rows and tensions amongst the founders. The habit is still followed. I've seen people shaking hands as they enter the lift, who may have played together on stage the night before or who will share an office when they reach their destination.

Misha is a little plumper than when I last saw him. He carries a walking stick and sometimes looks as though he may lose his balance; otherwise he has made terrific recovery from a massive stroke two or three years ago. Holding the position he does in the theatre, writer in residence, best friend and confidant of star actor Oleg Yefremov, who directs his plays, has been married to at least one of the leading actresses (as has Yefremov), suffers ill health – I can't help trying to recreate the old situation – Yefremov/Stanislavsky, Roshchin/Chekhov. Chekhov was introduced to the Art Theatre by his literary friend Nemirovich-Danchenko, Stanislavsky's founding partner and co-director: but Stanislavsky directed the plays in a way that often disappointed Chekhov, to the extent that he felt they had not been read properly. Why, if Beerbohm Tree, Sir Henry Irving, Bernard Shaw, Tolstoy and Tchaikovsky had themselves recorded on wax, didn't Anton Pavlovich? Couldn't he have gone round to see Chaliapin, who had a wind-up gramophone and must have been an early HMV waxist? I would give anything to hear the rich bass voice of the writer. Will something emerge from previously unexplored material when the Art Theatre Museum finally settles and unpacks in its new enlarged premises adjoining the theatre?

Misha's appearance at the Art Theatre, the half-dozen times that I've witnessed it, produces the feeling of a happy dovecote.

Cooing and wing-brushing, his friends and associates celebrate his arrival with surprised delight, crowding about him to gauge his health. Actresses wind themselves around him – while their husbands look on – owning him, stroking and kissing him, rubbing themselves against him like pussycats. His pleasure is manifest and I know he is in good credit for every caress.

Oleg Tabakov raced past, indicating affection but a tardy arrival. In the foyer, a member of the staff I had often met, made a shocking disclosure: did I know that today Oleg Nikolayevich had resigned? Misha approached with two programmes. Did he know that Oleg Nikolayevich had resigned today? No, his closest friend did not know that Oleg Nikolayevich had resigned. A lump of dread settled somewhere amongst my ribs.

Julia, the usherette with the bouffant hair who has often shown me to a seat during my ten years of visiting, raced forward, clearing a way for us.

'Mikhail Mikhailovich, where are you sitting? Are you together? Two, come, sit there.'

We found ourselves a few places along from Stanislavsky's named seat, about eight rows back. An open space in front. Plenty of leg room. Extra chairs were being squeezed in to accommodate the overbooking; people expected to enjoy themselves. As I prepared to settle down, my eye was compelled towards a lone man standing four rows back, hands on hips, elbows out, staring at me. Juvenaly Kalantarov.

'Good evening,' I smiled and sat down. My past is my present. Three photographs of Michael Chekhov filled the upstage area; as Gogol's Government Inspector, as himself and, I guess, as Hamlet.

It was, as promised, a galactic entertainment. As well as an excerpt from *The Government Inspector,* given by Alexander Filipenko, I watched virtuoso skills in individual set pieces. An actor from the Vakhtangov Theatre, standing at the side of the stage, did a half-hour monologue that built comedically until the audience was beside itself with laughter, yet it went on and on. Breathtaking. Unlike anything I had previously seen in a Russian theatre. It hardly mattered that I was not able to share the play on words. I had the pleasure, in company with hundreds of other humans, of melting to a master whose articulate body and vocal tunes would have seduced in any language. Comparisons? Fred Astaire, Joan Sutherland, Carl Lewis. Supreme in their field. Fast and light. I also remembered Derek Jacobi playing *Touchstone* at the Old Vic.

Oleg Yefremov and Victor Sergachev gave the Chekhov sketch which I had seen them play in Yalta. Oleg Tabakov read some letters of Michael Chekhov, in one of which he wrote, 'My mother and Anton Pavlovich loved each other, why did they not marry?' The performance was hosted by Yursky, another leading actor/director of the Art Theatre. He had the audience in stitches with his showpiece too. The bliss of prolonged uncontained laughter is something I feel starved of. Wouldn't fewer people die violently if we laughed more? It was an evening of glory for the theatre. I sat yearning more than ever to find myself on that stage with those talented performers.

I relish heroes; spent many hours before and into my teens, soaking up the tales of Greek mythology, and I haven't done with them yet. Russians make heroes of their own people. Pictures of Michael Chekhov were honoured with applause from stage and auditorium alike.

Delighted, relaxed people crowded out. Juvenaly was beside me to kiss my hand, as familiar as if I'd seen him yesterday.

'Have you come from England especially for this evening?'

'*Нет, конечно.*'[3]

'I had heard that you might be coming to play at the Art Theatre.

Is it true?'

I groaned internally.

'I know nothing. I have no definite plans.'

'There were some good things about our work together, it was not all bad?'

He needed a friendly response.

'Juvenaly, I believe, maybe, we didn't understand each other.'

'Well, I think you understood me, maybe I didn't understand you.'

---

[3] 'Of course not.'

He told me that he was going to Taganrog the following day to see *Cherry Orchard* and *Uncle Vanya*, which he had directed during the spring. Why don't I come too? This man really wants to mend whatever discomfort lingers between us. Maybe if there had been time for me to go with him I could have asked him the inadmissable question:

'Juvenaly, why do you treat your actors with contempt?'

Misha was worried about Oleg. He decided he must find him before he joined the party which had been laid on for the performers in one of the foyers. I entered with Oleg who had appeared through the pass door which separates the audience from backstage.

'Where's Misha?'

'Looking for you.'

There was, as usual, plenty of cognac, vodka and mineral water, but the food showed that the theatre's entertainment budget belt has been severely pulled in.

I congratulated two young actresses on the zest of their contribution. Was it an extract from a current production? No, they'd learned it specially and rehearsed only twice. I shivered.

I learned more about Vadim, the solicitous ticket giver. How many times he has shepherded me from the box-office window to a front stall. He feels himself always to have been connected with the Art Theatre. His mother was Oleg's first teacher.

Misha was amused to hear that I am writing a memoir of my Russian life and that he figures in it.

'Shall we be able to read it one day?'

'I hope so, Misha. Will you find me a publisher in Moscow?'

Oleg Nikolayich, having made his speech early on, had finally given himself permission to relax at the end of a long day. He was too tired to move when I kissed him goodbye. I didn't guess that I wouldn't see him again. This time.

I feel no qualm making my way home late at night. A hundred yards from the theatre, past Meyerhold's flat where his wife was murdered, to Gorky Street. Nip down into the underpass. I am a Moskvichka.

An excitable morning on the telephone to Taganrog. The evening of my arrival I had called Fedorovsky at home. I asked whether he could gather some of the actors for me to talk to one day. It is still scarcely a reality for me that I am able to speak to Russians in Chekhov's birthplace from their capital city, MOSCOW.

'Come and play in *Cherry Orchard* on Friday. We will fly you down. You can see *Vanya* on Saturday and return to England as planned on Sunday.'

Tatyana, *administratr,* made it sound so easy.

Amadeus by Peter Shaffer at MKhAT in the evening. I saw the last performance as Mozart of Roman Kozak. Recently appointed Director of the Stanislavsky Theatre, he is also an actor. Of stature. His passionate, raw portrayal blazed through the play, which itself seemed much more substantial and immediate than the conventional hit I had seen in London; I was reminded of another less felicitous away production of a home-hit, *My Fair Lady,* in West Berlin, in 1972. I found that heavy-handed; not least the Ascot scene where the Cecil Beaton repro frocks had two inches of shiny plastic round the hems to keep them clean.

Alyona had played two small parts immaculately. We waited at the outer stage door for Volodya and his star car. I feasted with them in the crowded room they share with their large parrot. They have named him *Попугай*/Parrot. They care for me as if I were a piece of Dresden china which unaccountably, makes me feel homesick.

41. Dom Kompozitorov: Sasha and Ksenia's flat. Left to right: humming fridge, Igor Yasulovich, Sasha, rubbish chute, and Ksenia.

At home in the flat, Ksenia, the Russian with the best colloquial English I know, and I, agree that some time must be spent in study of each other's tongue. Sasha, her biologist husband, is quietly humorous. He specialises in worms and insects; collects tea leaves and coffee grounds for them to eat. I am well trained to add my appropriate debris to the banquet he prepares for his proteges in two jars that stay beside the sink in the kitchen.

I was sitting in a make-up chair next to Michael Caine during the filming of *The Fourth Protocol,* when the shocking news came of an explosion at Chernobyl. 'Twenty thousand dead,' they said...

Sasha has made many visits to that site. His job is to inspect and record the reproductive habits of the worms since the accident. The state rewards him with free travel for life. He seems perfectly healthy. It hasn't stopped him being funny.

Our language sessions are of no interest to him. Ksenia believes that a language should be learned only through phrases, which accumulate to make sentences. You learn a phrase, you have achieved something. *Ursa appropinquat.* By taping sayings and sentences in English for Ksenia and trying to be exact in their meaning I can at least pay her back a little for her hospitality. She accepts a bean. Or a lentil. But money?

'No really, Caroline, it's not necessary.'

I like living in Moscow; waking up in a warm flat and pressing my bare feet into the floorboards; hearing the clack of wooden rings as I push open the bamboo-patterned curtains and take my first look at crystal snow, centuries-high sky and the brown and black stylised magpies. No sound of traffic. Quiet as a London Sunday used to be. I glance up at the Rostropovich balcony, at the ex-Shostakovich balcony. I pad down the passage to the kitchen, say hello to the fridge. There may be activity down the waste chute to make me aware of neighbours. Clap, bang, the daily newspaper flops onto the floor inside the reinforced front door. The risk of burglary has doubled in six months. When I go out, leaving the flat empty, I must double lock the front door after me making sure a small handle is facing exactly the right way. If I fail, no one can get in until the locksmith comes to break the door down. They have locksmiths. Things get done. People have lived in Moscow and got things done since 1147.

This building, Дом композиторов[4] (Composers' House), is home to many distinguished musicians. An expert pianist practises above after midday.

I make tea, tea, tea. Sometimes I even answer the long telephone ring; taking a message from a mother, father (they're divorced), mother-in-law; or friends who may rattle off their message too quickly for my anxious ear. A nickname – 'Ksyusha' for Ksenia can catch me out. The endless hot water is there to be enjoyed after a cultural tussle with the bath plug and a flannel. The cockroaches look quite friendly to me, they're not in a hurry – I am not horrified by dry creepy crawlies – but I know I must arrange for them to take a trip down the chute. A morning writing Christmas cards for Taganrog and Moscow gives me an additional feeling of at homeness. I am a free Western woman with dollars in my purse, a reason to be here and a reason to leave. No one can take from me the certainty that I am a part of this and I love it.

---

[4] House of Composers – one of the many clubs for distinguished persons involved in the arts in the former USSR and the Russian Federation.

The Braithwaites opened their ambassadorial arms again, so Amanda and I, driven by Valery, alert and acting a foreigner in his own country, joined the queue up the grand staircase to the annual Christmas drinks party for the British resident, mainly business, community; the sort of event I would loathe to host. The Embassy staff pulling their weight conscientiously. I have clear memory of the dutifulness of it from my time with the British Delegation at the UN. Here, as a guest, I had a good time with the Head of Security who belied any silly prejudice I might have had by being charming and knowing about Chekhov.

Valery made a comic meal of dropping his wife and me at our next engagement before going to an all-male birthday party. Valery, being Jewish, is a source of non-stop humour; both in gentle teasing from his wife – 'Jewish tears!' ('crocodile tears') and in his own gift for commentary on what the present holds. He lights up and delivers his observations like a professional, then he falls silent again. For ages. His audience rocks with laughter.

The familiar blue and white cloth covered the large round table in the Yasulovich living room. It was laid with a spread of pickled fish, chicken joints, mixed vegetable salad, hot boiled potatoes, bread and butter. Plain and spiced vodka. Jam in little dishes with the tea.

Igor and the family cat – on heat and howling for a mate – welcomed us. We found actor/director Dima Brusnikin; Sasha Semakin, the young writer of a play to be discussed; Ellie, an English post-graduate house-guest; and Natasha – in and out, delivering from the kitchen. Her warmth of welcome is wholehearted. She is shrewd and there would be no point in lying to her about anything.

We ate and brought ourselves up to date. How can we realise our wish to present a play, in which Igor and I will perform, to Russian and to English audiences? We tried to cut through the fantasies we have about each other's national artistic imperatives. I can see that, governmentally, they are seriously pushed for money, but believe that the innate cultural thrust is towards high-minded adventurous creativity.

'Wrong!' they shout joyously. 'We are a nation of stupid ignorant arseholes, with no interest in anything except money and vodka. Would it be possible for you to raise some finance for an exchange of this sort?'

'Finance?' I screech. 'They can't finance books for school children. We are a nation of scornful insular arseholes, with no interest in anything except money and scandal.'

We got that out of the way.

'Why don't you read the play?' Dima challenged suddenly. Amanda, who earns by translating, had made a substantial effort to provide a native text for me. We took a deep breath. Igor read in Russian, I in English. After some pages Dima asked me to read in Russian. Difficult for me to sight-read in Russian. Then Igor in English. Hard for him to sight-read in English. Hearty laughter from the replete diners. Plenty to mull over. The silences were those that come when a group of people feel they may be onto something quite novel and adventurous.

The cat, who all evening had been expressing the grievous agony of her frustration and getting no sympathy for it, saw us out again. Dima and Sasha stayed on the Metro with me until my stop.

19 December – Thursday

Could I get to the theatre to talk plans? I scuttled under Gorky Street – renamed Tverskaya – as it used to be in pre-Revolutionary times. Irina took charge.

'Oleg Nikolayich is unwell, but he wants us to fix dates because we must make announcements and plan publicity.'

I thought this was to be an in-house slide-in.

'Now, you will need two rehearsals.'

'Only two?'

'Let's go and see Tanya. She arranges these things.'

In her cramped office, Tanya masterminds the performance and rehearsal schedules for the two theatres within the building. She resolves a complicated repertoire, in which no play receives more than two consecutive performances. She has to accommodate nearly three hundred artists. Several productions are usually in rehearsal at any time. Some new, some revivals; actors and actresses are prepared for take-over in roles or as second and third cast in long-running productions. Opposite a character's name in the programme for *Seagull*, say, could be two famous names and one slightly less well known, with their status – People's Artist, Meritorious Artist – underneath. There is a pencil tick against the name of the artist we are to see tonight.

Tanya is as glamorous as any of the actresses in the company. Irina opened the conversation.

'Can you arrange three or four performances of *Cherry Orchard* in March or April for Carolina to play Charlotta Ivanovna?'

News To Tanya

The chequered sheet was spread out on the desk. Tanya stood on her side, Irina and I on ours. We bent our heads over the flimsy map of the Art Theatre's spring.

'You will need two rehearsals,' Tanya mused.

'Only two?'

'And one on the stage.'

Only one? But not out loud. I had become a Lilliputian in the face of these potentials.

'Oleg Nikolayich asked that Carolina should give a minimum of three performances,' said Irina, negotiating with huge charm.

Tanya was not finding it easy.

We left with two performances and three rehearsals (one on stage) pencilled in for the first week of March.

'Please could I have a copy of the text in the version you use? It is rather different from the one I am used to.'

'Is it?' Kolya was surprised. He promised he would get my role typed out so that I could take it to England.

I went, jubilant, to see a stylised, two-toned production of Dostoyevsky's *The Idiot* at the Taganka Theatre.

The hall felt drier and emptier than when I had visited it during the Lyubimov reign.

'Look who's here!' called Amanda, excitedly, as we collected our coats in the foyer. I was face to face with Julius Kagarlitsky. The first person ever to welcome me into a Moscow home. His Raya died after years of severe illness and pain, during which he nursed her with unquestioning devotion. He has a new younger wife, an ex-student of his, who patently adores him and he has spread luxuriously with emotional well-being. He was presenting how dreadful is the state of their country; no money, no food.

'Svetlana has had to stop working in order to queue for food.'

'Look at you!' I said, poking him affectionately in the chest. 'You're a millionaire.'

He was wearing a brand-new full-length sheepskin coat and a fox-fur hat. He laughed at the discrepancy between the visual and the spoken.

'Jewish tears,' chuckled those who know and love him best.

Tanya Lavrova drove me in her car to the Rimsky Market, used by local residents. It is housed in old solid structures which are set in a dishevelled courtyard. Out of doors, stalls fashioned from boxes or chairs offer second-hand tracksuits, mushrooms, wire, eggs, pliers, socks. There are clusters of smoking spivs, heads on the swivel, as one might expect near any street market in any country. And drunks, watery above and below the belt, agelessly incapacitated.

Tanya's son is a first-rate sculptor who yearns for exhibition abroad. Alyosha helped us carry the stinking pickles that were to make my relations head for the door when they were unwrapped at Christmas.

Cherry Orchard was conveniently scheduled at the Art Theatre for my last evening. Alyona was playing a tiny part of a little girl in a flashback sequence behind gauze. A call from the theatre invited me to come for a costume fitting an hour before curtain-up. They really do mean business. A stylish black-haired wardrobe mistress led me from the stage door to an empty dressing room, where a set of costumes were hanging waiting to be tried on. How can it be that a tall, thin actress had already played Charlotta Ivanovna and that the clothes, designed in a black and white production by Valery Levantal (whom I had met years ago at the Yasulovich house) should fit as if made for me? For the first and second acts, I will wear a cream wool skirt and jacket, immaculately sewn. The very slightest alterations were pinned and indicated with maximum professionalism and minimum fuss. You know at once if you are in the hands of a good dressmaker. The audience are led to believe in a blouse with long sleeves and a tie round the neck. If they were admitted to the dressing room during the interval they would see that the actress simply removes the composite jacket and sits in a camisole.

Costumes are often fashioned with a quick change in view. An actress must trust her dresser to get her back on stage in sixty seconds looking completely different, if that is required. It is an intimate, bonding relationship. You start undressing almost before you leave the stage. You helter, led by a hand in the dark, to a corner behind a screen where there is a light, a mirror and any jewellery or props you may need for your next entrance. You step out of the skirt which falls to the ground as you reached the screen – you've been undoing hooks and poppers as you ran. The new skirt is drawn up from the bundle on the floor where it has been carefully arranged with a space in the middle for you to stand on. As the waistband is pulled to and fastened, you step out of one shoe straight into another with either foot. You slide your arms into the new jacket, and while those fastenings are being attended to, you change your earrings, look in the mirror, reach for your prop, whisper, 'Thank you.' Then you skelter to the entrance and saunter onto the stage as lazy and bored as if you'd been playing dominoes in the next room for three hours. A skilled playwright crafts scenes so that quick changes are not inordinate.

I climbed into the fourth act two-piece. Another marvellous fit. I will be given pop socks to match and there seems to be no problem finding shoes big enough for my feet. The third-act party costume is also black and white. A man's tailcoat; a top hat, and a floppy black bow round the neck. Deprived of my blue and orange check and stripe clown outfit from Taganrog I hurried my brain to find details to support Charlotta's past. Her parents were travelling entertainers. She, as a child, had done somersaults and tricks at fairs. I wanted to introduce a bit of circus and sawdust. Maybe the trousers could be far too big around the waist, and the legs shortened by several inches to reveal striped socks? Black and white, of course. And could there be stretchy braces to twang and shoes with extra length at the toes to give that lovely flapping spatula look? Would Levantal approve? Lena, wardrobe, responded with enthusiasm, but the dresser was loyal to the status quo. Why all this upheaval for one performance? Two, two. Oleg Nikolayich must be consulted. Nothing should be changed without his permission. When I revealed that I had known the director for several years and that it was for and through him that I was making this unseemly commotion, she relented somewhat. I did everything I knew to gain her approval and acceptance. I felt like Babar's Friend Zephir when he tried to entertain the Gogottes. I even did an illusion with a silk scarf to make her laugh. Alyona flitted past on her way to get made-up. Kolya appeared with my precious text.

'Come and meet Tenyakova who plays Ranevskaya.'

This felt intrusive, twenty minutes before her performance began, but I was led in my tailcoat to her dressing room.

'This is Carolina who will be playing Charlotta Ivanovna.'

'Tonight?'

'Oh heavens, no!' I gasped. 'In March, I hope.'

'Good, good. Till we meet, then.' She smiled sweetly.

I did a comedy exit straight into the face of the actress who was going to be Charlotta in ten minutes. I bleached with shame, excused myself and hurried away to change, feeling I must get out of sight before I did any more damage. All the same I felt we had passed the point of no return. The meeting with Tenyakova had done it. It had been named out loud.

'This is Carolina, who will play Charlotta Ivanovna.'

I watched the play hawk-eyed for detail. The ACT III tricks were going to be a handful. Tonight we had Lyubshin instead of Smokhtunovsky, playing Gaev, Ranevskaya's feckless brother. Innokenti Smoktunovsky played Hamlet in a film that was shown in London in the 1960s. A time when anything Russian was rare and mystical. The Russians were our enemies, we were told. He was the best Hamlet I'd ever seen. I clearly remember choosing to stand near the graphic poster wherever it hung on any Underground platform. At one station someone had painted a huge penis sticking out from his tights. I'm a sucker for graffiti.

I came to admire Lyubshin more recently, in modern Mikhalkov seasons at the NFT. And here he was, glamorous as ever, with shoulder-length grey hair, playing Gaev. With which one of these heroes will I be acting?

Volodya was outside to take Alyona and me home for tea and a word with *Попугай*/Parrot. I had a request. Would they record my role in the Art Theatre version of the text for me? I had my cassette recorder and the four typed pages in my bag. Very clear and slow, please. No acting. Alyona was Charlotta. Volodya was everybody else and stage directions. Goodbye, Moscow. See you soon.

They say it's the journey that counts...

March 1992

Accustomed to the rough and tumble of the business community queueing for early morning flights to the continent, I was surprised to push the trolley Adam had found for me into a deserted check-in hall at Heathrow.

Is it a bomb scare?

'There is some go-slow with the security people. You will find the blockage a bit further on.'

I had been entrusted with another fur coat to wear and deliver. This one was rather grander than hitherto. Heavy black Persian lamb. It is easier to justify wearing fur in a country where the cold is an invading force. I'm more inclined to believe that regional conditions produce appropriate regional habits. My body is not trained to the cold any more than it is to the heat I yearn and search for in countries closer to the equator.

I cannot rid myself of the idea that I should come to Russia laden with gifts. I offered a quality second-hand wool dress to the wrong person.

'What is this fantasy?'

'I'm sorry. On television we see only queues and empty shops, and I'm told on the telephone from Moscow that you have nothing.'

'We can buy new clothes here. They are very expensive, but if we have the money we can buy them.'

In Taganrog the situation was clearly far worse than in Moscow. There was no resistance to second-hand denim and tartan there. I am still not quite ready to drop what feels like giving but can be perceived as patronage.

Of one thing I am certain. Alcohol and cigarettes are never refused. A clever whisky firm sells its produce in plastic bottles at the duty-free store now. I haven't seen the same for vodka. I knew that the weight of the bottles and cigarettes added to the coat, camera and cassette recorder were going to overload the last long trail to the departure gate. I asked for help. A push-into-shape cardboard box, suitable for housing a six-foot by three-foot pack of cards, was knocked up for me. I stuffed in the fur coat, a wodge of computer-related stationery for Sasha, the script of the play I will start to rehearse on my return to England, my notebooks, gloves and umbrella. I watched the ungainly start of its passage to the plane. The counter women had again, refreshingly, accepted that the overweight part of my luggage was food-aid in the form of sugar, rice, lentils, porridge oats and Cheddar cheese, and made no extra charge.

Security – no queue – passport control, duty-free. Once safely strapped into a seat, my only remaining task is to impress on the aeroplane silently that in order to fly it must leave the ground. Having accomplished this between us I can sit back, assimilate my neighbour's shape and texture and begin to think about food.

After little more than half an hour the pilot's voice was heard.

'Ladies and gentlemen, I have to tell you that a flap is hanging down from one of the wings so we are on our way back to England.'

There had been no sensation of turning round, but I saw the sun was now on the other side of the plane.

Nothing about a possible air disaster is funny. Nothing, nothing, nothing. Procedure, however, can be comic. There were extensive comforting messages.

'This is not an emergency. Everything is perfectly all right and there is no cause for concern. However we don't like flying with a flap hanging down and that is why, rather than continue the journey, we are returning to Heathrow. As I say, this is not an emergency.'

'Methinks he doth protest too much,' ventured my neighbour, drily.

During the initial safe half-hour, we'd learned each other's headlines. He was a businessman connected with the nuclear industry. Excellent the way travel helps me to face my prejudices.

The pilot continued to reassure us until we were on the ground. I noticed a fire engine standing by as we came to a halt. My seat by the window overlooked the wing in which was the offending flap. I conducted a running commentary for my new friend.

'They've brought some steps up to the wing. There are some engineers looking into the hole. They're taking Polaroids. An executive man in a suit and a man in a boiler suit, and a man who is half-boiler suit and half-executive and a fireman with fluorescent trimmings. One man keeps pushing the flap shut, but it doesn't stay shut. Now he has put his head right inside the hole.'

It was announced, after about half an hour, that it was probably possible to fix the flap. In order to find out whether the fixing was a success, it would have to be tested under flying conditions, which would mean roaring up and down the tarmac very fast to see whether the flap stayed shut. If it didn't stay shut it would be necessary for us to disembark and travel on another aeroplane; so it had been decided that it would be better if we disembark now. We would be taken to the departure lounge and given refreshments until a replacement, different-sized aeroplane – the only one that could do the return journey to Moscow – was available.

Why is any of that funny to me? Was it relief that we had landed safely? Without the expertise, experience and effort of those men our situation could not be resolved. They were conscientiously doing their jobs. Is it the littleness of people in the face of greater forces? And the courage? Samuel Beckett? Actually flap is a funny word. They were being serious about a FLAP.

The duty-free bags were dragged from their resting place overhead. I found a seat in the lounge and settled down to wait for the trolleys of turkey and lobster to be wheeled towards us. Nothing happened. No information. No food. It was about eleven o'clock. I was ravenous. On the plane I had moved my clock forward the three hours to Moscow time and my stomach had gone with it. Some passengers had made for the counter and were buying sandwiches and beer. Others congested at the telephones. I heard snippets.

'Well, we were nearly at Berlin when the pilot said there was a flap hanging down...flap...FLAP – yes, so we had to turn round...'

I spotted Natalia Makarova – a ballerina has an unmistakable stance – wearing a scarf draped cleverly in a T. E. Lawrence way. It hid her face and was wildly chic. Next to me was curled a lean, alert girl – anything from twelve to eighteen. She, too, could have been a dancer. And Russian. Elfin, no hips. She looked dangerously frail, as many dancers do. She was anxious about a large hoop that accompanied her. I guarded it while she made her telephone call. She was an English gymnast returning to Moscow for training. She hoped to be one of two chosen from three to be in the British Olympic team.

It was all quite good-natured. There is a splendid smile that people use in such situations. It encompasses, 'We might have guessed this would happen. This has happened to me before. I'm well up to this sort of thing. So are the people who are meeting me at the other end. All the same I rather wish we hadn't opened that second bottle of wine last night, I want to go to sleep.'

Eventually an announcement told us that we could procure a five-pound voucher if we brought our boarding cards to the British Airways desk. It felt second rate and typical of the bad old-fashioned English days when Lady Dartmouth had famously complained about a dirty teacup.

After three hours, at the time we should have been landing in Moscow, we took off again. A feeling prevailed that the inconvenience we had endured should have been drowned with champagne on the house. It wasn't. For lunch or tea or supper we had excellent salmon. We arrived in Moscow at ten p.m. local time.

The journey counts? The arrival, in this case, was part of the journey. The maw to the carousel delivered most of my bags faster than usual. I felt smug. I would get to the teenage guard at passport control first. Time passed. A few final stragglers were labouring to drag their cartoned washing machines past the formalities. My cardboard box had still not shown. The aperture that expels luggage has a modesty skirt of rubber flaps – that word again – to conceal whatever steaming shocking truths lie behind. I decided to make an indecent assault. I stuck my head and shoulders through the slits and called in Russian:

'Hello? Anyone? I'm waiting. More. I'm Anglichanka. Where is it? Please.'

One of the unloaders did the sort of gross, brutal gesturing me away with words to match that I haven't experienced in England recently, any more, even now, again, yet. Except from a yuppie when I didn't cross the road quite fast enough in front of his gorgeous red car, and from a plain-clothes policeman when I turned into a Fulham street to park and there was a serious incident happening a few doors along, possibly with guns.

I hung on. I'm a brave person in Russia.

'British Airways carton? Big. Very important. Moscow Art Theatre.' I used as many incentives as I could muster, apart from *Ambassador*.

The caved-in box was contemptuously ejected, open at one end. I scrabbled inside, fearing that the fur coat had been snatched or, even worse, that my precious four pages of Art Theatre *Cherry Orchard* text had gone. From then on my credentials carried me through in a flash to Vadim, waiting for the second time, with red tulips and the official Volvo. He had learned of the flight delay only when he reached the terminal in the afternoon.

As we travelled luxuriously towards the capital he outlined that I should rest tomorrow, I must be tired, and then we could plan rehearsals. I didn't want to rest. I wanted to get myself through that stage door and stay there day and night until the first performance. I wanted to watch rehearsals, hear the language spoken on stage, in the canteen, in dressing rooms. In short, I wanted to feel part of the company.

Vadim told me that Tanya Lavrova was playing in *Seagull* this evening; that tomorrow it would be played again with another Arkadina. I have sat in the audience twice to see this production. I begged that I might watch the performance from the wings. I want to have a sense of the stage looking outwards; to get inside the smell, the size, the backstage spaces, the sound effects. If I am to have only one rehearsal on the stage, I want to reduce the number of shocks. I must acquaint my body with every bolt and screw and curtain and lamp and speck of dust beforehand. They take horses to sniff the jumps before the Grand National. I too need to do some primitive sniffing. One more request. Could I, please, have some sort of official identification to get me daily through the stage door? Of course. I handed Vadim a spare passport photograph.

Sasha, Ksenia and I drink tea. Familiarity. Time is imaginary. Within an hour I feel as if I've been there all my life. The call came that I may watch at noon a rehearsal of *Bobok*, an amalgam of three stories by Dostoyevsky, and that Alyona will accompany me.

Actors, on show for the first time in wig and costume – particularly if the outfit is incomplete – are highly tuned to notice a foreign body in the environment. Alyona introduced me to her director, who understood my wish to be perceived a friendly supportive colleague, not as a sentencing judge.

A vehicle for the talented younger members of the company. It was a delight. An inventive, funny presentation. Andrey Panin, blond and of medium height and build – perfect for the actor who wishes to remain unstereotyped and free to choose from a wide variety of roles – gave a spectacular comic performance. I feel that he will fall into all the major Chekhov parts, should do *The Government Inspector* soon, and I'd relish him in *Charley's Aunt* before that. Plastic is the word Russians use to describe mobile, physically expressive acting. I am becoming accustomed to it. Andryusha was definitely plastic. When I met him in the canteen during the interval he spoke good American-English. Alyona sitting next to me had had to suffer the discomfort of watching another actress playing the part they share. I could feel the tension rising and falling as the hurdles were approached and taken.

Henrietta, next door in the Art Theatre Museum, was surrounded by her workmates. It was her first day back from Sevastopol where she had left her perilously ill mother in order to be of service to me in rehearsal. I learned this as she spoke. She was sharing with her colleagues the news that she had given in her notice and that it had been accepted – let's hope that is a false alarm like Oleg's resignation. I knew that there were differences of outlook between herself and the Director of the Museum, but not the extent of the difficulty.

To add to this, her rapt audience heard how a group of two hundred nationalist Ukrainians had clamoured publicly for the Russians in Sevastopol (Henrietta) to go home. Crimea has been reclaimed. Next they will take control of the Black Sea Fleet, which is based in the port. Meaty stuff for unionists who fear the thunderclap of nationalism with violence. A meeting, banned by President Yeltsin and Mayor Popov, has been planned for 17 March. The old guard will try to persuade the Deputies to put Humpty Dumpty together again.

'I have a present for you.'

Vadim placed in my palm a stiff red identity card, three inches by two. Impressed on the outside was the Art Theatre logo, a seagull on the wing; inside my photograph, officially stamped. I read that I am 'Actress' that I may be in the theatre from nine a.m. to midnight until 31 December 1992. The mirror of my delight was on Vadim's face. I would no more sell my pass than an Olympian their gold medal.

42. Caro's MKhAT pass (interior).

Alyona nipped into the lift with me. We went up several flights so that I might sniff the room in which I would be rehearsing tomorrow; then she led me to the side of the stage to await curtain-up. The stage manager found a hard-backed chair for me to sit on, beside the piano. The smiling pianist was already an acquaintance. She rubbed her knuckles in her palms as we waited.

Actors and actresses began to make their way into the shadows from the brilliance of the dressing rooms; coaxing their bodies into the state of character at which the play begins. There is no questioning the parallel with priests preparing for their rituals. Laying out props, hitching an outer garment, taking deep breaths while clearing the throat, trying somehow to empty themselves of unnecessary rubbish in order to be a channel for something clear and light. One actress busied towards me, dressed as a maid, her arms filled with linen. She was waving at me enthusiastically, still her offstage self. It was Tanya, the glamour girl who planned my schedule. She acts as well. After her welcome I made myself as invisible as I was able.

A technician turned the handle of the wheel that parts the famous curtains. *Seagull* began. The atmosphere seeped around me, soft as a silken shawl. The music is haunting. A two-adjacent-notes motif comes at times of uncertainty as a warning, accompanying the players like an unseen friend on a lonely walk, of similar quality to the light. This, with the voices speaking the sentences as the author might have heard them, made a profound impression on me. Although I had seen this production more than once, I had never been as touched by it as I was this time, sitting beside and behind the actors. I hardly shifted on my chair for the three acts that are played without a break before the interval. I was entranced by the magic of theatre.

I commented to the stage manager during the interval how the audience was noticeably quiet, sparing with their laughter. I was told that the production has been running for ten years. There are many productions of the play in Moscow. This is a great play from a great author. They've lived with it all their lives. Audiences want to see the work of modern authors who can write freely, who aren't part of the System. People are exhausted. They need something new, then maybe they can come back to this with more attention.

Oleg Nikolayich's son, Misha, played Konstantin Treplev, Innokenti Smoktunovsky was Dorn. The actors were quiet as they waited to make an entrance. They sat on wooden benches, occasionally exchanging a word; flicking a hand to relax it, looking at the floor. Listening. There were very few others backstage. These performers, all of whom I have watched again and again, are going to be my colleagues in less than twenty-four hours.

12 March – Thursday

The day of my first rehearsal was the first anniversary of my last performance in Taganrog. There are no accidents. The postcode for Taganrog – 347900 – almost exactly matches my Equity number – 34970. Accident? Please!

I woke with comfortable time to get ready. Anxiety came and went in thuds. These actors have been playing in this production for three years. I hope they will feel friendly towards me. I dressed in pale pink.

I'd asked Henrietta whether, before meeting me, she could buy two or four carnations. Flowers, in even numbers, are given when someone has died. The Art Theatre has recently lost one of its most senior actors, Yevstigneev. I'd watched his work in numerous plays at MKhAT. My memory insists he always entered from an upstage position to allow for maximum preview and anticipation of his first line. He carried as much size and history as a stately home. He progressed slowly to the centre of the stage, looking straight ahead, taking in the weather conditions, indicating without hubris, 'I'm here, folks, you'd better believe your luck.' Then giving us reason to. Fred Emney, when I was young, had the same effect on me, more recently Bill Fraser – now, it's Les Dawson.

The length of shared employment some of the actors have enjoyed within the company is remarkable. They play big parts, small parts, turning out night after night, year after year; very often being encouraged with an entrance round from the affectionate audience, and with carnations at the curtain call. The fun and reward of repertoire. This theatre company is a family as Stanislavsky intended. We all know that family life is not without problems.

Oleg Nikolayich has been at the Art Theatre for fifteen years. Some of these actors were with him at his Sovremennik (Comtemporary) Theatre. When I first met Oleg Nikolayich he was in charge of what they call the New Moscow Art Theatre, a large edifice on the Tverskoy Boulevard. Outside, the building looks like a piece of shrapnel, spikily uninviting. The interior lacks vitality. It tells me that it will be good for me to watch a play there. Our

National Theatre on the South Bank to me has a no-wish-to-please exterior, but I feel happy when I reach the foyer. I made a blunder to Oleg Nikolayich during the early days of our acquaintance – one of many. The historic Moscow Art Theatre is being restored to its original state. I sounded a hope that the work will soon be complete so that he can leave this horrible theatre. It took some uncomfortable minutes and re-wordings for me to understand that, for Russians, the word *theatre* means theatre company, not theatre building. When the Old Moscow Art Theatre re-opened, the company divided. Oleg Nikolayich went to the original building, putting the actress/director Doronina in charge of the carbuncle.

I wished, as my first action in his theatre, to offer Oleg Nikolayich flowers in memory of Yevstigneev. Henrietta told me that even more recently an actor had died from the Doronina Company.

'There will be a third,' I voiced the English superstition that theatrical deaths come in threes. Henrietta looked at me sideways. Is Carolina a witch? We made our way to the windowless room I had glanced into the evening before.

Stage manager Olya and Kolya Skorik, staff director in charge of the introduction of new actors into already running productions, were waiting for us, preoccupied with the air conditioning. If it was switched on, the roaring would make it hard to concentrate; if not, it might get stuffy. What would I like?

'Oh please, I don't want anything special.'

The first actor arrived wearing a smart, striped suit. He introduced himself with a surname, followed by a first name, Davidov, Andrey. He helped them to decide that we were better off without the air conditioning. Andrey is the taller son of a huge father. Golden haired, between thirty and forty, I would describe him as a watchable leading man who hints at Pan-like unpredictability, an actor who has charmed me with his impeccable drunk acting.

Drink, as a personal problem, is rather rare for actors and actresses in England. It is largely disapproved of, so drunk acting is something that has to be learned like a foreign body language.

In Russia, my impression is, everybody knows what it is like to be drunk. I mean drunk in a courageous, sustained, continuous, lasting way. Not in the girlish 'Two glasses of champagne and I'm anybody's' style that afflicts me. Both men and women appear to have staggering capacity for alcohol. They can talk, even listen and engage in convincing argument with a half a bottle of vodka inside each belly around the table. It's a tourist attraction. One man I met had a punishing attitude to drink. I watched him perform a ritual. He cut an apple into small pieces. He emptied the brimming glass of vodka and swallowed. The first breath he took after swallowing was inhaled through a piece of apple which he held tight against his nostrils. Then he ate the morsel. This format enabled him to keep on drinking. The fumes from vodka are disagreeable. Russians drink vodka for result, not for the taste. Hangovers are not much acknowledged. Perhaps it is a question of habit. They're used to drinking, we're used to hiding our feelings. Well, we were until the last day of August 1997.

Andrey – Andryusha – never believe the first name you are told, that is only the outer door; each has at least two diminutives to take you to the inner person, (Carolinochka fills me with the same intimate warmth as does Caro in England) – Andryusha excels at the weaving drunk. As Gavrila, the non-speaking manservant in *Ivanov,* he forced my eyes away from other performers as he glided towards Lyebedev, carrying a tray stacked with small glasses of vodka. The unseeing concentration on his task tells me that for every tray he delivers there is one sunk by him in the servants' hall offstage. Andryusha plays Yasha in *Cherry Orchard*; his friendly welcome was expressed in suave American-English. Sergachev/Firs came into the room, with Nevinny/Yepikhodov and Shcherbakov/Pishchik hard on his heels. Three People's Artists/Knights standing about in their relaxed, working clothes. We were awaiting Oleg Nikolayevich Yefremov – People's Artist *narodny artist*/Knight.

In England, Charlotta is a much sought-after role. One of our highly respected directors, Declan Donellan, hearing that I was to play her, told me, with professional naughtiness, 'Oh, it's a wonderful part, she never has to look at any of the other actors!'

Her desperate loneliness, isolation and eccentricity offer rich pickings to any actress who is prepared to spend time practising illusions. It may, indeed, have been the very Englishness of her unconforming nature that intrigued Chekhov while he was writing for the governess, as Oleg Nikolayich had indicated when he first suggested that I essay the role with his company. In 1903/4 she was certainly a highly valued character. Initial casting ideas had Chekhov's wife, Olga Knipper, giving her first life. Knipper had played Arkadina in *Seagull*; had created Masha in *Three Sisters* and Yelena in *Uncle Vanya*. She was the leading Chekhovian lady of the Moscow Art Theatre. In fact she took on Ranevskaya, the central role in *Cherry Orchard*. Charlotta was given to a less well-known actress, Sofia Khalyutina.

Chekhov wrote: 'People who bear their grief inside them for a long time and are used to it only whistle and brood a lot.' This notion could be applied to more than one character in the canon. Charlotta might indeed qualify for this sort of expression. Kalantarov had had none of this. Charlotta, in his view, had quite an extrovert way of being. She showed herself boldly, describing her progress through the play in an uncomfortably raw manner. Somewhat mad. Knowingly so. In each act my external mode was different.

ACT I. The outsider who needs and claims attention.

ACT II. The despair of the ignored cucumber-eating observer, howling her need for someone to talk to. Offended by the caterwauling of the wretched love triangle Yepikhodov /Dunyasha/ Yasha, grateful for Firs.

ACT III. Charlotta, the clown, tries to chivvy the lamentable ignorant group into enjoying the last-chance party which culminates with the news that the cherry orchard has been sold to Lopakhin. Charlotta's tricks charge the evening with vitality and humour only for as long as she can hold the attention of the guests.

ACT IV. Abandoned on the scrapheap, Charlotta begs Lopakhin for a job. She knows, the others seem not to have learned, that we are on our own, we must take responsibility for ourselves. Charlotta's judgment fell hard on Ranevskaya in Kalantarov's estimation of the play. It's a terrific part. Kalantarov, whatever I felt about his treatment of our colleagues, had made available a generous scenario for me to tackle as my debut in Chekhovian drama. I am grateful, Juvenaly.

'Carolina!'

The warm bass voice of Oleg Nikolayich.

I turned to see my employer, flanked by two assistants. Today, wearing a fine executive suit, he looked slight, almost fragile. He kissed my hand, welcomed me to his theatre, then moved to the director's position behind the table. I presented the flowers, asking him to accept them in memory of Yevstigneev. He spoke a few words to complete the little ceremony. Then he smiled at me.

'Well, do what you want to do?' He turned to the others. 'She has her own tricks. Let her do what she wants to do.'

I felt breathless.

'But Oleg, it's your production. I don't want to…'

'No, no, do anything you like. Feel free. I'm sorry I can't stay. I have to go to my own rehearsal.'

He went on his way.

'You will see him again on Monday,' Kolya hastened to reassure me.

'He will take your Dress Rehearsal in the theatre on the morning of the first performance.'

'Two rehearsals and one on stage.' This was how I had prised respectful disbelief from such of my friends in England as could still hear the word Russia without vomiting. Today is Thursday. We'd better get on with it.

We were rehearsing the picnic scene. I remembered Charlotta's hurrying entrance. Rather, it' is an exit from an offstage scene, she is escaping.

Viktor/Sergachev, playing Firs, is sitting motionless on a tombstone. His white hair, spun glass, hangs in irregular lengths onto the dark green shoulders of his livery coat. His knees are together, the cream breeches and stockings end in buckled patent leather shoes. A top hat – called a цилиндр/tsilindr – sits on his head. He could have been there for months, years. Firs is my favourite characterisation from this lean, experienced *narodny* actor. He uses a dry hollow voice, shouting his words, as some deaf people do, without cadence or musicality or even inflection. He would succeed in Samuel Beckett. He is absent and present the way a stone is; noble in the service of the family who will leave him to die, forgotten.

Sergachev had passed through the theatre in Yalta while we were preparing for our performance.

'Success!' he wished me, on the move.

'We have had no rehearsal.' I denied his optimism.

'Sometimes that can be better.'

And he was gone.

Not today. I had hardly started on my march away from the singing jackals in the wings when Sergachev spoke.

'The stage is very wide. Don't speak until you are at least halfway across.'

He was joined in helpfulness by the two remaining actors, Andryusha and Slava Nevinny. Shcherbakov/Pishchik was not needed for the scene and had gone home.

Slava Nevinny has had me as a fan for ten years. He is one of the widest men I've ever met, and one of the nimblest, with his unruly dark hair and the face of a young boy; his hold on an audience is such that he is able, on a crowded stage, to focus his public's attention on one funny finger joint. He will start a routine that taken to conclusion must bring the house down. His outrageous skill and confidence make it necessary for him to demonstrate fully only the first few seconds, after which the merest indication of a nod or blink takes the audience the rest of the way while he sits back – without having to put his tonnage to the trouble. You need a lovable personality to get away with such cheek. He has it in spades and can hardly enter or leave the stage without applause.

Between them, aided by Kolya from the prompt table, these generous men guided me through the act.

'The gun is rather heavy.'

'You will be in a better light if you stand there.'

When I produced my own props, Nevinny knew the right moment to do the silk scarf strangle. Sergachev allowed me to lift his top hat with my right hand, '*Ein*', lift my straw boater with my left; '*Zwei*', put them both back onto the others' head; '*Drei!*' Ten times at least. Leaving his hair completely awry. There was a hubbub of interruptive, supporting encouragement; sometimes all of them speaking together, at which Henrietta would step in to clear the wood from the trees. We were able to work at full speed because of her subtle ability to translate the essence of a sentence quickly.

We stopped after a densely packed hour and a half. They had been as I had most hoped they would be. Skilled playmates. Darlings.

The production that kept Oleg from us is *Горе от ума*,[1] a massive classic in verse by the early nineteenth-century diplomat and poet Griboyedov. A romantic statue of the writer stands on a small *boulvar* outside one of the Metro stations that I use frequently. He was murdered while doing a tour of duty in Tehran. I have heard the play talked of frequently in Moscow, not with particular affection; more with the anxiety and guilt felt about a distant, gracious relation who may, if visited, deliver a dazzling heirloom. I had heard the director Mikhalkov announce that he was planning to make a film of the comedy, more than five years ago.

I saw Tabakov coming out of the lift one day previously. He was late.

'Where is the rehearsal?'

As if I would know.

'*Woe from Wit?* There, may be,' I pointed. 'How are you?'

'I'm alive.' His eyes rolled to heaven before he darted out of sight. Rotund Tabakov darts.

Nourishment in the canteen was followed by a fitting in an upmarket dressing room. Valentina, the dresser from December, clucked briskly and kindly.

'Try these shoes, Carolinochka.'

I've been accepted.

A costume fitting is an exhausting process for the body, but helpful for the character. You watch yourself taking the shape the

---

[1] *Woe from Wit* – a comedy by Alexander Griboyedov, written in 1823.

audience will see. I owe it to Charlotta Ivanovna to look at the mirror in front and behind. Henrietta stood and watched by the window.

'I can't believe this is happening,' I marvelled.

'It has never happened before.' She should know.

The two flowers I had presented in memory of Yevstigneev still lay on the table in the rehearsal room. At the front of the theatre stood a picture of the departed actor. I put my offering amongst the collection of blooms that honoured his achievements.

'Have you seen the poster?'

Henrietta's face told me there was more in the question.

16, 17, 18 March
In the play of A. P. Chekhov
Cherry Orchard
Actress of the Theatre Royal Brighton (England)
Caroline Blakiston
In the role of Charlotta

Below, in letters half the size, were the names of the six People's Artists, two Meritorious Artists, and six Artists who will appear in the production also.

'No.' I moaned in disbelief. 'Oh no-o-o-o.'

'What's wrong?' Henrietta was worried.

From the biography that I had forwarded to MKhAT had been chosen the fact that I had recently played Lady Bracknell at the Theatre Royal, Brighton. I collapsed in reeling, rollicking laughter. They think I'm employed by the Queen.

Henrietta, once she understood, was helpless, too. 'They must change it.'

'No, please, they mean to do me honour.'

I went home in good spirits, excited by the work and the situation, looking forward to tomorrow.

13 March – Friday: Rehearsal 2

The room began to fill with large actors. The three allies from yesterday, rejoined by Petya Shcherbakov/Pishchik. There was another Shcherbakov, Boris.

'Borya,' he introduced himself. This actor looks the film star he is. His face has the symmetry of a classical statue. His eyes are set as far apart as eyes can be; his head topped by golden hair. He had played an appropriately young Trigorin in *Seagull*, two nights before, and I had watched his Lopakhin last year. Petya, known as Uncle Petya, and Borya made fun for me of their unrelatedness. Another handsome giant bounced into the room, bursting with energy and juice. Seryozha Shkalikov is the most successful Trofimov I've seen. Even the humourless straggly wig and spectacles, while disguising him, can't obliterate this intelligent amusing actor. His personality is engagingly subversive. He started playing with Charlotta's dog. This prop creature is formed from white nylon fur at the end of a stiffened lead such as my children brought back from Disneyland, not at all life-like. Shkalikov had it lifting its leg against Shcherbakov/Pishchik's trouser. Shcherbakov/Pishchik co-operatively extended the scenario. Polina/Anya and Natasha/Varya entered quietly, Kolya, also, hurried into the room. The six Huge Ones clustered round the prompt table, talking nineteen to the dozen, smoking, smoking. We waited and waited. We were attendant, I felt, on one of the Gaevs. Lyubshin or Smokhtunovsky. It was distinctly intimidating. News came through that something had not worked out with Smoktunovsky and a car. Kolya suggested, therefore, that we retrace yesterday's ACT II steps until he arrives.

The half-hour that followed was the most testing of the whole job. In front of such a distinguished audience it was hard to stop the feeling of the sand running out of my hollow legs. I was spared the ordeal of witnessing Smokhtunovsky's arrival.

When I turned at the conclusion of the scene I saw the doyen of Russian theatre sitting, legs crossed, chin cupped in his left hand, leaning sideways over the back of a wooden chair. A smile played gently. He stood to raise my hand to his lips.

'We are so pleased to welcome you to our theatre. We are delighted to have you here.'

The moment had grandeur and formality, as well as professional normality.

We started to rehearse the family return in ACT I.

'You follow me onto the stage.' Borya/Lopakhin set off.

We were in tow to an absent Ranevskaya (back from Israel tomorrow). For the first half-page of dialogue Charlotta stands, ignored, watching the backs of the celebrating family.

'During this bit,' indicated Kolya, 'Charlotta plays with her dog, lifting it into her arms and cuddling it.'

'But Ranevskaya is speaking. It would be distracting.' He didn't insist.

Pishchik has a handful of nuts, from which he picks and pops into his mouth. This gives Charlotta the handle with which to draw attention to herself.

'And my dog eats nuts/*Moya sobaka i oryekhi kushayet.*'[2]

'*Sobachka!*' came the chorus. OK.

'And my *little* dog eats nuts.'

Her first line, followed soon by her first exit. Chekhov loved Charlotta.

Yesterday's bustle of helpfulness continued. When I get into a bath I have to fill up with hot water at least three times so that my body is warmed through to the bone marrow, no difference between it and the water. This was how I felt in rehearsal. They were heating me through and through, so that I was as much part of the scene as they. The advantage of this is obvious; it means that each actor will get the response from the audience that they are used to and deserve. There's nothing more annoying than a laugh missed through ignorance.

---

[2] Charlotta's line in Russian from *Cherry Orchard* is: 'Моя собака и орехи кушает.'

43. Smoktunovsky with me in rehearsal.

Smoktunovsky soon took the lead in my schooling – he is a most delicate man, making suggestions, dropping hints about the role, the play, the author; then immediately seeming to retract in case it is an intrusion.

'Or no?' His head bends enquiringly like a robin.

The second entrance in the first act includes the first trick. Ranevskaya is smoking. Lopakhin, seeing Charlotta standing at the door, apologises for not having greeted her properly before. He tries to kiss her hand. Her response is worldly.

'If you are allowed to kiss my hand, you will want to kiss...' She indicates elbow, shoulder and anything the director thinks suitable. Then Lopakhin asks her to do a trick. Ranevskaya and the others take up the cry to the court jester. She declines.

In the Yefremov production she distracts attention from her refusal to amuse them by pointing out the bad habit of smoking. She removes the cigarette from Ranevskaya's mouth, looks around, sees a convenient handkerchief in Lopakhin's breast pocket, pulls it out, shows it front and back to the assembled company, lays it over her left hand and proceeds with the Disappearing Cigarette illusion. After which she exits the stage.

She has regained power by unexpectedly entertaining them and by immediately leaving them to go to bed.

'To sleep,' she declares to each character she passes on her way, 'Sleep – sleep – sleep'. Her voice continues out of sight.

We know we have been watching an unusual woman. Our appetite is whetted. People who do what they do are interesting.

I'd watched the two other actresses who play Charlotta succeed with the Cigarette Trick convincingly. I was going to need more practise than I could expect the colleagues to endure. I managed the principle, but needed time to make it look easy. Smoktunovsky joined in from behind me.

'Do it very delicately, then when the cigarette has disappeared wave the handkerchief gently to show how beautiful and fresh the air is now.' He demonstrated with a beatific expression.

There is no religious attitude towards the text. 'Sleep, sleep, sleep,' was not indicated by Chekhov. Yesterday's ACT II material was an amalgam of original and re-write Chekhov, with additional '*Ein, zwei, dreis*' thrown in. How would this be looked on by Anton Pavlovich?

We moved on to ACT IV. The family are leaving their home for ever. The cherry orchard is being cut down. I was handed the rug that Charlotta bundles up and uses to suggest a baby. She alternately makes the crying noise and sings a lullaby. Both at Taganrog and here I sang, 'Bye Baby Bunting'. It has a sunny, repetitive tune and is without Russian undertone. I was fortunate to have a clear memory of the stage picture. I placed myself at the bottom of the imaginary staircase. Innokenti Mikhailich once more stepped from his position to guide me. Charlotta uses the baby to reproach Ranevskaya who deceives herself when she tells her daughter, Anya, that she will return one day. He wanted me to understand the most important moment in the play for Charlotta. It comes after she throws down the imaginary baby in disgust, dredges up her courage, and asks Lopakhin for a job. Then, he told me, she is completely real and exposed. This is her moment of truth. She has to leave his side so that he will not see her crying. As the greatest Hamlet I have ever seen described this episode to me, his eyes filled with tears. His face was transparent with feeling. He was Charlotta in her predicament.

Innokenti Mikhailovich Smoktunovsky is a person unlike any I have met. His presence is astonishingly light; airy, weightless, spiritual. I feel that I could invite him to step onto my fingertip and lift him as high as I will. He is neither tall nor short. His hair is soft and greyish. His thespian face is territory over which battles have been fought and won. I cannot guess his age. I shall never forget that internal soliloquy as he pushed his way through the crowded hall at Elsinore.

He is at my side, counselling me with this delicacy on the tiniest sensory detail.

'Carolinochka! One more little suggestion. May I?' Finger to lips, as if asking for quiet. 'Maybe?' Robin head. 'Or not?'

I try to describe one of the heroes of my life, and the best image I can find is that of Alicia Markova, genius too, in the second act of *Giselle* – thistledown.

When my turn came to plead with Lopakhin, I welled too, and had to move away so that the new owner of the cherry orchard would not see into my breaking heart. I made my exit, dragging the rug after me. Kolya reminded me that I should leave through another opening in the set.

'No, no!' remonstrated Innokenti Mikhailovich. 'She should do exactly what she did. Let her go off there. That's the way.'

Kolya agreed. 'After all,' Oleg Nikolayich had said, 'Let her do what she wants. Whatever makes her comfortable.'

Blakiston Caroline was feeling support on every level. Of course the rehearsal was for me and my work; I found myself in a living space they were creating for me. I had no sense that they had all been doing it for three years. I felt that they were first-timing with me.

After a period of heavy concentration a body needs nourishment.

We repaired to the canteen for some rice.

To my surprise I saw Dima/Ivanov sitting at one of the tables. Back unexpectedly from the West Indies. I had learned during December that he was to be away on a tour managed by Arkady, while I was undertaking my Art Theatre engagement. A bonus. We might be able to continue discussions for our Yasulovich project. As he got to his feet, I saw that he had a leg in plaster and was holding a stick.

'An accident on stage.' He brushed it aside. 'When can we meet?' I pleaded purdah until my performances were over. Of course.

I went home and lay down, stiff as a board, going over the gratitude I feel for those men. The girls, Polina/Anya and Natasha/Varya, modestly stayed in the background during rehearsal, watching but no suggestions. They show plenty of affection for Innokenti Mikhailich; tease him respectfully, do imitations of his walk. He leads them on with little skittish movements. They play like dolphins. It was everything I want to be a part of. Serious, important work, lightened by silliness.

'Is everything all right? Is there anything you want? We'll do it for you, no problem.'

Reassurances are what I meet at every turn.

I'm getting more rehearsal than I had been promised. I brought the Disappearing Cigarette illusion home to practise with. A couple of hours drudgery with an umbrella understudying the rifle, and sleight of hand with smelly cigarette butts should lift lurking anxieties and set me free to enjoy ACT III on stage. I was looking forward to it like anything.

14 March

This time last year I was celebrating my daughter's nineteenth birthday on the train from Taganrog, wondering whether the London florists had delivered as ordered, and whether the telegram sent from Taganrog had arrived. Both had. This year again I remember her beauty and her warm velvety personality with gratitude and longing. Her thick dark hair hangs in a curtain to below her waist. Happy birthday, darling Char. Perhaps she'll telephone later.

ACT III was my favourite in Taganrog. I was indescribably happy in my clown costume. The unpredictable, magical, somewhat dangerous side of Charlotta can take hold. I was released in an androgynous world. Man? Woman? Both? Neither? I could draw on the extremes of each. Cruel or compassionate without warning or justification. Free to show all the grief I've ever known, all the joy. It's a seductive habitat.

I used to fear clowns when I was taken to the circus as a child. Those huge painted *papier-mâché* heads struck me with dread. Please God, don't let us have seats in the front row or the gangway. The clown without an extra head is even worse. His face is painted to make me feel sorry for him. He is tearful, vulnerable. But let him near and he reveals savage heartlessness. He might look deep into my soul with the small wet eyes that sit behind the exaggerated make-up, and ask me to stand up and be exposed in the blinding searchlight that follows him around. Please God, don't let him come this way.

I knew my need to be an actress before I was eight. 'Caroline wants to be an actress. She'll help the conjuror.'

'No, God, please, God, no.' I rooted in unending paralysed blush, eyes welling as the man dressed in black and white held up an umbrella and then a sheet of newspaper.

'Here is an umbrella and here is a sheet of newspaper. What shall I do with them?'

Why is he asking me? Doesn't he know how to do the trick? Please, God, don't let the tears run over until I'm sitting down again.

He tried again, showing the audience with a look that he had chosen his assistant badly.

My mind blanked out by terror and shame, I waited for the agony to end.

'Wrap them up.' He prompted, eventually, seeing he had a flop on his hands.

'Wrap them up.' I whispered.

Everything was prepared and waiting for my introduction to the third act. The steep stairs had been rolled into place. Helpful lighting warming things up. The musicians were waiting in the wings, as was the house composer – brilliant Vassily Nemirovich Danchenko. His sounds have captured my imagination with every production that I have seen, and I've carried away snatches to

England, where I pick them out on a piano or simply relive them in my head.

Olya, the stage manager, was showing me the tables, one on each side of the stage, behind the proscenium arch, that hold the props Charlotta uses in the third act.

Then I saw Iya Sergeyevna Savvina, People's Artist/Dame, famous in the film *The Lady with the Little Dog*, accustomed interpreter of Charlotta; she was neatly dressed in blue jeans and checked shirt, with her hair tied back from her face – Doris Day. She was smiling.

I thought: 'You've come to destroy me.'

I said: 'You've come to help me.'

She said: 'I've come to help you.'

I said: 'Oh, thank you, thank you!'

It is Charlotta's energy that motors the beginning of the Act. Savvina took me through every entrance, more than once, clearly, wholly practical. I salute and thank her. Iya means Violet, a rare name in Russia.

Natasha Tenyakova/Ranevskaya arrived through the stalls and climbed up onto the stage, clearly unwell.

'I'm just back from Israel,' she explained wryly. 'I immediately caught a cold and lost my voice. But I'll be all right.' She sank into her coat looking wretched, but worked without complaint.

I took friendly Uncle Petya Shcherbakov/Pishchik to one side and asked whether he would like to join me in a card trick to surprise the others, one that is not usually part of the proceedings. This smiling man agreed at once.

The only unsolved issue was the 'dangerous' three-foot sparkler that I entered with to get the act off to an exciting start. The music came bouncing from the orchestra in the wings but try as he might the prop man was unable to get the firework to ignite. Oh well, I'm sure it will work on Monday.

Sergachev/Firs, who stands motionless for ages beside a column with a chandelier on top, invited me to stick one of my six wands into his clenched fist as a way of disposing of it in a hurry. I found myself *Chef d'Orchestre* throughout the Act. Starting and stopping the music at will. Henrietta had been set in the front row with pad and pencil to be my memory.

We practised the quick change into the ACT IV black and white skirt and jacket. Perfect. Another go with the rug-baby and that was it.

'Any problems, any worries?' asked Kolya, kindly, when the rehearsal ended. I felt cheerful and panicky.

'No. No. Well, yes. I need more rehearsal.'

'You will remember everything. No problem.'

A bonus had been watching Andryusha/Yasha sitting in a corner trying to work out the mechanics of the Silk Scarf Choking Illusion using his own woolly one. I still owe him the secret.

15 March – Sunday

In my Moscow home, the normality of domesticity cools the rising barometer of creativity. Sasha and Ksenia are a devout couple. Lent is experienced fully in church-going and fasting. Plain food is to my taste so no changes are necessary for me and there is always enough. Ksenia came home, one day, gleeful at having succeeded in buying fresh yeast. This was crumbled onto a tray in the kitchen and left to dry on the windowsill above the radiator. It will stay there, a temptation to straying playing fingers until she makes her Easter cakes for the family. I know one or two houses in north and south Russia where pictures of the last tsar are displayed alongside religious icons. Back in this quiet, family apartment, I wonder about the Revolution and wish I knew how many people were involved in it. I can't picture it in numbers. Would they constitute a full house at Wembley? Similarly the French Revolution. I imagine the great FA stadium packed with *perruques, jabots, redingotes* – eating cake – it doesn't give me an answer.

I slept long and deep. I had been offered a rehearsal room from eleven o'clock. There I found Olya setting out the props, and a new functionary – *suflyor* – prompter, Natasha; dark-haired with interested eyes and a broad smile. She was sitting behind the table with the fat script. I forgot that Sunday in Moscow is not a day off.

'Please, go home, I am happy to work alone.'

'On the contrary...' pretend schoolmistress face. 'I have to be here, it's my job to see that you don't make a mistake.'

I know actors and actresses who pay their children, first of all sixpence, then in line with inflation, to take them through their part. I hadn't the nerve to offer mine that tedium, though Charlotte did once save me from despair when I was learning technical jargon for a Treasury training film.

Natasha gave me the cues again and again. She sat on Firs's tombstone and endured *tsilindr* on, *tsilindr* off.

'Don't you want to kill me?' I asked, after an hour.

'No, I enjoy it. It's really interesting to watch the different way each actress works.'

We went to renew ourselves in the canteen. Coffee is made in a long-handled Middle-Eastern pot. The grounds and cold water are put into the container and moved about on a bed of sand so hot that the water boils. Expert and delicious. I also chose beetroot salad and plain boiled kasha (buckwheat) onto which a dollop of butter was dropped. A slice of black bread completed the repast.

'I feel so happy and excited,' I blurred to Isolde as we passed her table. She delicately spat sideways three times, equivalent to crossing fingers for luck. It's common practice.

Usherette Julya had nipped upstairs from her duties in the stalls. A children's matinee of *Ondine*. She joined Natasha and me with her cup. We shared tales of motherhood and, she – grandmotherhood.

I find the door to the stage and peep through. Bare. Abandoned, after the matinee. The auditorium half-lit. I walk to the prompt corner, take a chair to the edge of the stage and sit down. In my own time I will get the feel of it, find my point of command. I send my message systematically to every seat in the auditorium. Some technicians wearing soundproof slippers, come to change the rods that hold the black velvet drapes, preparing for the evening performance. They acknowledge me with friendly nods. It is very warm. Trouble is taken to make the theatre comfortable for the people who work in it. I take some photographs and collect a few loose splinters from the boards. They will make good first-night presents for special people who understand my illness.

At home, I spend three hours sorting socks and tights – unromantic, but eternally scarce – and writing cards to thank the cast and associated people for their help and kindness.

Ides of March. Bed.

16 March – Monday

A bright morning. The snow on the trees in the courtyard below is a dry scattering of sugar.

As I gently negotiate entry into this climactic dream-of-a-lifetime day, there is time to open my pores and strengthen myself with the ordinariness of some of my recent experiences. I must be looking to some degree native. I was stopped in the street by a young man asking for the Moscow Art Theatre Studio.

'I'm going there myself.'

And by a very dishevelled out-of-town old man.

'Is it this way? Is this the way?'

I couldn't make out where to.

'I'm sorry, I'm *Anglichanka*.'

He forgave me, laughing. Sometimes I bump into someone I know in the wide Tverskaya Street underpass. I came upon Isolde treading carefully. We walked arm in arm because it was the first day of snow and the granite steps can be treacherous. One afternoon, I met, coming up from below, Slava Lyubshin. Film star, heart-throb, on his way to play Tartuffe. He pulled the collar of my coat closer round my neck.

'You must keep warm. It's very cold.' He was dressed in jeans and ski-hat, the same as any other passing worker. No question of presenting himself in the street to be recognised. I guess it's hard to preen in four inches of slush.

Events. Events take charge. I arrived at the theatre to prepare for the Dress Rehearsal.

'We have great sorrow,' said the woman, taking my outer clothes from me. 'Shcherbakov has died in the night.' She shook her head in disbelief. Shcherbakov/Pishchik, Uncle Petya. Not an old man. The third actor dies. A friendly co-operative colleague, with whom I have scarcely brushed wings, has called it a day. I saw at once this is a family loss for the theatre.

I made my way to the warm, cheerful dressing room. Tanya appeared. No commiseration seemed adequate.

'Maybe they'll cancel the performance?'

'No, everything will go ahead. Oleg Nikolayich has been rehearsing since nine o'clock with Kashpur.'

'Has he played Pishchik before?'

'No.'

'No understudy?'

'No.'

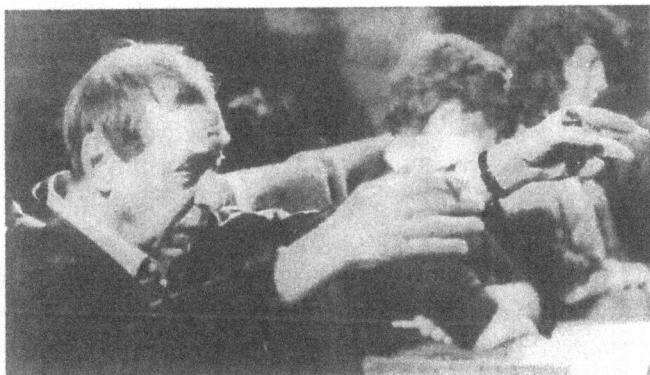

44. Yefremov in rehearsal, 1994.

Overwhelmed, she fled down the passage.

The dressing room is at the stage end of a long curving corridor. It is stylishly set out in rather a grand way. The actors are treated to the same pale wood as the audience. I found a dressing table with drawers and four small standard lights. A bed to lie on, a wardrobe. My costumes were hanging, waiting.

When Valentina had dressed me, we were silenced by uncertainty; I went down onto the stage.

One or two of the actors were standing inert, invaded by the news. I saw others being poleaxed as they arrived. I had watched

Kashpur/Pishchik in *Seagull* a few nights ago. He came onto the stage now, hugged and kissed me. Polina/Anya was sitting at the bottom of the stairs, wiped out. I approached her tentatively.

'I'm with you.'

She nodded, speechless.

They were all open, affectionate, hurt. Tenyakova, completely overwhelmed; Nevinny could hardly speak, but everybody hugged me, and I hugged them. Smokhtunovsky, sitting at the side, jumped to his feet to greet me.

'Please, please,' I begged.

It's an archetypal theatrical happening. A death. We go on anyway. There's no business like show business.

I was the only one in costume and make-up. A table had been erected for Oleg Nikolayich in the stalls. A glass of tea and an ashtray ready. When he came into the auditorium, very formal, 'Let's start, let's start', it became clear that he is going to take a full rehearsal. He must go through the whole play for the new Pishchik, not just my scenes, but he is also giving direction to other actors, probably to calm them down, to make them feel ordinary. He asked for concentration and for people to get inside their roles.

I felt I should offer not to play tonight. One of their actors is being introduced to a role he has never played before, in drastic circumstances. They should have one of their own playing Charlotta. Henrietta felt it wouldn't be accepted, but would tell Kolya who could suggest it to Oleg Nikolayich. The answer came. This is theatre, we carry on as planned. There has been a lot of publicity. Some people will be coming to see Carolina. They must see Carolina.

Lyosha Zharkov was rehearsing Lopakhin and will play tonight. This is a complete surprise. We'd journeyed to Vladimir together last year, he having a walking stick to aid a broken leg. I noted it cured, as we hugged.

After my first line and exit I stood in the wings. Tenyakova/Ranevskaya indicated a chair for me to sit on.

'I'm fine, thanks.'

'Sit down! SIT DOWN! I'M TELLING YOU!' She took my hand, fiercely kind. Everything is going to be heightened today. I sat in the wings. Oleg was finding something to say to each actor. I looked to see whether Zharkov had his handkerchief for the Cigarette Illusion. He had. Kolya came round with a useful reminder: 'Don't forget that first you refuse to do a trick, then you change your mind and do one.'

Yefremov stays mostly in the stalls, speaking from there. On stage Shkalikov/Trofimov is being practical. He leads Kashpur/Pishchik from place to place. Gradually the atmosphere relaxes. Actors begin to be able to hear each other's attempts at jokes and laugh a little. The possibility of future re-enters the arena. Russian adaptability. It takes the pressure off. The feeling that we're going to survive anyway stops the over-dramatic do or die sensationalism. It'll be all right, we'll improvise. It's the Russian credo. It's what they're made for. It's what they're training for always.

Back in my dressing room to change for ACT III, I was visited by Alyona who had been watching to see that the costume and make-up were all right. She told me I can be heard at the back. The Tannoy call came, structured and polite, not so different from England: 'Everyone down for the beginning of the second half, please.'

A special call for me.

'Carolina, we beg you to come to the stage.' I ran down to check my wands.

I felt confident for all six entrances. The practice paid off. The music came when it should. Kashpur/Pishchik took on the extra card tricks without a murmur. I was taken by the hand in the dark for the quick change into the black dress for the last entrance. It was exciting to find myself asking for a job from Zharkov, a Lopakhin I had not acted with before. A coiled spring. He listens well and gives strong response. Smoktunovsky had taken a personal interest in this exchange from the start. While I was speaking the speech, he was doing commentary from behind me.

'Yes. Y-E-S. Very good.' I went off into the wings. He followed and stuck his head offstage after me. 'Very good. V-E-R-Y good!'

'I lo-o-o-ve you!' I laughed back at him in English. It was uplifting.

An unforeseen demand comes near the end of ACT IV. The family have got their coats on to leave. They sit down together, as is traditional before a journey. Pishchik arrives in a flurry to pay back some money he owes. He is unaware that a major departure is at hand. When it hits him, he too, on the verge of tears, must find somewhere to sit. The only vacant space (in this production) is the family rocking horse. Michael Frayn gives us:

'Well, there we are... There we are... Be happy... God give you strength... There we are, then... To everything in this world there is an end... And if one day the rumour reaches you that the end has come for me, then remember this old... this old horse, and say: "Once on this earth there was a certain Simeonov-Pishchik... God rest his soul..."' Kashpur, reading from the script, bravely kept going. Many of the actors began to cry. Nevinny/Yepikhodov, sitting there, huge, sweating. His great wounded face suddenly streamed with inconsolable tears. The actors looked at the ground. They looked anywhere rather than at the rocking horse where their friend had sat.

The Dress Rehearsal finished before four o'clock. Henrietta came to the dressing room with her notebook and read me Oleg Nikolayich's remarks. A reporter arrived to interview me. The press come at any time, it seems, without warning. I quite like it. It makes for spontaneity although, in this case – she was newer to the shock than I – the conversation was short and mournful.

In the canteen Oleg Nikolayich was sitting, smoking. Responsible. Available. It was the first time today that I had seen him close up. When I approached he got hastily to his feet.

'Можно?[3]' I asked, and gave him a hug. 'I'm sorry about everything.' His shoulders were too heavy to shrug.

'Что делать?'[4]

To spare him further expense of spirit, I went to a table by the window to eat with Henrietta.

---

[3] 'May I?'

[4] 'What is to be done?' Also, the title of a famous nineteenth-century novel by the Russian philosopher, journalist and literary critic Nikolay Chernyshevsky.

During the meal break, my belongings had been moved into Savvina's star dressing room across the lobby. Her name is on the door. It is a much bigger, personal room. Iya Sergeyevna's chosen pictures and photographs hang on the walls. Potted plants stand between the bed and two armchairs. A private shower and Ж lead off the cubby-hall. The main staircase to the dressing rooms is wide and grand, made of creamy marble. The Art Nouveau, decorative banisters are executed in bronze. These respectful gestures towards the employees of the Art Theatre elevate them and give them status.

Alyona, light as a feather, was dusting around my every need. She flicked from me the effort of delivering cards and presents, dashing to each dressing room in turn.

Thus, also, the draining exchanges were avoided that would have happened in this supercharged time, which would have helped neither donor nor receiver. An undisguised blessing. She brought me an armful of pale pink roses. Such a sight is almost unknown in Russia, where the cost of three or five stems eats into a week's wages. Her sweet, unthinking generosity and care were among the most valuable supports of the day. In a vase the roses were reflected three times in the dressing table mirror.

I asked that I might rest in the dark, alone. A rug was laid over me, but I continued to feel cold. Nevinny/Yepikhodov knocked and entered, full of apology, carrying a card and a small bottle of brandy. Polina/Anya likewise. Her watchfulness in rehearsal had felt deeply supportive. She has the frail intensity of the ballet dancer she used to be. She brought a wicker basket to hold a hot glass of tea. A bottle of natural herb oil was given me by Tanya who is standing by in case I need her hair services after all. Tenyakova/Ranevskaya – a big presence, feminine and warm – what a lot there is to learn about womanliness from these Russian actresses; they go, uninhibitedly, with their feelings. I'd admired her Ranevskaya from the first. She wears her own dark hair in a shoulder-length bob. She inhabits this play. She, nearly paralysed with shock, brought me a crucifix from Jerusalem made of hard, probably olive, wood. And a carnation. Kolya Skorik came with a bunch of flowers. Perhaps the most emphatically theatrical present of all was from Vadim. He arrived with a personalised Moscow Art Theatre poster overprinted in the writing they use to advertise a play. It celebrates me/Charlotta for treading the boards of the Moscow Art Theatre and finishes with their version of 'Break a leg' – 'No down, no feathers.' (*Ни пуха, ни пера.*) No performer wishes a cracked femur, no hunter wishes an empty bag. '*К чёрту!*/To the Devil!' is the obligatory response I had learned in Taganrog. At the bottom a fine bunch of tulips has been painted. We hung it on the dressing room door for me to enjoy luxuriously now.

Henrietta's connection with the Art Theatre is so close and her awareness so acute that I was surprised to hear her ask, 'When do you give presents, before or after the first night?'

'Now.'

She shyly lifted from her bag a small parcel. Inside I found a picture which she had commissioned especially for this occasion. It is a most delicate montage made from birch bark, wood shavings and filigree leaves to show an exquisite tiny Russian snowscape with a road leading to the horizon. I could tell Henrietta immediately where she will find it when she and Gennady visit me by the sea.

Three bells, two, one – signalled the decreasing time to curtain-up, as in Taganrog.

There was no time for me to feel nervous for myself. It was historic and given full value by top professionals.

Olga spoke quietly into the Tannoy as we stood bunched to go through the narrow entrance. 'Everything is about to begin.'

Just do it.

Debutants Kashpur and I got our bearings in the short first entrance. In the second the Disappearing Cigarette disappeared and got a round of applause. Charlotta's long scene in ACT II went splendidly.

I was led to my dressing room to change before the interval, given a glass of tea and sat listening to the actors finishing the act which I've seen them play from the front and am now a part of. Astounding, frankly.

I had a flying visit from Alyona, herself in performance in the Studio Theatre down the hall.

'How's it going?' Her eyes were alight with excitement for me.

'Fine. How's yours?' I laughed.

'Fine. See you later,' she squealed and dashed to make her next entrance.

The feeling in the theatre is receptively warm. The stage is flat. No rake. I have no sense that there is a bridge to cross to reach the audience. The front row is very close to the stage. It's a heart-to-heart situation.

ACT III

Kashpur/Pishchik made a tiny transposition of lines during one of our exchanges. He was full of unnecessary apology, as if he had ruined my chances. The huge experience of this compact actor added to his courage, meant that the audience could not have known the crisis conditions of his performance. I heard no announcement before the play began. Throughout the evening Shkalikov/Trofimov conducted him. He whispered lines to him, said, 'Sit down now.' Made himself a back-up shadow. I found that responsible comradeship one of the most moving aspects of the night. There was also Olga and my суфлёр,[5] Natasha, on either side of the stage with a prompt script for him to dash to between entrances or from which they could call a line if all else failed. It didn't. For the harrowing rocking-horse section he sensibly carried some papers along with the money. Amongst the papers were a few sheets of script.

ACT IV

After the rug-baby and asking Lopakhin for a job I have quite a long wait in the wings before the final appearance. I was joined by Tenyakova/Ranevskaya and Smokhtunovsky/Gaev. Innokenti Mikhailich asked me whether I would like to sit down. Terrified of missing the entrance, I declined and stood clutching the rug. He stayed beside me.

'It's not a very good day to have your première.'

---

[5] Prompter.

'I am glad to be here with everybody. Will you play tomorrow, too?'

After confirming that he would play again, he tried out some of the English that he has been learning for four months. He has a daughter living in America. To speak English is also useful for making international movies. He talked of a film made in Italy with 'One of your great stars, Tom Conti. Also Isabella Rossellini. She's a very good actress. So it was Tom Conti and Isabella Rossellini – and me.' He gave a self-deprecating, pussycat smile.

I played, 'No, no, it was YOU and tomcontiandisabellarossellini' Caught out in flirtatious sycophancy, I thought I heard silence on stage. I've missed it! I dashed forward.

'No, no, no, no. Not yet, not yet.' He saved me. 'You're far too early. There's lots of time. Ages.'

'A week?'

'A month.'

I feel he enjoys chit-chat, danger, intimacy and silliness, like the rest of us. I'm hooked. He's wonderful.

At the end of the play, Firs, forgotten and abandoned, appears alone; he realises that the family has gone without him and settles down to accept his fate. Tenyakova/Ranevskaya gave in at last to the feelings she had controlled all evening. She sobbed and sobbed. The others were raw with misery.

They do an operatic curtain call. Actors come through the gap in pairs, receiving individual applause. I was with Kashpur/Pishchik. We came on third. Flowers were handed to me from the stalls by Igor and by Gennady. In the general line-up Sergachev /Firs took me beside him. More flowers from Andrei Tarkovsky's sister, Marina. Then – everything taking me by surprise – onto the stage walked Vadim, representing the management, with a large ribboned bouquet. He kissed me and murmured, 'Умничка!'[6]

I wanted to give a flower to Kashpur/Pishchik, who in ordinary circumstances would have been the centre of attention for saving the day. He wouldn't accept. Absolutely not.

---

[6] 'Clever girl!'

The actors, emptied of everything, hugged me and went away to grieve. Igor and Natasha Yasulovich were waiting in the lobby, supportive.

There, suddenly, was Oleg Nikolayich, a tear in the corner of his eye. I leaned my head against his chest and let my own feelings overflow.

'*Поздравляю!*'[7] he said gently. He was mourning his friend.

At such a time the person, who in this case was me, is suffering a degree of shock and needs to be led, told what to do. Henrietta and Gennady guided me to my dressing room, bringing with them a journalist from *Izvestia*. I learned from the questions she asked that having a real foreigner playing Charlotta Ivanovna makes them understand more about the part than they previously had. She sensed the loneliness. She felt that Charlotta is an aspect of all the characters in the play and holds up a mirror to them. She was putting into words exactly what I've been trying to do: to make the woman in some respects the Chorus.

'Let's hope that's what Chekhov wrote,' she said, adding that she had never seen such a relationship between Firs and Charlotta. Sergachev/Firs responds delightfully to the way I do the hat exchange. I play with him like a child. His dear blank, stone-deaf face broke into a seraphic ear-to-ear smile as he realised he was being taken account of and included in something. He had not done it in rehearsal. What a reward for Charlotta/Carolina. He even mouthed the word '*Госпожа*.'[8]

That's it. I don't know if I have any ambitions now. I've done what I wanted to do.

Henrietta reached into her bag.

'Here is your first payment. You have to sign the paper. They are giving you more than you thought.'

I had to be transferred slowly back into my own clothes. We picked up the flowers – all but the roses – the Nevinny cognac, and left. So late were we that Alyona had had to collect master keys to lock up the dressing room.

---

[7] 'Congratulations.'

[8] 'Madame.'

A rather battered photograph of Shcherbakov had been placed on a ledge inside the stage door. I laid two carnations in front of it.

Volodya, Alyona's husband, my Russian son, was patiently waiting in his car to drive me the few hundred yards home. It is necessary to go halfway to the Pushkin Statue before you are allowed to make a U-turn in this six-lane highway, the main artery to the Kremlin.

'I'm sorry we don't have a party for you.' Ksenia was putting food onto three plates. 'This is a party.'

We sat on stools in the kitchen. Sasha, of aristocratic lineage with Celtic features and colouring, poured nips of Nevinny brandy.

In bed, I did dozens of re-runs of *A Day in the Life of an English Actress*. I stopped when I reached a frame which told me that I had neither wrapped socks nor written a card for Uncle Petya Shcherbakov. Only for him had I not.

17 March – Tuesday

I woke feeling comfortable and relaxed. Another fairy-tale morning; the snow is more solid, inches-thick cake icing. The strength of the sun, however, contradicts the freeze and water drips from the melting crust at the top of the building. It descends like slow rain, each drop a smooth, illuminated crystal as it falls past the window.

This is the first anniversary of the referendum held to decide whether or not to keep the Union together. I was interested, as we prepared for our Gala at the Hermitage Theatre this day last year, to discover that it seemed not to be of great moment to my colleagues. Some told me that they had voted before leaving home. It would have concerned me hugely to be involved in voting for the separation of Scotland, Wales, Northern Ireland and England. I found that I was far more excited by the issue than they were. The national decision had been to retain the Union. Now, a year later, that vote has been blotted out. A meeting was called to lobby Deputies from all over the CIS to persuade them to reunite. The old Moscow lags were talking of two hundred and fifty thousand demonstrators outside the Manezh (the customary meeting place beside Red Square), of tanks on the streets, barricades. Added to this we were told that an unknown number of Deputies were arriving secretly at an undisclosed destination south of Moscow for their deliberations.

I decided to gain fresh air and exercise by watching the Changing of the Guard, then by mingling with the crowd, hoping to take photographs of patriots voicing their views.

Ksenia accompanied me for the midday ritual at the Mausoleum. I was feeling happy. I felt sure that with my newly earned riches she would no longer be able to refuse some contribution to the housekeeping.

'Could we talk about that tomorrow?' She won't hear of it.

I told Ksenia there are two best days for an actress. One is when you have been offered a job and the play is good, the part – good, the cast – good, the director – good, the money – good, the billing – good, and you haven't yet started working on it, so you are still free in your head. The other is the morning after a pleasing first night.

The Kremlin was glittering gold domes to its glory. We ambled around the high walls of the great fortification.

'Let's go inside,' suggested Ksenia. 'We can stroll through and out again. I haven't done that for a long while.'

'Can we just walk in?' I remembered paying.

'You only pay to enter the churches and museums.'

Closed today. We sauntered past the Flame of The Dead Soldier as we returned to the open space where small groups were already collecting. Red flags with hammer and sickle – how harmless they look without the might of the System behind them. A woman, sixtyish, was a Stalin supporter. Her commitment and agitation gave me a good view of her silver teeth. The demonstrators were mostly far from young. They were urgent and distressed. Posters and placards had been carefully written out. A photograph of Lenin leaned against a parapet, guarded over by a woman with a traditional floral scarf tied under her chin. Women figured equally with men.

The television cameras were looking for extremes, but not finding anything likely to spark fisticuffs, let alone tanks. I have only marched once in England. Democratic humour was strong.

Here, there were noisy pockets of undirected anger clustering for comfort, but with nowhere to channel their rage, neither numerous nor menacing, they were watched tolerantly.

I raced, obedient to an urgent call from Irina, to be interviewed in my dressing room for television. The lengthy exposure was stopped only when it was announced that the curtain would rise in ten minutes. I had to whoosh the invaders from my room.

What it is to be surrounded by actors who know what they are doing.

'How are you today?' I asked Kashpur/Pishchik.

'Worse.' Climbing Everest two days running, with a sense of humour. I love actors.

I stayed by the side of the stage throughout ACT I, partly to consolidate myself in the atmosphere because I didn't want to miss the sights and sounds. I noticed the little red light of the television camera flicking on and off whenever I spoke. It had not been indicated that they would be in the front row, a yard away.

During the interval, a tap at my door revealed Andryusha/Yasha's father wearing his Director of the Art Theatre Museum hat. He was hosting Richard MacMahon from Illinois. This American has achieved a translation of *Cherry Orchard* which he claims shows unseen material from the days when Stanislavsky, believing that the audience would have difficulty with the second act, was trying to realise the original production of the play.

Vadim appeared again with a bouquet for me at the curtain call. Tenyakova handed on the flowers she was given and would take none from me in return.

I had begged Alyona to ask tactfully whether I might take a photograph of the entire cast on stage at the end of the performance. By the time the applause stopped an armchair had already been set upstage against the nursery window. Innokenti Mikhailich pressed me to sit down. The actors generously stayed to crowd around me as if they were my family. Alyona snapped with my camera.

Oleg Nikolayich disclosed something extraordinary in rehearsal yesterday. All of Chekhov's dramatic works were fed into a computer in the United States. The information came out that his writing is of the rhythm and style found in the chants and liturgy of the Orthodox Church. This revelation added to an awkward sequence of thoughts that have been accumulating in my mind. I have been excited by the small exchanges I have with Zharkov/Lopakhin. Alyosha Zharkov is an actor of highly tuned intelligence, of compressed energy and speedy reaction. Thin and dangerous. I might be able to describe an English actor thus and hope to see him in a play by Noel Coward. Not Zharkov. I cannot imagine him playing in *Private Lives*. Why? Because he's Russian. I have found myself coming up against something I don't want to face. A growing uncertainty about how foreign actors can play convincingly in Chekhov. Zharkov is a definitive Lopakhin. Why? Because he is Russian. He comes from the right place to play Lopakhin. The place that Chekhov wrote from, Russia. I write this with discomfort. I know that the greater the apprehension I gain of Russia and her people since living and working here, the greater is my anxiety about the translation of a classic from one language to another.

'Tell us something new, Caroline.'

In England, we pride ourselves on our Chekhov. I've seen splendid productions with glorious performances. We love him because we believe his characters speak in an ordinary, natural way, like us. For Russians now he is writing about the past; a time before the Revolution, which is rather ancient, a period of nostalgia for some. But even when he wrote, it was heightened language; not free and naturalistic, the way we perceive. When we watch a visiting Russian company, we note the Russianness and feel satisfied. We aren't Russian, so we must find our own way into the universality of the characters and take what we can from it. It is not because I am giving a Russian performance in *Cherry Orchard* that people tell me they gain insight into Charlotta Ivanovna. It is my un-Russianness that opens their eyes – nothing to do with me. I know that Pam Gems and Michael Frayn have opened doors for me, and a recent *Uncle Vanya* by Richard Briers appealed to me with tragi-comic believability beyond any I've seen here or there. A long-ago Yelyena from Rosemary Harris is etched in my mind's eye – and I always revert in homage to

Smokhtunovsky's sizzling Hamlet. So shut up. Everything is defined by its opposite.

18 March – Wednesday

The funeral of Petya Shcherbakov in the theatre at noon. I was not sure that my presence would be appropriate. It might be intrusive. I must judge that when I get there. I need to be with them. I carried four carnations. Tanya Lavrova was parking her car near the stage door. We hugged briefly. She shook her head. Her arms made a disjointed movement. Speech was out of the question. I followed her inside.

Vadim, wearing a black tie, put his hand on my arm. 'I'll take you in.'

'It's all right. I'm meeting Henrietta. Thank you.'

Asya and Andrey Myagkov and his wife stood together. His cold hand lifted mine to his lips in salutation. Andrey is a richly comic actor on any other day. Lyubshin, expressionless, inclined his head in recognition. The leading actors mustered in a stricken gathering, within which each stood separate in their sorrow. I am received with dignity. In this stark moment I am not family.

It was nearing midday. The secretaries and backstage workers were all wearing black. I removed my thick coat because everyone else had done the same. I found a dark skirt to wear but no dark jersey and had chosen a green sweater which I could cover with the black one Henrietta was bringing me from Gennady, but I felt self-conscious. I'll just have to put the coat on again. The attendant couldn't understand why I was leaving before the ceremony. I explained my predicament. She peeled off her plum-coloured cardigan.

'Will this do?'

'Thank you. Oh, thank you very much.' I pulled it on.

I was led into the auditorium where the lights were at half-strength. I was astonished to see three or four hundred people sitting in the stalls.

A large blown-up photograph of Petya Shcherbakov hung against black velvet drapes, a small black mourning curtain swathed across one corner. In the centre of the dimly lit stage, tilted up on a raised dais, rested the open coffin which held the embalmed body of the actor. The coffin was lined with red silk, banked around with enormous wreaths, several similar of which were standing sentry across the stage. Three rows of chairs were set a few yards from the coffin on either side. On these sat family mourners, Oleg Yefremov, Innokenti Smoktunovsky and other senior actors. Solemn music was playing. It was a concentration of devotion and regret.

The widow, a small black lace shawl covering her head, was leaning over her husband. She seemed to be speaking to him. The intimacy of a domestic relationship was being brought to a close in public.

Oleg Nikolayich was speaking as I joined a queue which led to steps onto the stage. I asked my neighbour what I must do.

'You walk up and lay your flowers. Stay there a while.'

The doors to the street had been unlocked. Passers-by were walking into the theatre, sitting quietly, paying their last respects in company with the theatre family.

Four men stood at the corner of the bier. Two others were acting as ushers. Three times – eight people climbed onto the stage, divided, and stood four on each side of the coffin for five or six minutes. They were led away down the steps as another group took their place. Within twenty minutes I was adding my flowers to the quantity that already lay loose over the body. Daffodils, carnations, roses. I walked past the foot of the coffin and became the fourth on the left-hand side.

The only embalmed face I have looked at previously is that of Lenin, behind glass, so I found nothing shocking in the sight, but I was thoroughly upset. To the side of me Mrs Shcherbakova was being given, like a child, sips from a small glass held by a young woman. She maintained a low moaning sob. I put the back of my hand to my mouth and kept it there. The tears ran down my neck into the borrowed cardigan.

The armband was transferred from mine to another's as I left the stage. I saw Henrietta perched on a back stall. Her handkerchief was wet. We watched the ritual for another hour. I've never seen anything like it. It was theatre – there was a large compliant audience. I cannot imagine such a scene in England. Oleg Nikolayich rose from time to time to introduce a speaker. Several of the *Cherry Orchard* actors tried. Shkalikov's voice broke as he struggled to get his words out. They loved him. Innokenti Mikhailich spoke last, drew his palm across his forehead as if to wipe away some of the pain, wrung his hands repeatedly. When he had finished, many of the mourners hurried up onto the stage again. The actors went back to have a last look. Some of them kissed Uncle Petya, they loved him.

'Now they will take his coffin to the cemetery,' explained Henrietta. The banks of flowers must be moved, the great red lid which was leaning against a wall in the foyer must be fixed in place.

The outside window, previously filled by a photograph of Evstigneev, now framed Shcherbakov. Anonymously given flowers lay on a ledge in front of his picture. They stay until they shrivel or are blown away.

I returned the cardigan. My benefactor understood. She'd been able to give, I'd been able to take. Thanks were unnecessary.

Zharkov and Lyubshin were sitting on the edge of a banquette, knees touching, hands hanging. Forsaken little boys facing a lifetime of separation from Uncle Petya. I knew that Zharkov had given his last performance, it would be Borya Shcherbakov as Lopakhin tonight, and maybe Lyubshin as Gaev. It was not possible for me to speak to them.

Henrietta and I had some business to attend to in her office. I must dedicate a photograph to the Art Theatre Museum. We were wretched, unable to talk properly. So we parted. Scholar and valued commentator, Ksenia patched me up as soon as I came through the door.

'Congratulations on your performance. It was REAL CHEKHOV.' The last phrase let loose the tears again.

The truth is that the torrential flood of experience that I have converged with has been an illumination beyond describing. Davidov had said, 'Because you are a real foreigner, we see everything differently now.'

It's as if what Charlotta does to the characters in *Cherry Orchard*, is what I've done to some people here. The conflicts and creative struggles that Azat, Kalantarov and I had wrestled with during 1991 were part of a combative process of barrier breaking, where the crumbling of established patterns appeared to be the personification of destruction, where we each felt wounded to the quick. I upset them and showed them things about themselves that perhaps they weren't conscious of. Charlotta does that. They certainly humbled me, showed me things about myself that need adjustment. At the Art Theatre all my responses are positive.

I had a bath, then lay on my bed. Crying doesn't half dry me out. Exciting to think I may be performing alongside an actor that I have neither rehearsed nor been on stage with before. I'm flattered that they take my adaptability for granted. The only disturbance was a telephone call from Bill Millinship of *The Observer*. May his photographer come to the theatre this evening?

I got to the theatre in plenty of time for an interview with Время – the nine o'clock news. I was determined that I would not be entrapped as I had been the previous night. They didn't turn up. Valentina, dresser, brought me a small figure carved from horn. A fisherman, as described in a Pushkin story. The tea-maker presented me with a set of postcards of Melikhovo and of Yalta. I was glad of extra time to season myself for this last performance. My eyes were needing help. I was not rushed.

Henrietta turned up. Vadim came to say goodbye. He is also an actor. He won't see me again. Away on tour tomorrow, in a play. I hadn't known this. Olya, the evening's stage manager, and Natasha who had allowed me to use and abuse her person in rehearsal on Sunday, were at the door. Olya carried carnations, Natasha – a collection of poems by Boris Pasternak and a little book about the Art Theatre, in which she had written a message. She started to read that I am a proper MoscowArtTheatre-ichka. I dissolved, waved at them, shaking my head.

'Please, I'm sorry, please, I can't...'

They backed out, apologising for distressing me. In bounded Shkalikov/Trofimov.

'Carolinochka, do you mind very much, we're going to...'

I began to sob.

'We're going to make an announcement before the performance that we buried our friend today. Do you mind? I'm so sorry.'

He hugged and kissed me, anything to stop the flood.

'It's all right, please don't be upset. Darling Carolinochka, it will be all right.'

I couldn't stop. Valentina and Henrietta looked on helplessly. I thought, 'I'm not going to be able to get down to the stage. I'm not going to be able to speak.'

I took some deep breaths, tried to find something to frighten myself with. Miss Medley's disapproving voice, as she spoke the Notices at supper a couple of days before I played Darcy in the school production of *Pride and Prejudice?* A friend had clipped my shoulder-length hair to an approximation of Jane Austen's hero. The result was there for the whole dining room to see. 'Will the *girl*' (pronounced *gel*) 'who left a pile of hair' (acidly drawn out) 'in the French oral examination room, please come and see me after supper in the staffroom.' That's better. More deep breaths. I shook my shoulders and flicked my hands. I spread a line of blue on the lower lids of my eyes, inside the lashes, next to the eyeball. The windows need to be open for people to see in.

Down at the side of the stage, the rest of the cast were already assembled. Exhausted, but still able to acknowledge me with their benevolence. I noticed that Gaev's exquisite cream woollen coat was being worn again by Innokenti Mikhailich. Borya Shcherbakov/Lopakhin squeezed my hand as he went to take his place. I've learned since I last saw him that he is married to Tanya/actress/glam *Administratr.*

A camera crew suddenly swept through the pass door, switched on a very bright light and photographed me pacing up and down with my little dog. Not a word. How odd. I carried on mouthing my lines. I felt them during the play in the auditorium as well as in the wings. There were cameras clicking in the front row.

During the interval my room filled up. The camera crew expected to interview me, the Russian photographer working for *The Observer* needed to get his pictures. There was impasse. *The Observer* negotiated first slot. The television interview, conducted in Russian, was reasonably haphazard. I feel reckless in this situation. An F-word could be thrown in and would be understood by a large number of viewers.

'And is there anything else you would like to do while you are in Moscow?'

'Yes, I'd like to meet Mikhail Sergeyevich (Gorbachev).'

'Oh? And what would you say to him?'

'Thank you.'

Alyona came to report how she finds it from the front. I had recovered my composure, thanks to Dr Footlights. The part delivers maximum effect without being burdensome. It is energetic and athletic, but not stressful. LOVELY. I dragooned Alyona to record all the remaining music excerpts from the wings. I am on and off the stage all through the ACT III. Nemirovich-Danchenko, the composer, acquiesced, so Alyona sat beside him as he conducted his band.

In ACT IV, I sang to my rug-baby, threw it down and begged for a job from the man who, by buying the cherry orchard, had thrown me out of work. Shcherbakov/Lopakhin contacted strongly with me in this moment. He took a huge step sideways and turned his back to the audience so that all the attention should be on me. It's the most graciously noble gesture I've ever encountered on stage.

The curtain call can be relived. Alyona took my cassette recorder into the stalls. Borya/Shcherbakov continued his gallantry, leading me forward again. In place of Vadim – walking painfully and slowly with a stick – emerged Dima/Ivanov, carrying the official bouquet.

This surprise, instead of making me cry, delighted me.

'Dimchik! Thank you.'

'Carolinochka!'

The audience also responded with glee at seeing one of their stars in cords and sweater instead of in black, shooting himself at the end of the fourth act of *Ivanov*. He trekked off again. Smoktunovsky led the rest of the cast offstage. I was left alone. In consent to my outstretched arm, the two leading men returned for a final call. Innokenti Mikhailich waved his hands for quiet.

'Today we said goodbye to an old friend. Now we have a new friend and colleague, Carolina. I hope she will come back.'

For the last time, I savoured the warmth of the space in which I feel no Me and You, only Us, audience and actors joined. I had responded to acting at the Fenice in Venice in the same way. In both places, and in no other, have I had an intuition of what it may be like to be a man wanting to fill a woman with himself and his seed to achieve union.

Shkalikov was at the door.

'Please, Carolinochka, will you come to our dressing room. We want you to be with us for a minute.'

'I must have supper with Oleg Nikolayich and our Ambassador and his wife.'

'Please, try for one minute.'

Henrietta told me that, following a funeral, a wake is held in honour of the dead person. Tanya, actress/Admin., was in charge for the official party. She led me first to the dressing room where Alyona, Shkalikov/Trofimov, Dima/Ivanov, Sergachev/Firs, Yanna/Dunyasha, Polina/Anya were sharing refreshments. They gave me a small glass of cognac. Shkalikov/Trofimov looked as if he was about to make a speech. I knew the danger and I needed to say something quickly before I... but it was already too late. My floodgates opened. If there's a drought get Caroline and be kind to her, she'll give you enough water to drown continents. I gulped what I must tell them before I leave their shelter.

'I have never met such friendship and warmth and love. Please, I want you to understand that what has made me feel part of your family is that you have allowed me to share your grief..'

Poor people. What could they do? In a surge of fellow feeling, Yanna/Dunyasha reached for her necklace, took it off and put it around my neck.

Tanya was waiting. Oleg Nikolayich was waiting. The Ambassador was waiting. We hugged around the room. I never heard what Shkalikov/Trofimov was going to say.

We set off for the next engagement. My eyes had to fend for themselves in the hurly-burly of social life.

In Oleg Nikolayich's room a banquet to bankrupt a tsar was laid on the table. A young man in a white coat was at hand to pour the wine. This was to be my last meeting with Rodric and Jill Braithwaite before their occupancy of the Embassy expires. They have kept the eaglest of kind eyes on my enterprise. They are famously successful in London and Moscow for having humanised this prestigious diplomatic post. Innokenty Mikhailich was present, relaxed in a patterned shirt – without jacket. There, also, were Kolya Skorik, the director who had encouraged me in rehearsal and another, darker Kolya, the spectacled young Administrative Director of the Theatre who had been present at the meeting the very first time Oleg Nikolayich had suggested that I come to play in his Theatre, and Irina Korchevnikova, prime manager of visa and travel, with whom I have hardly spoken except on the telephone during this intense time, and Henrietta – earning a feast, if no money, for her devotion, and of course Oleg Nikolayich. It could not have been guessed that this morning mourning was the whole concern. The opening speech by Oleg Nikolayich came quite quickly. I grabbed it on tape. A bit later Innokenty Mikhailich began to speak charmingly. Alyona's enthusiasm for cheers and applause meant, unfortunately, that the tape ran out. You can't have everything. The diplomats and I were given a commemorative bronze plaque each.

Henrietta came to help me out of my dressing room. This unassertive, compassionate woman should have been at home with her husband, packing to return to her dying mother, but her loyalty to my situation put her needs at the bottom of the pile. She epitomises unreligious goodness, if anyone is looking for an example.

Well past midnight, my cardigan friend was still at her post by the stage door. I daren't ask her how she would get home. Oleg Nikolayich and Irina live one flat above the other in the same block. Henrietta and I joined them in the cream Volvo for the crow-fly two-hundred metre trip. My address is twenty yards from there. A taxi chanced to be at the corner for Henrietta. It cost her a tenth of her month's wages to go home. About the distance from Charing Cross to Kingston. I'm not sure how it is that the Theatre didn't see that her selflessness had earned her a ride home. An offer from me would have been unacceptable.

I padded about in the flat, put my flowers in water, made tea. Calm, happy and fulfilled. Life consists of people doing what they do.

19 March

Waiting to hear from Taganrog held me at home instead of going to the theatre to be paid. Bill Millinship kept me entertained for two comfortable hours in the afternoon, while he gathered material for his *Observer* article. He'd watched the last performance.

'I've never seen anything like that in the theatre before. I can't understand why you didn't cry.'

'You were watching the only time in the day when I wasn't crying.'

We drank tea and agreed about plenty of things. He promised to ring my home on his special telephone.

Tatyana from Taganrog was on the line.

'You will come by air tomorrow. The Theatre will tell you what time and will bring you to the airport. I will be at the airport and will travel with you so you are not frightened.'

Me, frightened? Never. Ksenia took over and gleaned that it will be a special aeroplane from Taganrog. Back on the line I spoke with Fedorovsky.

'Happy birthday for yesterday!'

It was the anniversary of our gala performance at the Hermitage.

'We'll be there to meet you.' said Volodya/Trofimov.

'Wonderful! What's the weather?'

'Warm. Southern spring.'

At Igor's and Natasha's house, Dima and they were already tucking into the feast. We took our own story a stage further. We need an English playwright, not just a translator, to make a version of Sasha's piece for England.

On the Metro coming home, I asked how it was that my name had been bill-boarded Las Vegas style but I had only been granted three rehearsals.

'The actors are paid very little. For them to come to rehearsal was a matter of great kindness to you and to the occasion.'

Suddenly I understood.

I was woken in the night. Charlotte, calling from London, had been horribly burgled in her flat of a month's rent and other treasures. My builder's number travels in my diary... 081-... I tried to reassure her across five countries and a sea. She's exceptionally gutsy.

20 March

Vadim, still here, came for me in a car which carried us for a good hour to a small provincial airport, Vykova. We were well past the departure time. Tatyana waited with open arms.

'I don't believe it!' went the dialogue, while we hugged to make sure we were really us.

It was a thirty- to forty-seater. Ten of us travelled first class. That is to say we sat, Tatyana and I, facing each other with a young German couple beside us; at another table, sideways, like a London bus, sat four more. No question of wearing seat belts. An open door to the back cabin, where people crowded to smoke, flapped (that word again) and banged on take-off. The moment the travellers were seated a bottle of wine and a bottle of cognac were produced. Six handy glasses were found in a small cupboard where I would have stored the first aid box. Sandwiches, sausage and eating accoutrements appeared from bags for a community picnic. They were all invited to see the play tomorrow night, *gratis*. It was jolly in the way the critics' forum was not. Tatyana had travelled three and a half hours from Taganrog in the morning. This is the Taganrog shuttle. She said the journey home would probably be shorter, because we're going south... downhill?

We flew first over encampments, divided into clusters of dachas. Later over snowy flat country through which flowed the Don. This great river curled an enquiring path across the steppe, which is marked out in large square sections. It's the amount that seems spectacular to my island eyes.

45. The plane to Taganrog, sans seat belts.

It had been arranged that the pilot would get ground control to telephone to Sasha/Pishchik when we were near and he would be there with his car. The improvisational family feeling is what I enjoy. Humans, not corporations.

Halfway, the view changed its character. The ground had the quality of material. The snow lay in fine drifts. I was reminded of an upholstered tapestry chair. The seat has been used so much that the wool has worn away. You see the canvas – threadbare.

'For goodness' sake, don't wear black tights,' had warned an English journalist in Moscow. 'There's a Taganrog Ripper. The victims are always clad in black tights. He's been around for a while. They can't seem to catch him.'

Before we took off, I'd noted that the wheels of the plane were satin smooth. We flew in over the melted sea and landed perfectly on a cracked concrete runway. A dog came bounding to welcome us. I climbed down onto the ground and saw Sasha/Pishchik and Volodya/Trofimov walking towards me.

Both men were as I remembered them. Sasha/Pishchik's laugh and girth were as generous as ever, and Volodya/Trofimov's tresses would make Rapunzel weep. The two sets of blue eyes were mirroring my delight.

Taganrog without snow was going to take a while to get used to. On the road to the hotel, the actors brought me up to date. Things are bad at the theatre. The cinema costs fifteen roubles, the theatre seats – six. Yet the theatre is empty. They believe themselves lucky if they have an audience of forty to fifty. The Saturday performance will be at five o'clock, in response to pleas that people have difficulty getting home afterwards. She indicated that we might do the play twice on Sunday, it would depend on the bookings.

'I'll come for you at nine thirty to rehearse at eleven,' Sasha/Pishchik offered, as we unpacked the car.

'I will need lots of time to practise the dances.'

The thought of this was enough to cause another eruption of *товарищеский*[9] laughter.

Volodya/Trofimov helped me to designate socks/tights, lipsticks and smokes. He was knowledgeable about the ages of the children of the company members. He approved a yellow car and a foot-long pencil for six-year-old Anton. Then we crossed the road to his attractive apartment where Olga, innately chic, and her son were making a tall pile of pancakes. We soon found ourselves talking about Kalantarov who had been back to do a production of *Uncle Vanya* during the autumn. I still had unresolved feelings about him I needed to air – after a year. I must look into his eyes and ask the questions or I shall have no peace.

The pancakes were eaten with rich strawberry jam. My proffered bottle of vodka was packed back into my bag after we'd each had a nip, and a giant jar of pickled tomatoes was put alongside to carry over the road. I tried out the rusty Chopin on their well-tuned piano. It was a kindly domestic start.

Although I stole the covers from the second bed, the cold kept me awake for a large part of the night. My electric element for

---

[9] 'Comradely/friendly.'

boiling a cup of tea can restore circulatory optimism and it did, when light came round the corner again.

The small, black, stage-door dog waited in his normal sausagey way. Waggy-waggy. Peter, who'd snatched me from rehearsal in Vladimir to visit Suzdal, was standing beside him. Fedorovsky, bigger than ever. His son, back from National Service – a best-of-both-worlds offspring of his father and mother/Ranevskaya. One by one the actresses and the actors and the stagehands. Finally the musicians. We merged and surrounded each other.

'It's like yesterday.'

I was shepherded to my accustomed waiting room with the plush couch to lie on. Suddenly Zhenia and Kolya. Maybe I am a little plumper, too.

Volodya/Trofimov and Sasha/Pishchik took turns in the stalls as director. After the picnic scene, which they watched together, they said, 'Carolina, what you are doing is Moscow Art Theatre. It's different. You used to be eccentric and crazy here. It was better. Do you want to do it again?'

'Do you want me to do it again?'

'No. Just if you want to do it.'

I felt I remembered nothing of the dances, but as we raced through them the steps began to come. We hastened through the tricks. It was over in an hour and a half, leaving me distinctly nervous.

The company dissolved for a meal break. I stayed on stage, the theatre smaller than I remembered. The musical stagehand told me his piano playing has got into arrears. He is going to study philology.

Vera, the Literary Director of the theatre, had been the companion of my tears in the car returning to Moscow from Vladimir. Her trim, trousered figure was at the side of the stage. The brill-red Joan of Arc haircut was matched by a scarlet mouth, she carried pickled cabbage and prepared chicken from her mother. I had already ordered cucumber salad, which arrived accompanied by fresh cranberries from next door.

'No black bread,' warned Zhenia.

No black bread to be had in Taganrog? Yes, everything here is much worse. The shortages. *Кошмар!*[10] Tatyana came to my room to announce the arrival of my old friends Rostov TV – and Taganrog TV which, last year, had not been born. I proceeded to the stage where bright lights were in place. The crystal Vladimir vase, filled with flowers, was given pride of place on the stage. I walked through the set to meet the reporter, whom I knew well from last year.

'What was it like at the Moscow Art Theatre? Was it better or worse than Taganrog?'

'Different and, of course, we had the tragedy of the death of Shcherbakov.'

'Carolina, you must rest, now.' Vera was insistent. She threw her fur coat over my feet. Is this the way opera singers are treated? Their concern for my Vitamin C intake was provided for by finely chopped chunks of orange and lemon peel in sugared water.

Fedorovsky delayed my siesta by asking me to sign a contract. We started to laugh.

I lay back on the hard Edwardian (tsarist?) couch. The theatre is spick and span, very warm. There is hot water in the tap which there hadn't been last year. I hope this is not a spurt of extravagance for my sake.

Vera's mother brought hot borscht to the dressing room. Lilya/Varya has changed her hairstyle and is a bouncing tumult of corkscrew curls. Valya/Anya looks cruelly thin and frail, subjecting herself to the full rigour of Lenten self-denial.

'Maybe you should eat more when you are working so hard?'

'For the old and the children and the sick we don't insist.'

Amongst the actresses, as from Ksenia, I heard how the importance of their religious devotion governs the way they live. The cleansing of mind and body in the Great Fast, leading to the most important time of the year, Easter. Following the celebration it is almost a disappointment, a clouding, to return to less austere ways.

My clown wig had been cleaned and was dressed to its full ridiculous height. As we climbed into our familiar costumes, I felt

---

10 'Nightmare!'

again the *terra firma* of known practice. My nerves left me. I felt part of it and not part of it. Operatic. Here today, gone tomorrow. We drew an audience of about three hundred.

Next Day

After watching the keep-fit leotard girls on breakfast TV and a stretch of 'Christian Television', the weather forecast is a fairy-tale, sparkling with magical names. Moldavia (+13 to 17), Armenia (0 to 6), Central Region, Ukraine, Archangelskoe, Volga, Byelorussia, Georgia, Azerbaijan, ending with St Petersburg and Moscow. This, in turn, followed by children's TV. *Old Kind Tales.* Mediaeval. A knight on horseback galloping across the sky. A dragon breathing fire. Ancient and romantic, beautifully photographed.

I like being alone in a foreign place with time to reflect and record. I returned to the Art Theatre in my mind. Smoktunovsky had offered me another of his delicate garnishings. Following 'Gi's a job!' to Lopakhin as I leave the stage – repeat of Charlotta's mannerism '*Ein, zwei, drei!*'

'Or maybe not?' The Art Theatre is not a museum. No inhibition regarding a sacred text. He is interested to continue the work until the last possible moment. Robert Stephens, similarly, had ideas for improvement between the last matinee and evening performances of a West End play we ran in together. Acting is 'work in progress'. The more I think about it the more I realise how lucky I was to have so much concrete help from the actors. They didn't just make space for me to do my stuff; they watched, listened, connected and built on it.

'I can't bear Jewish directors because they don't understand Russian people.'

Thus exploded an actor out of the blue during my 1992 visit to Russia.

'Is Oleg Nikolayevich Yefremov Jewish?' I asked, diffidently.

'No, absolutely not. That's why he is the number one, top first-class Russian director.'

I am intimidated by the baldness of such an extreme expression. I must sit quietly and examine my own prejudices.

Discover how many I have and whether I would state them so candidly. It is not the first time that I have been shown that the non-integration of Jewish people can make a Russian feel anger.

The actors had new tunes up their guitar strings. I was treated to them all, every one. Borya/Yasha won my prize this year. His song carried centuries of broken-hearted loneliness and a yearning for beauty.

I wanted my last full day in Taganrog to be spent walking. I wanted the pleasure of covering the old ground without the blanket of snow. It is still a little early for green shoots but the sun was dazzling. My guard, Zhenya, her son, Kolya, and I came across Borya near the theatre.

'I would like you to see where I live.'

He led us a couple of hundred metres from our workplace, through a wooden-paled gate to a yard around which hunched low dwellings with reconstructed roofs. Washing was hanging outside. I had an expectation – not realised – of chickens pecking. We passed through the door of a thick-walled building. In the outer space a heavy iron gas cooker was burning low from all its jets to warm the apartment. The windows in the living room are set deep in the walls, guaranteeing protection from the extreme of summer heat. It is the room of an artist of slender means. My eye was drawn immediately to an intriguing set of decorations that Borya had suspended from the ceiling. His books and other belongings are on shelves near at hand. The improvisational style of his home confirms my feeling that what goes on inside a Russian is generally of greater import than external display. After we left him, Zhenia explained that Borya lives apart from his wife.

We continued our walk across the town to the great pebble and sand *plage* where Taganrogers bathe in season. A small kebab hut was closed. The outlines of dismantled beach shelters stood as reminder that here summer is hot. A young fisherman was wading out to his net. We three sat on granite blocks a yard from the lapping water, tearing at a loaf of black bread we had bought, while Kolya got himself an ice cream at another counter. We watched the catch being retrieved. One trout-sized fish. The bite of the wind was sharper even than the brilliant sun's response. We needed a hot drink.

We passed two disintegrating dog corpses on the uphill road to Chekhov Street. The *domik* birthplace was shut. It was Monday. The Cherry Orchard Cafe, next door, opened as we approached. When coffee is available, it is of unswerving high quality. Kolya's good nature is a blessing. He chortles at the first opportunity. Most of our journey must now be uphill away from the sea before we go down again towards the sea on the other side of the tiny isthmus. The shop from which we had bought the bread now had a substantial crowd outside.

'Are you waiting for vodka?' called Zhenia. She was answered by smoke-filled nods. Word of a shipment gets round as quickly as news of a carcass to jackals in the tundra.

We found ourselves passing Zhenia's block of flats. 'Please may I see your home?'

A hall, kitchen, bathroom and living room are what she shares with her growing son. I understand why a notion of privacy is rare in this country. I am admiring of how much sacrifice is made in accommodation to the other's needs. Mother and son are good friends. If their television screen was divided into two and if it were possible to do so, each could watch the programme of their choice simultaneously and have as big a picture as any I have in my house.

The complex of flats are built around a playground which was packed with children enjoying half-term almost as much as were the endless unidentifiable breeds of dog. Far more dogs than in England. I saw a Pekingese for the first time.

It was nearing six o'clock when Zhenia rang the theatre.

'They have been waiting all day for Carolina to collect her money.

Now everyone has gone home.'

Oh dear, something had been expected of me on this tranquil free day. We had passed our time without obligation; it felt the closest I had been able to sense in myself the natural rhythm of a local person. A really important, indigenous day.

We were sauntering through the great laid-out public gardens. These are surrounded by ornamental railings, which add a grandeur to the recreational strolling place of the townsfolk. Walking just ahead of us we recognised Fedorovsky. He showed no irritation at having been kept waiting all day. We tramped together through dusk to dark for nearly an hour until we reached my hotel. Fedorovsky had yet further to go. My day companions turned round cheerfully to return to their own unprivate lives. Four hours walking, which was what I had wanted, put paid to any further socialising.

Fedorovsky had intimated that the Mayor had something to say to me. I stayed an extra happy day. I did not know whether I would be leaving by the evening plane or – my preference – the overnight train. Sasha/Pischik chauffeured me around that I might return to favourite places and photograph them more and better. The places are still there. The people are still there. I expect the people I know in America and Australia and Spain and France and Wales and Manchester and Brixton are still there, too. Doing what they're doing. It's very odd. Some of them are asleep, and some of them are standing on their heads, I was brought up to believe.

'I understand that last year you were a correspondent for the BBC.' Mayor Shilo got straight down to brass tacks. What chances were there of me advancing Taganrog as a place with investment potential? Already there is interest from England and America.

'Nothing would please me more. Unfortunately, I am only an actress. I have tried without success to effect a twinning between the Dramatichesky Teatr in Taganrog and the Royal Shakespeare Company in Stratford-upon-Avon, whose policy, sadly, is to remain single.'

I left with a promotion cassette in my bag, feeling foolish. I have not a single connection in commerce. Six of us were feasted at the expense, but without the presence, of the Mayor.

The message came that the actors were waiting to say goodbye. Still not knowing how I should travel, we found Valya/Anya and Lena/Ranevskaya at the stage door. I haven't seen enough of them. Sudden news: I will return by train. Zhenya and Kolya, too, so that I am not robbed or raped.

Goodbye theatre. Hug all. Pat dog. This can be done again.

The railway station at Taganrog is large and architecturally imposing. It cannot be much changed since the time when Anton Pavlovich alighted at this stop.

We picked our way to the farthest pier, the platform being level with the track makes the arrival of the train more awesome than usual. Ours, from Turkistan, burned in regally; towering black and green.

'Oh, thank you for everything. I love you.'

46. Caroline crossing the railway lines at Taganrog station.

Sasha, Tatyana, Fedorovsky. HUG, H-U-G, H-U-U-G-G. Trains set off slowly. Waving is a kindly method of parting.

Extra money must have passed hands to secure our cabin, Zhenya asserted. The train was full. Someone had been persuaded to travel another day. How else could a two-berth compartment be available?

This train scenario suits me better than anything I can think of. Eighteen hours at sixty miles an hour. One thousand and eighty minutes of bliss. Leaning against two fat pillows, facing the window, with nothing to worry about and cheerful caring companions.

The train has been moving for nearly twenty-four hours already. Taganrog is the thirty-second of forty-six stops from Makhachkala to Moscow.

Being told that an English actress is next door usually produces an invitation of some sort. I agreed reluctantly, jealous of the inroads being made into my carefully counted minutes of heaven; fearing also that I must sing for my supper and be charming and talkative. Zhenia insisted that nothing was required. Purpose of visit? Greed. We sold our female company for sturgeon roe.

The darkish, middle-aged-ish chaps in their blue tracksuits had already half-emptied a bottle of cognac and three-quarters of a bottle of vodka had gone down someone's throat. Some fizzy water and a bottle of Pepsi-Cola remained untouched.

47. Leaving Crimea on the train: guests of Magamet
and Magamet with caviar.

They brought out a tin and told us it was from the Caspian Sea: it was the same shape – at least half the size again – as that of a Camembert cheese. Packed solid with black juicy caviar. On another plate were laid thick chunks of smoked sturgeon. There was rich home-made brown bread. They jostled the caviar generously onto the bread and handed it over, their eyes shining like jet beads. There was also cucumber. Not satisfied with their level of hospitality, they opened a tin of crab.

'*Давай!*[11] Come on, tuck in.'

Zhenia was provocative and attractive to these men. She chatted easily to make them talk, delighting them with her lusty extrovert behaviour. She wound them up into a daze. I had real admiration for the confidence with which she gave these guys their ups and downs. She is about thirty. As a physically trained private detective she is capable of throwing a man twice her size. She is of average height; has a friendly face with a wide mouth and eyes that show plenty of hurt when she forgets to cover up. Her hair is her crowning glory. It has golden highlights on chestnut and is a mane past her shoulders. She wears it the way film stars used to when I was young. Layers of opulent waves. They're doing it again now. Her long nails are often brilliantly painted.

I learned halfway through the meal that our hosts were *musulmen* from Daghestan, which is one side of the Caspian Sea, after Azerbaijan and Astrakhan. They were both called Magamet in Russian. In other words, we were in the company of two Muslims called Mahomet. They called on Allah to give us good health as we drank (I'm sure I was brought up to believe that Muslims don't touch alcohol). One rashly, and with a naughty look in his eye, admitted to having three or four wives. The other said that being a Muscovite, he has only one wife. I asked how many husbands the wives had. The joke was wasted. They didn't understand the question. Suddenly, they were in trouble. Zhenia challenged them. She pounced. She's dangerous. The multi-wifer shrank as she spelled out the imbalance. She beat him into the ground.

'Oh yes, a man can have five, six, seven wives, but if we ask how many husbands the wives can have...'

He was cowed and terrified.

'Look how ashamed he is.'

It was as if she was suddenly the controlling mother. She wasn't really being terrifying, just, he'd been found out. She ruled the roost at the supper party. She managed her share of the brandy.

---

[11] 'Come on!'

When she felt that I had had enough to eat and was no longer understanding what their thickened tongues were uttering, that was it.

'*Давай!* Let's go.'

Basic sexist behaviour, I suppose. I believe I have never seen it this way round before.

There had been conversation as well as discipline. Many-wived Mahomet aired his anti-Gorbachev sentiments enthusiastically. He chose the wrong audience.

'From my point of view, the President has saved the world from East-West enmity,' I countered. 'He insists on change, and he listens.'

'But our life is so terrible.'

'I feel the same way about Mrs Thatcher as you do about President Gorbachev.'

This was hard for him to focus on.

'Nobody has any money. We have beggars.'

Points to him, he believed.

'I've seen more beggars in London than in Moscow. People sleep on the street in cardboard boxes.'

Match point...

'Why?'

He left an empty court.

'Mrs Thatcher.'

Unfair advantage. I've been in both countries. At first it was beyond belief. He thought about it. His face was a question mark. He went over it a few times. He declared that it was really interesting to talk to me. He meant it.

The Mahomets gave us strong tea before Zhenia led me to safety next door. She stayed only long enough to make sure that her son was sleeping. She had the stamina for a few more rakish hours yet.

I withdrew into thoughts on the differences between the Moscow and Taganrog *Cherry Orchards*. People try to draw me on which was better. One production about provincial people was done by provincial actors in a provincial theatre. The other by metropolitan actors in a metropolitan theatre. Chekhov was from the provinces. Provincial is not a word I feel comfortable with, it is derogatory. Regional would be better. When I heard a distinguished Moscow writer describe the English as provincial, I felt humiliated for us.

The silvery sun gleamed over Oryol, Turgenev's stop. Fine buildings. Classical pillars decorated with clusters of grapes calmly face the passing trains. Zhenia jumped down from the carriage and returned with a pile of hot boiled potatoes, wrapped in newspaper. Anything more welcome and delicious could not be imagined.

The last stop before Moscow was Tula. This town has been famous for its iron and steel products; train engines and sewing machines. One of the musicians at Taganrog showed me a hundred-year-old sturdy samovar which originated in this Sheffield of old Russia.

Our daylight Daghestanis were pressing us to visit them during summer months to sun ourselves and eat more black roe. The tracksuits discarded in favour of jeans and jackets. Mahomet/Henry VIII was wearing a belt fastened by a handsomely ornamented silver buckle, which he said had been in his family for several generations.

We emptied our carriage and pack-horsed our luggage through rainy Moscow. Sasha is away being a biologist and Ksenia is in Zagorsk, supporting a close friend who is about to become a nun. I have the flat to myself. We had tea in the flat before Zhenya took Kolya to her sister. These two are for ever. I have been in privileged care with these two young friends.

An important occasion was being marked in MKhAT. It was the first time that *Игроки*[12] by Dostoyevsky was in repertoire since the death of Yevstigneev, whose last performance was in this play. The play is set in modern times, by the sea, gangsterish. I had not seen Nevinny/Yepikhodov in modern dress on stage before. Tenyakova/Ranevskaya played a maid. She had a cigarette hanging from her mouth and did a marvellous sluttish walk. I saw Kalyagin for the first time. He, like Nevinny and Tabakov, has only to walk onto the stage for the audience to collapse. The stars have spent years earning that. I remember being cross with Jack Benny for playing

---

[12] *The Gamblers.*

the reward that he hadn't earned from me because I was too young to have seen him in his prime. It was a stylish production, an actor's dream. I laughed and laughed. It carried all the dangers of a successful classic where five or six of the theatre's leading comedy performers are on stage at the same time. Sitting as close as I was, it would have been difficult to miss seeing the struggle some of them had to keep a straight face. Yevstigneev's part was taken by Yursky, the director of this hit. He sensibly played without frills. I saw actors that were new to me. Several of them got entrance rounds. They are an impressive co-operative of experienced performers.

Volodya/son had to consult my map of Moscow when I begged to be taken, in the dark, to see the White House, where the blockades had manifested during the Coup. A nasty tangle of metal is memorial. It will stay. We banqueted – four courses – under the blinkless, lidless eye of *Попугай*/Parrot.

Next Day

Before noon. I felt like fresh air.

I rang my old employers, Tovarichestvo Rezhissyorov – The Directors' Association – and invited myself along for half an hour.

'We're very busy and the place is in a filthy mess.'

It was Volodya who had taken me to the airport at a time of debacle.

I had written and sent, with the utmost sincerity, the two letters requested by Azat.

Volodya arranged for me to be met at Pushkin's statue, 'Hello!'

They were still there. All of them. I was welcomed with tea, we reminisced good-naturedly. Not an inkling of ill will.

'Have you spoken to Azat?'

They implied no hidden agenda.

'No.'

'He's not so much involved with theatre now. He's a businessman.'

'And Borya?' (My trustworthy friend from Vladimir.)

'He's around, involved with films.'

They are initiating plans for the autumn Chekhov Festival. Maybe they could set up a production...

Their attitude is adventurous. They take people and things as they come. And go. I'm learning.

Borya rang as I returned to the apartment; he had a new haircut but the energy was the same. He was carrying a picture wrapped in a green plastic tablecloth.

'I've had it for a year. As soon as I saw it, I said I must buy this for Carolina.'

It's a brilliantly coloured, New Age oil painting of Vladimir. Like Azat, Borya is a pioneer, though he has an untroubled nature in this new society.

'I am always happy.' He laughed his way into his coat and boots and bounced off down the stairs.

After knowing him for ten years, I want to say goodbye to Oleg Nikolayich and thank him for what I've been allowed to do in his theatre. I made an enquiring visit to the third floor of the building. Irina was sorting through the recent photographs of *Cherry Orchard*, choosing which should go to the Museum for posterity.

'Oleg Nikolayich is going away tomorrow. He is not at all well.'

'Can I say goodbye to him now?'

'He's not in the theatre.'

'Shall I telephone him at home?'

'Better not. He's not well enough.'

She handed me half a dozen prints from the collection to take home.

I am invited to watch a morning rehearsal of *Platonov*. This is directed by Dima Brusnikin. He also plays the title role in the production which is soon to set off for Crimea. Alyona is essaying a new part. Again, I find myself intrigued by the easiness with which Russian actors play characters who are drunk. Their familiarity with alcohol is intrinsic. The way they hold a bottle, a glass, the way they slap it down. Men and women are equally comfortable with the idiom. It is not something they have to consider at all. I have noticed swollen hands, faces which have extra water under the skin. The eyes in the morning are not always clear.

'It's part of the theatre tradition here that actors and actresses have a capacity for drink.' I was told categorically. 'The women in this country, particularly, use drink because they are so badly treated.'

My response was that I have not yet had experience of any country where the women are incontrovertibly well treated. Nor men either, of course. The model I consulted on whom to base my transsexual role in the BBC's *Rides* – herself a one-time, twice-married man said, 'It was not until I became a woman that I realised to what degree women are second-class citizens.'

Amanda took me in a taxi to have tea with Julius and Svetlana Kagarlitsky. This occasion was notable for the astonishing way in which the party of five grown-ups was taken over by the six-year-old child of Julius's radical political son, Boris. The bespectacled, curlyheaded boy sat at one end of the table, opposite his grandfather, and pronounced on this and that issue. His arms followed the gestures of intellectual discourse, his hand coming to rest occasionally under his chin. It was impressive. He was not patronised by the elders. He was the centre of attention. The proper place for a genius. Hilaire Belloc would have had a field day in verse with Georgy.

At home I ran a bath. For the first time in ten years of Moscow experience the water was cold. 'A journey is indicated.'

Something has been working away in my undergrowth. It finally surfaced. I dialled a number.

'Allwo?'

'Azat?'

'Yes.'

'It's me, Carolina, from London.'

'Oh, Carolina, how are you?'

'Azat, I need to tell you something.'

'Yes?'

'Azat, I want you to know that I know it was because of you that I came to Russia to act in Chekhov in Russian. I want to thank you. You were the first to make it possible for me to be the first.'

'It makes me very happy to hear you say that, Carolina.'

'Our problems were perhaps because we didn't understand each other enough. It was very difficult and very interesting and I am really happy that it happened. Thank you, Azat.'

'Oh, now I remember how I felt when we first met. Thank you for calling.'

My state of mind had not allowed me to make that call one minute before I did. I was grateful. I dialled another number.

'Allwo?'

'Sasha?'

'Yes.'

'It's me, Carolina, from London.'

'Oh, Carolina, how are you?'

'I'm sorry that I haven't seen you and Olga this time. I want to say hello and goodbye.'

'When are you leaving?'

'Tomorrow.'

'We'll come to the airport with you.'

Oh, my goodness.

It was cheering to see Misha Roshchin out of hospital in the anteroom to the Director's Box when I returned to the Art Theatre before the performance of *Amadeus* in the evening. Yefremov's son, Misha, was making his debut as Mozart. Roshchin was standing in for the absent father. This unwell writer is a man whose humour balances every extreme. It is impossible to imagine him boring. In the present chaos of society, he suggested, there are only three questions.

'What can be done? (Chernyshevsky); Who is to blame? (Herzen); Who shot the goal?' (vox-pop).

The bells went for the start of the performance. I left the theatre.

A last supper with Igor and Natasha to try to resolve a difficulty; my constantly expressed anxiety about an English audience's reluctance to accept wordy, translated Russian playwriting.

Dima grasped the issue: 'What we have is literature. What we need is theatre in two languages. Two characters. "How do you do?" "How do you do?" A reason for them to stay on stage (and the

audience in the audience) for a couple of hours, then, "Goodbye."
"Goodbye."'

'You're a genius, Dimchik, thank you.'

Igor closed the evening with three or four special requests from
me. He has a stock of mime set-pieces which I ask for every time.
I know them backwards and wait like a child for the pay-off. We
were all crying. With laughter.

The Last Morning

I used my pass to enter the Art Theatre for the last time. Farewells
flew in and out of open doors. Irina apologised that the Volvo
would have to drop me at the airport and leave immediately. Is
there anyone who could go with me to the airport?

'Sasha Smirnov.'

'Fine.'

'Thanks for everything, Irina.'

I carried a small Christmas tree decoration in the shape of a
heart. We went together and placed it, with a note, on Oleg
Nikolayich's vacant desk.

Ksenia and I watched an American film on cassette. There were
slangy phrases thrown out of the corner of a mouth as someone
turned a street corner, or ate a hamburger. It was as hard for me to
retrieve them as for her. She is a perfectionist and we went over
and over tiny sections trying to mine every jewel.

Amanda came to share a last plateful in the kitchen. I am
beginning to miss these affectionate women already.

At the second they said they would, Sasha and Olga Smirnov
arrived at the door. This imposing actor and journalist had played
Rasputin in a television film. Our paths crossed fruitfully in
London, and he had watched the Hermitage Gala in 1991. Dressed
in an overcoat that reached nearly to the ground, today he was
looking more magnificent than ever. His hair was tied back in a
long tail. His face shone with a particular radiance. I was meeting
his wife for the first time. She, too, tall and exquisitely dressed,
exotic. The white streak contrasted the beauty of the rest of her
raven hair. Her creamy skin glowed with well-being.

Leaving Ksenia and Amanda had to be practical, love without tears.

Sasha drove his car alongside the Volvo. Olga and I sat together in the back of the comfortable limousine. I learned that she is a doctor who specialises in homoeopathic and alternative forms of healing.

There was time to spare in the empty airport before the flight. My shining guardians took me over. They held my hands. They stroked me.

'You've touched Russia. You belong to us, now.'

Every bit of the departure was fated to succeed. Ours was the shortest queue. Sasha was allowed to push my trolley past the barrier. With the lightest of hearts, I was leaving home to go home. I turned to wave for the last time and saw a flow of love coming from two angels.

48. Sasha Smirnov.

49. Poster on MKhAT billboard announcing the death of Oleg Yefremov.

Introduction to the Gelman Poem

In the summer of 2018 a friend from Moscow handed me a poem by the distinguished playwright and sage, Alexander Isaakovich Gelman. It is written in memory of his close friend Oleg Nikolayevich Yefremov, Director of the Moscow Art Theatre until his death on 24 March 2000, aged seventy-five. Discovered on Facebook, translated into English, I found myself, as I read it, in company again with the Oleg Yefremov I got to know as a deep friend during the fourteen years of my visits to Moscow.

Immediately, I wanted to ask the poet, whom I had met with Oleg, whether I might have the honour of his permission to print it in *Travelling Towards Chekhov*. His consent came flying back with a modest request that it might also be printed in Russian and could he have two copies.

50. Alexander Isaakovich Gelman.

In Memory Of Oleg Nikolayevich Yefremov.

By Alexander Isaakovich Gelman

После смерти, Олег, кто угодно
может с тобой делать все что угодно,
одни говорят – ты был не совсем на высоте,
на меньшей высоте, чем от тебя ждали,
другие – ты был на недосягаемой высоте,
на гораздо большей – чем от тебя ждали.
О, эти, которые стоят с рулеткой в руках,
отмеряют с точностью до миллиметра,
кто недопрыгнул, кто перепрыгнул...
Как их много, Олег,
как они довольны
результатами своих измерений,
скушать готовы друг друга,
но свой замер не позволят
изменить ни на один миллиметр.
Властью своей над ушедшими
они пользуются умело, азартно, бесстыдно,
с такой уверенностью в своем праве,
что это не может не вызывать восхищения.

Воздух; который ты вытеснял
Своим телом,
в местах, где часто бывал,
помнит тебя,
хранит тебе верность.
Когда я попадаю случайно
в эти дыры пространства, -
сердце вздрагивает.

Ты уходишь все дальше, все дальше,
а время твое возвращается, возвращается.
Ты знавал очаровательных дам:
Цензуру Никитичну,
Цензуру Леонидовну,
теперь у нас Цензура Владимировна.
Опять востребован твой лукавый талант
обращения с начальством,
опять надо притворяться шутом
или напиваться,
чтоб не видеть выражения
собственных трезвых глаз,
слово «опять» от частых употреблений
с каждым днем набухает, тяжелеет –
вот-вот сорвется,
упадет нам на голову.
Ты уходишь все дальше, все дальше,
а время твое возвращается, возвращается.

English Translation of Gelman's Poem

After your death, Oleg, anyone
can do anything they like with you –
some say that you were not quite up to the mark,
accomplished less than they expected of you,
others – that you achieved the unachievable, much
more than they expected of you.
O, these creatures/beings, who stand with a measuring
tape in their hands,
taking precise, down to the last millimetre
measurements,
those who didn't leap far enough, those who out-leapt
themselves...
in defiance of people's expectations...
How many of them there are, Oleg,
how pleased they are
with the results of their measurements,
ready to gobble each other up,
but not allowing their assessment
to be altered by even a millimetre.
Their power over the departed,
they use to good effect, boldly, shamelessly,
and such is their conviction that they are within their
rights
it cannot but arouse our admiration.

The air which you displaced by your body,
the places where you often hung out,
remember you,
remain loyal to you.
When I occasionally find myself in these holes in
space,
 – My heart misses a beat.

You are receding further, further into the distance
but your time is returning, returning.
You were acquainted with charming ladies:
Nikitichna's censorship,
Leonidovna's censorship.
And today we have Vladimirovna's censorship.
Again your cunning talent
of negotiating with the authorities,
is in demand,
again one has to act the role of jester
or get drunk,
so as not to see the expression
in one's own sober eyes,
the word 'again' from frequent usage
as each day passes swells out, becomes heavier·–
at any moment, it will explode,
fall on our heads.
You are receding further, further into the distance
But your time is returning, returning.

51. Oleg Nikolayevich Yefremov.

Index

www.ingramcontent.com/pod-product-compliance
Lightning Source LLC
Chambersburg PA
CBHW060238100426
42742CB00011B/1569